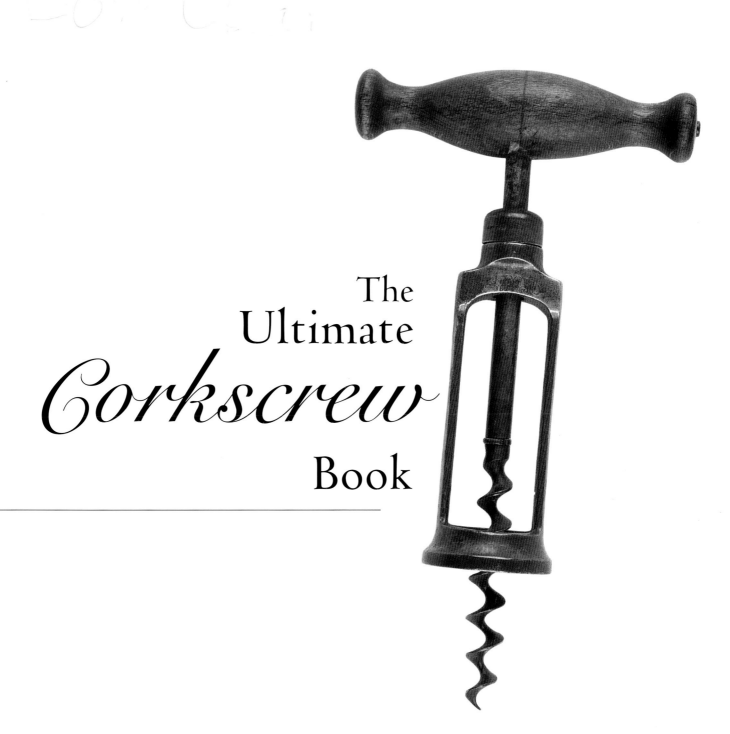

The
Ultimate
Corkscrew
Book

Donald A. Bull

Schiffer Publishing Ltd

4880 Lower Valley Road, Atglen, PA 19310 USA

Bull, Donald.
    The ultimate corkscrew book / Donald A. Bull.
        p.   cm.
    Includes bibliographical references and index.
    ISBN 0-7643-0701-0   (hardcover)
    1. Corkscrews--Collectors and collecting--United States.
I. Title.
NK8459.C67B86   1999
683'.82--dc21   98-38891
                                                        CIP

Design by Blair Loughrey
Type set in Snell BT/Venetian 301

ISBN: 0-7643-0701-0
Printed in China
1 2 3 4

Published by Schiffer Publishing Ltd.
4880 Lower Valley Road
Atglen, PA 19310
Phone: (610) 593-1777; Fax: (610) 593-2002
E-mail: Schifferbk@aol.com
Please visit our web site catalog www.schifferbooks.com
or write for a free catalog.
This book may be purchased from the publisher.
Please include $3.95 for shipping.

In Europe, Schiffer books are distributed by
Bushwood Books
6 Marksbury Rd.
Kew Gardens
Surrey TW9 4JF England
Phone: 44 (0)181 392-8585; Fax: 44 (0)181 392-9876
E-mail: Bushwd@aol.com

Please try your bookstore first.

We are interested in hearing from authors
with book ideas on related subjects.

Dedication

To my sons, John and Michael.
They will inherit my collection one day and say "Why?"
And to my wife, Bonnie.
She has been saying "Why?" for many years.
And to Howard Luterman and Ron Maclean.
They say "Why not?"

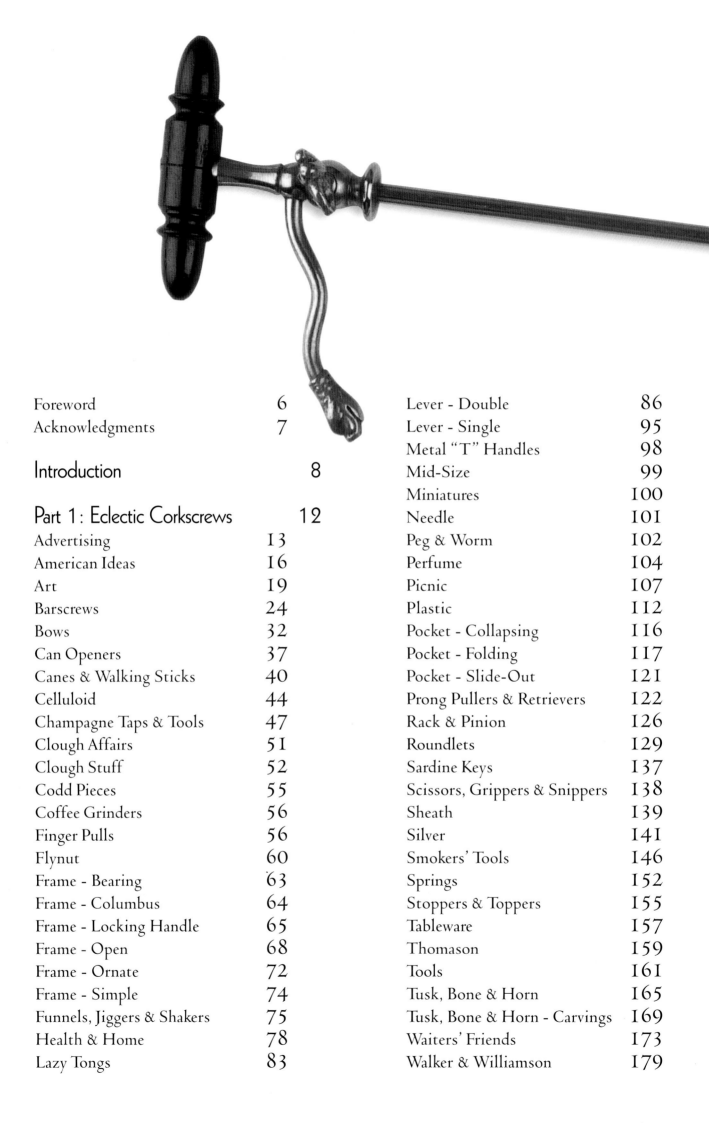

Contents

Foreword

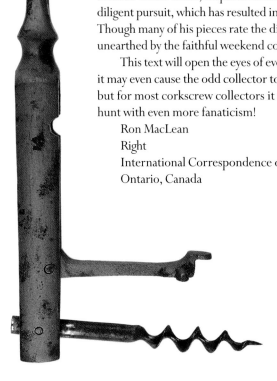

Although many claim greatness, this fine edition from the pen of Don Bull truly merits such a distinction.

This volume is the armchair guide to corkscrews. By perusing the 3600 illustrated and documented examples, it is possible to gain an understanding of the diversity and creativity that occurred in the past several hundred years. Perhaps a more suitable name for this book would be "Everyman's Guide to Corkscrews," as it covers the entire range of this twisted hobby!

The wisdom contained within these pages is mind boggling in both depth and scope. Don Bull has succeeded in accurately cataloging and illustrating a variety of objects so diverse that many lesser mortals might have thought the task impossible. His text covers a broad variety, from items of quantity to those of quality, from the mundane to the exquisitely rare.

Remarkably, all the examples presented come from one source: the author's personal collection. These items, acquired from around the world, reflect the labors of a relentless and diligent pursuit, which has resulted in one of the most comprehensive collections ever amassed. Though many of his pieces rate the distinction "truly unique," a significant number can still be unearthed by the faithful weekend collector.

This text will open the eyes of every devotee, from the novice to the true addict. In the end it may even cause the odd collector to abandon the search for corkscrews as a hopeless pursuit, but for most corkscrew collectors it will revitalize their energy and provide the motivation to hunt with even more fanaticism!

Ron MacLean
Right
International Correspondence of Corkscrew Addicts
Ontario, Canada

Acknowledgments

T here are hundreds of corkscrew collectors to thank for the knowledge they have provided through books, articles, submissions to newsletters, and private photos with researched comments. Readers should study the list of authors in the "Resources" section at the back of this book. All of them deserve a special thanks for the information they have provided. For fear of omitting an individual, I thank the entire past and present membership of the International Correspondence of Corkscrew Addicts (ICCA). Their annual "Six Best" photographs and corkscrew tales continue to help build a fascinating library of corkscrew facts and anecdotes. I also thank the members of the Canadian Corkscrew Collectors Club (CCCC) who choose to disseminate "Six Best" information and also contribute to this growing library.

The editors of club publications are a very dedicated and special breed, needed to assemble newsletters on a regular basis. In addition to writing most of the newsletters themselves, they are constantly begging the membership to submit articles and data. Deserving a special recognition are Joseph Paradi, Editor of *The Bottle Scrue Times* (ICCA); Jane Wlochowski, Editor of *The Quarterly Worme* (CCCC); and John Stanley, Editor of *Just for Openers* (JFO).

The busy pens of Herb Danziger, Brother Timothy Diener, Frank Ellis, Ron MacLean, Don Minzenmayer, the late Bob Nugent, Ferd Peters, Philly Rains, Lehr Roe, Bernard Watney, and Joe Young have created some in depth studies of special corkscrews and corkscrew collecting.

I especially want to thank Howard Luterman and Ron MacLean for their valuable assistance with this book. Each spent many hours checking content and assisting with value guidelines.

The individuals at Schiffer Publishing were all extremely helpful. When I first met Peter Schiffer, he looked at my 700+ photographs and said they were good but would be better if done as slides. His suggestion led to two marvelous weeks at Schiffer where I had the opportunity to use their fabulous studio to rephotograph all the corkscrews. A special thanks to Peter for encouraging me to reshoot them and allowing me the use of his studio. I also thank Bruce Waters who gave me a quick and valuable education in their cameras and lighting systems.

Everybody needs direction to stay on the proper path at all times. My editor made certain that I did not stray. Thank you Jennifer Lindbeck.

Introduction

A Fairy Tale

O nce upon a time there were two winemakers, Ron and Howard. They put their wine up in jugs and used corks as stoppers. They always took great care to leave enough cork above the jug rims to grasp by their fingertips or teeth for removal.

One Sunday afternoon, Ron and Howard took several jugs of their wine to an outing. They were attending a mudball game, which turned into quite a wild affair. Ron and Howard overindulged, getting bloody drunk. Upon returning to their carriage, the boys stretched out for a nap, but while doing so, Howard leaned on a jug of wine and pushed the cork down flush with the top.

They spent the night sprawled in the carriage. The next morning when Ron awoke, he looked for a little of what was then known as the "breath of the hare that zonked him." Ron grabbed the jug with the cork pushed in flush. "Howard, what the hell have you done?" yelled Ron. Howard woke up with a start. He looked at his dastardly deed and sorrowfully shook his head. All their other jugs were empty.

Determined to open the jug, Ron began to study the situation. Several minutes passed. Finally, Ron proclaimed "Eureka!" Howard thirstily waited for details. Hurriedly, Ron ran off to the vineyard at the side of the road, returning with an old piece of grapevine root. He then took out his knife and unscrewed a long screw from one of the carriage boards. Next, he screwed that screw through the grapevine.

Grasping the grapevine firmly, he picked up the jug of wine and screwed the screw into the cork. He gave it a little tug. The screw came out with a little piece of cork. He screwed it in again. He pulled. A little more cork was removed. The screw was tearing apart the cork. Several more attempts brought up pieces of cork and finally the remainder was forced down into the jug. Seconds later, the winemakers were drinking again!

Ron knew he was on the verge of finding a better way to extract a cork than by teeth or fingertips. He *knew* that he could fully seal wine with a cork and remove the cork. On the way home, they passed by a blacksmith. Ron looked at his grapevine root with a screw running through it. He thought if the blacksmith could turn him a fine worm for his root, he could turn it into a cork without damaging the cork. The worm would engage the cork on each turn and pull it out without a problem.

The blacksmith and Ron made a corkscrew that worked. And that is how the corkscrew came to be.

Other Tales

Many articles have been written with thoughts and theories of the earliest corkscrew. In *Corkscrews and Bottle Openers*, Evan Perry wrote the "idea, almost certainly, came from the 'worm' or 'screw' on a ramrod or cleaning rod used to draw a gun's charge from the gun barrel." These "worms" were known from the early 17th century. In their colorful introduction to *Corkscrews for Collectors*, Watney and Babbidge also explore this idea, proclaiming "The corkscrew may well have been an English invention."

According to Bert Giulian, in *Corkscrews of the Eighteenth Century*, the earliest mention of "scrue" was by William Morice in 1657 and "worme" was brought up by Nehemiah in 1681. Giulian says Claver Morris referred to a "cork-drawer" in 1686 and, in 1702, the word "Bottle Screw" first appeared in the *Philosophical Transactions of the Royal Society of London*. Giulian also refers to Nicholas Amhurst's 1724 poetry for the first mention of "cork scrue."

This hand colored print from *116 Patents Granted by the United States* by Sackett & Wilhelms Litho Co., New York takes a rather humorous look at the evolution of the corkscrew:

"The corkscrew was unknown to our forefathers two hundred years ago.

Various methods of extracting corks were resorted to in olden times, such as winding a cloth or handkerchief tightly around the cork, and with a peculiar jerk pulling the stopper out of the bottle; breaking the neck of the bottle was common practice, and many persons became very expert in removing corks with teeth.

The earliest mention of the corkscrew is in an amusing poem entitled *The Tale of the Bottle Screw* in a collection of poems by Nicholas Amhurst, published in 1723. Bacchus is described in the poem, and among other things, it is said of him:

> 'This hand a corkscrew did contain,
> And that a bottle of champagne.'

Yet at the time 'bottle screw' appears to have been the common name of this useful article, for the poet concludes his tale with the following lines:

> 'By me shall Birmingham become
> In future days more famed than Rome;
> Shall owe to me her reputation,
> And serve with bottle screws the nation.'

The modern corkscrew came into use about the beginning of the last century, and was for many years called a 'bottle screw.'

Corkscrews, like corks, are to be found, in some shape or other, in all parts of the civilized world."

So how and when did the corkscrew really come to be? The *Ron and Howard Fairy Tale* took place "once upon a time." As there is no real evidence of the origin of the corkscrew, it is as likely as any that Ron and Howard "invented" the corkscrew. And then it was re-invented thousands of times.

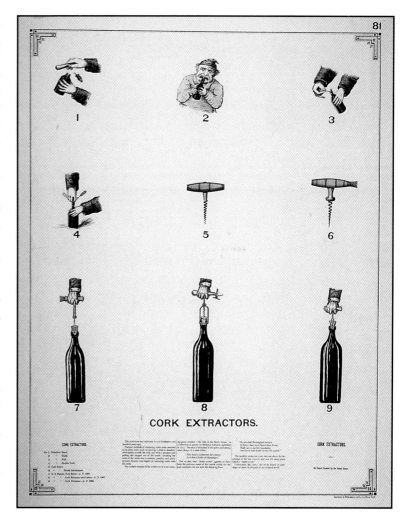

CORK EXTRACTORS.

This Book

This book is about all types of corkscrews — antique corkscrews and modern corkscrews, iron corkscrews and plastic corkscrews, simple corkscrews and complex corkscrews, fancy corkscrews and plain corkscrews. In this book, I have attempted to place corkscrews in categories in which they fit best.

For years, I have heard debates and suggestions about classification systems for corkscrews. Thoughts of categorizing by worm and handle type abound. Categorizing by time period is another thought. I have not heard anyone talk about color though. And how about categorizing by small, medium, large, and extra large? I viewed the exercise in much simpler terms.

I just took corkscrews and grouped them with related corkscrews regardless of age, material, or color and that became their category. There are double levers of metal and of plastic, old double levers and new double levers. Pigs are grouped with other pigs. Cats are grouped with other cats with a couple of mice thrown in because we associate mice with cats. Dogs are grouped with dogs. Yes, you might find a stray dog in the "Syroco" category. Or you might find a waiter's friend in the "Celluloid" category. Yes, there are corkscrews that cross categories, but we're never going to get it perfect, are we?

Why categorize corkscrews this way? With talk of corkscrew sources "drying up," it seems that more and more collectors are specializing. Some collect only mechanicals, some only wood handles, some carvings, some figurals, and some knives. The categories in this book will help the collector know what is available in his area(s) of interest.

I have attempted to make the book as user friendly as possible. It has been divided into four parts and, with the exception of the fourth, all categories within the parts are in alphabetical order. Most corkscrews are individually valued and described. In some cases value ranges apply to a group of corkscrews within a photograph or to all corkscrews in the photograph. Patent and manufacturer markings are listed in ALL CAPS. Advertisements, slogans, and other promotions are listed in quotations. All markings and advertising copy appear as spelled. Punctuation has been added occasionally for clarity.

Other Books

I have a rather large library of corkscrew material including manufacturers' catalogs, auction catalogs, brochures, photographs, articles, newsletters, and books. The number of books on corkscrews is overwhelming. Take a look in the "Resources" in the back of this book to see how many great corkscrew works have been published. A number of these books cover patents of given periods or countries in great detail.

It is not my intention in this book to go into great detail on individual corkscrews with worm pitches and diameters, complete patent details or detailed histories. Rather, my intent is to offer an overview of developments in many of the more important categories and give some general information in the photo captions. As a collector becomes more addicted to corkscrews, he should seriously study the many other wonderful corkscrew information resources.

Values

V alue ranges are based on past sales both public and private, prices advertised in the media and at shows, prices realized on internet sales, and gut feelings. In cases where prior sale information was not readily available, value is based upon relative scarcity versus known values.

Factors that bring values down:
- Broken parts
- Missing parts
- Cracks and chips
- No markings or poor markings
- Uneducated sellers
- Apathetic buyers

Factors that bring values up:
- Two or more collectors lusting after the same corkscrew at an auction
- Over zealous buyers
- Inflation
- Low supply and high demand
- Increased awareness and interest in corkscrews

When selling a corkscrew, a collector is most likely to obtain the best price by selling to another collector, provided the selling collector is in a position to find a buyer.

The easiest way to dispose of a collection of corkscrews is to sell it to a dealer. Bear in mind when selling to a dealer, the price offered will be much less than the "list priced." The collector must understand that the dealer already has the market for the product and needs to make a profit. It is the business he has developed.

Please note that the value ranges in this book represent estimates of current selling prices of corkscrews in very good condition. Neither the author nor the publisher will be responsible for any gain or loss experienced by using the value guidelines.

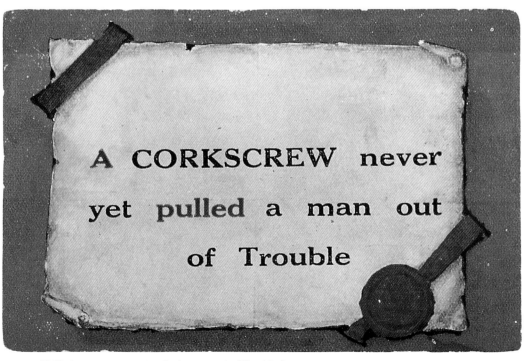

"A Corkscrew never yet pulled a man out of Trouble."

Contact

If you have comments or questions about corkscrews, please write to the author at:

P. O. Box 596
Wirtz, VA 24184
USA

You may also send boxes filled with corkscrews to that address!

Part I
Eclectic Corkscrews

Advertising

The corkscrew collector who specializes in advertising examples will find a very long list of available types. Barmounts, wallmounts, picnics, bows, roundlets, knives, waiter's friends, can openers, and sardine keys are just a few. Wood handle direct pulls and bell types were among the most popular in the late 1800s and early 1900s. Hundreds of different names can be found on them, but the advertising corkscrew collector must remember that he is competing for these prizes with collectors of general or specific advertising. The specific brand name advertising collector is likely to drive the prices higher than values shown in this category.

A trade card from Heims Brewing Company of East St. Louis, Illinois.

Left to right: An example of advertising that could easily be overlooked - cast into the top of the button is "Schlitz Brew'g Co., St. Paul." $80-100; A Walker wood handle with a rare instance of a notched button secured by a cotter pin. "Saginaw Brewing Co., Saginaw, Michigan." $150-200; Another button with cast in advertising "Bergner & Engel, Phila." $80-100.

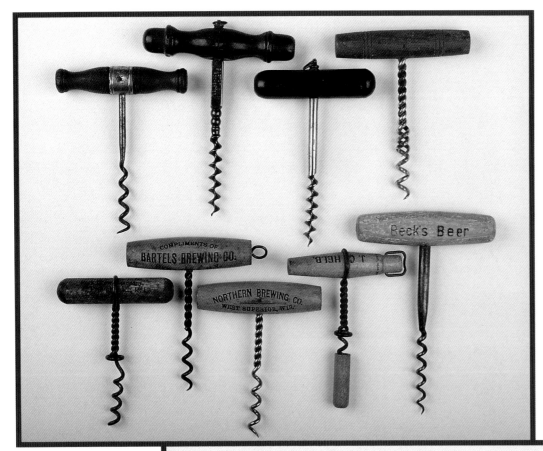

Wood handles on direct pull advertising T's were produced in many styles. Some did a poor job of getting the message across.

Top row left to right: Manufactured by Haff with barely noticeable advertising on the brass band - "St. Joseph Brewing Co., St. Joseph, Mo." $150-200; Advertising on the square shank is "Bartholomay Rochester." $100-150; It takes a very close look to see that this one is impressed on the handle with "Genesee Brewing Co." $80-100; The twisted wire worm has "Anheuser-Busch" imprinted in very small block letters on the handle. $60-80.

Bottom row left to right: A Clough type from Park Brew Company. The advertising on this corkscrew is quite worthy of note: "Park Brew Food Products, Ales, Lager, Porter, Malt Extract, Chemists find them Clean and Pure. Park Brew Co., Providence, R. I." $60-80; Bartels Brewing with hanging ring. $50-70; Northern Brewing Co. $40-60; Clough with short sheath and decapitator advertising "J. C. Helb, East York, Pa." $60-80; Big and bold "Beck's Beer." $30-40.

Simple direct pulls *from left to right:* "Northwestern Extract" with WILLIAMSON on shank. Rounded handle. $30-50; "Elgin Eagle Brewing Company" with wire helix. $30-40; "Moerlein" with web helix. $20-30; "Engesser Brewing Co." with speed worm. $50-60; "Val Blatz Brewing" plate attached to top. $80-100; "Phillip Kling Brewing Co." on flat handle with web helix. $50-60; "Stroh's Beer" on flat handle with wire helix. $40-50.

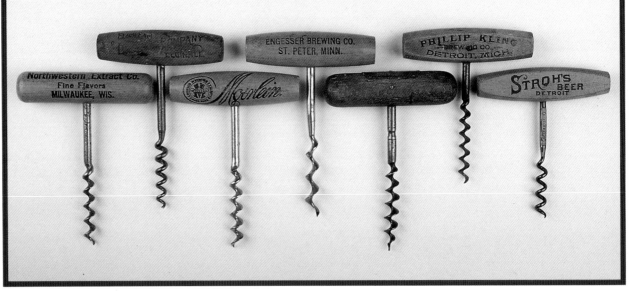

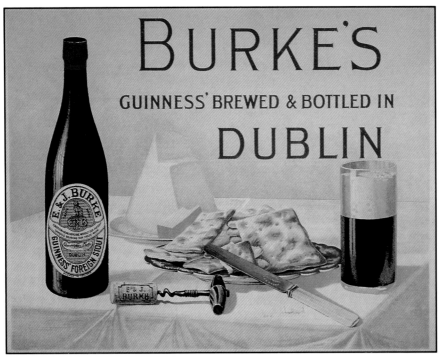

A framed 25" x 19" advertising lithograph for "Burke's Guinness Brewed & Bottled in Dublin." The table is ready with crackers and cheese, a bottle of Guinness Foreign Stout and a corkscrew.

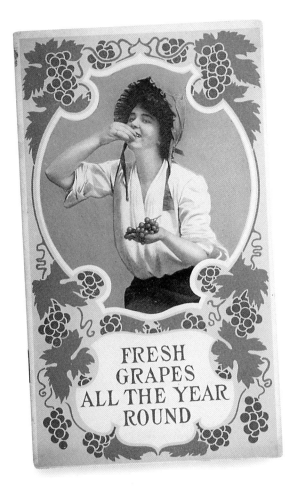

The "Fresh Grapes All the Year Round" brochure was copyrighted in 1905 by The Welch Grape Juice Company. It discusses the company history, vineyards, grapes, production of grape juice, grape juice as a tonic and for communion wine, and drink recipes. The reward is on the last page: "A Self Puller. Corks in Welch's Grape Juice are difficult to draw, for it is necessary to make a perfect seal. Do you want a self-pulling cork-screw? Send us one quart or two pint labels from Welch's Grape Juice (no repeats) or 10c in stamps and receive a self-pulling corkscrew by mail. The Welch Grape Juice Co., Westfield, New York, U. S. A." The corkscrew is marked WILLIAMSON'S on the shank. $40-50 for the set.

10" x 12 1/2" tin litho printed by Wedekind & Co. of London for Thos. Grant & Sons Distillery, Maidstone, England. There is a wood handle corkscrew on the table. The conversation is:
Mʀ WELLER, SENʀ: "Samivel my boy, Grant's Cherry Whisky is tip-top and salivating."
SAM: "You're right, Guvnor, it's first rate. If you feel bad, it makes you feel WELLER."

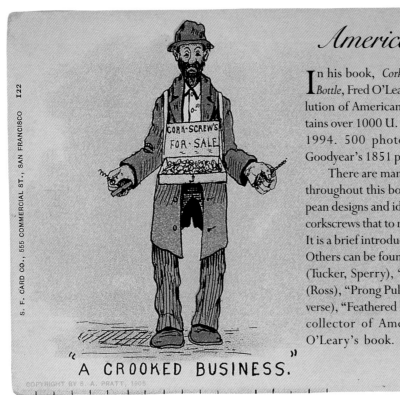

American Ideas

In his book, *Corkscrews 1000 Patented Ways to Open a Bottle*, Fred O'Leary gives a detailed history of the evolution of American corkscrew designs. His book contains over 1000 U. S. patents issued between 1851 and 1994. 500 photographs show corkscrews from Goodyear's 1851 patent to Cellini's 1994 patent.

There are many U. S. patented corkscrews shown throughout this book; many of which resemble European designs and ideas. In this category I have included corkscrews that to me have an "American look and feel." It is a brief introduction to early American corkscrews. Others can be found under categories "Lever - Single" (Tucker, Sperry), "Lever - Double" (Smythe), "Pigs" (Ross), "Prong Pullers & Retrievers" (Mumford, Converse), "Feathered Friends" (Avillar), etc. The advanced collector of American corkscrews should study O'Leary's book.

Top row left to right: Thomas Strait's 1883 conical self-puller bell marked PAT. JUNE.12.83. $700-1200; Charles Chinnock 1862 self-puller marked CHINNOCK'S PATENT MAY 27, 1862. Open barrel. $400-700; Unmarked Chinnock with closed barrel. $200-300; Unmarked Chinnock . Frame. $60-80.

Bottom row left to right: The "Burgundy" frame with locking handle. Shown in 1946 Williamson catalog at $18 per dozen with the claim "Will not agitate contents of bottle." $100-150; Wilbur Woodman 1886. Spur on handle locks handle. WOODMAN'S PATENT and PAT'D JAN.Y 6.1886 cast into handle. $1000-1200; Joshua Barnes 1876 marked PAT. JUNE 27 76. $400-800; Unmarked Chinnock type. Frame. $60-80.

Top row left to right: William Bennit's 1883 self-puller with fixed bell marked PAT. MAY 15TH 1883. $150-200; Another Bennit marked with patent date and MAGIC CORK SCREW. $275-325; Unmarked cast iron handle with rotating bell. $100-125; Thomas Curley's 1884 self-puller with slotted bell cast with handle and machined. Handle marked T CURLEY TROY NY and PAT'D MAR.22.84. $500-700; Marked on band HICKS & REYNOLDS TROY, N. Y. The slot that is used on the Curley bell is in the shank under the bell. $400-600; Curley with slotted bell. Marked on the band PAT. APR.22.84. $500-700; Walker's Schlitz Bell. *$150-250.

Bottom row left to right: Edward Haff 1885 direct pull with two piece pinned metal handle. $75-100; Haff marked on band PATENT APPLIED FOR with two piece two color wood handle. Salesman's Sample? $80-100; Light color handle Haff marked on band HAFF MFG. CO. NEW YORK PATD APL. 14, 85, MAY 5TH 85. $40-60; Dark handle with same mark. $40-60; A fine corkscrew marked on shank J. H. SCHINTZ. A San Francisco manufacturer. $150-250; Another fine San Francisco corkscrew marked M PRICE. $150-200.

Top row left to right: A very unusual speed worm T-handle with two fret wire cap lifter mounted in end of handle. Bottom of handle is marked WALKER. $150-200; William Williamson's 1898 "Cap Lift" without bell. These small versions were produced without a bell. It is not simply missing. End of handle is marked WILLIAMSON CO. NEWARK, N. J. PATENTED DEC 13 98. $40-60; Wire wrap through handle finishing above worm with two wire cork grips. This is an English corkscrew made after the introduction in England of Clough's twisted wire corkscrew manufacturing machines. $75-100; Unmarked winged handle with cap lifter. Shown in 1946 Williamson catalog at $3.60 per dozen. $15-20; Winged cap lifter marked A & J MADE IN U. S. A. with a wooden sheath. $10-20.

Bottom row left to right: Unmarked Bennit's Magic type fixed bell with brush in handle. $150-200; Unmarked cast iron handle with rotating bell. $150-200; William Williamson's 1897 Bell with flat top handle and advertising. Marked on end of handle PATENT PENDING. $300-500.

A great piece of early beer advertising from Williamson Company of Newark, New Jersey. The top of the handle is flat with a celluloid plate affixed with four small nails. The plate reads "Compliments of The Gottfried Krueger Brewing Co., Newark, N. J., U. S. A." Krueger was founded in Newark in 1852 by Braun & Laible. The company went out of business in 1961 and is probably best remembered as the company that introduced canned beer in 1935.

*The Schlitz self-puller was made by Erie Specialty Manufacturing Co. for Schlitz between 1888 and 1891. The globe in the center of the handle represents the Schlitz trademark used extensively in their advertising. It says "Schlitz Trade Mark." The sides of the handle read "Schlitz, Milwaukee, U. S. A." The word "Schlitz" is cast into the half globe bell. The end of the handle is marked E.S.M. CO., ERIE, PA., WALKER PAT. APPLIED FOR. This was the forerunner to Walker's 1883 patent.

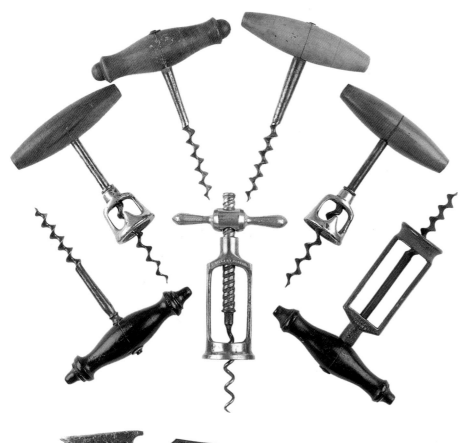

The Murphy Company was founded in Boston, Massachusetts, in 1850 and later relocated three times to surrounding communities. Murphy manufactured a wide range of cutlery products. In addition to corkscrews, its products included knives, chisels, cigar box openers, cheese testers, burnishing irons, and more. T-handle Murphy corkscrews are normally marked on the shank. Frame types are marked on the top of the frame. Apparently, the only patent issued to the Murphy Company was John Murphy's in 1901. He added a spur to the collar of the bell (pointing up) for use as a cap lifter and wire breaker. The patent also shows the spur on a button type.

Top row left to right: Murphy patent marked PAT. APR. 23 '01, R. MURPHY on shank. $80-120; Acorn handle marked MURPHY on shank (earliest Murphys were marked only MURPHY; later examples were marked R. MURPHY). $70-100; Marked R. MURPHY, BOSTON. $50-80; Another like the one on the *left.* $80-120.

Bottom row left to right: Dark acorn handle marked MURPHY. $70-100; Frame with locking handle. Frame marked R. MURPHY, BOSTON. $75-100; Acorn handle with frame marked R. MURPHY, BOSTON. $80-100.

NOTE: Some of the Murphy patent bells are marked on the bottom of the collar R. MURPHY, HARVARD, MASS., PAT. APRIL 23, 1901. These were made prior to those marked on the shank. $100-130.

A mean looking piece of cutlery. Marked near the handle "FOUR-IN-ONE" WARRANTED CAN & BOTTLE OPENER KNIFE, PAT. FEB. 10, '03. The openers are marked CAP LIFTER and CAN OPENER. The handle is the sheath for the wire worm. The blade is sandwiched by a fine wood handle and secured with three brass rivets. $150-200. A more common version has a round handle. $100-150.

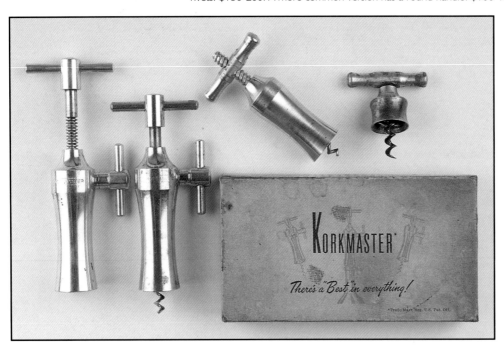

Marshall T. McDowell was granted Design Patent Number 148,810 on February 24, 1948 for his rack and pinion design. His application had been filed almost two years before on April 25, 1946. World War II had helped make aluminum a household word and that was the material McDowell chose for his corkscrew. On the *left* is McDowell's rack and pinion corkscrew shown with rack raised and lowered. This one is marked TRADE MARK KORKMASTER PAT. PENDING. It came in the box shown. The patent drawing is of this design. $75-100.

The corkscrew at *middle right* is marked KORKMASTER JUNIOR. The collar rotates to lock the handle for turning the worm into the cork. "Unlocking" the collar allows the handle to turn to extract the cork. $60-80.

The corkscrew on the *right* looks like it might be homemade. However, several have been found by collectors. Upon close examination, it appears to be a McDowell production. The shape of the barrel is exactly the same as the top of the Korkmaster barrel. This one is simple. There is a short barrel with a worm and stem passing through the top. The handle is fixed to the stem and does work extremely well in loosening the cork. With a slight tug, the cork is liberated. $60-75.

The original Korkmaster box proclaims THERE'S A "BEST" IN EVERYTHING. On the side panel is: The Korkmaster Co., 1060 Broad Street, Newark, New Jersey. And we learn how to use it:

Pull out top handle of "Korkmaster" as far as it will go.

Place "Korkmaster" on top of bottle.

Hold lower neck of "Korkmaster" and upper neck of bottle firmly with left hand.

Turn Top Handle clockwise, exerting a downward pressure to set point of corkscrew into the cork and continue to turn as far as possible.

Turn side handle clockwise with right hand and cork will pop.

Drink Heartily.

The instructions in the box describe the uses:

To remove crown caps - Place machine on crown...and lift up. This is the "U-Neek" way.

To remove milk caps - Push one pin through base and insert in far side of cap. Do it with ease.

To remove large corks - Place machine on top of bottle, then push pins down. Turn slowly and draw out cork. Do it gently. To release stopper - pull pins up.

To remove small corks - Push pin through base until points enter top of cork then push pins into stopper and turn as for large corks. Don't pull the "U-Neek."

Wilson Brady's 1917 patented unique U-NEEK. The box says "Manufactured Only by the Unique Necessites [*sic*] Corporation, 316 St. Paul St., Baltimore, Md., Don't Pull The 'U-Neek' (Trade Mark) Full Directions Inside Pat. Jan. 23, 1917 Other Patents Pending. Will Remove Corks, Crowns, Milk Bottle Caps Etc. with a simple twist." $1000-1500 (complete with three pins and retainer).

Art

Although the diehard corkscrew collector thinks of all corkscrews as works of art, there are some that should simply be classified as "Art" corkscrews. Some are poor works of art and others have a bit more interest. Some are good ideas: like outstretched arms, which make a perfect T-handle puller. Some are not so good: such as the nude holding a wreath, which is a bit difficult to grasp (although, it does feel good as a cap lifter). There are no mechanical patents on any of these "art" works.

Above: Many brass two finger pulls have been produced in England with a wide variety of handle designs. Some have convenient hanging rings and some have English registration marks to date them. Values range from $15 to $50 with registration marks bringing higher values.
Left to right: Bear standing on a log; Seated man R℞ 767310 (1931 registration); Reindeer marked R℞ 637121 (1914).

Left: Although many of the brass two finger pulls were sold individually, some came in a set with cap lifter, bottle recorker, and stand. *Left:* Souvenir of "The Old Curiosity Shop." $60-80. *Right:* The ribbon below the lady says "Esmerelda." $60-80.

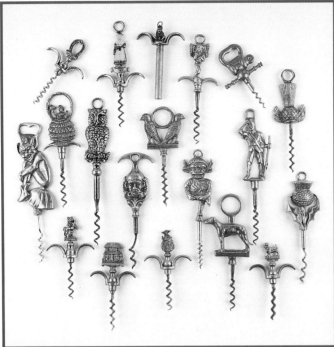

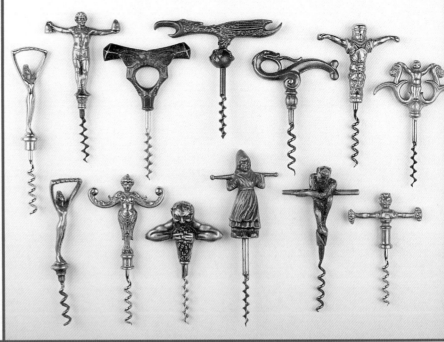

More English brass figurals.
Top row: Horseshoe (marked "Good Luck"), Unusual painted version of lady ("Jenny Jones" REG 700096 = 1923), Seated Pixie (unusual with sheath and cut worm), Standing Smiling Pixie, Buckle.
Second row: Large Seated Pixie, Lady ("Esmerelda"), Birds (this one is not English - marked MADE IN BELGIUM), Scout, Thistle.
Bottom row: Cat playing fiddle ("Cat & Fiddle"), Building ("The Old Curiosity Shop" marked PEERAGE ENGLAND), Lady with wide dress bottom, Pixie Face, Greyhound Dog, Horned Oriental Bust, Small Dog ("Sealyham"), Thistle with large leaves, Castle ("Abbey Gateway, Thetford").

This is a group of German and Scandinavian designs that are a bit better quality than the English two finger brass pulls. *Top row left to right:* Brass Nude with Victory Wreath (GERMANY). $50-60; Weight lifter. $150-180; Howling Dog. $100-125; Roadrunner. $125-150; Serpent. $80-100; Decorated Boy (recent). $40-50; Cherub with flowers. $150-200.
Bottom row left to right: Chromed Nude with Victory Wreath. $50-60; Decorated Lady (GERMANY). $75-85; Bacchus crushing Grapes (C.V.H. ROSTFRITT. initials for C.V. Heljestrand Co. corkscrew manufacturers in Eskilstuna, Sweden). $125-150; Dutch Girl with Yoke. $125-150; Bear Holding Bar. $110-130; Man Holding Grapes with outstretched arms (GERMANY). $65-75.

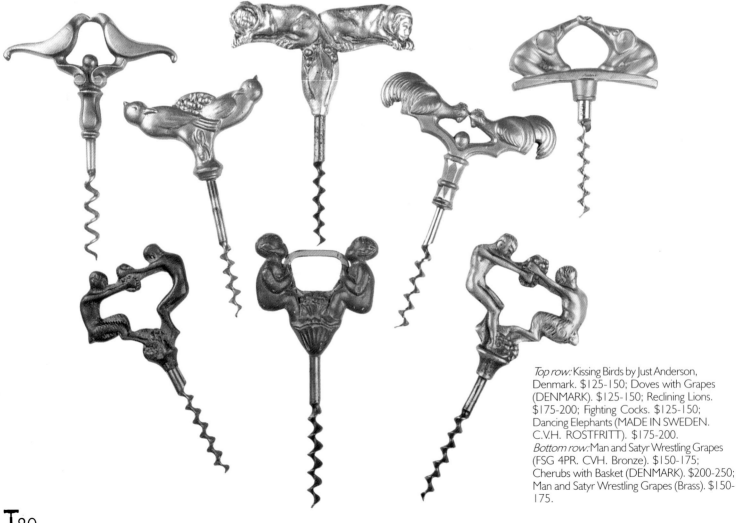

Top row: Kissing Birds by Just Anderson, Denmark. $125-150; Doves with Grapes (DENMARK). $125-150; Reclining Lions. $175-200; Fighting Cocks. $125-150; Dancing Elephants (MADE IN SWEDEN. C.V.H. ROSTFRITT). $175-200.
Bottom row: Man and Satyr Wrestling Grapes (FSG 4PR. CVH. Bronze). $150-175; Cherubs with Basket (DENMARK). $200-250; Man and Satyr Wrestling Grapes (Brass). $150-175.

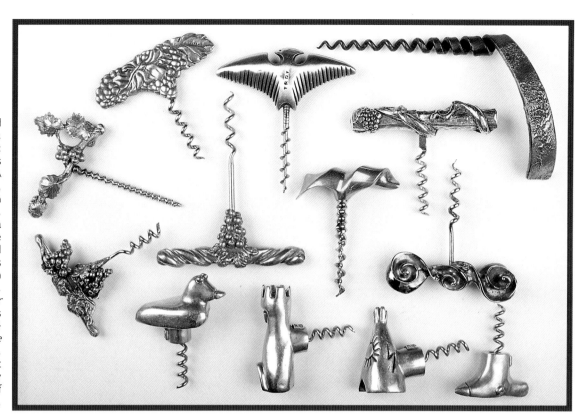

Various artists have created corkscrews in their own special way. Here are a few of their ideas: The grape handle design at *top left* is marked ©1989 SEAGULL. A product of Seagull Pewter, Pugwash, Nova Scotia. $25-30. The Eagle in the *center* is marked TROY. $50-60. The log with grapes and vine was a recent find in Atlanta. $15-20. The corkscrew with tapered worm and right angle handle at the *top right* was designed by artist Brian Cummings in the 1980s. $65-75. The three grape designs at *left center* are unmarked. $30-40. The brass twist handle is marked SAMSON #4 '89. $40-50. Bow design at *middle right* is marked PMC. $15-20. The four unusual pewter designs at *bottom* are marked © ROUX . They were designed by Steve Vaubel of Brooklyn, New York. $60-90.

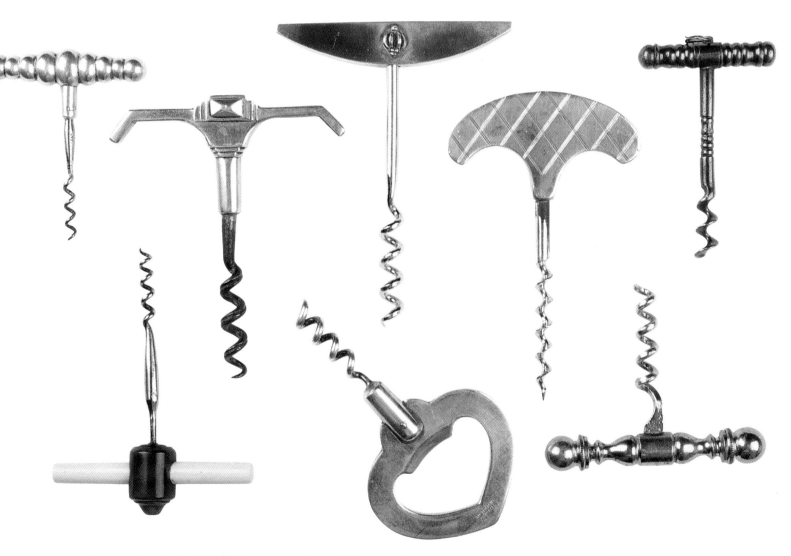

Top row left to right: English 1876 Hallmark on handle and STEEL marked on shank. $200-250; Mark of Wakeley & Wheeler of London with a 1906 Hallmark. $350-400; Marked MOLTKE STERLING. 300 of this Dane's design were produced in 1975. $250-300; Mark of Towle Silversmiths, Newburyport, Massachusetts. $200-250; 3" tall steel T-handle. $65-75.

Bottom row left to right: Unusual celluloid handle with delicate worm. $150-200; Silver heart marked NAPIER SILVER PLATE. $75-85; Unmarked brass T-handle. $50-60.

Top row left to right: Silver Plate Swedish wreath marked with letter P in circle. $100-125; Two Roosters marked MADE IN AUSTRIA. $150-200; Unmarked grape, leaf, and vine handle. $100-125.

Middle row left to right: T-handle with grapevine and grape design marked SKS ZINN SSX. $50-65; Unmarked grape design. $65-75; Heavy grapevine design casting that came in presentation case. $800-900; Pewter with grape bunches on ends marked DENMARK. $50-60.

Bottom row left to right: Unmarked two finger pull. $65-75; Unmarked double hole grapevine design with extra gripping power. $300-350; Similar feel to *left middle* but marked WMF ZINN. $85-95.

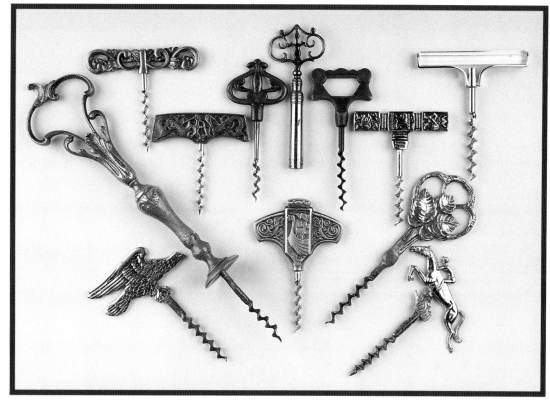

The four pewter handle corkscrews were purchased in a department store in Oslo, Norway in the early nineties. *Second from top right* is marked TINN-PER NORWAY, STOPT-TINN PEWTER. It sells for $69.50 with a matching cap lifter. The pewter handle at *bottom center* is marked TINN PEWTER, NORWAY, H. S. $20-30. The T-handle with glass bar affixed to a gold plated handle was purchased in an Oslo gift shop. $65-75.
Top center: Copper plate. $50-60; Steel with sheath $200-250; Brass with opener. $75-100.
The *bottom* four "corkscrews" are all suspected to be fakes.

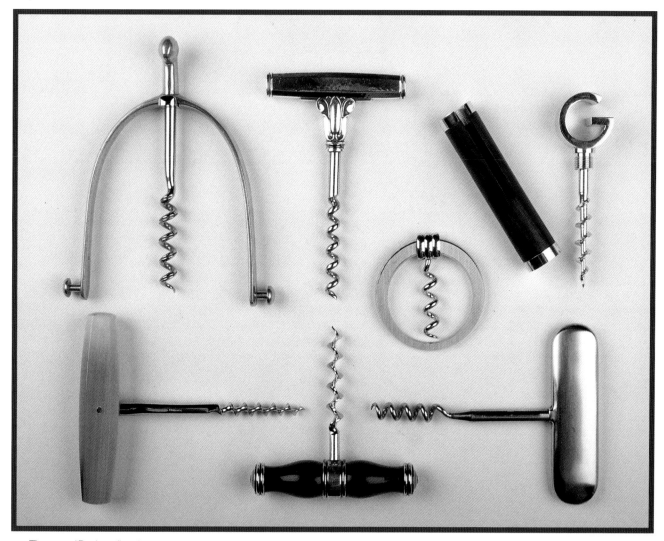

These are "Designer" corkscrews.
Top row left to right: Spur marked HERMES PARIS, MADE IN FRANCE, DEPOSE. $350-400; T-handle marked GEORG JENSEN, STERLING DENMARK. $350-400; Circle folding bow marked MUST DE CARTIER, MADE IN FRANCE 003042 with Cartier Hallmark. $350-400; An unusual picnic style in which the threaded sheath has a slot up the center to mate with the center portion of the G. Marked GUCCI ITALY. $250-300.

Bottom row left to right: Pinned bone handle marked on shank DUNHILL, ELOI FRANCE. $175-200; Ebony handle marked EBENE and silver fittings marked CHRISTOFLE FRANCE with hallmarks. $200-250; Heavy steel T-handle marked WILKENS with crown. $125-150.

Barscrews

Barscrews are heavy cast iron or brass corkscrews that mount by either clamps or screws on the bar top. Some are designed to remove a cork by first turning the worm into the cork then pulling a lever. Others turn the worm into the cork and extract it in one continuous motion. A 1902 Sears catalog contains several models targeting the saloon, soda fountain, restaurant, club, and hotel market. Of all corkscrews, barscrews are those most frequently favored with names. These include Acme, Ajax, Bacchus, Blitz, Cedon, Champion, Crown, Cyclop, Daisy, Don, Eclipse, Enterprise, Estate, Express, Extractee, Famlee, Favorite, Handy, Hektor, Helios, Hero, Infanta, Invincible, Little Quicker, Meriden, Merritt, Modern, New Era, Phoenix, Pullmee, Rapid, Rimo, Safety, Samson, Shamrock, Shomee, Simple, Slam, Swift, Unique, Victor, Vintner, Yankee, Zeus, and the Quick and Easy Cork Puller.

In advertising for a barscrew, by Andrew Muir of London, to describe the ease of operation, it states "the leverage power is such that female assistants can draw the tightest Corks without effort." 1885 reviews in the trade press included the following comments:

> a delicate girl can draw without effort . . .
>
> . . . the operation is so simple, that it can be effected by ladies . . .
>
> . . .a positive boon to the barmaid, the sight of whom painfully struggling with an obdurate cork cannot be pleasant to the feelings of any chivalrous beholder.

Aren't men lucky that such an invention helped women pull their corks? And it was done "by this single movement a spiral corkscrew is propelled forward and retracted, of course carrying with it the cork, which is in turn expelled from the machine by the return motion of the hand lever" (*The Caterer and Hotel Proprietors' Gazette*).

A Champion barscrew is mounted at the left end of the bar at New York's Gallagher's Steak House. It clamps to the bar with a flange extending over the top with room enough for an advertising plate, which would be visible to the customer.

Given the great numbers of these that turn up, The Arcade Manufacturing Company of Freeport, Illinois evidently produced a lot of "Champion" barscrews. They are frequently found marked CHAMPION, PAT. SEPT. 7, 1897 and DES. PAT. JUN 9, 1896 for patents issued to Michael Redlinger. Values on regular Champions range from $75 to $150. Here are some more interesting Champions. *Left to right:* A later Art Deco version. $150-200; Champion with advertising plate for "Theo. Hamm Brewing Co., St. Paul, Minn." $300-500; Al Capone's Champion originally used in his Chicago bar on Van Buren St. and later at his estate in Lake Geneva, Wisconsin. *$Rare.*

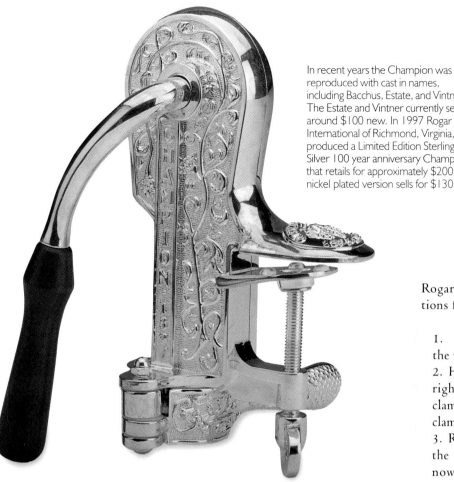

In recent years the Champion was reproduced with cast in names, including Bacchus, Estate, and Vintner. The Estate and Vintner currently sell for around $100 new. In 1997 Rogar International of Richmond, Virginia, produced a Limited Edition Sterling Silver 100 year anniversary Champion that retails for approximately $200. A nickel plated version sells for $130.

Rogar International's instructions for using the Champion:

1. Position the handle all the way to the rear.
2. Holding the bottle in the right hand, place between clamps until it stops. Grip clamps firmly with left hand.
3. Rotate handle forward all the way down. The cork is now cleanly removed and your wine is ready to serve.
4. To remove cork, rotate handle to the rear and cork will drop in your hand.

The "Yankee 7" is based on Raymond Gilchrist's design patent of 1905 and mechanical patent of 1913. This one has an advertising plate reading "Kessler Brewing Co., Helena, Mont." $125-175 without advertising. $400-500 with advertising.

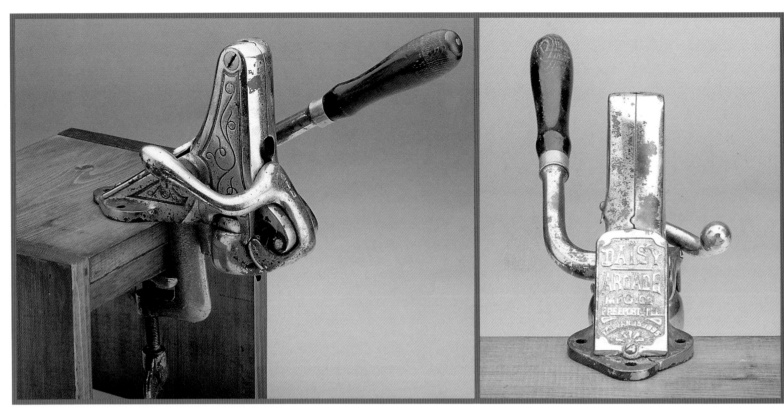

Two views of the "Daisy" marked on plate DAISY, ARCADE MFG. CO., FREEPORT, ILL. PAT. JAN 15 1895. Patent by Charles Morgan. $250-500.

Edwin Walker's 1891 patent. Screws to the bar top with interchangeable advertising plate exposed to the patron. $250-500.
Left plate: "Albany Steam Bottling Works, Hinckels Brewing Co's Lager Beer."
Right plate: "Erie Specialty Mfg. Co., Erie, Pa."

The "Quick & Easy" from Walker's 1894 and 1895 patents. Screws to bar top. Four examples with different advertising plates and different design marks. $250-350.
Advertising/design marks from *left to right:* Goetz Brewing Co., St. Joseph, Mo. / 1897 DESIGN; Quandt Brewing Co., Troy, N. Y. / 1895 DESIGN; Minneapolis Brewing Co. / 1893 DESIGN; The Cleveland Faucet Co. / 1896 DESIGN. The design dates are marked inside the handles.

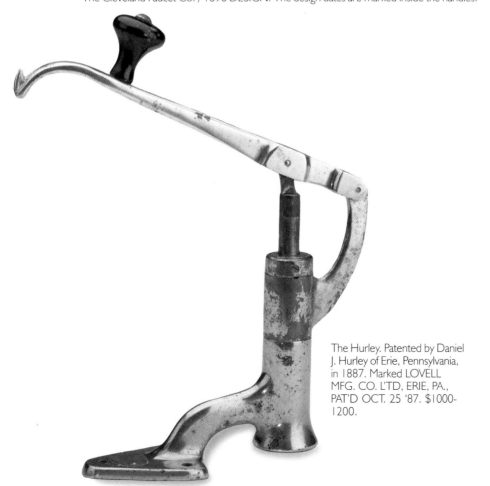

The Hurley. Patented by Daniel J. Hurley of Erie, Pennsylvania, in 1887. Marked LOVELL MFG. CO. L'TD, ERIE, PA., PAT'D OCT. 25 '87. $1000-1200.

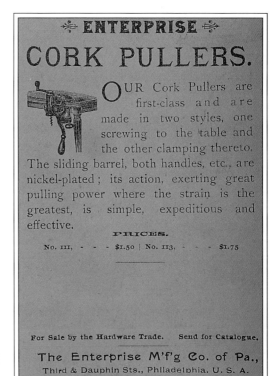

The Enterprise Cork Puller from the Enterprise Manufacturing Company of Philadelphia. The spike on the back is a wire breaker. The fine print on the second trade card has a copyright date of 1893. The reverse says "In seventeen hundred and eighty three, By the treaty of Paris, our states were made free, And the Enterprise Cork Puller helped on the cause, while the Patriots drank to our land and its laws." No, the Enterprise was not around 100 years before the copyright date of the card, but the poetry makes good advertising copy. $700-1000.

The "Rotary Eclipse" is an engineering wonder and a sight to behold. Hold the bottle firmly to the collar, rotate the handle and the cork is extracted. Patented in England, France, Germany, and the United States. The Rotary Eclipse has a left-hand speed worm. $1200-1500.

Above: Marked THE DON. $400-500.

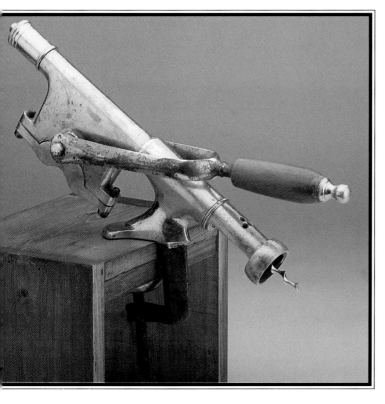

Left: The "Acme." Marked G. EDMONDS & SONS. $400-500.

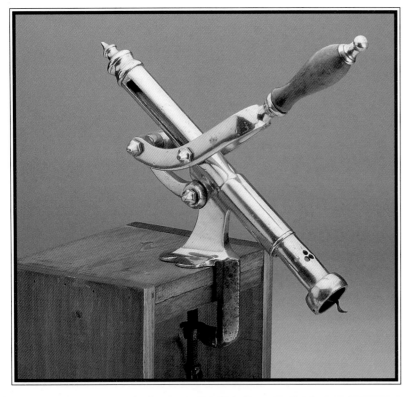

Left: Unmarked. Scalloped bar plate. $200-300.

Lower left: Cast iron marked RAPID, SWISS MADE. $150-200.

Lower right: Brass colored. Marked RAPID, SWISS MADE. This model has been sold in the United States for several years in brass colored and chromed versions for about $150.

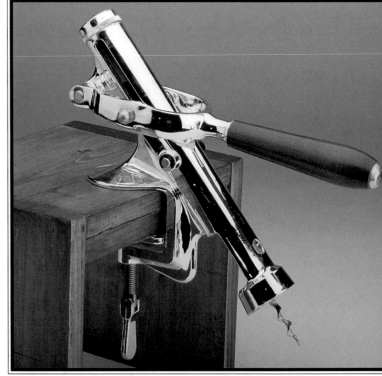

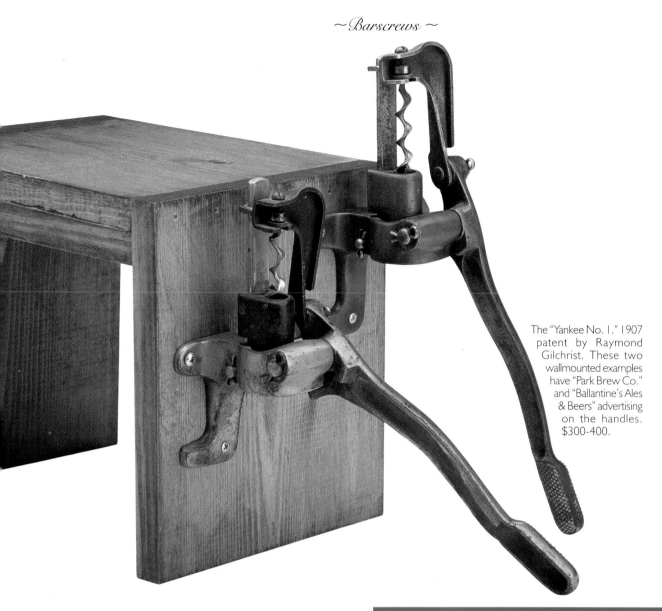

The "Yankee No. 1." 1907 patent by Raymond Gilchrist. These two wallmounted examples have "Park Brew Co." and "Ballantine's Ales & Beers" advertising on the handles. $300-400.

The Gilchrist Co. of Newark, New Jersey, marketed the Yankee wallmounted cork puller as "A household necessity." Advertising copy says "Should be in every home. Don't let any woman struggle with a corkscrew to open tightly corked catsup, olive, pickle, medicine or any other bottle. The Yankee is screwed against any upright surface: Icebox, Sideboard, Door Frame or Wall. It's always there. No hunting for a corkscrew, always ready to draw the tightest cork from any bottle." For those who thought corkscrews were used only for wine - your list has expanded even further.

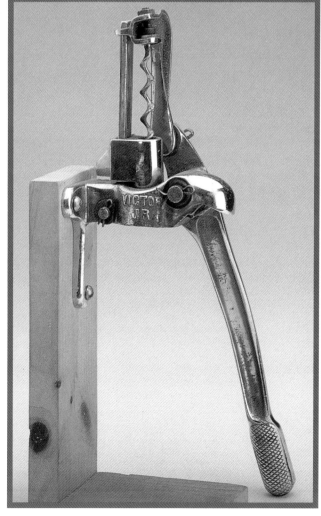

Wallmounted corkscrew marked VICTOR JR. $400-500.

Bows

One of the first bows a new corkscrew collector is apt to find is a rather simple worm that folds out from the center of the bow with the bow becoming the handle of the cork remover. This chapter shows some of the hundreds of sizes, shapes, and configurations of folding bows, which have been produced since the 18th century.

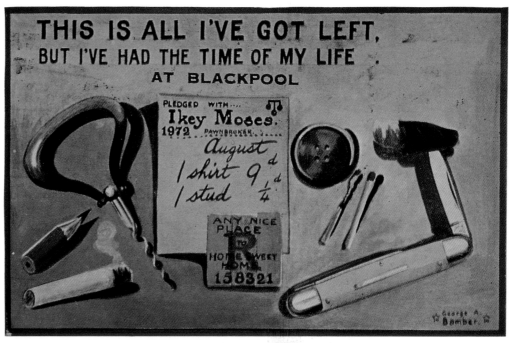

"This is all I have left, but I've had the time of my life." Thankfully, the poor soul still had a corkscrew! Interestingly the pawn ticket says 1972. The postcard was mailed in 1918!

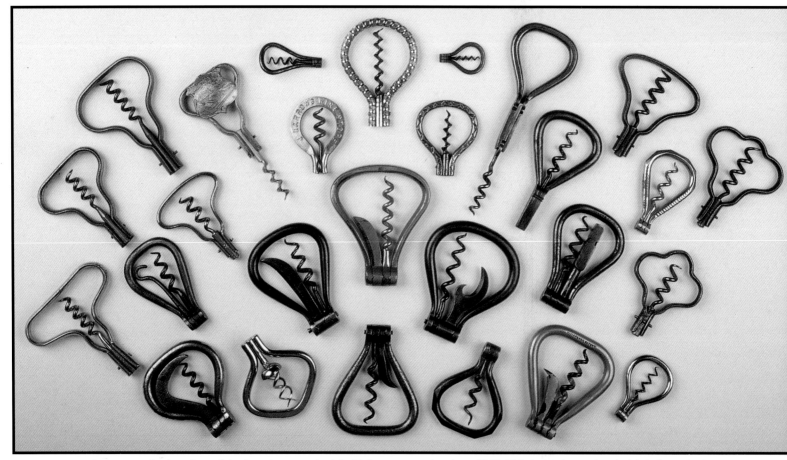

A close examination of any of the three bows on the *left* with flat handles will excite the collector when they note that they are marked WILLIAMSONS on the top (Cornelius T. Williamson's 1883 American patent). Williamson was a manufacturer in Newark, New Jersey. $25-30. When examining the three on the *right* plus the flat handle one under the corkscrew with shield, the collector will find the mark PAT. OCT.10.77. That is George Havell's American patent of 1877, which comes in many sizes and configurations. A 1913 Williamson catalog illustrates 10 different sizes and shapes. $50-100. There are also baby bows like the two delicate examples at the *top*. $50-70. The bow in the *top center* is an ornate silver plated design. $125-150. A rarity is a bow with advertising - there is one to the *left* of the silver bow that says "J. Darrow's Wine Store, 1146 Washington St." $75-100. The souvenir plate variety says "Chicago Union Station" and has a picture of the station. $60-80. There are some with nicely faceted handles. $50-100. Others have manufacturers names such as the small bow at the *lower right* marked R. JONES & SON. $80-100. The closed and open bows with square end are carriage keys. $250-300. At the *bottom* is a double helix marked D.R.G.M. $80-100.

The hunt for bows continues and one quickly learns that they were produced with multiple tools. In this photo are a number with a second tool added - a foil cutter/wire breaker in the *middle* marked GERMANY with Henckel's trademark on the handle. $100-125. Another foil cutter to its *left* marked R. JONES & SON on the blade. $150-200. Yet another *below* it marked BAKER & CO. $125-150. The one with folding carriage key is marked LUND. $250-300. Other two tool corkscrews include a button hook, a horse hoof pick, and a cap lifter. $100-150. The bow with foil cutter at the *lower right* is very unusual and rare in that it has gripping teeth at the top of the worm. This is marked C. VIARENGO PATENT, an 1898 English patent. $300-400.

All of these are quite collectible. Most desirable are those that have complete worms that are neither tipped nor bent. Accompanying tools should be complete and a manufacturer's mark always adds value.

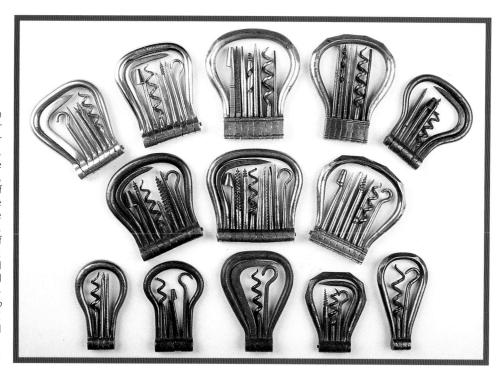

Even harder to find are folding bows with multiple tools. A good value rule of thumb for bows with three or more tools is $50-75 per tool.

In the *bottom row* we have moved up to three and four tool bows, including button hooks, hoof picks, awls, and leather punches. None of these have manufacturer's marks (as is often the case in multi-tool bows) but they are all quite desirable.

Six, seven, and eight - those are the number of tools in the bows starting with the *top left*. We've added saw blades, screwdrivers, and rasps. The bow in the *center* has ten tools! All so elegant yet, except for two, the manufacturers left their marks off. The *second from left, top row* is simply marked HILL & HAYMARKET. The eight tool bow in the *second row* is claimed with the mark EDWARDS & SONS, 161 REGENT ST., W.

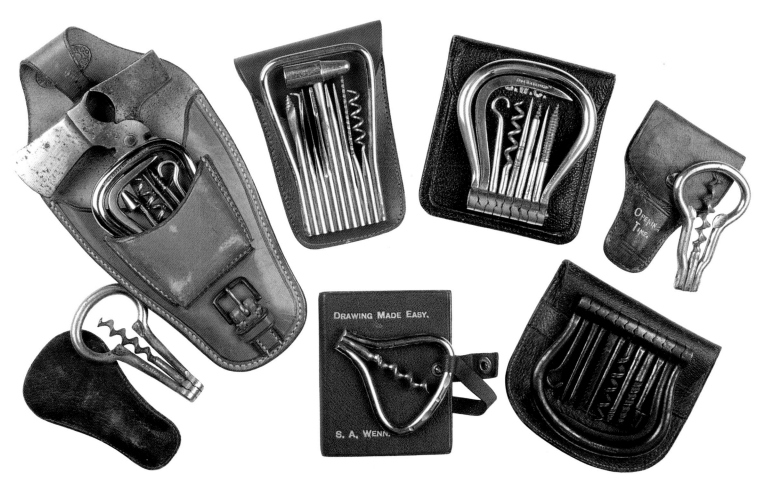

Another challenge is to find folding bows in their original leather cases. The case at the *left* is from Holtzapffel & Co., 645 Charing Cross, London. It has an additional multi-purpose tool in the back of the case. A 1909 English Plant's catalog lists the functions of this tool as hammer, hatchet, pincers, wire cutters, screw driver, and nail driver. The six tool bow in the front pocket is marked HOLTZAPFFEL 64CHARING†. $600-700. The next case is marked TOOLMASTER with a tag reading "Gadgeteers, Box 172, Orange, N. J." A 1940s order form lists the tool at $3.95 and shows the nine functions: Corkscrew, Saw, Awl, Screw Driver, Hammer, Bottle Opener, Knife, Can Opener, and Augur. Louis Strauss was granted an American patent for this multi-tool in 1949. $150-175. The black case is marked MADE IN ENGLAND with gold applied initials C.W.C. $500-600. The hoof pick on the seven tool bow is also marked MADE IN ENGLAND. $400-500.

At *top right* and *lower left* are corkscrew bows that have frets in the bow for use as a cap lifter. The one at *lower left* is marked D.R.G.M. GERMANY (Ernst Wahl's 1926 German patent No. 959,374) and the unmarked one comes in a leather pouch marked OPENING TIME. $80-100. The bow inside the "book" is marked simply FOREIGN. Inside the cover of the book is a block of wood with a space carved out to fit the bow. The book's cover reads "Drawing Made Easy, S. A. Wenn." $400-500. The bow at *lower right* has 10 tools and is marked HOLTZAPFFEL 64CHARING†. The leather case is a perfect fit for the bow. $550-750.

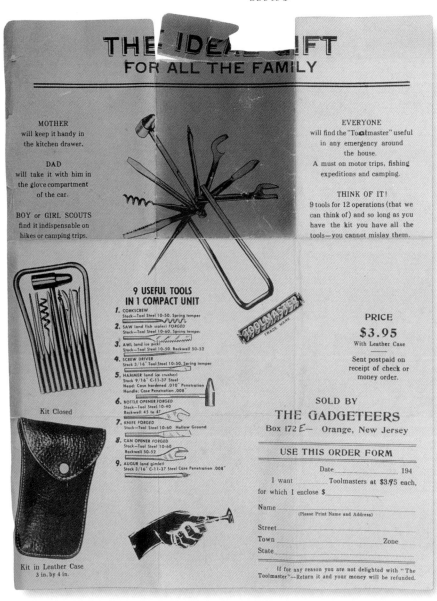

An order form for the Toolmaster that:
"Mother will keep handy in the kitchen drawer.
Dad will take it with him in the glove compartment of the car.
Boy or Girl Scouts find it indispensable on hikes or camping trips.
Everyone will find the 'Toolmaster' useful in any emergency around the house. A must on motor trips, fishing expeditions an camping."
...and don't forget the wine!

A group of nine different two tool bows varying in width from 1 1/2" to 2 3/4." $80-120.
The bow in the *center* is marked GERMANY with the Henckels Company twins trademark. The bow *below* it is marked F. PIGALL, RUPERT ST.

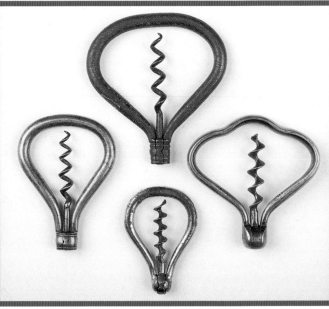

Four c.1800 folding bows from 1 1/2" to 3" wide. Note the rounded or detailed outside edges on the joints. $80-120.

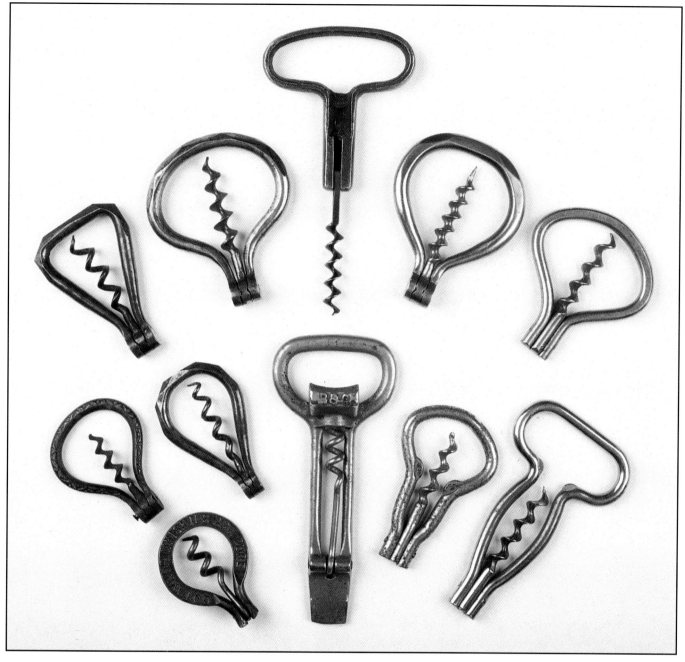

The discerning corkscrew bow collector might want to ferret out some of the more interesting examples. For a little practice, find in the photo: Four faceted bows. $50-75; Bow with detailed scrollwork. $60-70; Bow advertising Taylor Whiskies. $75-100; Simple with flats on bow. $30-40; Two with fret style cap lifters. $60-80; Marked B & C with cap lifter and lid prier. $75-90; Unusual design with worm folding into a channel. $150-200.

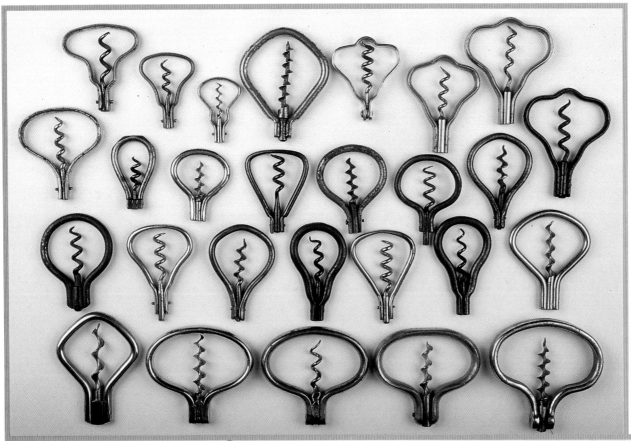

A stranger once called me and said he was excited to have heard that another corkscrew collector lived nearby. He said he only collected one type and was anxious to show them off. I invited him to visit. Twenty minutes later, a motorcycle came roaring down the driveway. I went out to greet him just as he was unstrapping a large mayonnaise jar from the motorcycle's rear package holder. The jar was filled with simple folding bows. He said he was buying every one he could for under $20. Most looked like these. He was buying at the right price - under $20.

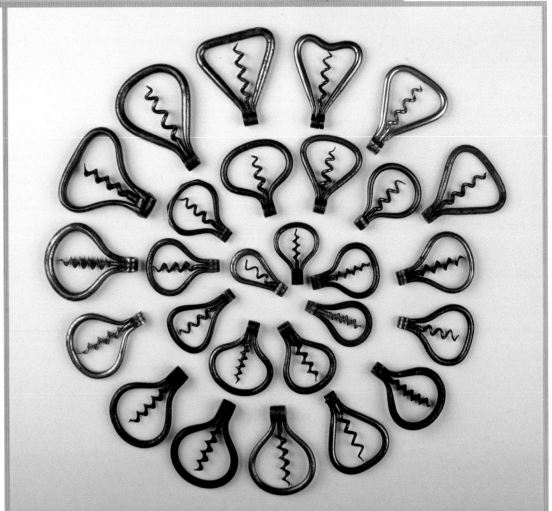

A group of folding bows varying from 3" to 6" in length when unfolded and ready for use. None are marked and they would probably half fill a mayonnaise jar. Under $20.

Can Openers

A well dressed cat waits anxiously for someone to grab the tin can opener on the table and open the can of cat food. The cat is not waiting for someone to open a bottle of wine with the corkscrew.

How many times have you hunted through a box of kitchen utensils only to be poked with the end of a seemingly ordinary tin can opener with simple folding worm? As the blood flows, you shun it and dig deeper, still hoping. Or maybe you seize the opportunity to expand your

corkscrew collection with that "ordinary" tin can opener. Hopefully, when you are done looking at the many "can openers" in this category, you will understand that there are some worthy "keepers."

Millions of combination can opener/ bottle opener/corkscrews have been made and sold in housewares in stores. They still are. You can buy them for under $1.00— New. But they aren't as collectible as the rusting lot in these photos. If you are starting a can opener collection, your first hundred varieties will be easy and cheap. How much you are willing to pay after that will depend upon how deeply you get involved with can openers.

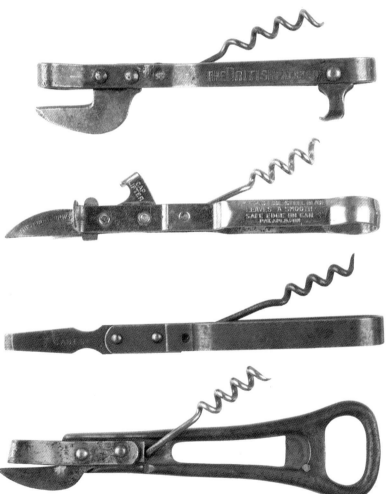

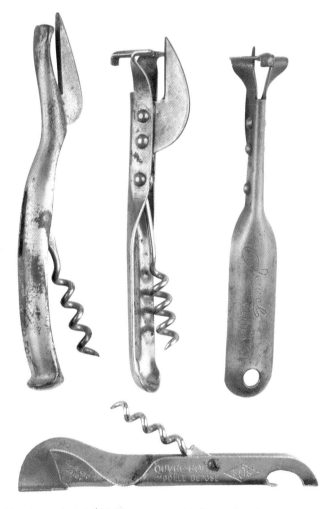

Left side from top to bottom: Marked BRITISH MADE PAT 11360, MADE IN ENGLAND. Frederick Sunderland's 1909 patent was for the piece on the tail end marked CROWN CORK OPENER. $30-40; Can opener designed to "leave a safe edge on the can." $15-20; Where's the can opener? An unmarked screwdriver in can opener style marked CAST STEEL. $40-50; Marked HENN on a chicken trademark. $35-50.
Upright three left to right: Casting slotted with a backspring to keep the worm tight when unfolded. $20-25; Well marked PAT JUL 10 - 23, THE JEWEL CAN OPENER, UNITED NOVELTIES, INC., YORK, PA. 1923 patent by Lewis Roberts. $20-30; Marked only JEWEL PATENTED. $20-30.
Bottom: A French can opener marked with SOS trademark MODELE DEPOSE. At the can opener it reads "Acier cemente" and at the worm "Ouvre-Boites." $20-30.

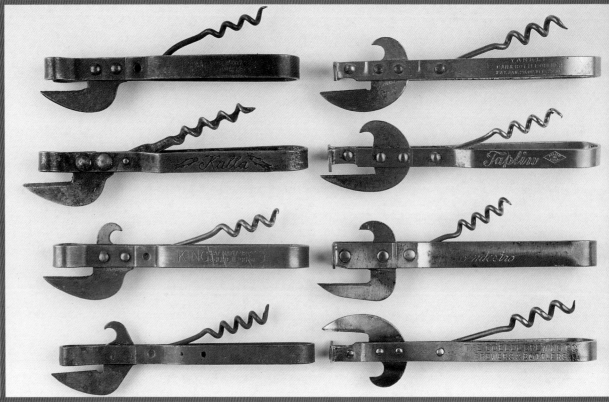

Ordinary looking at first, but . . . *Left side from top to bottom:* Two made without a cap lifter. Wire helix and web helix. $20-30; The "King" by Turner & Seymour Mfg. Co., Torrington, Connecticut, with cap lifter backward and the "King" with cap lifter forward. $15-20. *Right side top to bottom:* The "Yankee" by the Taylor Manufacturing Co., Hartford, Connecticut. $10-15; The "Taplin." $5-10; The "Indestro" by Indestro Mfg. Co., Chicago. $10-15; The "Yankee" with an unusual bit of advertising: "The Goebel Brewing Co., Brewers & Bottlers, Goebel Beer, Detroit, Mich." $75-100.

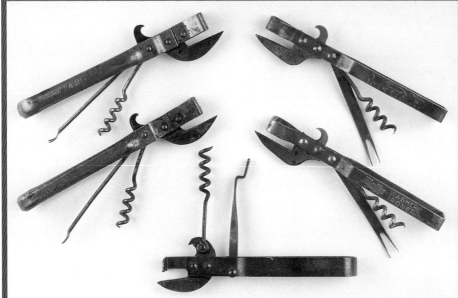

Here are some great ones you may have missed by not looking closely. The *top* four all include a folding cocktail fork. These are worthy of further exploration: *Top row:* Marked EASY GRIP 4 IN 1. $40-50; Marked ROBERTS MADE IN U. S. A. with flat fork. $30-40. *Second row:* If you find the "Mound City Malt Syrup" advertising unusual on the first, try the second: "Maytag Washer Ironer." $40-50. At the *bottom* is the true reward for looking closely at all can openers. This rare example is a waiter's friend! The worm is riveted to the cap lifter so it will be in the proper position when the neckstand is folded down from the handle. $100-150.

Left side top to bottom: Marked QUINTUPLET KITCHEN UTILITY. A 1936 American design. $25-30; Vaughan's. Made by the zillions. $1-2; Lots of chrome. $1-2; The "Re-Cap-O" from Ransom Company, Detroit. $10-15. Right side: For the thumb guard collector. All different with three marked on the protective shield THUMB GUARD and two HAND GUARD. $2-3.

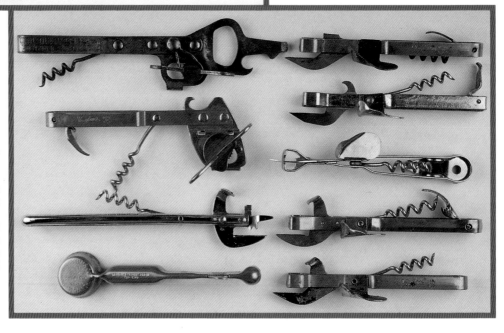

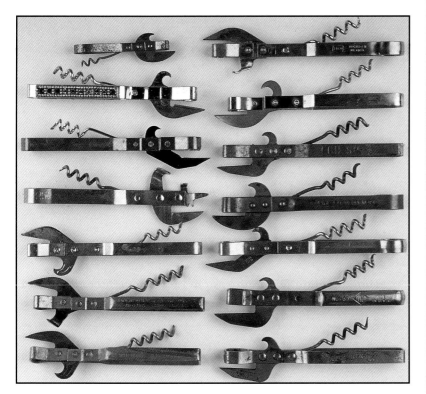

Here's an assortment you might want to pass up unless you are *really* serious about corkscrew can opener collecting. They include: A 3" with "J. A. Bennett, The Brown Line from Kingston," a bejeweled example salvaged from the junk pile and sold to a collector, and others made in Canada, England, Hong Kong, Mexico, and the United States. Various can openers: $0.50-2.

From top to bottom: Brushed stainless steel and wood can puncher with cap lifter and corkscrew. Marked VERNCO, STAINLESS STEEL, JAPAN. $5-8; A crude Russian can opener/cap lifter/corkscrew. $5-7; Multi-purpose tool marked BARLOW STAINLESS JAPAN. $6-7.

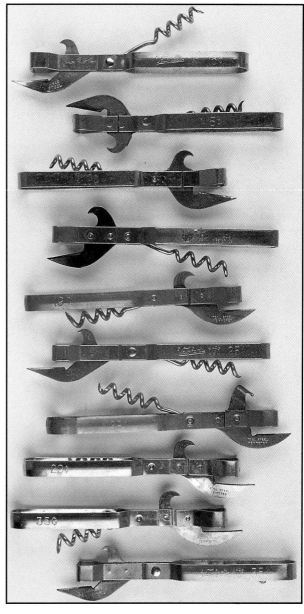

What price will a dealer put on a corkscrew that already has a price on it? Do you pay the tag price or the stamped price? Here's a collection that starts with a 15¢ marking at the *top* and goes up to 35¢ at the *bottom*. They all have only a can opener, bottle opener, and worm that folds into the handle. They vary in prices (15¢, 19¢, 25¢, 29¢, 35¢), manufacturers, and design. The hardiest is the *fourth from the top*, which is marked PATHOS-COMPLET and R/R 19¢, MADE IN WESTERN GERMANY. Made for the U.S. market. $15-25.

Top: Cast cap lifter marked COMBI with small thin wire worm. A can opener marked H C STAINLESS STEEL is riveted on the end. $30-40.

Middle left to right: A lot of metal stamping, bending, and riveting went into making this dime store orange combination corkscrew, cap lifter, and can opener. Turkey, c.1988. $10-12; Heavy stamping combination tool with knife, corkscrew, cap lifter, and can opener marked TURYSTA, MADE IN POLAND, U.R.Z. PAT NO. 12185, 13817, P.R.L. $15-20.

Bottom: Marked PATENTED ENGLAND, HOME WARE, CANS, CAPS, CORKS with key design. $15-20.

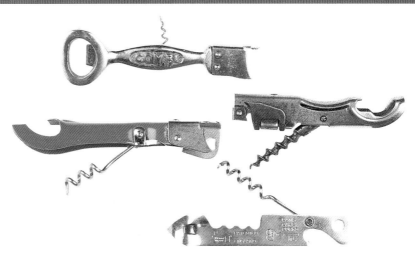

Canes & Walking Sticks

Are they real corkscrews? That seems to be one of the first questions asked about canes with worms attached to the handles and concealed in the sticks. There are stories about dealers who take canes with various hidden implements and change them to corkscrews. And there are those who say that the only genuine corkscrew canes are those with a bayonet fit and all threaded ones are fakes. The answer is simply that some were originally intended to have corkscrews and others were re-fabricated! But they are all cane and walking stick corkscrews! A corkscrew cane will uncork a bottle and another bottle and another and if you drink it all, it will help you walk home.

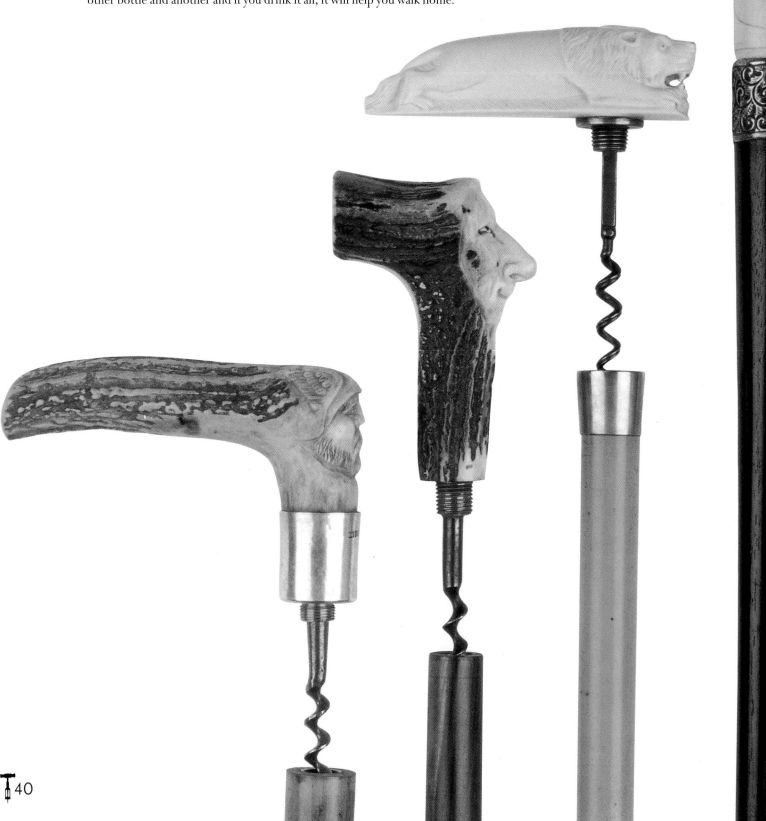

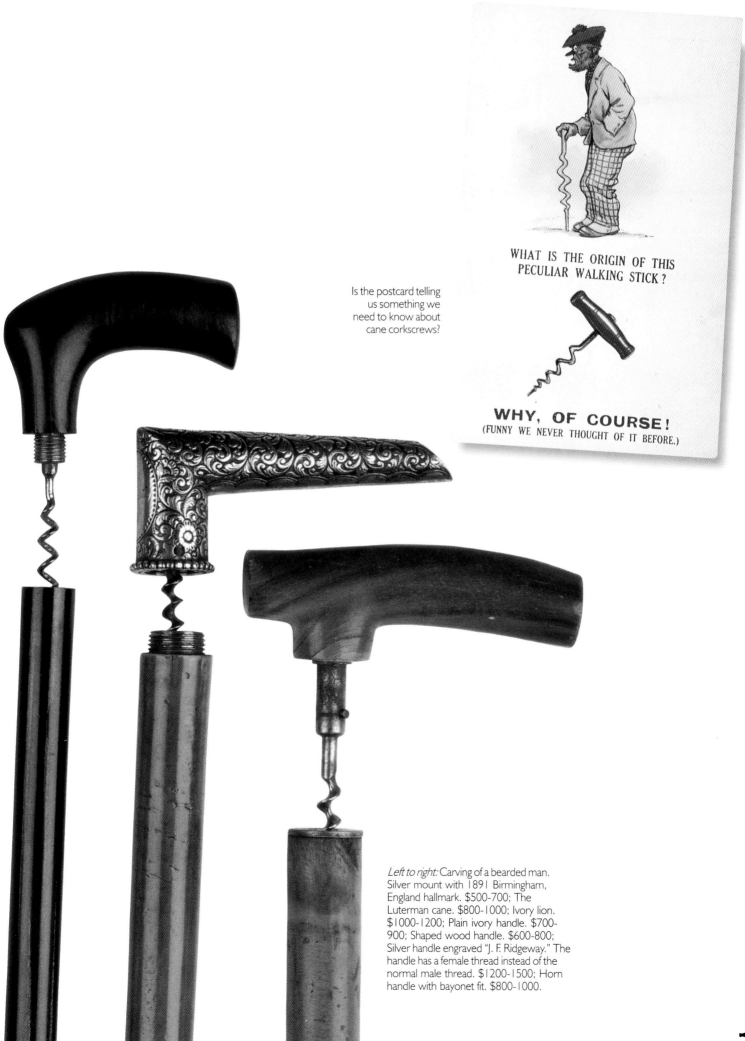

WHAT IS THE ORIGIN OF THIS
PECULIAR WALKING STICK?

WHY, OF COURSE!
(FUNNY WE NEVER THOUGHT OF IT BEFORE.)

Is the postcard telling
us something we
need to know about
cane corkscrews?

Left to right: Carving of a bearded man.
Silver mount with 1891 Birmingham,
England hallmark. $500-700; The
Luterman cane. $800-1000; Ivory lion.
$1000-1200; Plain ivory handle. $700-
900; Shaped wood handle. $600-800;
Silver handle engraved "J. F. Ridgeway." The
handle has a female thread instead of the
normal male thread. $1200-1500; Horn
handle with bayonet fit. $800-1000.

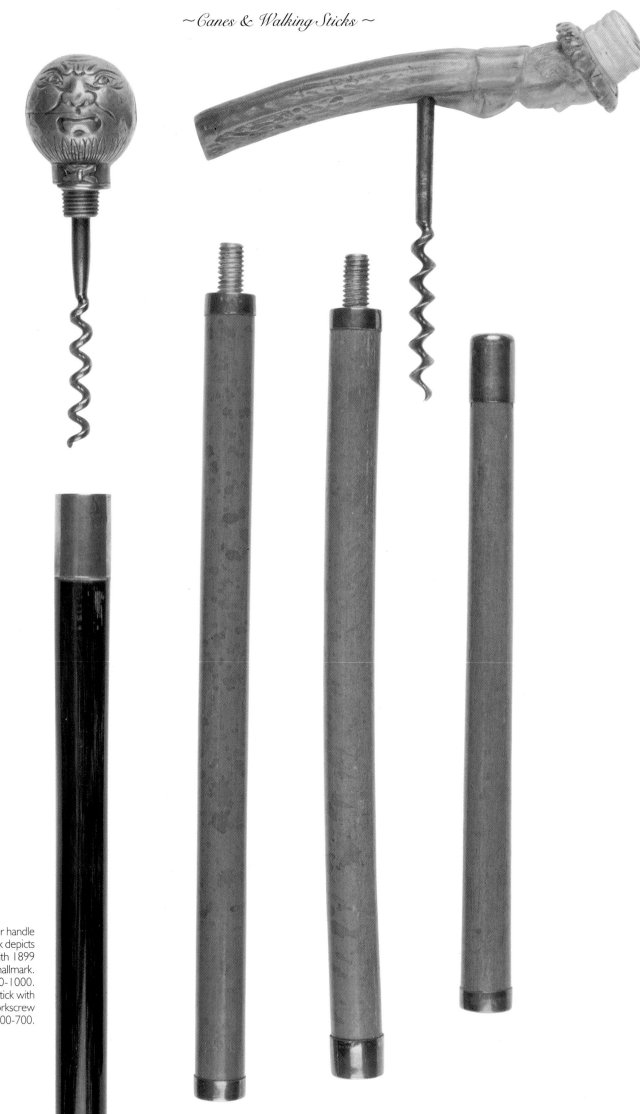

The silver handle walking stick depicts John Bull with 1899 London hallmark. $800-1000. Three piece stick with friction fit corkscrew carving. $600-700.

Corozo nut carving walking stick. $800-1000.
For more on Corozo nut carvings see the "People" category.

A walking stick with beautiful ivory carvings with mating ivory threads. The top is removed to reveal a perfume screw. $1200-1500. Can you just imagine someone's grandmother sitting in her chair and resting her hands on this as she scans the bottles of perfume on her dresser for a selection?

Celluloid

Celluloid was the first synthetic plastic material. In 1856, it was synthesized by British Chemist Alexander Parkes (1831-1890). John Wesley Hyatt (1837-1920) of Starkey, New York, developed it as a commercial product in 1869.

Celluloid is produced from a mixture of cellulose nitrate and camphor. It is a strong, durable product that can be produced in many colors. It was even an inexpensive substitute for ivory. Common products made from celluloid include combs, brushes, dentures, billiard balls, photographic film, and, yes, handles for figural corkscrews!

Here are a few of the corkscrews with celluloid handles in the shapes of legs, mermaids, alligators, kissing couples, and shoes. Marks and patent data are noted. Manufacturers marks noted are detailed at the end of this category. The gay nineties legs are German patent 21718 issued to Steinfeld & Reimer January 1, 1894. A 1910 Norvell-Shapleigh Hardware Company catalog calls the legs "Ballet" and offers them at $14 per dozen.

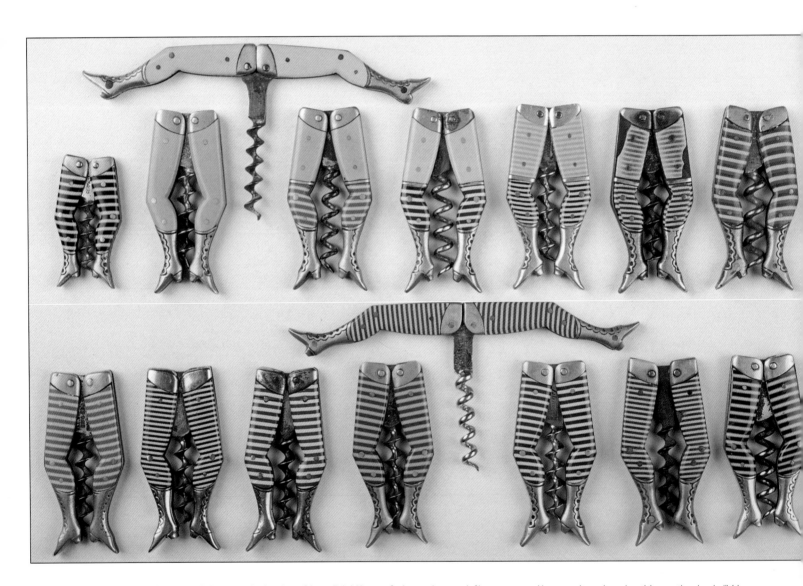

Top row left to right: Mini legs are the hardest of the celluloid legs to find. The pair at *top left* is 1 7/8" long. $650-850; Rare bare flesh tone. $450-550; Three pair of half flesh tone, half stripes. $400-550; Two different stripe pairings on each side. $600-750; Tri-color wavy lines. $500-750.
Bottom row: The most common color stripes for legs are pink/white, green/white, and blue/white. $250-350. However, the pink/white at *bottom left* is very unusual because it carries advertising on the shank: "Val Blatz Br'g Co." and is marked MADE IN GERMANY. $400-450. Other two color versions are valued at $300-$400. Markings on legs include: GERMANY; GESETZLICH GESCHÜTZT; SRD (with arrow through it) GERMANY; MORLEY & SONS GERMANY; HUGO KÖLLER SOLINGEN; REGISTERED GERMANY; GRAEF & SCHMIDT MADE IN GERMANY; HENRY BOKER; LUNAWERK SOLINGEN GERMANY; D PERES GERMANY.

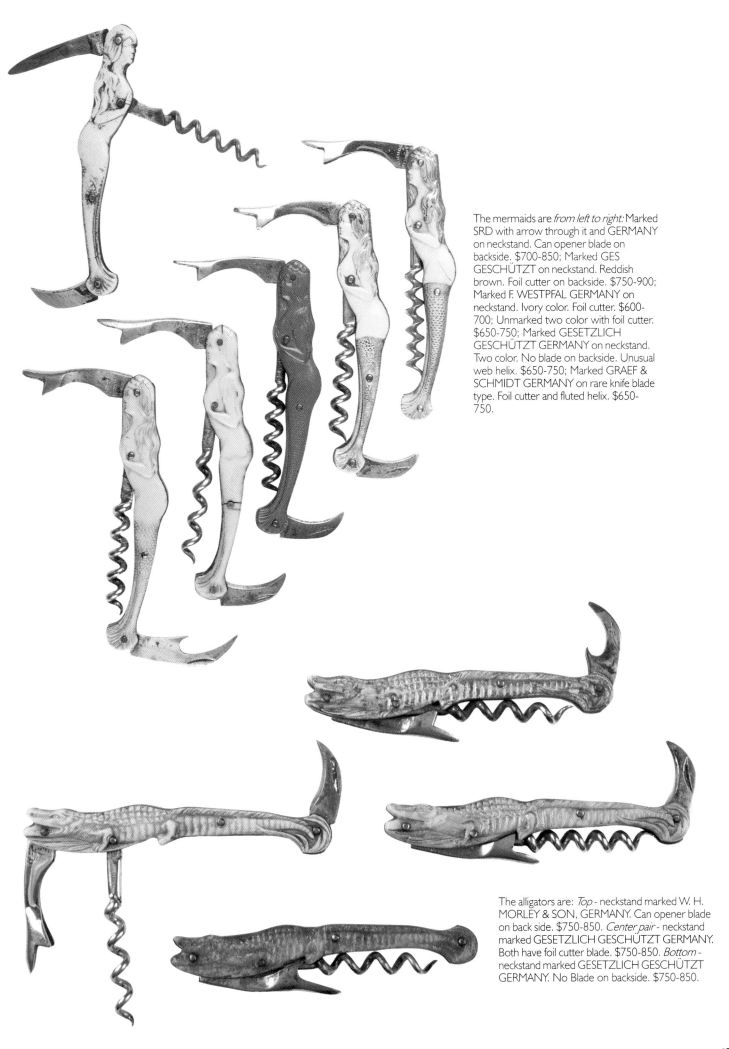

The mermaids are *from left to right:* Marked SRD with arrow through it and GERMANY on neckstand. Can opener blade on backside. $700-850; Marked GES GESCHÜTZT on neckstand. Reddish brown. Foil cutter on backside. $750-900; Marked F. WESTPFAL GERMANY on neckstand. Ivory color. Foil cutter. $600-700; Unmarked two color with foil cutter. $650-750; Marked GESETZLICH GESCHÜTZT GERMANY on neckstand. Two color. No blade on backside. Unusual web helix. $650-750; Marked GRAEF & SCHMIDT GERMANY on rare knife blade type. Foil cutter and fluted helix. $650-750.

The alligators are: *Top* - neckstand marked W. H. MORLEY & SON, GERMANY. Can opener blade on back side. $750-850. *Center pair* - neckstand marked GESETZLICH GESCHÜTZT GERMANY. Both have foil cutter blade. $750-850. *Bottom* - neckstand marked GESETZLICH GESCHÜTZT GERMANY. No Blade on backside. $750-850.

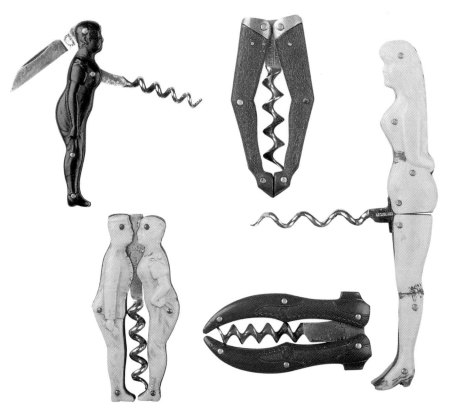

Top row left to right: Lady with blade marked A ANDERSON, ESKILSTUNA. An Anderson advertisement calls this "svart celluloidskaft" - black celluloid. It has at times been incorrectly identified as Bakelite. Bakelite is a thermosetting plastic resin invented by Leo Hendrik Baekeland (1863-1944) in 1909. He was a U.S. chemist and inventor born in Ghent, Belgium. $900-1100; Satyr legs are marked REGISTERED GERMANY. $600-700; The woman folds in the middle and is marked GES. GESCH. $1200-1500.
Bottom row left to right: Marked AMOR GERMANY, D.R.G.M. 105407. The German patent was issued to Carl Bewer of Solingen on November 31, 1898. This corkscrew is sometimes referred to as the "Kissing Couple" and was produced with celluloid and all metal handles. $750-1250; The shoes are Ernst Lesser's German patent number 82028 of September 4, 1897. Marked WEYERSBERG & SON GERMANY. $550-650.

Companies and marks found on corkscrews in this category:
- A ANDERSON, ESKILSTUNA: Located in the Swedish cutlery center Eskilstuna.
- VAL BLATZ BR'G CO: A Milwaukee, Wisconsin brewer. The name Val Blatz was used until Prohibition (1920).
- HENRY BOKER: A large cutlery manufacturer in Solingen, Germany, founded in 1867 and still operating.
- GESETZLICH GESCHÜTZT: German for Legally Registered.
- GRAEF & SCHMIDT GERMANY: New York City agent for J. A. Henckels of Solingen, Germany, located at 29 Warren Street from 1883-1908, The firm changed locations several times before going out of business in 1952.
- HUGO KÖLLER SOLINGEN: German cutlery manufacturer founded in 1861.
- LOERZEL BROTHERS, SAUGERTIES, N. Y., CELEBRATED LAGER: Founded in 1874, the Loerzel Brothers name was used from 1888 to 1893.
- LUNAWERK SOLINGEN GERMANY: A. Feist & Co. founded in Solingen, Germany in 1903 used this name from 1928 to 1948 for its New York office.
- W. H. MORLEY & SON, GERMANY: Offices in Germany and New York City 1913-1927
- D PERES GERMANY: Founded in 1885 in Solingen, Germany, and still operating
- SRD (with arrow through it) GERMANY: Mark of Severin R. Droescher, an importer located at 77-79 Warren Street, New York City 1891-1924.
- F. WESTPFAL GERMANY: Frederick Westpfal, Importer, 186 East Houston Street, New York City 1884-1928.
- WEYERSBERG & SON: Founded in Germany in 1787.

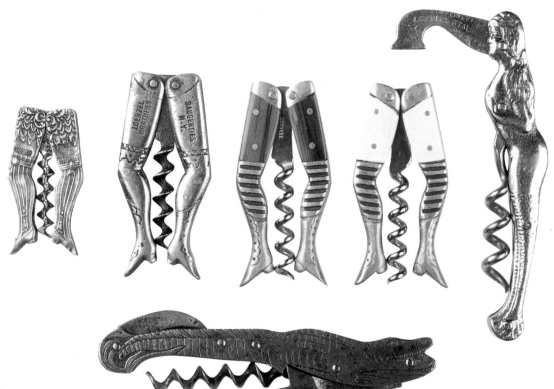

Non-celluloid.
Left to right: Mini legs. The top of the worm is marked REGISTERED GERMANY. The handles are marked STERLING. $1200-1500; All metal handles advertising "Loerzel Brothers, Saugerties, N. Y., Celebrated Lager." $600-800; Two 1970s productions marked GERMANY. Plastic thighs and stripes are painted in the grooves. $100-150; Cast mermaid waiter's friend marked DAVIS "IMPROVED" PAT. JULY 4-91, OTHER PATS PEND with advertising "Compliments of Charles Staebler, 257 Beaubien St., Detroit, Mich." Staebler operated a saloon at that address. $1000-1200.
Bottom: Steel alligator. Marked GESETZLICH GESCHÜTZT GERMANY on neckstand. $800-1000.

Champagne Taps & Tools

Champagne or soda water taps date to the early 19th century. An English example with 1807 hallmark was made by Phipps & Robinson of London. The first tap patent was issued in France in 1828 to M. F. G. Rever.

Taps are designed to penetrate the cork of a bottle containing gaseous liquid. A valve allows the user to draw off as much as wanted, then close the valve and keep the contents bubbly. There are six basic versions:

1. One piece which is threaded into the cork until holes in the base of the thread pass through.
2. One piece which is pushed through the cork until holes in the base pass through.
3. Two piece threaded into the cork with the center spike removed to form the opening.
4. Two piece pushed into the cork with center spike removed to form the opening.
5. Two piece which has a point attached to the threaded shaft. The point drops off in the bottle after it passes through the cork.
6. Two piece with the point attached to a shaft running through the tap and connected to the top button. Moving the shaft up and down allows passage of liquid around the point.

All but the sixth have a valve to control the flow of liquid. The flow in the sixth is controlled by opening and closing the tube by moving the point.

A seventh? In an 1880 English patent, Frederick Hooper and Arthur Luke offer a version without a valve. It is threaded into the cork with the holes penetrating the cork. To stop the flow of liquid the tap is backed off so the holes are within the cork—a cheap, but impractical, approach.

A look at tap boxes and cases reveals the secrets of using taps. Bear in mind that taps in original packaging have higher values than stray taps.

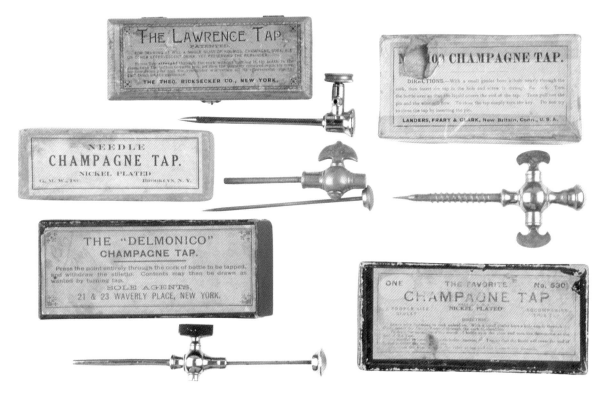

The Lawrence Tap is an 1876 American patent by William and Richard Bentley. To use it: "Force Tap straight through the cork without turning it, tip bottle to the glass, turn the button towards you, let flow the quantity required; quickly turn button from you and the remainder will retain all its effervescent quality. Don't let the gas escape." The button is marked THE LAWRENCE TAP and the top is marked BENTLEY'S PAT. OCT. 17. 1876. $125-175.
The Needle Champagne Tap is from G. M. W. Inc., Brooklyn, New York. $60-80.
The Delmonico Champagne Tap instructions are: "Press the point entirely through the cork of the bottle to be tapped,

and withdraw the stiletto. Contents may then be drawn off as wanted by turning tap." $80-100.
The Champagne Tap from Landers, Frary & Clark of New Britain, Connecticut, tells the user "With a small gimlet bore a hole nearly through the cork, then insert the tap in the hole and screw it through the cork. Turn the bottle over so that the liquid covers the end of the tap. Then pull out the pin and the wine will flow. To close the tap simply turn the key. Do not try to close the tap by inserting the pin." $80-100
The "Favorite" Champagne Tap manufactured by Williamson has an interesting added instruction: "Leave wire fastening to cork unbroken." $80-100.

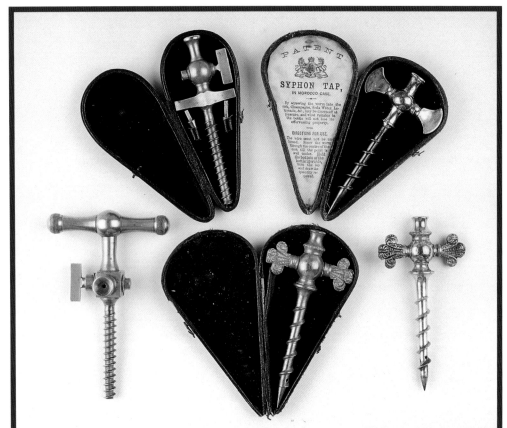

Here are three taps in coffin-like cases. Milne's tap at *top left* comes with two points. The point drops into the bottle when the cork is penetrated. Directions for use tell us: "When the Tap is screwed into the cork and once in use the bottle should be kept turned upside down and placed in a tumbler or jug with a little water in it, this will prevent any escape of Gas through the tap." $100-125.

The directions of the Syphon Tap at *top right* tell us that "The wire must not be unloosed." $100-125.

Maw's Prince of Wales Soda Water Tap at *bottom center* is another marked tap: S. MAW & SON LONDON. To use it "Screw the tap through the centre of the cork, until the holes in the stem have passed beyond it into the bottle, then invert the latter and draw off the quantity required." $100-125.

Maw's tap without case is shown on the *right*. $75-100.

The tap at *bottom left* has storage space for the points in the handle, which are accessed by removing the end balls. $100-125.

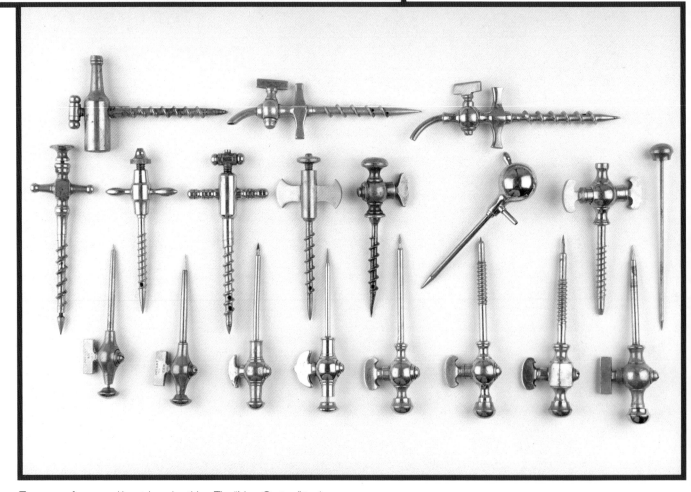

Taps were often named in catalog advertising. The "New Century" tap by Williamson Company is at *top left*. The "Beacon" is *to its right*. The "Hub" is at *far right in the second row*. The "Abyssinian" is at *bottom left*. An assortment of one and two piece taps. $50-100.

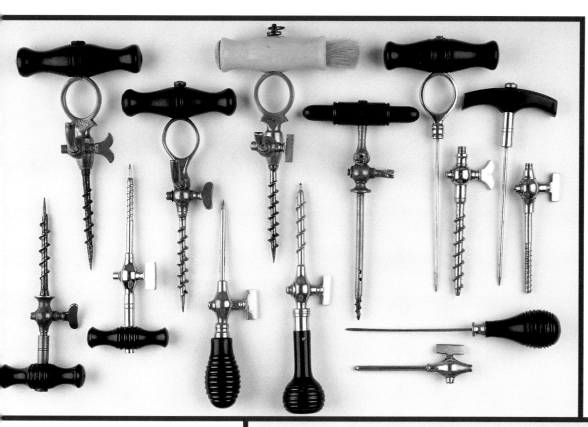

These taps function like their all metal cousins but are a lot more pleasing to have and hold.

Top row left to right: Wood handle. Marked HOLBORN CHAMPAGNE SCREW. $100-150; Brass valve and fittings. Unmarked. $80-120; Bone handle with brush. Marked HOLBORN CHAMPAGNE SCREW plus an 1877 registration mark. $150-200; French tap with serpent head spout. $80-100; Two piece Holborn type with spike attached to handle that unscrews from the tube. $100-150; Two piece with spike attached to two finger handle. $100-125; Note that the *first three* have holes at the bottom of the thread and a valve to control flow.

Bottom row left to right: Two 5 1/2" two piece taps. Note difference in threads. $75-100; Three different round handle two piece taps. $80-120.

The three long taps with serpent design spouts and valves are French. They have a short thread on the end that forms a passageway in the cork to be followed by pushing the tube all the way into the bottle. The holes for flow of liquid are just above the threads. $150-200.

The cork is marked "Dry" and PATENT 7431 on the sides and "Heidsieck & Co., Reims" on the bottom. The steel shank is marked M^CBRIDE'S PATENT. Hugh McBride's 1888 patent was primarily to provide a champagne wire or string breaker at the bottom of the worm and a handle shaped and slanted for better grip. He chose a champagne cork design for the handle. $200-300.

The tool with separate wood turning grip is the "Indus" from Barcelona, Spain. It is marked INDUS PATENTADO. The acorn at the top unthreads to allow liquid to pass. Patented in Spain and the United States (1928) by Alfonso Oliveras Guerris. $150-200.

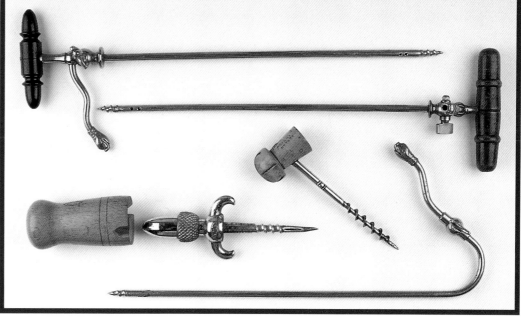

A number of tools have been produced for breaking wires and strings on champagne bottles, removing wax and dirt, and safely popping corks. Safety does take the fun out of popping corks with thumb pressure.

Note: A very common method of opening a champagne bottle is to break it over the bow of a ship.

49

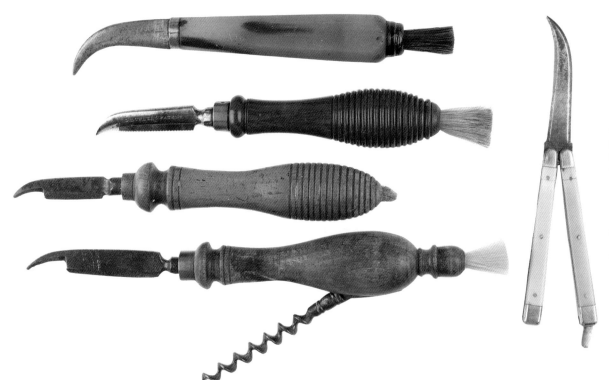

19th century champagne knives were usually designed with a hook at the end to break wire or string and a serrated blade to ease the cork out of the bottle. *Top to bottom:* Horn with blade marked RODGERS CUTLERS TO HIS MAJESTY. $100-150; Blade marked G. DOWLER'S PATENT. $150-200; Unmarked boxwood handle. $75-100; A rare example with folding corkscrew. $600-800. *Right:* Folding champagne knife marked T & C PARIS, BREVETE S.G.D.G. The catch locks the handle when folded up. $200-300.

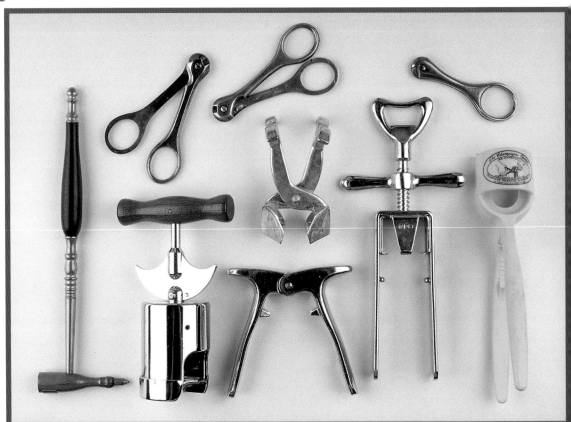

Across the top are three folding wire cutters with the *first two* including a cigar clipper. $20-30. At *left* is an ice breaker with champagne bottle head. $40-50. The other five tools are various designs for gripping and lifting a champagne cork including: *Bottom left to right:* A 1985 American patent with cam action. $30-40; The "Champagne Key" - an American 1984 patent. $20-30; A patented Italian flynut. $50-60; A plastic 1977 American patent from Champagne Products of Monrovia, California. $20-30. The two finger puller above the "Champagne Key" was made in China. $5-10.

In 1850, Frenchman Seraphin Bossin patented a cork removing machine. This archimedean corkscrew was placed in a bayonet chuck in the machine to pull a champagne cork. $125-150.

Clough Affairs

In 1875, William Clough invented a small wire one finger pull corkscrew, which in the ensuing years would undergo several changes in appearance as well as manufacturing processes. The corkscrews shown in this photograph had nickel plated brass sleeves that were usually stamped with advertising or events promotions. Apparently Clough welcomed the turn of the century American expositions and several of these are souvenirs of Atlanta, Chicago, San Francisco, and St. Louis expositions.

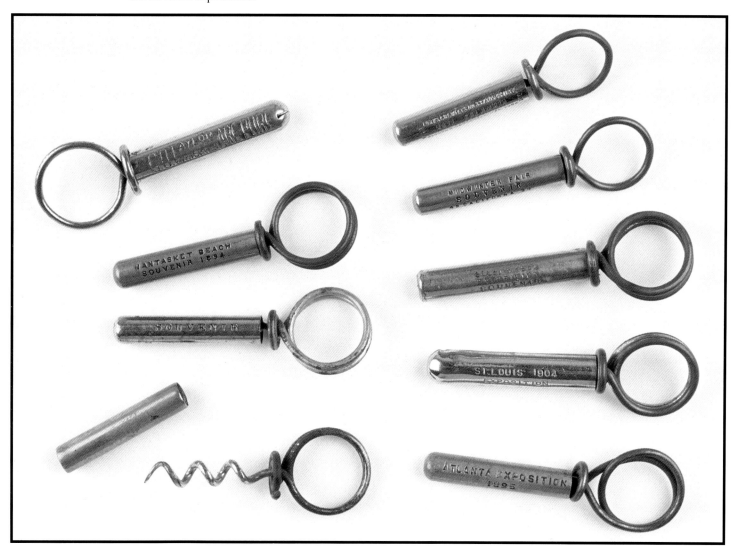

The corkscrew sheath at *top right* is marked CORKSCREW PATS NO 337309 441137, HAIL COLUMBIA 1492 1892, CLOUGH & MACONNELL, NEW YORK. The first patent refers to William Crabb's 1886 for a scarf cut point. Clough's earlier designs were for a ground point. The second patent refers to William Rockwell Clough's 1890 patent for a "Machine for Making Corkscrews." The event was the Columbian Exposition of 1893 which celebrated the anniversary of Columbus' discovery of the New World. It had opened one year late in Chicago. The first Ferris Wheel was built for the exposition and electricity was first shown at an American exposition to the delight of over 21 million attendees. The snack food Cracker Jacks had its debut at this exposition. The present Jackson Park was part of the exposition area. $80-100.

The *second corkscrew on the right* is marked MIDWINTER FAIR SOUVENIR 49 CALIFORNIA 94, PAT NO 337309, THE CLOUGH WIRE CORKSCREW CO., ALTON N.H. The event was the 1894 California Midwinter International Exposition held in San Francisco's Golden Gate Park. Two of the remaining structures from the event are the Japanese Tea Garden and the de Young Museum. $125-150.

The *fifth* corkscrew sheath is marked ATLANTA EXPOSITION 1895, PAT NO 337309, THE CLOUGH WIRE CORKSCREW CO., ALTON N H. The Atlanta event was the 1895 Cotton States International Exposition. The country's first movie theater opened in Atlanta at this event. $125-150.

The *third and fourth on the left* with slightly different sheaths are marked ST. LOUIS 1904 EXPOSITION, SOUVENIR, ROCKWELL CLOUGH CO., ALTON, N.H. U. S. A, PAT. OCT. 16, 1900. The patent date refers to Clough's new machine for making corkscrews. In 1904, St. Louis was celebrating the Louisiana Purchase centennial with this exposition held in Forest Park. The first large automobile display was seen at this fair. $125-150.

The *second corkscrew sheath on the right* is marked NANTASKET BEACH SOUVENIR 1894, PAT. NO. 337309 THE CLOUGH WIRE CORKSCREW CO., ALTON, N.H. Nantasket Beach is in Hull, Massachusetts, and no major industrial exhibitions were held there. Nantasket Beach may be best known for the first night baseball game played there in 1880 and for a giant roller coaster in Paragon Park. $125-150.

The *top right* corkscrew sheath advertises "G. O. Taylor Whiskies are Pure" and is one of many such advertising sheaths produced by Clough. $25-40. The *third* corkscrew has only Clough's marks on it and the *fourth* is unmarked. $15-25.

Clough Stuff

T wenty three patents for corkscrews and corkscrew producing machinery were issued to William Rockwell Clough of Alton, New Hampshire. In 1875, his first corkscrew patent was issued covering his small wire corkscrew used for medicines, inks, and other products with small corks. His last in 1920 for a "Pocket Implement" pictures a knife with a folding worm and other blades. His most successful invention was in October of 1900 for a "Machine for Making Corkscrews." Millions of corkscrews were produced with a wood sheath indicating the October 16, 1900 patent date for the machine. The wood sheath was a very popular form for all types of advertisers from breweries and distilleries, to haberdasheries, to insurance companies, and even laundries. As frequently as they turn up, one would suspect that thousands of companies used them.

Ten years after the invention of the machine, Clough patented an important refinement for his wood sheath corkscrew. He added his "Decapitator" for removing bottle caps. These turn up far less frequently than the plain sheath. This can be attributed to the dying market for that form of advertising by the second decade of the 20th century.

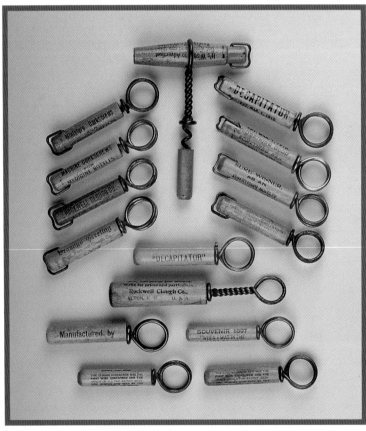

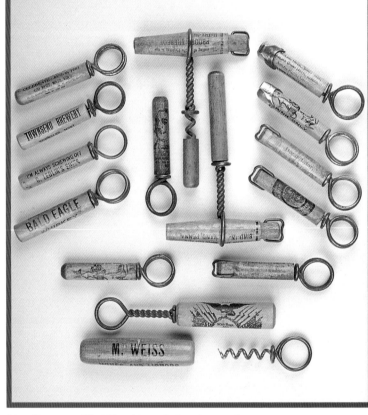

The Rockwell Clough Company took full advantage of their own products as a means to advertise their own products. All of these corkscrews carry Clough advertising and they are all different. Values range from $10-50.

Here are some examples of Clough advertising copy:
"Sure winner as an advertising novelty."
"Decapitator, Something Good, Something New."
"Miniature Corkscrews for Medicine Bottles and other bottles, sold by the millions all over the world."
"It's Wise to Advertise! Get wise and use this Newire Combination Corkscrew and cap-lifter. The Best we Ever Made."
"Seasons Greetings" (in green lettering).
"Put your name on 1000 of these decapitators. You'll find it the best ad. that ever happened to you."
"Advertise!!! That is business these days. This device is a great-strong-ad. New, and patent just allowed. Write for prices and particulars. Rockwell Clough Co., Alton, N.H. U. S. A."

It is quite apparent that Clough's products and promotions were a success. Every type of corkscrew that carried the Clough advertising can be found with advertising and promotions of others. Value is very much influenced by the advertising on the corkscrews and the interest of specific advertising and local interest collectors. $1-50.

Included in this lot are souvenirs of a couple of celebrations - "Celebrate - Aug. 6, 1902, 42d Regt., Mass. Vols." and "Memories of Port Hudson, 50th Regt. and 4th Battery Reunion, Salem, Aug. 26, 1909."

Evidencing Clough's claim to worldwide sales is a wood sheath marked "I'm always screwing off, C. Ledlin's Suits, Tailor & Mercer, Bathurst" supplied by "Pratten Bros. Sydney" (Australia).

A matched set. A cork top bottle of Davis Maryland Rye Whiskey and the matching advertising corkscrew. $50-75.

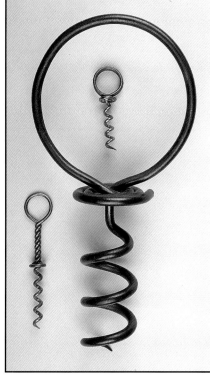

Left: An 11 1/2" Clough corkscrew from a point of purchase display. $150-200.

Below: A mere two dozen of the millions of Clough wood sheath advertising corkscrews. $1-30.
My favorite advertising on these is: "From J. M. Cotton, Headquarters for Portsmouth Brewery, also Anheuser-Busch Beer, wines and liquors of all kinds for medicinal and family use. Your patronage solicited. Ashland, N.H."
The sad thing about this Clough type corkscrew is that, unlike the picnic corkscrew, the sheath is not a snug fit in the hole at the top of the worm.

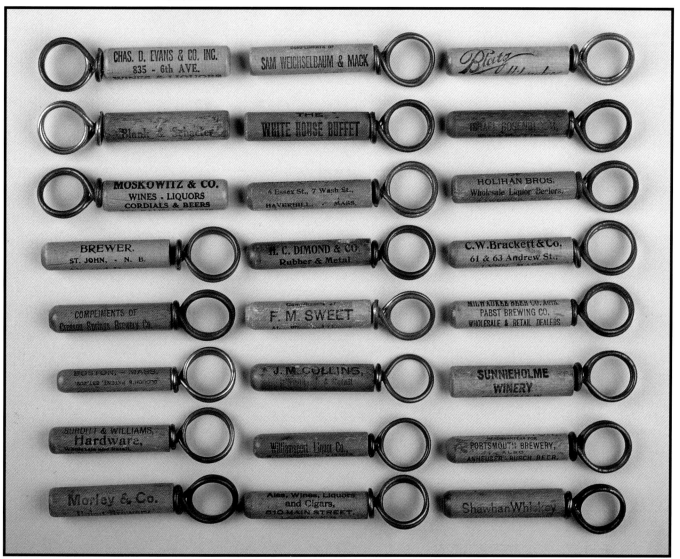

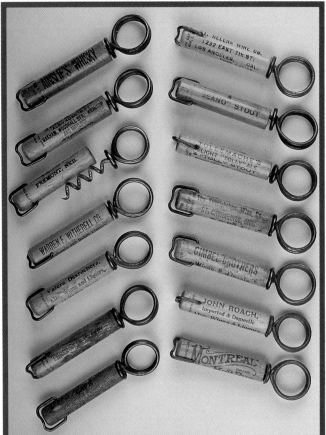

Left: Clough's 1910 patented and Trademarked "Decapitator." They are harder to find than those without the cap remover. All of these have different beer, wine, or liquor advertising. $5-50.

Below: The box reads "Pat. April 30, 1901, Oct. 16, 1900, the 'All-Ways' Handy Combination Bottle Opener & Corkscrew, No two ways about this being useful, it's useful in four ways - Pulling a Cork, Taking out Aluminum Stopper, Removing a Seal, Lifting a Crown Cap." The box contains the "All-Ways" with unusual paper label advertising "Just a little better than what you thought was best, Altpeter's Root Beer and Ginger Ale, Factory 217 Maple Street, Baraboo, Wisconsin, Telephone 230."

The 1900 patent reference is Clough's machine for bending wire into a corkscrew. The 1901 patent is John Baseler's patent for a "Stopper Extractor." The patent was for the cap lifter with the point at the front end of the crescent designed to punch a hole in the cap so it could not be re-used. A 1916 *Western Brewer* magazine advertisement from A. W. Stephens Company of Waltham, Massachusetts, proclaims "One of these openers hung up in the kitchen beats a hundred of the other kind scattered on the cellar floor."

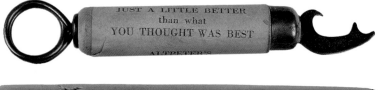

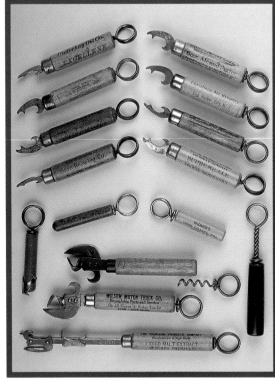

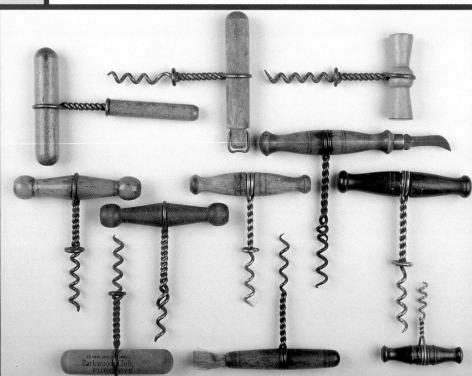

Left: The *top* eight corkscrews are the "All-Ways" with a variety of advertisements. Supplier names are usually included in small print and often with the incorrect patent dates March 30, 1901 and April 30, 1910. $20-50 depending upon brand name advertised.

The red sheath corkscrew at *lower left* is an English version of Clough's decapitator. $15-20. The black sheath on the *lower right* protects the worm of a single extended wire, single loop corkscrew. $25-35. The red sheath has French advertising and is thinner than the typical American sheaths. $30-40. The green sheath advertising "Widmer's Wine Cellars" turns up in droves with the incorrect cap lifter/corkscrew combination. $50-75.

The two short can openers are marked BULL-DOG TEMPERED. $50-75.

At *bottom* is a can opener patented in 1904 by Frank White and Fred Winkler. It is marked "SURE-CUT" CAN OPENER PAT 7-10-04 . It has a sliding adjustable blade and incorporates the Clough wire corkscrew in the handle. $50-75.

Right: A variety of Clough corkscrews many of which were manufactured by the Williamson Company of Newark, New Jersey.

Top row left to right: Plain handle and sheath. $20-30; Handle with decapitator. $30-40; Bowtie handle. $25-35.

Second row left to right: Clough's 1899 wood handle design patent in lacquered oak. Wire finishes in a button above the worm. $40-50; 1899 patent with mahogany stain, no button. $35-40; Clough's 1876 patent. Marked WILLIAMSON'S on top of wire wrap. 3 3/4" handle. $25-35; A rare unmarked example with foil cutter. $75-100; Top of wire marked WILLIAMSON'S. 4 1/4" handle. $25-35.

Bottom row left to right: Wire wrapped wood handle with advertising. $20-30; Cigar shape handle with brush. $50-75; Midsize with 2 1/2" wide handle. $10-15.

Codd Pieces

In 1870, Englishman Hiram Codd introduced an internally stoppered bottle. The bottle has a glass ball molded into a chamber in the top. A rubber "O" seats in a ring molded inside the top lip. When the bottle is filled with liquid, the pressure of the gas holds the glass ball against the rubber seal to maintain the pressure until released.

This Codd bottle is marked W H DIXON EAST GRINSTEAD. Hiram Codd registered his first opener for depressing the glass balls in the necks of his bottles on May 10th 1872. The "openers" are wood rounds hollowed out and leaving a stud in the middle to depress the ball in the bottle. One is marked L. VALLET, MAKER, LIVERPOOL.

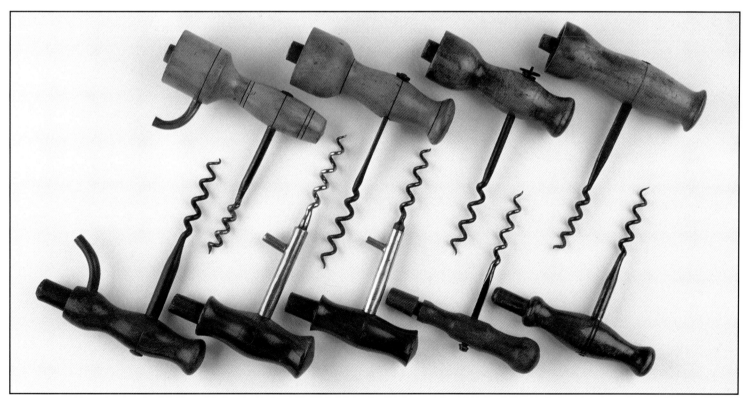

A Codd bottle opener added to a corkscrew handle was a useful accessory. The boxwood handles in the *top row* vary slightly with the *first* having the added advantage of a pouring spout. These are a few of the many variations of the 1881 English registration of J & W Roper of Birmingham. $100-150.

In the *bottom row* all have the depressing mechanism cut into the handle without the benefit of a bottle collar. The *first* has a pouring spout placed like the one above it. $100-125. The next two are Matt Perkins 1884 English patent in which the liquid runs through a part of the handle to a spout in the tubular shank. Both are marked CONEY'S PATENT. $150-225. The two at *right* are a simplification of the mechanism. $75-100.

Coffee Grinders

Because of its appearance, this type of corkscrew has been dubbed "Coffee Grinder." Coffee Grinder corkscrews were produced as early as the late 18th century. In the late 19th century, J. H. Perille produced one he called the "Manivelle" (the Crank). The two shown here are 20th century Italian. $300-500.

Finger Pulls

Finger Pulls are designed to fit two, three, or four fingers. Most are English. With a couple of exceptions, brute force is used to remove the cork. I have only included metal pulls in this category. Each photo contains pulls that vary in size or design. Some are very slight. A keen eyed pull specialist will, no doubt, be able to root out many more.

Health Wealth and All Prosperity

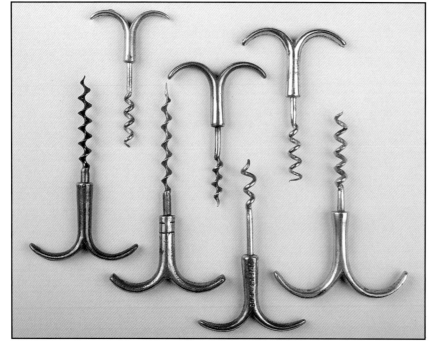

These pulls range from a 2" wide handle for two finger comfort at the *top right* to a 3 1/2" span at *lower right* for a full grip. *Bottom left and right and top row* are unmarked. $20-30. In the *bottom row the 2nd from left* is marked C. T. WILLETTS L᷁ᴰ. $70-80. The *3rd* is marked COMMERCIAL and was a product of G. F. Hipkins. $30-40.

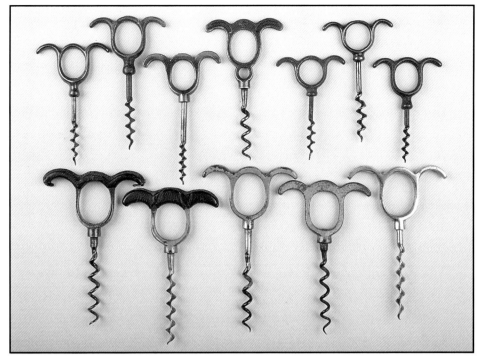

Three finger pulls with handles ranging from 2 1/4" to 3 1/4" span. These are often called "eyebrows" for obvious reasons. The pull at *top center* is marked THE LEVER SIGNET and can be used by itself or with a lever (see "Lever - Single" category). Value of unmarked plain handle examples is $5-25. The two at *lower left* have leather covered handles with the *first* marked LOFTUS. The leather is wrapped and stitched. $75-100.

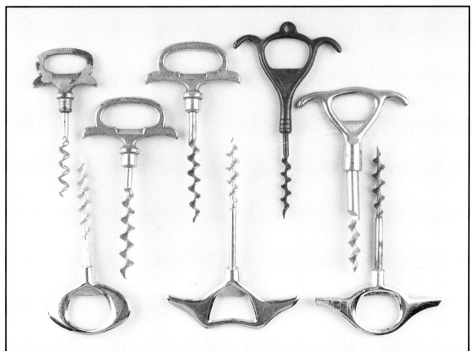

Two and three finger pulls with a cap lifter added. The *first three in the top row* are marked R⁰ N⁰ 713438 (English registered design of 1925) with the *third* further marked MALING & C⁰ L™. These are also found with nickel plated brass sheaths. $30-40. The *fourth* has a hanger hole added. $40-50. On the *top right* is a crudely cast handle with a poorly cut worm. From Eastern Europe. $5-10. The three designer pulls in the *bottom row* have bright chrome plated handles. The last is marked LEVER. $25-35.

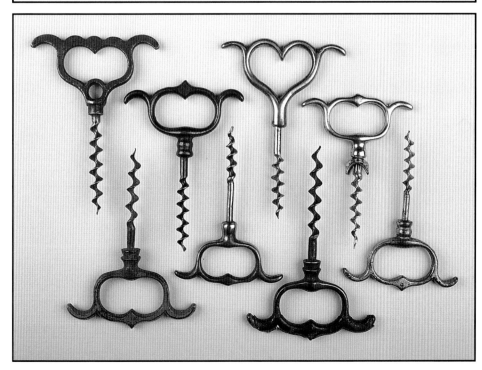

Four finger pulls.
Top row left to right: For use independently or with a lever. $40-50; Leather wrapped handle $100-125; Heart shape handle. $75-100; Teeth added above worm. Marked L B. $125-150.
Bottom row: Four iron unmarked pulls. $25-35.

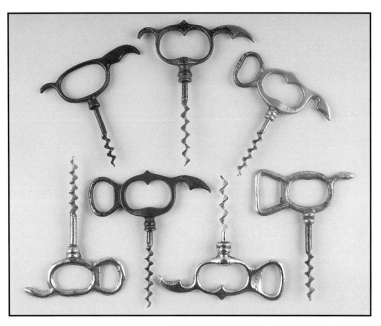

"I'M PULLING MY WEIGHT" ALL RIGHT

Above: The two four finger pulls at *top left* have a foil cutter/wire breaker added. The *first* is different in that it does not have the divider for the middle two fingers. The remaining five have a cap lifter added to the design. $50-75.

Right: *Left to right:* Three finger with button and fine wire worm marked UNIVERSAL, G. F. HIPKINS. $75-100; Four finger pull with reeded button. $60-80; Four finger pull with plain button and wire helix. $50-75; Three finger pull with scalloped top with fancy shaft and finished with gripping teeth. $150-200; Three finger pull with plain button and web helix. $60-80.

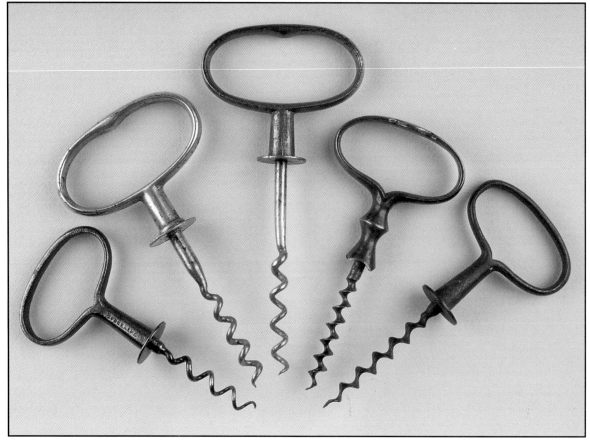

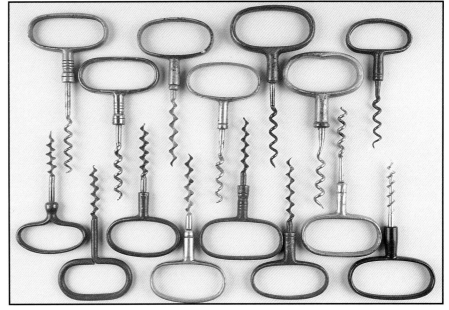

Various full grip pulls often referred to as the "Cellarman's Corkscrew." Unmarked examples valued at $10-20. Marked examples are: *Top row second from left* is marked FOREIGN at the base of the grip. $20-25; *Bottom row fourth from left* has "Apollinaris" advertising on top. $75-85; *Sixth from left* is marked DENT & VAIZEY, CROSBY SQUARE LONDON on top. $80-100; *Bottom row second from right* is marked FARROW & JACKSON LTD LONDON below the grip. $100-125.

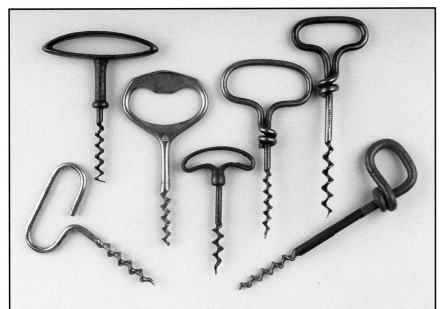

*The Dirilyte Company was located in Kokomo, Indiana, and began marketing flatware and hollowware under the trade name DIRIGOLD in 1926. The gold color metal, not plated, was developed in Sweden in 1914. Because it contained no gold, the U.S. Patent Office objected and the name was changed to DIRILYTE in 1937.

Top row left to right: Squashed design four finger pull. $60-70; Two finger pull with cap lifter. Engraved with initials "C.N.E." and marked DIRIGOLD. *$80-100; Squashed design two finger pull. $40-50; Three finger pull formed from one piece of metal shaped and wrapped. $30-40; Two finger one piece marked ZEITZ. $50-60.
Bottom row left and right: Cheaply done one piece. $5-7; One finger, one piece knot marked STUBAIMARWA. $30-40.

Three French two finger pulls with elegant design. The pull on the *left* has teeth above worm. These grip the cork to assist in breaking the seal with the bottle by continuing to twist after the worm is inserted. $75-100; The Perille trademark is stamped on the shaft of the other two. $100-150.

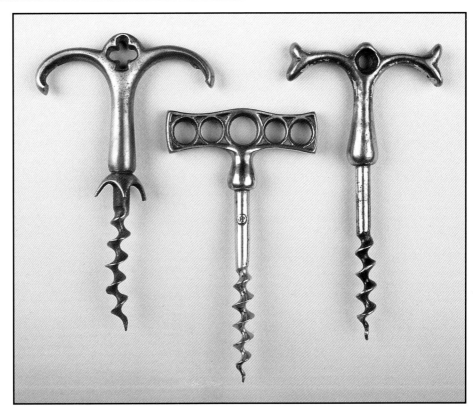

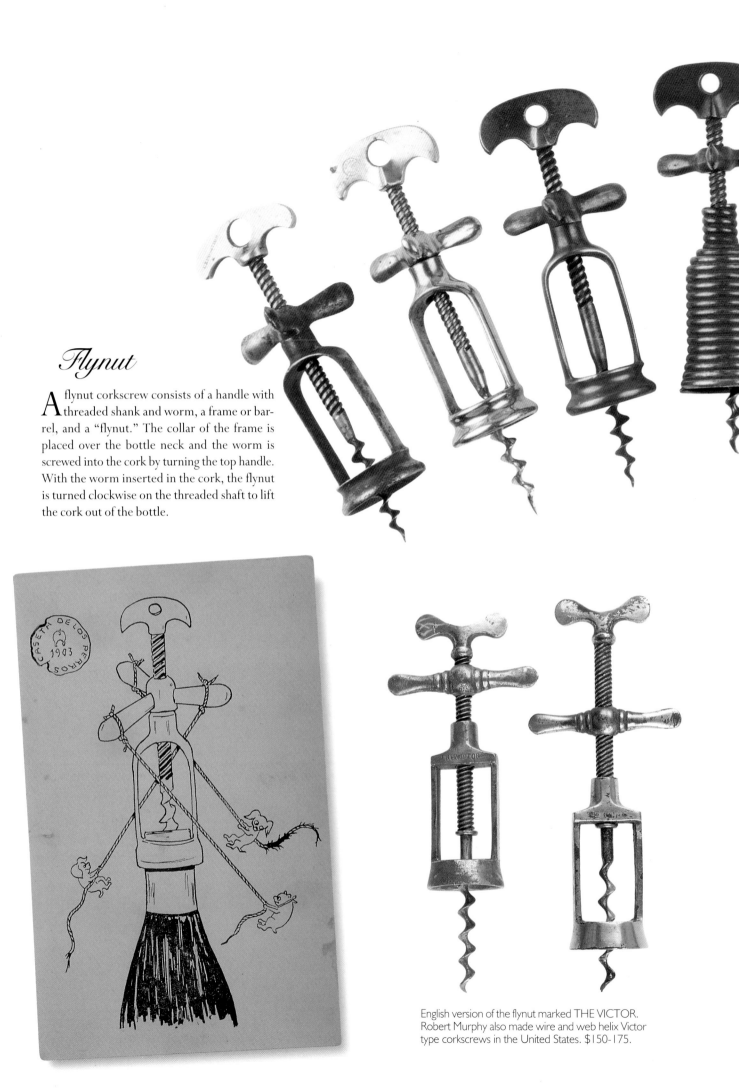

Flynut

Aflynut corkscrew consists of a handle with threaded shank and worm, a frame or barrel, and a "flynut." The collar of the frame is placed over the bottle neck and the worm is screwed into the cork by turning the top handle. With the worm inserted in the cork, the flynut is turned clockwise on the threaded shaft to lift the cork out of the bottle.

English version of the flynut marked THE VICTOR. Robert Murphy also made wire and web helix Victor type corkscrews in the United States. $150-175.

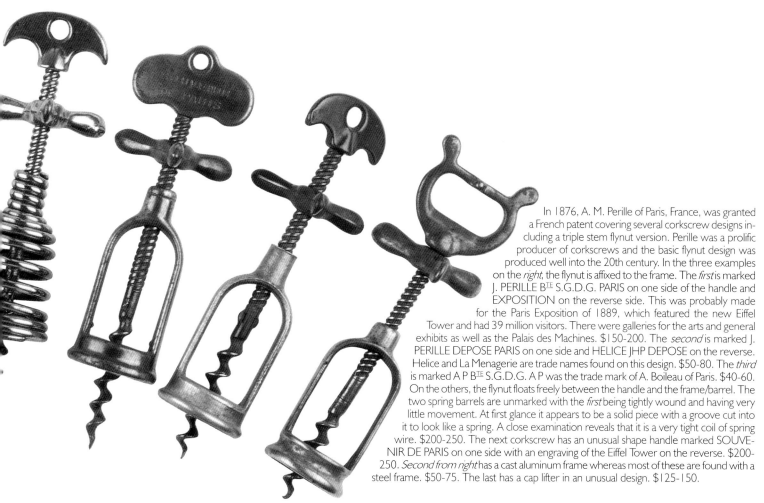

In 1876, A. M. Perille of Paris, France, was granted a French patent covering several corkscrew designs including a triple stem flynut version. Perille was a prolific producer of corkscrews and the basic flynut design was produced well into the 20th century. In the three examples on the *right*, the flynut is affixed to the frame. The *first* is marked J. PERILLE B^TE S.G.D.G. PARIS on one side of the handle and EXPOSITION on the reverse side. This was probably made for the Paris Exposition of 1889, which featured the new Eiffel Tower and had 39 million visitors. There were galleries for the arts and general exhibits as well as the Palais des Machines. $150-200. The *second* is marked J. PERILLE DEPOSE PARIS on one side and HELICE JHP DEPOSE on the reverse. Helice and La Menagerie are trade names found on this design. $50-80. The *third* is marked A P B^TE S.G.D.G. A P was the trade mark of A. Boileau of Paris. $40-60. On the others, the flynut floats freely between the handle and the frame/barrel. The two spring barrels are unmarked with the *first* being tightly wound and having very little movement. At first glance it appears to be a solid piece with a groove cut into it to look like a spring. A close examination reveals that it is a very tight coil of spring wire. $200-250. The next corkscrew has an unusual shape handle marked SOUVENIR DE PARIS on one side with an engraving of the Eiffel Tower on the reverse. $200-250. *Second from right* has a cast aluminum frame whereas most of these are found with a steel frame. $50-75. The last has a cap lifter in an unusual design. $125-150.

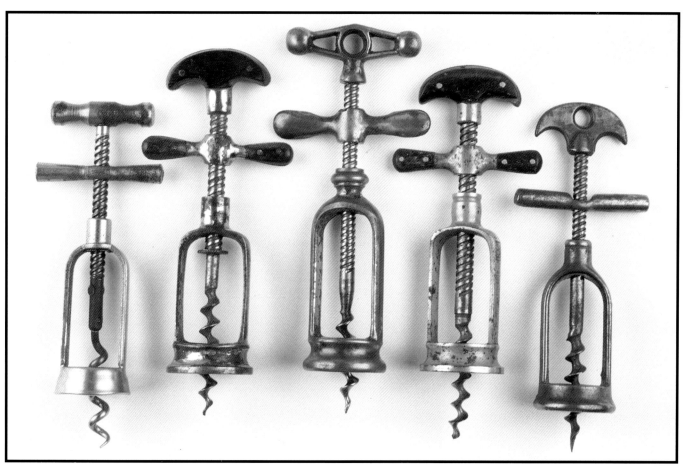

Another Perille type design is the flynut with two legs. At *right and left* are two unmarked simple bar flynuts having differing handles and worms. $75-90. The corkscrews to the *right and left of center* have wood embellishments riveted to the handle and flynut. The one on the *right* was made in Czechoslovakia. $100-125. In the *center* is Perille's "Aero" marked AERO on the flynut and JHP DEPOSE PARIS on the frame. $175-200.

Here is a brass Italian version of the flynut corkscrew. It is marked EDWIN JAY MADE IN ITALY. The marking is on top of the center hub of the flynut, which in an unusually inconspicuous spot for an Italian corkscrew. $75-100.

Above: Five "flynut" designs. In the *first four* the top handle is connected to the worm by a smooth stem. This stem floats in the fixed second handle mounted on an externally threaded stem. The *fifth* has a flynut traveling the threaded stem of the worm.
Left to right: Marked ITALY, BREVETTATO. $40-50; Brass colored, marked on top handle VALEZINA. Bottom of middle stem is marked MADE IN ENGLAND, PAT. PEND., REG DESIGN NO. 857383. Although it is marked with a 1949 English registration, this corkscrew was patented in England in 1943 and in America in 1944 by American inventor John Miller. $100-125; A silver colored "Valezina" additionally marked CANADIAN R. D. NO. 112-17645 without PAT PEND. The Valezina was also made in red and blue. $100-125; Hourglass barrel with a tag on the underside of the lower handle reading "Spain." $50-60; Unmarked and poorly silver plated. $10-15.

Left: She's a Perille type corkscrew and she has been perfectly fitted with head, upper body, and skirt. Each of the three carved rosewood pieces is secured with a wood pin. The head is secured to the handle at the top (you can see part of the metal handle - her earrings), the upper body to the flynut which has been trimmed to accommodate it, and the skirt to the frame. The bottom of the skirt is marked "Made in France." $100-200.

Frame - Bearing

In 1901, Ernst Scharff registered a design in Germany for a frame corkscrew with an enclosed bearing at the top of the frame to assist in smooth extraction of the cork. G. Usbeck had a similar design in 1909 with an exposed bearing at the top of the frame. The Usbeck design was produced in several forms and is still being made by the Monopol Company in Marburg, Germany.

Left to right: Usbeck design with ornate handle marked D.R.G.M. GERMANY, MONOPOL UNIVERSAL. Unusual tapered frame. Cap lifter in the handle. $150-175; A cheap imitation of the first marked A & Z and O N A in a triangle. $120-130; An even cheaper imitation marked SANDRIK, WSKOV, MSI, PONIKI. $100-120; Same handle and marks as the *third* but intended as a two finger direct pull. $50-60.

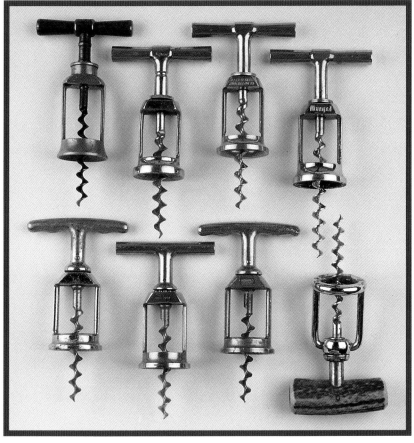

Theordor Kämpf's 1926 German design. Top of frame marked RECORD GERMANY/D.R.G.M. $80-120.

Top row left to right: Scharff design marked on frame SOLON / D.R.G.M. Nº152004. $100-125; Usbeck design marked GERMANY on the handle. $20-30; Usbeck design marked MONOPOL on the frame. $20-25; Usbeck design marked J. A. HENCKELS ZWILLINGSWERK on the frame. $30-40.
Bottom row left to right: The *first three* are Swiss made marked VOSS CUTLERY, SWISS MADE, and LADOR. In the Swiss type the handle and stem to the bearing are one piece pinned on the worm shank. $15-20; The stag handle on the *right* is a cheap imitation. $3-4.

Frame - Columbus

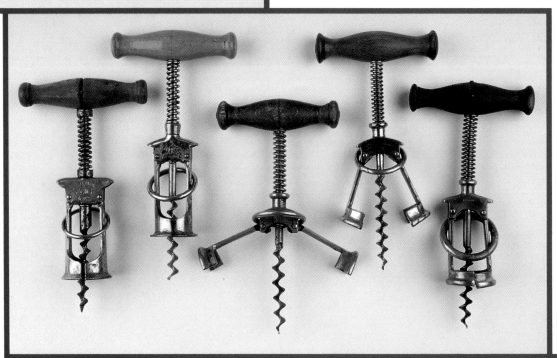

In 1893, Eduard Becker of Solingen, Germany, invented a corkscrew with a split frame to facilitate removal of the extracted cork from the worm. To use it:

1. Secure the frame by sliding the ring to the bottom.
2. Place collar over bottle neck.
3. Turn worm into cork until cork is lifted into the frame.
4. Invert the corkscrew. The ring will drop to the stops on the arms which will open.
5. Remove the cork.

The spring between the handle and the frame assists the extraction by exerting pressure on the handle to gradually withdraw the cork. Becker was issued German patent 70879 in March 1893. An English patent was issued in September followed by an American patent in April 1894.

Why is it called the "Columbus"? Although I have seen no written record, the Columbian exposition took place in Chicago in 1893 and it is possible that it was named to commemorate that event.

Top left: A large number of variations of the Columbus corkscrew exists. *Left to right:* Marked COLUMBUS ORIGINAL on sheet metal frame. $50-75; Marked D. R. PATENT NO. 70879 on one side of steel frame top and COLUMBUS on the other. $60-80; Large stag horn (8 1/2") marked COLUMBUS on one side and GERMANY with the trademark of Müller & Schmidt, Solingen, Germany. $150-200; Marked D.R. PATENT NO. 70879 on one side of frame, other side blank. $60-80.

Center: *Left to right:* A cheap version with maple handle, sheet metal frame, and a Trident trademark. $30-40; A Columbus from Argentina marked INDUSTRIA ARGENTINA, GAUMEN, M. REG. (for registered mark) on one side of frame. Gaumen is the manufacturer. $75-100; Two unmarked. $30-50; Last one marked only GERMANY. $35-55.

Right: The corkscrew in the *middle* with bamboo handle is marked ORIGINAL - BACCHUS at top of frame. $125-175. The other two have a bearing assist in the top of the frame. The one on the *left* is marked SAXONY and the one on the *right* LANGBEIN GERMANY. $100-150.

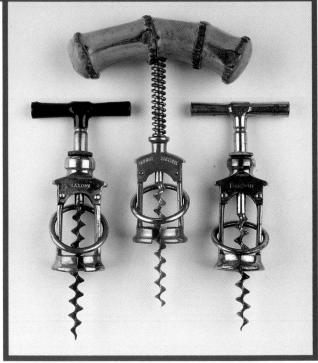

Frame - Locking Handle

Since the middle of the 19th century numerous inventions and designs have addressed a mechanism for locking the handle on the worm shank. The "locked" handle is used first to screw the worm into the cork. Once it is screwed down to the frame, the handle is unlocked. Continuing to turn it will lift the cork. Compare this to the "flynut" corkscrew. A fixed handle attached to the shank is used to screw the worm into the cork. A second handle, the "flynut," is then used to lift the cork.

Left to right: Marked WULFRUNA, PLANT'S PATENT NO. 5549. In Stephen Plant's 1884 English patent, a sliding-plate covers the top of the shank to lock the handle in place. $150-200; Marked PATENT and G. R. on the brass sliding collar lock. This is an 1891 German registration by Heinrich Ehrhardt. $200-300; The "Bodega," an 1899 German patent by Ernst Scharff. When the handle is raised, the arms pivot down on a nut, closing its opening and locking the handle. When the arms meet the frame, they are pushed up and "unlock" the handle. $500-600.

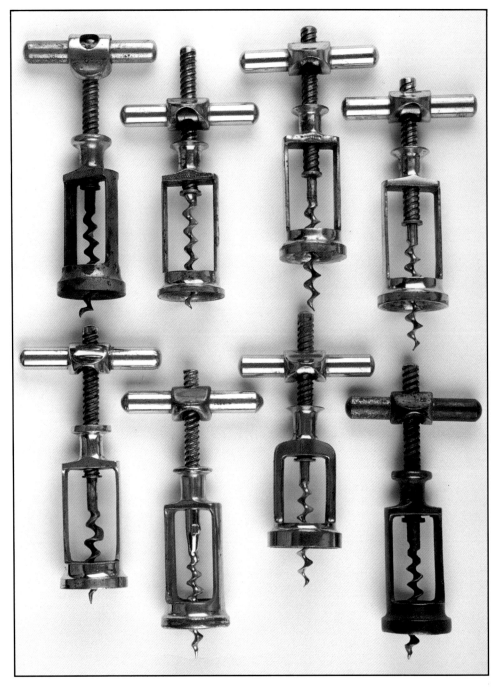

In May of 1891, Heinrich Ehrhardt in Düsseldorf, Germany, patented a locking collar that had an elongated hole on the underside and a "nose" on the front. The elongated hole allows the handle "nose" to drop down and lock the handle when it is threaded up to the top of the shank. When the nose comes in contact with the top of the frame, it is pushed up causing the handle to "unlock." Continuous turning will then extract the cork. These eight corkscrews all have the Ehrhardt collar and are marked at the top of the frame (except when noted). Value range is $40-80.
Top row left to right: GARBARINO BROS. (New York importers) MADE IN GERMANY; J. A. HENCKELS, SOLINGEN; H. BOKER & CO., GERMANY, SAXONY.
Bottom row left to right: CZECHO-SLOVAKIA; G M T C⁰, FRANCE marked on handle (note that this one does not have the small "button" at the bottom of the thread); Short frame, not marked; ACIER.

In addition to the patent, Heinrich Ehrhardt registered a design for a locking revolving collar in February of 1891 (the sliding collar is shown in the first photograph in this category). In this earlier version the collar did not have the weighted nose and had to be locked and unlocked manually. Six examples of the manual revolving lock are shown here. Value range is $35-75.
Left to right: Unmarked narrow 2 1/2" handle; GRAEF & SCHMIDT (New York importers) GERMANY; Marked WESTER BROS., M.I. GERMANY; Marked only GERMANY; Marked THE CHALLENGE; A modern Russian version.

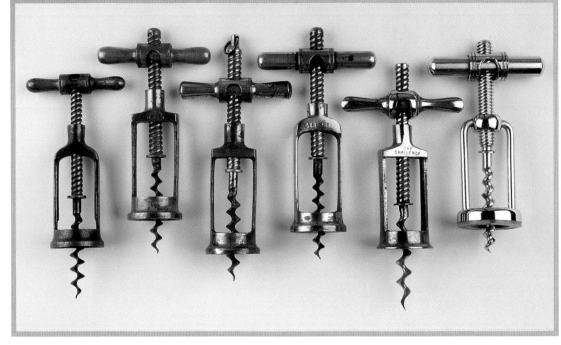

Here are four examples of Ehrhardt's 1891 patent idea with wide column frames. Value range is $60-80. *Left to right:* Brass marked EDWIN JAY, MADE IN ITALY on the locking collar; Unmarked nickel plated; Unmarked chrome plated; Unmarked. The last has teeth below the thread instead of the button to keep it from freely pulling up through the frame.

Right: The locking handle frame on the *left* is marked MONOPOL WEST GERMANY on the handle. It has a left-hand worm and comes in the box that says it is a left-handed model. Instructions on the box, however, are for a right-handed model. $30-40. The *middle* corkscrew is a right-handed version of the first marked on the handle B. ALTMANN & CO., NEW YORK, MADE IN GERMANY. Altmann was a New York department store. $40-50. Note: "Altmann" is spelled with two n's on this corkscrew. Another in the "Waiters' Friends" category is spelled "Altman."
On the *right* is a wide frame with verdigris finish and twelve astrological signs on the frame. $30-50.

Below: Here are three examples of the locking collar with closed barrel. The *first* is in a box marked "'Lifetimer' Automatic Cork-Puller, copyright by Gadgets of California, 'The gift for a lifetime.'" $40-50.
The *middle* corkscrew is the same as the "Lifetimer" except it has an elliptical collar. $25-35.
The corkscrew on the *right* has a wood and brass barrel and handle. $20-25.

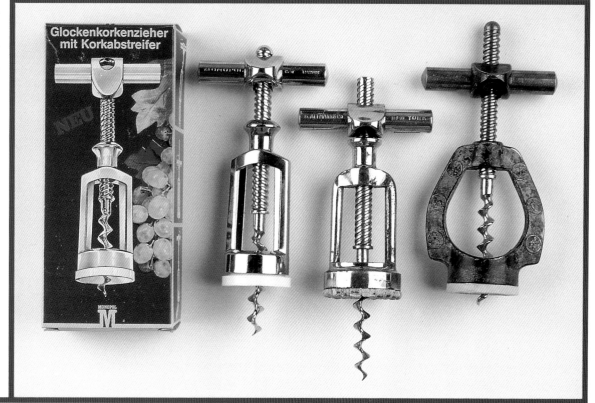

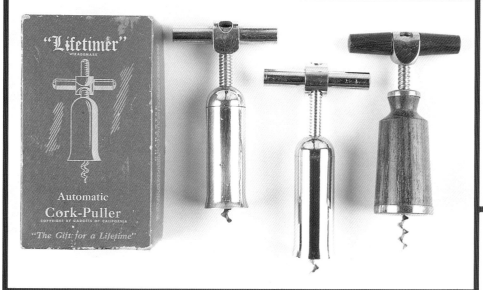

Instructions included with the "Lifetimer:"

1. Turn the handle to top of the drawscrew. Collar will automatically lock in position.

2. Insert the corkscrew fully into the cork by clockwise rotation. Lift and hold the locking collar with the thumb and rotate the handle one turn clockwise.

3. Release the collar and continue to rotate the handle clockwise and the cork will be drawn from the bottle.

Willy Fritsch uses
a frame type
corkscrew to
open a bottle.

Willy Fritsch

Frame - Open

Corkscrews with open frames have been made with a wide variety of "better mousetraps" to pull the cork or remove the cork from the worm. The bottom of the frame is flared. In some instances the frame is placed on top of the bottle before turning the worm into the cork. In others as the worm is turned into the cork, the frame descends to meet the neck. Continuing to turn the handle, unlocking the handle then turning, turning a secondary handle, and reversing the rotation are different methods employed to lift the cork into the frame. With the open frame, the cork can be grasped as needed to remove it from the worm, if there is no mechanical means of doing this. Examples of frames with internal mechanisms with two exceptions are shown in this category.

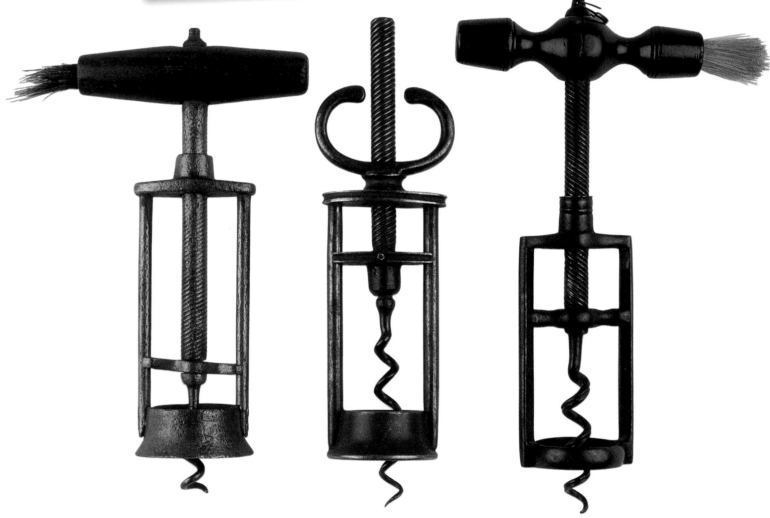

English frame corkscrews
Left: In John Coney's 1854 English patent, the threaded stem passing through a two post frame is hollow and receives the stem of the worm. The frame is placed on top of the bottle first. When entering the cork, the notches on the bottom of the threaded stem and projections above the worm engage and they disengage when the rotation is reversed. A pin on the worm stem is then engaged to lift the cork guided by a crossbar riding on the posts. $700-1000.
Middle: In this design, the worm is inserted into the cork first by grasping the frame and handle. The frame descends to meet the bottle. The handle, which has an internal thread and is attached to the top of the frame and rotating freely, is then turned. The stem and guide are lifted in the frame and the cork is extracted. Reverse the handle to lower the worm and remove the cork. $1200-1500.
Right: The action is the same as in the *middle* except the internal thread is in the top of the frame. Turning the handle after penetration, lifts the cork into the frame. $1000-1200.

French frame corkscrews.
Left: Two marked DIAMANT PARIS with the trademark of Perille. The "Diamant" is based on an 1876 French patent by Jacques Perille. On the *left* is a typical Perille handle and on the *right* a bone handle. The stem of the worm is smooth passing through the stem of the frame, which has an external thread. The worm is turned into the cork and a jaw clutch below the handle engages the internally threaded collar to lift the cork. $250-350.
Right: Two marked on the top of the button L'EXCELSIOR, A. G. B^{TE} S.G.D.G. PARIS. A. G. is Armand Guichard and this is his 1880 French patent. The worm is inserted into the cork and the frame descends to meet the bottle neck. Reversing the rotation lifts the cork in the frame. $250-350.

German frame corkscrews. Georg Usbeck's 1902 registered design had a crossbar with double hooks that hook over the top of the frame as a locking device. When the worm is screwed into the cork, the handle and frame are locked for self extraction of the cork. The lock is undone to drop the cork below the frame for removal. A spring assists in extraction.
Left to right: Marked BONSA. Usbeck design with wire spring. $125-150; Marked D.R.G.M. with slots in frame to lock crossbar. $125-150; Marked D.R.G.M. with slots in frame, machined spring. $150-175; Button design like the French L'Excelsior. Marked GERMANY. $100-150.

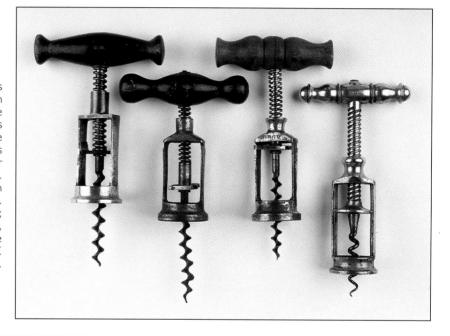

Left: A pair of unmarked English Coney type corkscrews with centering button. $250-350.
Right: A nickel plated and two "Farrow and Jackson" type unmarked butterfly handle corkscrews with centering button. $150-250.

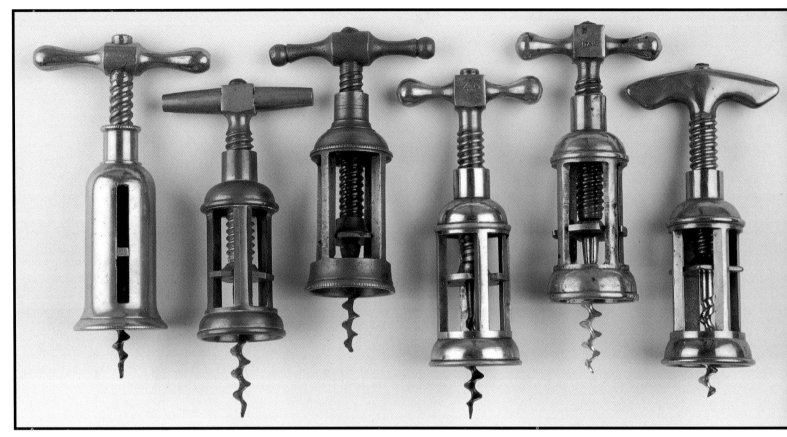

Italian frames with centering button.
Left to right: Slotted barrel marked CAPPELI, BORGOMANERO. $150-200; Three column brass frame with triangulated button. $80-100; Four column brass frame with reeded edges. $100-125; Four column nickel plated brass frame with handle marked MADE ITALY [*sic*]. $70-80; Four column brass frame with handle marked ITALY. $70-80; Four column brass frame with square centering device. $80-100.

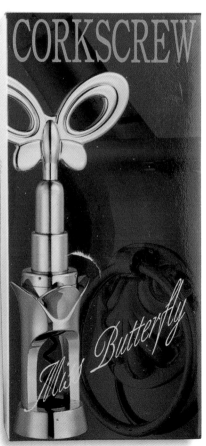

"Miss Butterfly" is a heavy 8 1/2" corkscrew from Taiwan. It is surprisingly well made with a coated worm and spring inside the top shaft to facilitate self-extraction. Continuous clockwise rotation of the handle removes the cork from the bottle, turn counter-clockwise to remove the cork from the worm. Available in Paris in 1997 for 150 French Francs.

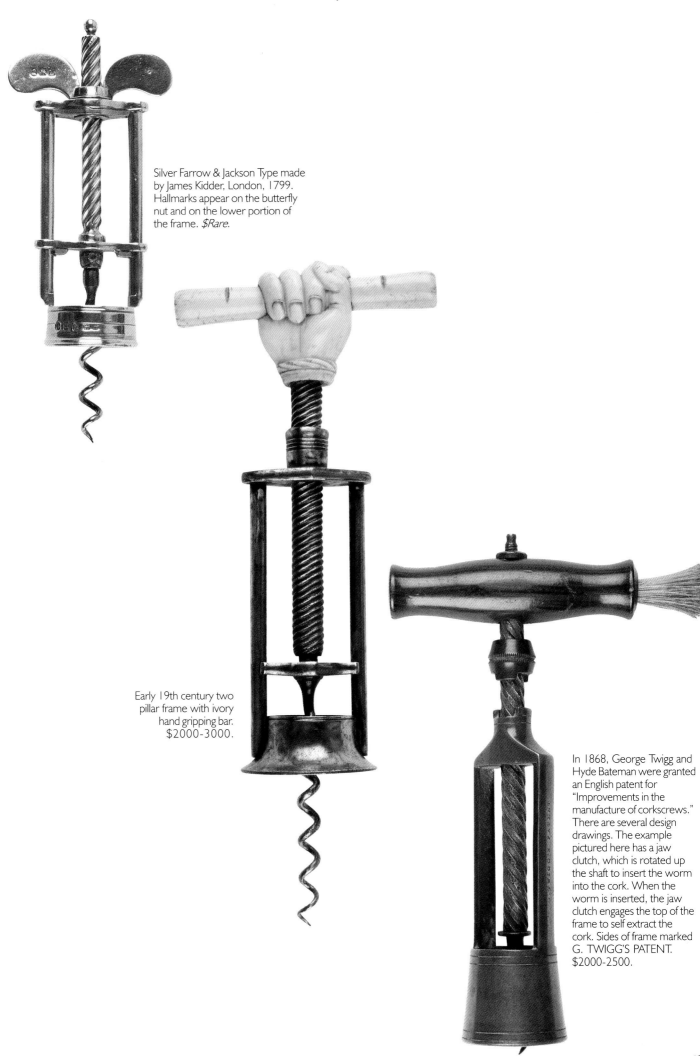

Silver Farrow & Jackson Type made by James Kidder, London, 1799. Hallmarks appear on the butterfly nut and on the lower portion of the frame. *$Rare*.

Early 19th century two pillar frame with ivory hand gripping bar. $2000-3000.

In 1868, George Twigg and Hyde Bateman were granted an English patent for "Improvements in the manufacture of corkscrews." There are several design drawings. The example pictured here has a jaw clutch, which is rotated up the shaft to insert the worm into the cork. When the worm is inserted, the jaw clutch engages the top of the frame to self extract the cork. Sides of frame marked G. TWIGG'S PATENT. $2000-2500.

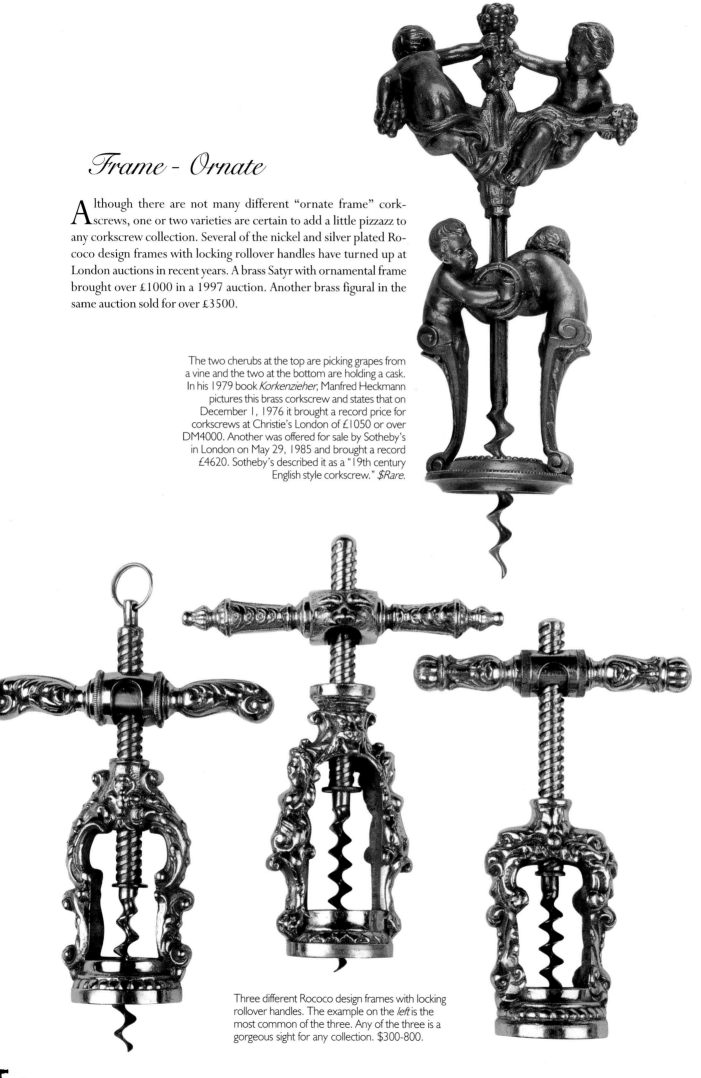

Frame - Ornate

Although there are not many different "ornate frame" cork-screws, one or two varieties are certain to add a little pizzazz to any corkscrew collection. Several of the nickel and silver plated Rococo design frames with locking rollover handles have turned up at London auctions in recent years. A brass Satyr with ornamental frame brought over £1000 in a 1997 auction. Another brass figural in the same auction sold for over £3500.

The two cherubs at the top are picking grapes from a vine and the two at the bottom are holding a cask. In his 1979 book *Korkenzieher*, Manfred Heckmann pictures this brass corkscrew and states that on December 1, 1976 it brought a record price for corkscrews at Christie's London of £1050 or over DM4000. Another was offered for sale by Sotheby's in London on May 29, 1985 and brought a record £4620. Sotheby's described it as a "19th century English style corkscrew." *$Rare*.

Three different Rococo design frames with locking rollover handles. The example on the *left* is the most common of the three. Any of the three is a gorgeous sight for any collection. $300-800.

Left to right: Two different Italian brass ornate frames. Worm lengths are different and a close examination reveals differences in design. Modern. $50-60; A copper colored "frame" with rollover handle. Back to back shields showing a mortar and pestle are separated by the collar and top of frame. The handle ends are in the shape of wine barrels. Marked ITALY. $60-70; Verdigris with gold tone finishes on ornate frame with rollover handle. $80-100; A nickel plated version of the first two with slightly different design. $50-60.

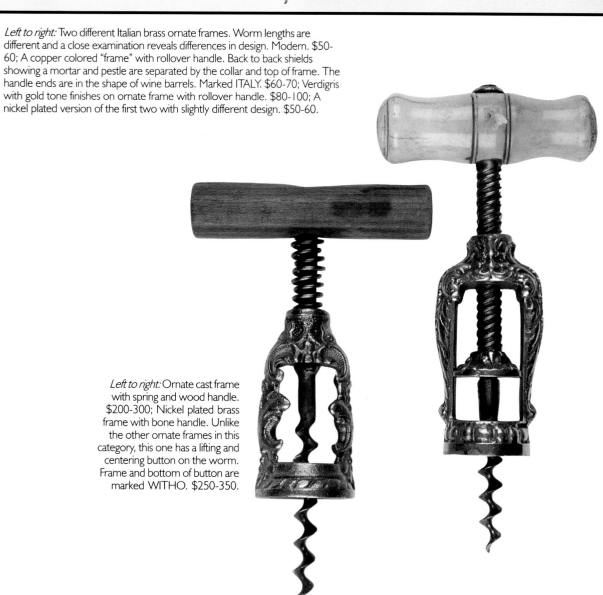

Left to right: Ornate cast frame with spring and wood handle. $200-300; Nickel plated brass frame with bone handle. Unlike the other ornate frames in this category, this one has a lifting and centering button on the worm. Frame and bottom of button are marked WITHO. $250-350.

Frame - Simple

This is a group of very simple corkscrew frame designs that consist (with one exception) of a handle, shank, and worm mounted in a frame. The simplicity of the designs makes workable, inexpensive to produce corkscrews.

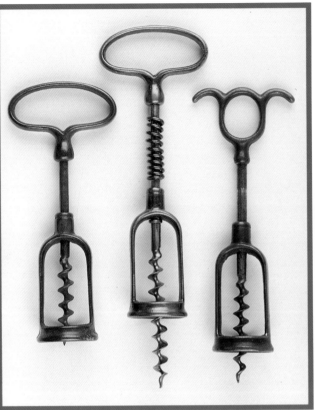

Above: *Left to right:* Frame with three finger oval handle. $75-100; Three finger oval handle with spring on shank. Exceptionally long - 8 1/2" from worm tip to handle top. $125-150; Three finger handle with frame. $100-125.

Left: Three examples of the "Perpetual." Criss cross grooves on the shank engage with a guide pin in the top of the frame causing the shank to continuously move up and down as the handle is turned. In use, the worm will be driven into the cork, the pattern in the grooves will be reversed, and the cork will be extracted. This is an 1884 German patent by Ernst Demmler.
Left to right: Reeded bands on handle and top of bottom of frame. $125-150; Wood handle with copper plated frame. $150-200; Sleek steel design. $125-150.

Left to right: Stag handle with rubber retainer at top of worm to prevent worm from being pulled through frame. Shank marked ENGLAND. $15-20; Marked THE SURPRISE at the top of the frame and REGISTERED 13185 on the handle. This is George Willet's 1884 English registration. Copper plated. $75-100; Marked R N° 692453. A 1922 English design including a cap lifter and wire breaker. Sides of the frame marked G. M. THURNAUER CO., MADE IN ENGLAND. $150-200; Nickel plated marked SURPRISE with surprising advertising on the sides of the frame: "Buchan's (Rhymney), King's Ale." $100-150; An unmarked European version of the American Chinnock patent. $40-50.

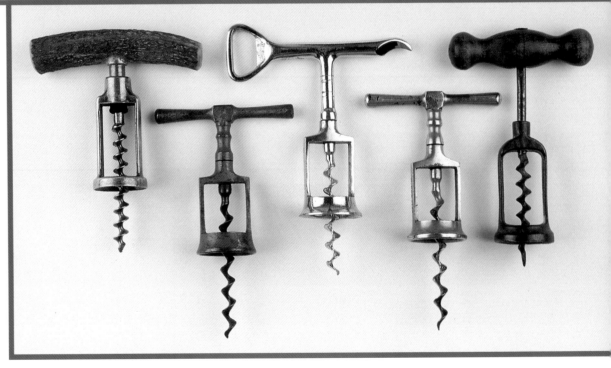

Funnels, Jiggers & Shakers

I n a 1941 Chase Specialty catalog, the "Bar Caddy" is described as "a combination jigger, bottle opener, corkscrew and ice breaker. The jigger is marked off for measuring 3/4 of an ounce, 1 ounce, 1 1/2 ounces, and 2 ounces. The jigger bottom is extra heavy metal, so you can crack ice cubes with it. The handle is a crown bottle-cap opener. A corkscrew is concealed inside the handle, when assembled." What more could the home bartender ask for? Such tools do turn up quite frequently at flea markets for bargain prices. Less common and more desirable are the combination tools with funnels. Many of these have been found with initials engraved or as awards given at special events.

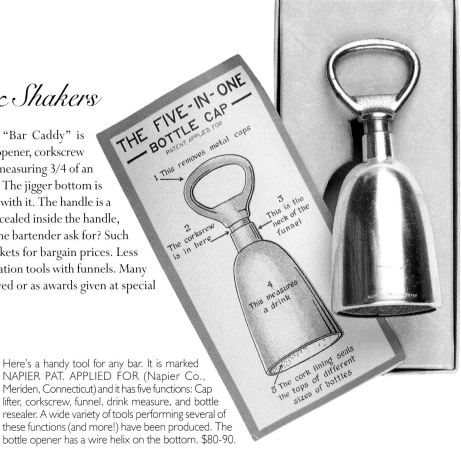

Here's a handy tool for any bar. It is marked NAPIER PAT. APPLIED FOR (Napier Co., Meriden, Connecticut) and it has five functions: Cap lifter, corkscrew, funnel, drink measure, and bottle resealer. A wide variety of tools performing several of these functions (and more!) have been produced. The bottle opener has a wire helix on the bottom. $80-90.

Here are three more Five-In-One tools. The one at *left bottom center* is similar to the tool described above and it is marked NAPIER SILVERPLATE PAT. PEND. In both of the Napier tools, the opener/corkscrew is a friction fit. The two at *top center* have a threaded fit with a web helix. The *right center* tool is marked + STERLING 3102 and the one on the *left* is unmarked, but has a fancier design on the measure/funnel. $60-75.
The Sterling cap lifter/corkscrew at *top left* appears to be a cover for a container (I have never seen it with a container). $65-75. Another Napier production is the small shaker with funnel, measurer, cap lifter, corkscrew, and funnel at *bottom left*. $150-175.
In the *middle of the bottom row* is a funnel with one cup, which is probably a part of a more complete set. $90-110. Three cups, a funnel, and corkscrew/opener marked GERMANY fit in the leather case. $100-120.

Above: Six combination tools. The funnel on the *left* has three nesting cups marked MADE IN GERMANY stored inside the funnel (1926 Schmidt & Co. German patent). The cap lifter has the trademark of Müller and Schmidt of Solingen. The wood grip on the next tool is the sheath for the worm attached to the cap lifter. The other end is a shot cup. There is no funnel. The funnel of the *third* is marked STERLING 2208 with the Eagle trademark of P. H. Locklin & Sons, manufacturers in New York City from 1920-1930. *Fourth and fifth* are marked STERLING 7309 with the trademark of R. Blackinton of North Attleboro, Massachusetts. The *fourth* is engraved with the initials J W G. The *sixth* is marked only GERMANY. $100-150.

Right: These five traveling funnels come complete with cap lifter, corkscrew, and carrying case. *Top left* was made by Müller & Schmidt in Solingen, Germany, and is a 1925 patent by Gustav Mössner. *Lower left* has a hammered finished and is unmarked. The two on the *right* also have a hammered finished and have the trademark of Webster Company of North Attleboro, Massachusetts. *Lower right* is engraved with the initials H. T. P. *Bottom center* has the Blackinton trademark, a picture of a golfer putting and the engraved initials B. W. J. $100-150.

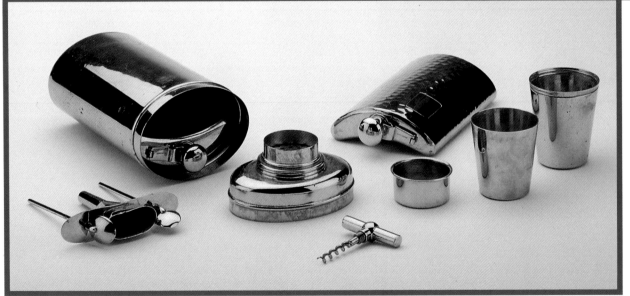

Here's a set that does everything. It comes in a leather case and is 10" high. Two cups and a cover are nested on top of the shaker. In addition, there are two flasks, two mixing spoons, a funnel, a picnic type corkscrew, and a cocktail strainer. The bottom of the shaker is marked D.R.G.M. 951628 (1926 German registration). All parts are marked MADE IN GERMANY. Now all we need is booze, a blanket, and a picnic lunch! $300-400.

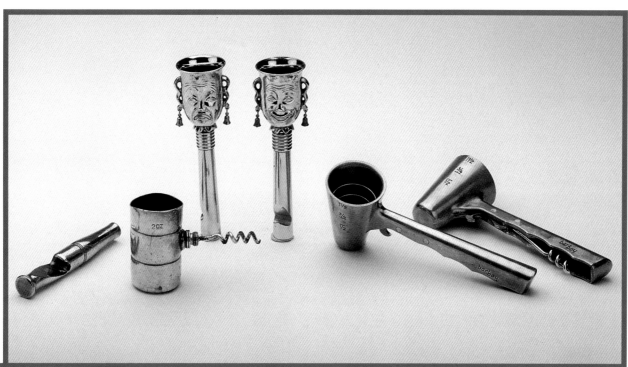

Above: Both jiggers in the *background* have an "A. M." sad face on one side and a "P. M." happy face on the other. The handle with machined in cap lifter unscrews to reveal the worm. $10-20.
The jigger with opener sheath on the *left* is silver plated and marked CAMBRIDGE, E. P. C. 711. $60-75.
The two on the *right* are the "Bar Boy" by Tempro Incorporated. $15-25.

Left: *Top:* "Bar Boy - the six-in-one appliance" from Tempro Incorporated, New Haven, Connecticut. Instructions for use state: "This corkscrew is designed in accordance with the best information obtainable on the subject of corkscrew construction." *Now that's quite a claim.* Further instructions: "To position corkscrew for use, hold cup open side up in right hand and strike handle with sharp blow against open palm of left hand. This will permit corkscrew to be pulled into the vertical position." *So that's how you get the worm out of the cavity!* Final instructions: "Insert point between inner side of bottle-neck and cork, turn until worm of corkscrew has penetrated cork. Draw cork from bottle with a straight upward pull." *Where* do I insert that point?
Bottom: "Mr. Bar Laddie" from Modern Sales Company, Los Angeles, California, is an ice pick, bottle opener, seal breaker, ice crusher, 1 & 2 ounce jigger, corkscrew, and muddler.

Twenty one different bar caddies. $2-12. Jiggers come in 1 1/2 and 2 ounce sizes. Four have cap lifters inserted or machined into the end and have lists of drink recipes accessed by turning the handle. The recipe type was often used for advertising purposes. The ARCO advertisement on one has a great reminder "When you stop to think, don't forget to start again."
Manufacturers' names on the jiggers include: Apex Products, Dania, Florida; Mr. Bartender Products; Cavalier by National Silver; Irvin Ware, U. S. A.; Chase, U. S. A.

Health & Home

In his 1883 catalog, C. T. Williamson has the following copy for his "Dose Cup and Cork Screw Combined, Patented March 7th, 1882:"

"A great want in the sick chamber overcome by the combination of Dose Cup and Cork Screw, thus serving a double purpose; the want either one causing great inconvenience and delay in administering to the immediate needs of the sick. There are times when delays are dangerous. Time lost looking for a cork screw, or something to extract the cork from a bottle of medicine, and then for a suitable article to measure out *prescribed quantity*, often causes vexation not only to attendant but nervousness and over-excitement on part of the one whose life may depend upon quickly and promptly receiving a dose of medicine. *The physician will use it with joy*. It should accompany each bottle of medicine requiring ACCURATE MEASUREMENT. If not, ask your druggist for it."

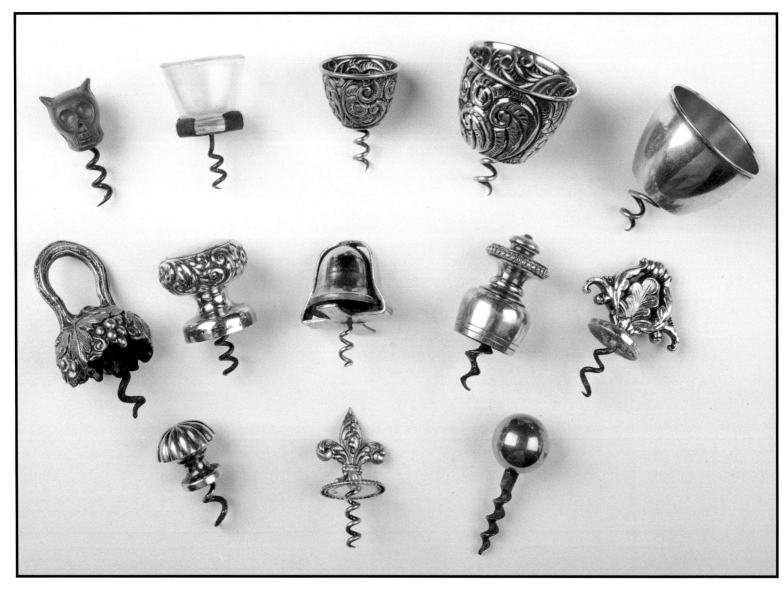

Williamson's advertisement is enough to scare anyone into purchasing one of the dose cup corkscrews in the *top row*. The 1882 patent was granted to Henry Zeilin. His patent calls it a "Dose Cup Bottle Stopper." The *first* is glass mounted in a tin holder. $200-250. The next three are silver and have the trademark of the S. Cottle Co. of New York City (1865-1920). $200-300. On the *left* is a cork puller that one would leave in a bottle as a poison warning. It is marked with crossed bones and the letters H R S D on the back of the skull. $75-100.
The eight ornate tops would be used for medicines and, possibly, perfumes, inks, shoe polish, other home remedies, and horse liniment bottled with small corks. *Second row left to right:* Grape and grape leaf design. $75-100; Floral design with the Cottle Company trademark. $100-125; A bell so one could hear if nosy hands are lifting the recorked bottle! $150-200; A stopper marked CHRISTOFLE. $175-225; An unmarked ornate leaf design. $100-125.
In the *third row* are two simple pullers on either side. $75-100. And, in the *middle*, a fleur de lis marked on the underside C B & H STERLING (Codding Bro. & Heilborn of North Attleboro, Massachusetts, 1879-1918). $125-150.

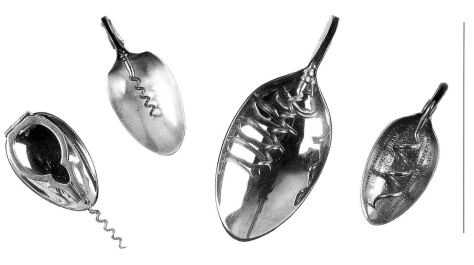

In September 1882, Cornelius Williamson received his own patent for taking medicine - a spoon with folding corkscrew handle. Although the three at *right* are similar to the patent, none have been found with the Williamson mark. The spoon with two folds on the *left* is marked STERLING 12 with the trademark Currier & Roby of New York City. $300-400. The *second* spoon has a lot of advertising in the bowl - "Tabloids of Compressed Drugs, Hazeline Cream, Keppler Extract Essence of Malt, Keppler Solution of Cod Liver Oil, Digestive, Demulgent, Strengthening, Hazeline Beer & Iron Wine." It is also marked PATENTED. $150-175. The *third* spoon is marked STERLING 8689 with the trademark of George W. Shiebler & Co. of New York City. $250-300. The spoon on the *right* is for a tablespoon size dose of medicine. It is marked STERLING 10 and has a gold wash in the bowl and the worm is gold plated. $300-350.

On June 7, 1881, William Rockwell Clough of Alton, New Hampshire, was granted a patent for a corkscrew that would revolutionize advertising for health and home remedies. His small corkscrew was designed to remove the small corks from bottles of patent medicines and the like. The cork-screws were made in wire bands that would accommodate for advertising. These could be given out with the bottle as a constant reminder of the manufacturer's name. Many manufacturers included a plain wire corkscrew with their product rather than spend the additional money on advertising. Clough had patented these in 1875. As a result, one is more likely to find a miniature corkscrew without advertising than with. If you didn't have a corkscrew, you could still remove the cork - In an 1886 booklet entitled *Professor Horsfords Phosphatic Baking Powder*, we are told "Scrape off the wax and carefully draw the cork with a corkscrew or common iron fork."

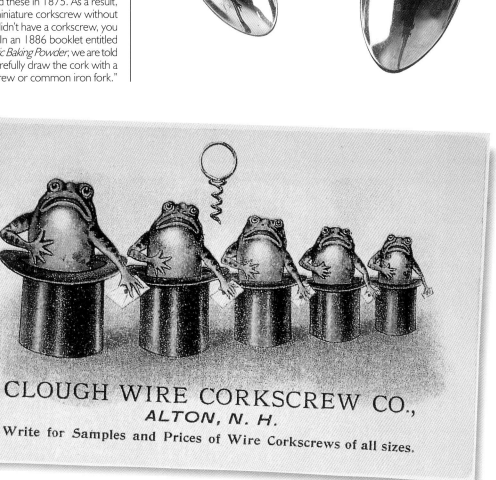

CLOUGH WIRE CORKSCREW CO.,
ALTON, N. H.
Write for Samples and Prices of Wire Corkscrews of all sizes.

In 1884, Clough patented the flat band corkscrew. A rarer version was patented by William Williamson in 1889. The rarest Clough advertising corkscrews are the two at *right and left of top center*. These were a 1903 patent by William J. Lowenstein. They have a hanging ring for more visible advertising. Only four names have been cataloged: Bailey H & C Pure Rye, Great A & P Tea Co's Extracts, Hance Bros. & White, Philadelphia, and Pearl Wedding Rye. The clock at *top center* can be rotated so the user knows the next time to take medicine. It is marked CLOUGH'S PATENT MEDICINE DIAL with Roman numerals.
A word on values: The wire and flat band corkscrews vary from $5 to $50 depending upon condition and the brand advertising. Having the corkscrew with the matching bottle can double or triple the value depending upon the condition of the bottle. The corkscrews with hanging advertisement are $100-125. The Medicine Dial is $150-200.

A challenge for any corkscrew collector is to find the bottle that matches the corkscrew advertising.

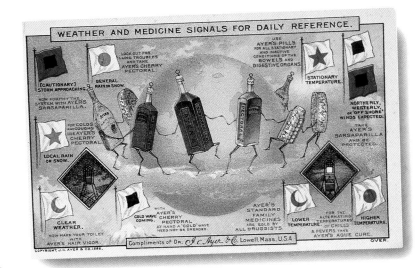

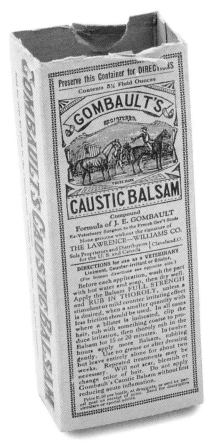

An even greater challenge is to find full bottles in the original box with the corkscrew. The Gombault's came with a plain wire corkscrew.

A twenty page booklet entitled *Our New Navy* from Perry Davis & Son, Providence, Rhode Island. Throughout the booklet are examples of the Davis Pain Killer successes. The bottle is shown on front and back covers with a wire corkscrew screwed into the cork. Evidently Davis supplied their product with a plain wire corkscrew for none has been found with the Davis name.

Extra large folding medicine - 2 1/2" closed. Nickel plated brass. Decorative markings and CLOUGH'S PATENT, JULY 22, 1884. $200-300.

Here is a check list of *wire type* Clough corkscrews that have been cataloged (sizes may vary):

o Bailey's H & C
o Bell-Ans (Indigest.)
o Benetol
o Bovinine
o Bull's Cough Syrup
o Caustic Balsam
o Clar-O-Type
o Clover
o Devoe & Co., N. Y.
o Eugene Ltd.
o Gargling Oil
o Glover (for animals)
o Goff's (Cough Syrup)
o Goff's (Min. Water)
o Goldmans Restorer
o Gottschall Products
o Guadalupana Med.
o Horsfords Acid Phos.

o Huxley
o Jiffy
o Jomavar-Girardo
o Kemp's Balsam
o Kendall's
o Kennedy, Donald
o Kikara
o Kohn, David, Phila.
o Lambert's Syrup
o Listerine
o Lloyd Brothers
o McLean Med. Co.
o Minards Linament
o Mother's Friend
o Mizzy
o Mufti (Dry Cleaning)
o Nonspi
o Nujol (Mineral Oil)

o Nye, William F.
o Packer's Charm
o Paragon
o Paris Med. Co.
o Pompeian
o Prickley Ash Bitters
o Remington Oil
o S.S.S. for the Blood
o Seigel's Syrup
o Severa
o Ship-A-Hoy
o Sirop Matheiu's
o Solyol (Disinfectant)
o Taft's Asthmalene
o Tippy Canoe
o Wampole's
o Weiss & Rauscher

Here is a checklist of *flat metal type* Clough corkscrews that have been cataloged (size, color and advertising copy vary):

o Adamsons Cough Balsam
o Aster Vanilla, Say
o Baileys Pure Rye
o Big G (Chemical)
o Boschees German Syrup
o Bovinine
o Brown's Iron Bitters
o Bull's Cough Syrup
o Carter's Inks
o Clough's Patent, July 22, 1884
o Cummings Sarsaparilla
o Emulson de Scott
o Ferroleum
o Goldman's Gray Hair Restorer
o Green's August Flower (Catarrh)
o Gunst & Co., Richmond, Va.

o Heller & Co., B., Chicago
o Herskovits
o Jefferson Club
o Judson's Gold Paint
o Kepler Solution Cod Liver
o Koch's Pepton Bouillon, Dr.
o Lactopeptine for Dyspepsia
o Listerine
o Listerine, Lambert Pharmacal
o Lung Tonic Cures Coughs
o Maconnell, James M., New York
o Magee's Emulsion, C. K.
o Merrel, Jacob L.
o Mount Vernon Pure Rye
o Panopepton

o Pat. July 22, 88
o Rawleigh Man (Cough Syrup)
o Red Star * Cough Cure
o St. Jacobs Oil
o Sanmetto for Kidneys and Bladder
o Scotts Emulsion (Cod Liver Oil)
o Sirop Mathieu's
o Sirop Mathieu's Syrup
o SSW
o Straus, Gunst & Co.
o Wakelee's Camelline
o Warner's Log Cabin Remedies
o Warner's Safe Cure
o Youth-O-Lede Hair Coloring
o Z. M. O. for Pain

A bottle of Lavender Water distilled by Ferd. Mülhens, Cologne, Germany. The case is fitted for the bottle. There is a pocket for a small folding bow corkscrew on the side. The top is removed to access the cork. A hinged bottom allows the owner to replace the bottle as needed. $125-150.

Lazy Tongs

The Lazy Tongs corkscrew is often referred to as a Concertina, Compound Lever, or even by the well known trade name ZIG ZAG. The United States patent classification for the type of action in this corkscrew is Lazy Tongs. The English patents of Wier (1884) and Armstrong (1902) refer to the mechanism as Lazy-Tongs. In the lazy tongs corkscrew design, the worm is affixed to the lowest linkage in a series of bars, which add a mechanical advantage to cork extraction. With the tool compressed, the worm is inserted into the cork until the collar comes to rest on the bottle neck. By pulling on the handle top, the cork can easily be removed with little effort.

The most common Lazy Tongs is the ZIG ZAG. It was patented by Marie Jules Leon Joseph Bart in France on March 29, 1920, French Patent Number 503957. Bart's English patent application also refers to these as "Lazy Tongs." In Bart's design, there is a spring in the handle that closes the lazy tongs when not in use. The 1920 patent does not have cap lifters on the upper arms. The caplifters were added in Bart's 1928 patent. This is an early Zig Zag in the original box complete with instructions. The corkscrew is marked ZIG ZAG BTE S.G.D.G. FR & ET, M&M DEP. Bottle cap lifters are on either side of the top links. A later box is shown at the *bottom*.

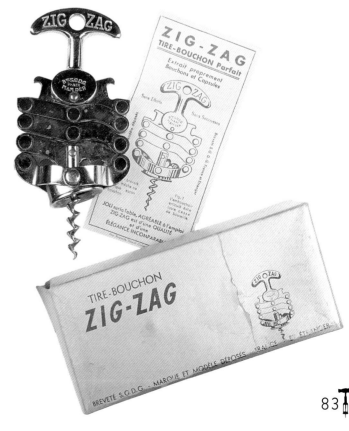

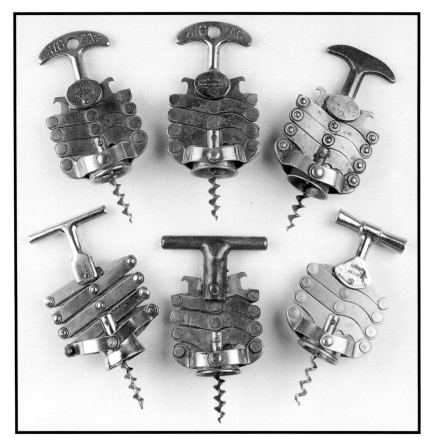

Many variations of the ZIG ZAG have been produced, which differ from the way the links are attached to each other to names and markings. An Illinois collector once showed me over 30 different variations of those called ZIG ZAG in his collection (shades of numismatists!). Note the very simple unmarked handle on the *upper right* and the very heavy unmarked cast handle at *middle bottom*. The example at *lower right* has the same type of links without the cap lifters at the top. It is marked SOUPLEX, P. P. P., MADE IN FRANCE. At *lower left*, the links are straight, the cap lifters are absent, and the top link is marked ECLAIR A P. ZIG ZAG. Values vary from $30-100 depending upon age and marks. Seven decades after Bart's invention, the ZIG ZAG has not lost its popularity. In 1990, Pati Hillis of Massachusetts created the "Pullman" designed after the ZIG ZAG. It retailed for $50-65. Another similar design called the "Lazyfish" currently retails for $25-40.

The ZIG ZAG curved links appear again in the corkscrews to the *left and right of top center*. At *left center* is the difficult to find "Kis-Ply" that has a wire spring in the circle at top. It is marked KIS-PLY PARIS, BREVETE DEPOSE, UNIVERSAL CUTLERY CO., FRANCE. This is Jean Thomas' 1932 French patent. $150-200. At *right* is a similar cheaper version without spring and with flat metal handle. It is not marked. $60-90. The *top middle* also has the flat handle but with straight links and no marks. $60-90. The unmarked example at *right* has a cast handle. $80-100.

Cap lifters are integral parts of the lower links on all three of the lazy tongs in the *bottom middle*. At *left* is a cheaply made example marked MADE IN FRANCE. $20-30. The other two are marked LE POLICHINELLE with one having an extra set of links and mounting for the worm between links instead of attached to the outside of links. $75-100.
The lazy tongs on the *left* are marked GERMANY and have a four finger grip on the top. These four finger grips are normally found on direct pull corkscrews. $100-125.

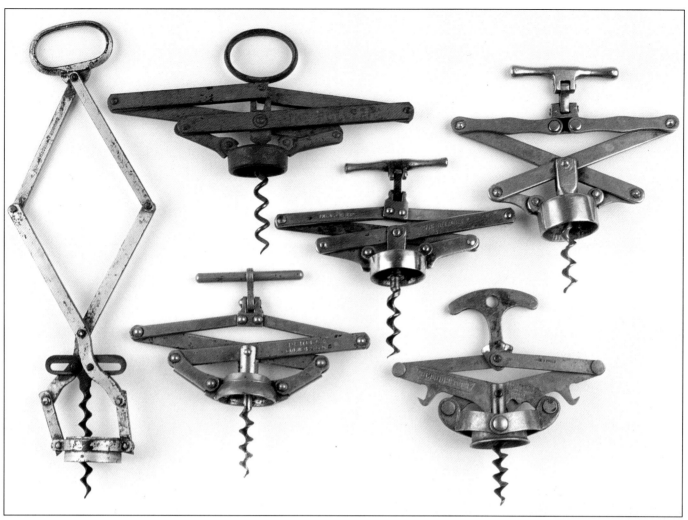

In 1902, Henry Armstrong was granted two English patents for two variations of lazy tongs. In the first (*top middle*), he made the upper links longer than the other links to increase the mechanical advantage and the top link has a slot so that the other arm would pivot on it for complete closure. His patent drawing shows two sets of the shorter links unlike this single set copper plated version marked THE "PULLEZI" and HEELEY'S ORIGINAL PATENT. The Pullezi was James Heeley's copy of Armstrong's patent (Birmingham, England). If it is a copy, why does it say "Original Patent?" The Pullezi does not have the pivot hole on the top link and Englishman Marshall Wier had already patented the lazy tongs with varying links. Wier was granted an American patent for this in 1885. The corkscrew in the *center* is Wier's and it is marked PAT. NOV. 10 1885 "THE RELIABLE."

Note the similarity to Heeley's ORIGINAL PATENT Pullezi! And Heeley *was* the manufacturer of Wier's patents. $150-300. Armstrong's second patent is shown on the *left*. It is marked H. D. ARMSTRONG PATENT and here again the patent drawing shows two sets of short links. In this patent, Armstrong added a crossbar with two slots to the top of the screw for connection to the links. $150-200. The remaining three corkscrews are: *Bottom center* is a French version of Wier's 1885 patent marked PERFECT BREVETE S.G.D.G. $125-150. *Lower right* is another French version marked DEBOUCHTOUT, BTE S.G.D.G., MARQUE ET MODELE DEPOSES FRANCE ET ETRANGER. This one has the cap lifters on the bottom links like the Le Polichinelle. $150-175. *Top right* is a much heavier unmarked version of Wier's patent. $100-150.

The father of the lazy tongs corkscrew was Marshall Wier. Here are two versions of his first patent issued in England in 1884. An abridged version of his patent specification reads "The screw is attached to a centre pin of the lowest pair of cross-bars of the lazy-tongs, and the ring, which passes over the bottle neck, is hinged to the side bars, suitable stops being provided to prevent lateral motion when the corkscrew is closed. A suitable handle is hinged at the other end of the lazy-tongs." The corkscrew on the *right* is shown in the patent. This one is copper plated and every link is marked. Patent and manufacturer information reads: PATENT WEIR'S PATENT 12804, 25 SEPTEMBER 1884, HEELEY & SONS, MAKERS. And in this rare instance there is advertising: "Gabriel Sedlmayer, Brauerei Zum Spaten Munchen" on one side and on the other - "Spaten Beer, 17, Phoenix St., Charing Cross Road, London, W. C." $175-250.

On the *left* is a rare corkscrew with two sets of links connected by rods in the middle. It is marked WIER'S PATENT, DOUBLE NO. 4283, J H S B (for James Heeley & Sons, Birmingham). The corkscrew is referred to as "Wier's Double." $1500-2000.

Is the father of the Lazy Tongs Corkscrew "Weir" or "Wier"? The patents say "Wier." The Heeley manufactured corkscrews say "Weir."

Lever - Double

The Double Lever is rather simple to use and can make cork extraction a pleasurable experience. The arms are raised to expose the worm below the frame. The worm is turned into the cork, and by simply lowering the arms, the cork is extracted.

WHEN
WHAT
HOW

A Guide to the Combining of Food and Wine to Produce Gastronomic Harmonies

CHARLES KRUG WINERY
EST. 1861
St. Helena, California

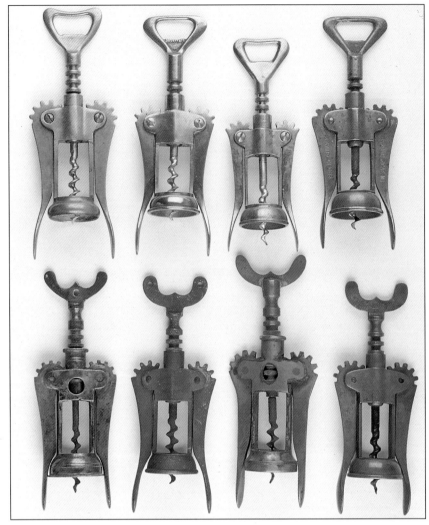

The most common double levers are the brass and chrome plated varieties with a cap lifter in the handle (*top row*). These are quite often marked ITALY and may have advertising on the levers. $15-30. Those in the *bottom row* are a little earlier and more difficult to find. $25-50. These are all very similar to Dominick Rosati's American Cork Extractor Patent (1930). Similar French patents were issued to Amedee Desbordes (1928), Baptiste Fedrici (1930), and Victor Fouque (1949).

Brass and chrome plated Italian double levers in their original boxes. Both boxes read "Cavatappo A Leva Con Levacapsule" (Lever corkscrew with cap lifter). The *left* has a red and white design reminiscent of a pack of Winston cigarettes. The *right* is decorated with grapes and in use picture.

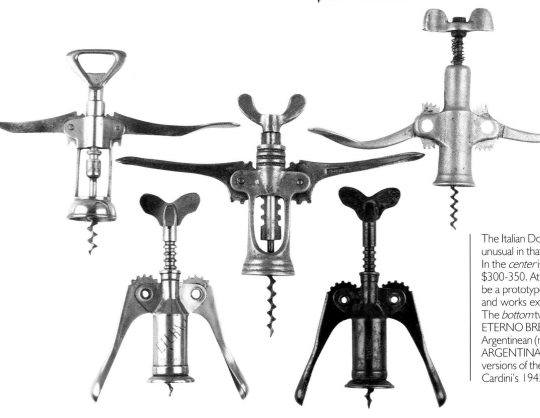

The Italian Double Lever at *top left* is unusual in that it is silver plated. $250-300. In the *center* is a French Double Lever. $300-350. At *top right* is what appears to be a prototype piece. This is cast aluminum and works extremely smoothly. $500-700. The *bottom* two are Italian (marked ETERNO BREV. CARDINI OMEGNA) and Argentinean (marked INDUSTRIA ARGENTINA ELESAN MAR. REG.) versions of the Eterno. The Eterno is Ettore Cardini's 1945 Italian patent. $200-300.

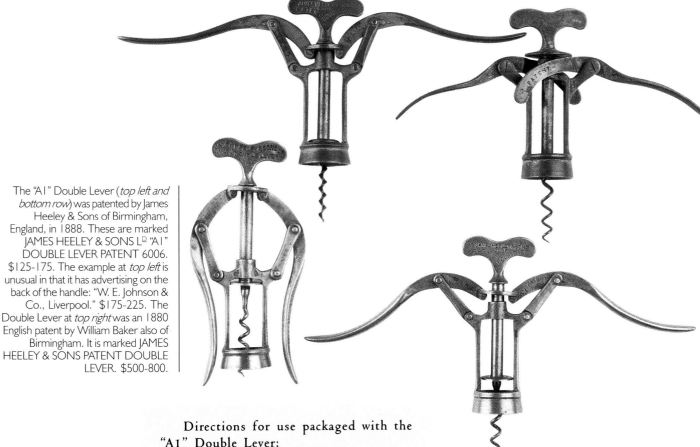

The "A1" Double Lever (*top left and bottom row*) was patented by James Heeley & Sons of Birmingham, England, in 1888. These are marked JAMES HEELEY & SONS L^D "A1" DOUBLE LEVER PATENT 6006. $125-175. The example at *top left* is unusual in that it has advertising on the back of the handle: "W. E. Johnson & Co., Liverpool." $175-225. The Double Lever at *top right* was an 1880 English patent by William Baker also of Birmingham. It is marked JAMES HEELEY & SONS PATENT DOUBLE LEVER. $500-800.

Directions for use packaged with the "A1" Double Lever:

1. Place the bottle on the table, open the levers wide and place the corkscrew frame on the bottle.

2. Screw the worm right down until the button at top touches the cork.

3. Then press the levers steadily down and the cork will be drawn with ease and safety.

NOTE: Always screw worm in as far as it will go before pressing down on levers.

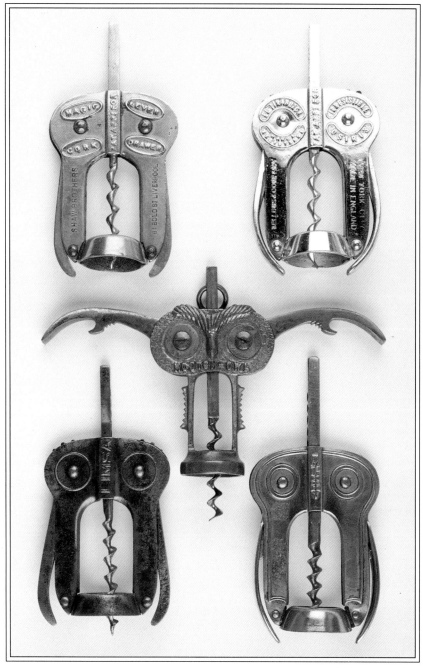

A highly desired Double Lever is the Hootch Owl pictured in the *center*. This is Richard Smythe's American Design Patent Number 98,968 of March 17, 1936. It is marked HOOTCH-OWL and has the appearance of an owl staring at us. On the backside, there are two slots at the eyes so the owl appears to be sleeping. The arms also can be used as cap lifters. In addition to the design patent, Smythe was issued Mechanical patent 2,115,289 on April 26, 1938 for this type. $1000-1500.
One should not confuse the Smythe design with the more common chrome double levers with similar appearance. Somewhat difficult is the English corkscrew at *top left* marked MAGIC LEVER CORK DRAWER. $100-125. A number of other types from Spain, Italy, and Portugal have been noted. Markings include LIMSA and BOJ (a trademark of B. Olanta y Juaristi in Spain). $50-75. Note: A new chrome BOJ now sells for approximately $10.

Another "Owl" double lever by Metalkay currently sold in department stores in Madrid, Spain.

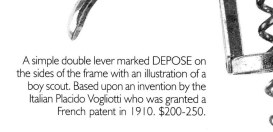

A simple double lever marked DEPOSE on the sides of the frame with an illustration of a boy scout. Based upon an invention by the Italian Placido Vogliotti who was granted a French patent in 1910. $200-250.

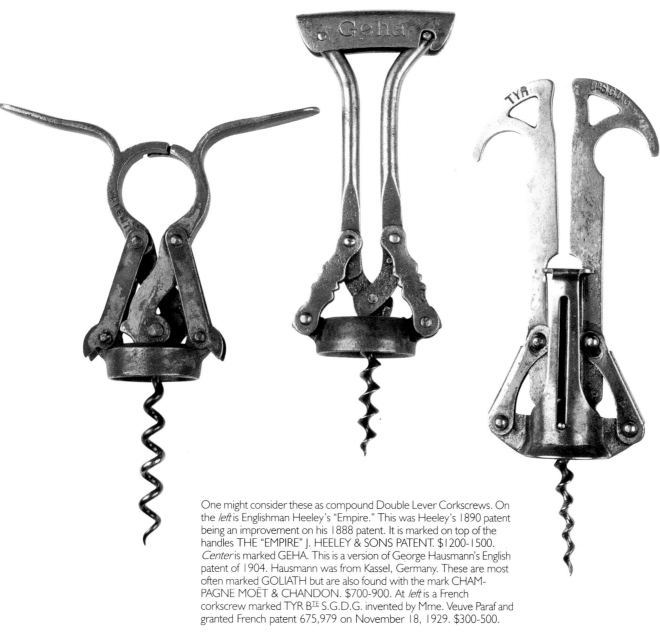

One might consider these as compound Double Lever Corkscrews. On the *left* is Englishman Heeley's "Empire." This was Heeley's 1890 patent being an improvement on his 1888 patent. It is marked on top of the handles THE "EMPIRE" J. HEELEY & SONS PATENT. $1200-1500. *Center* is marked GEHA. This is a version of George Hausmann's English patent of 1904. Hausmann was from Kassel, Germany. These are most often marked GOLIATH but are also found with the mark CHAMPAGNE MOËT & CHANDON. $700-900. At *left* is a French corkscrew marked TYR B^IE S.G.D.G. invented by Mme. Veuve Paraf and granted French patent 675,979 on November 18, 1929. $300-500.

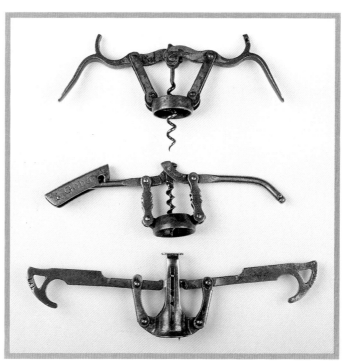

The Empire, Geha, and Tyr with levers pulled down.

~Lever-Double~

No they are not Larry, Moe, and Curley Joe. The fellow on the *left* is the Sommelier and it is Italian designer Aldo Colombo's American Design Patent Number 274,974 of August 7, 1984. In the *center* is a Monk Cellarmaster with cellar key hanging from his sash. On the *right* is Bacchus. They are all silver- plated. $30-40.

These Italian Double Levers are from the late 50s through the early 60s. They are aluminum and usually have toasts in several languages on the backside. They are variously known as the Clown, Barman, and Barmaid. The clown is the rarest of the lot. All have a cap lifter incorporated in the mouth. Based on Gemelli's design patent. $50-90 (except clown $150-200).

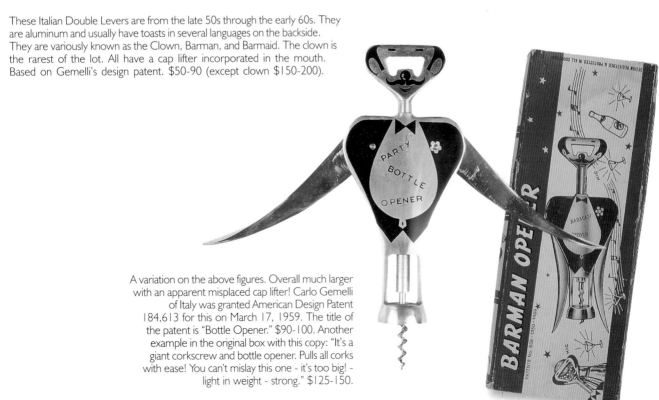

A variation on the above figures. Overall much larger with an apparent misplaced cap lifter! Carlo Gemelli of Italy was granted American Design Patent 184,613 for this on March 17, 1959. The title of the patent is "Bottle Opener." $90-100. Another example in the original box with this copy: "It's a giant corkscrew and bottle opener. Pulls all corks with ease! You can't mislay this one - it's too big! - light in weight - strong." $125-150.

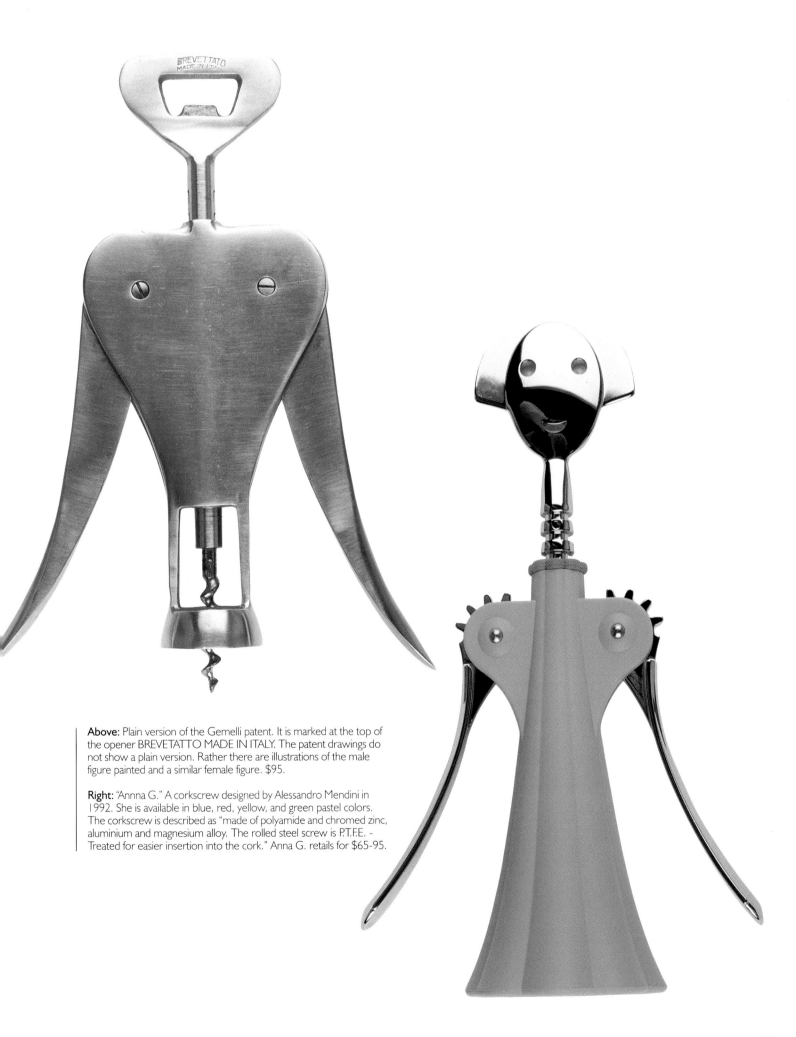

Above: Plain version of the Gemelli patent. It is marked at the top of the opener BREVETATTO MADE IN ITALY. The patent drawings do not show a plain version. Rather there are illustrations of the male figure painted and a similar female figure. $95.

Right: "Annna G." A corkscrew designed by Alessandro Mendini in 1992. She is available in blue, red, yellow, and green pastel colors. The corkscrew is described as "made of polyamide and chromed zinc, aluminium and magnesium alloy. The rolled steel screw is P.T.F.E. - Treated for easier insertion into the cork." Anna G. retails for $65-95.

IL CAVATAPPI

BIG

Campagnolo

A large 12" well-engineered double lever from the world famous Vicenza, Italy, bicycle manufacturer Campagnolo. The corkscrew was designed in the 1960s by Tullio Campagnolo. It is currently produced in brass and satin finishes and sells for about $100.

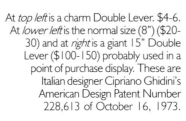

At *top left* is a charm Double Lever. $4-6. At *lower left* is the normal size (8") ($20-30) and at *right* is a giant 15" Double Lever ($100-150) probably used in a point of purchase display. These are Italian designer Cipriano Ghidini's American Design Patent Number 228,613 of October 16, 1973.

On the *left* is a left-handed version of a double lever by the Monopol Company of Germany. The box describes it as "Bell corkscrew with forged and tempered steel thread. With cork ejector." The "Design Plus" version on the *right* is for right-handers. It is described as "Lever corkscrew with corc [*sic*]. Superfine polished nickel-plated and satin-finished. With elastic center ring which sets itself on to the bottleneck. Steel thread forged, tempered, sharpened and polished. Very easy to turn into the cork." $20-30.

A colorful collection of modern double levers. Yellow and white are unmarked. Blue is marked FRANMARA ITALY. Black advertises Benson & Hedges (cigarettes) on the levers. Red is marked PHOENIXWARE at the bottle collar. $15-25.

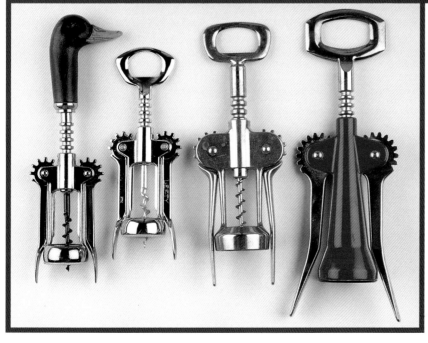

More modern double levers. $20-40 The chrome plated example on the *right* has a left-hand worm. The duck plus a dog, fox, eagle, golf ball, and horse with hand painted resin handles are currently marketed at $30-40. The levers are made in Italy and the handles are made in Wallsall, England, by Thomas Blakeman Limited.

The blister package says "Left-Handed Corkscrews. Confuse all your wine drinking Friends! Challenge the Experts with wine's best novelty." Currently produced in China and selling for $7-11.

The modern plastic versions of double levers seem endless. Here are ten variations in design or color including open frame and barrel types. The three similar open frames in the *top photo* are marked with a PW logo and MADE IN U. S. A. PAT. PEND. The one to the *right of center* has a plastic worm. The *center* piece is marked LIESSE and is rather unusual because the levers actually fold into the frame. The white one on the *right* is marked HOAN. In the photo to the *left*: FARBERWARE; unmarked; LIESSE (set); unmarked; BAR-TECH. $10-25.

One of the most sought after single levers is the Hull's Royal Club. Although a number of them have turned up in recent auction sales, the price continues to escalate as the battle to fill that hole in collections grows. Charles Hull was granted a patent in 1864 for two designs - one with a cam action on the handle and the other with a roller. The attached plate reads "C. Hull, Patentee Birmingham Royal Club Corkscrew." $2500-4500.

Lever - Single

Like the double lever corkscrew, the single lever is rather simple and easy to use. Instead of having two arms to raise the cork after the worm has penetrated, the user has a single arm leverage. The most common type of single lever corkscrew is the "Waiter's Friend," which is covered in that category. Some of the most difficult to find single levers are shown here.

I need to relate a "corkscrew find" story....several years ago my wife and I visited a newly opened consignment shop. When we entered, I went directly to some shelves in the corner that appeared to have a number of small things. There I spotted a worm. I moved aside the covering rubble and saw my prize. My hands were trembling as I read the price tag. $4.00! I grasped it tightly in my hand waiting for my wife to finish rounds of the store. I went to the cashier and, without even bargaining, I forked over my $4.00 (plus tax). Safely in my car with my new found treasure, I showed it to my wife and asked her if she would have purchased it if she had come by herself. She responded that it looked like a brand new kitchen implement and she probably would pass it up. The "kitchen implement" is in mint condition. It is an American patent issued to Alfred Sperry of Wallingford, Connecticut, in 1878. It is distinctly marked May 28, 1878. Simmons Hardware of St. Louis, Missouri, offered "Sperry's Improved Lever" in their 1881 catalog for $1.25! Current value: $2500-3500. If only I had more such stories to tell!

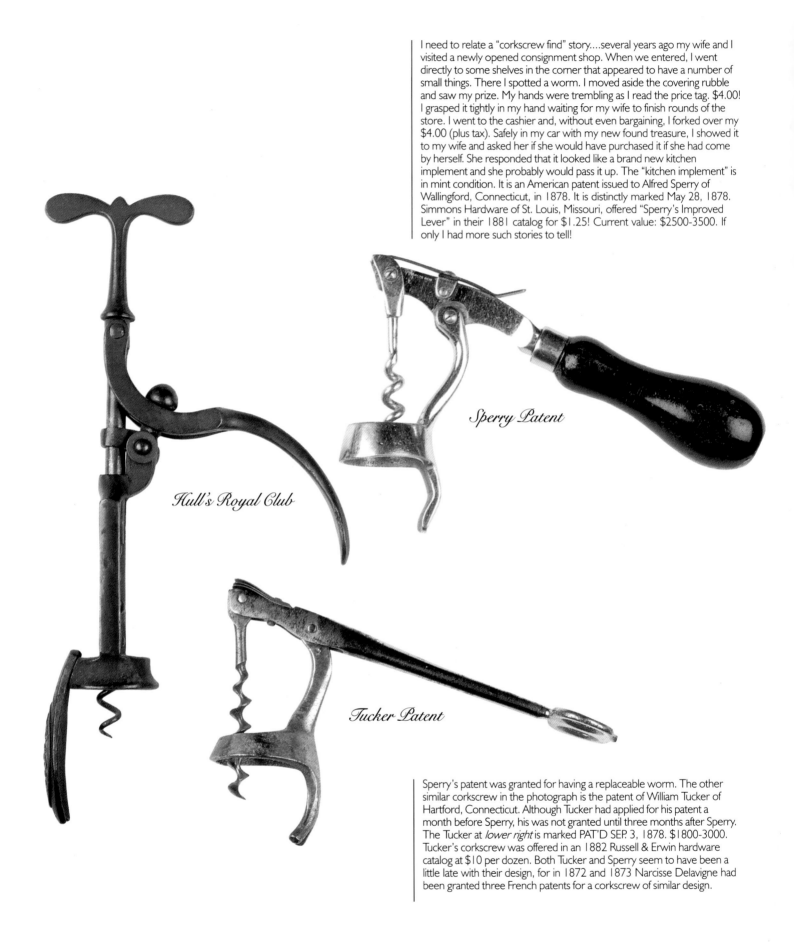

Hull's Royal Club

Sperry Patent

Tucker Patent

Sperry's patent was granted for having a replaceable worm. The other similar corkscrew in the photograph is the patent of William Tucker of Hartford, Connecticut. Although Tucker had applied for his patent a month before Sperry, his was not granted until three months after Sperry. The Tucker at *lower right* is marked PAT'D SEP. 3, 1878. $1800-3000. Tucker's corkscrew was offered in an 1882 Russell & Erwin hardware catalog at $10 per dozen. Both Tucker and Sperry seem to have been a little late with their design, for in 1872 and 1873 Narcisse Delavigne had been granted three French patents for a corkscrew of similar design.

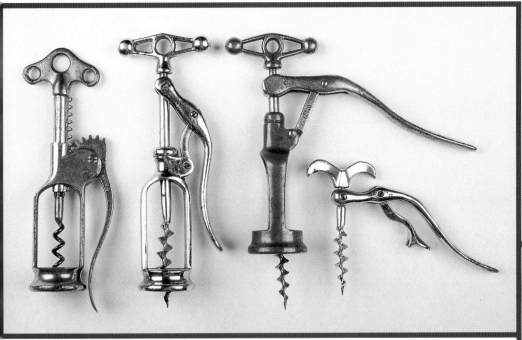

While the Tucker, Sperry, and Delavigne were being produced, the French firm of Perille was producing a different form of single lever corkscrew. The corkscrew *second from left* is Perille's "Le Presto." It is marked LE PRESTO PARIS JHP DEPOSE. This nickel plated brass model was designed by Victor Rousseau in 1905 and produced until 1953. $250-500.

To the *right* of the Le Presto is a later mechanical design marked LESTO and FRANCE. In this corkscrew, the lever has been moved to a position opposite the opening of the frame. $200-300. On the *left* is a single lever employing a rack and pinion extraction method. It is marked MADE IN FRANCE. A 1928 advertisement refers to the corkscrew as "Le Parfait." $250-500. On the *right* is Perille's "Subito." It is marked DEPOSE PARIS JHP and was supplied in a case marked TIRE-BOUCHON "SUBITO." $900-1200.

Early versions of Perille's corkscrews have a "crown" at the top of the handle.

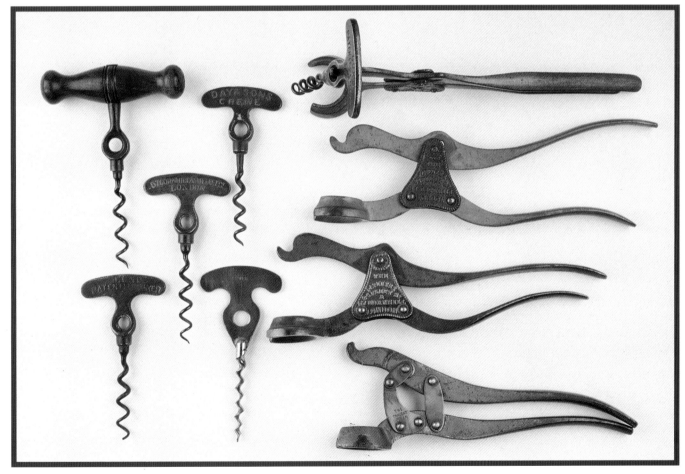

The whole idea of a single lever was nothing new even when Hull received his patent. Nine years earlier, in 1855, William Lund and William Hipkins had received a patent for three corkscrew designs including a lever handle that would lift a cork via a rather simple worm screwed into the cork separately. And...even Lund was not the first - in 1854 Edmund Burke patented a lever in which the corkscrew was permanently mounted to the lever. Other two piece levers were patented by Wolverson (1873) and Goodall (1885 and 1889). In the photograph the *top* three levers are by Lund and the *bottom* is Wolverson's "Tangent Lever." $100-250.

Metal "T" Handles

The idea of an all metal corkscrew with shank and worm connected perpendicularly to a fixed handle is one of the simplest forms of corkscrews. They were cheap to produce, impervious to fire, and susceptible to rust. Hundreds of variations exist and, like their wood handle cousins, many 20th century examples were used for advertising purposes.

6" x 8" framed print of white cats with metal T-handle corkscrew on the table.

Top right corner: Unmarked nickel plated cast handle with wire worm. $15-20.
Bottom left corner: Onion cap handle with poor wire worm. $8-10.
Top row diagonally left to right: A nickel plated 3 5/8" wide brass handle tapped to mate threaded shank of worm. $30-40; Steel handle with wire/ice breaker spike. $50-75; Shank marked J. PAYNE & CO. Shank penetrates handle and is peened on top to secure. $40-60; Three simple steel handles, the first two shanks secured by peening on top. $20-30.
Bottom row diagonally left to right: Three unmarked brass handles (one nickel plated) $15-25; Steel handle with machined concentric designs. $40-50; Steel handle marked S & P in the center. $20-25; Steel handle marked S & P in the center and SPIERS & POND on the shank. $35-45.

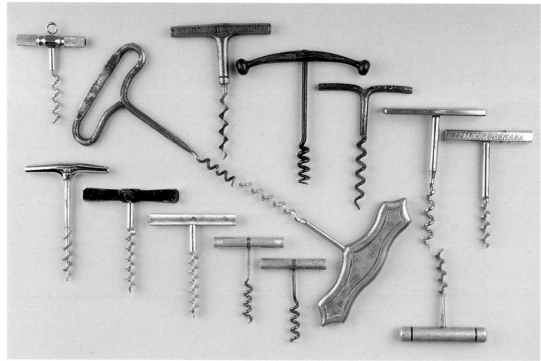

Top row of five diagonally left to right: Advertising for a corkscrew go-with: "E. Marwood & Co. Liverpool & Blackburn, 'Perfecta' Waxed Corks." $65-75; Iron. c.1800. $150-200; One piece marked J. A. HENCKELS with twins logo (the German manufacturer) and GRAEF & SCHMIDT (the New York City importing firm). $75-100; Top of heavy flat bar has advertising for "Thorne's Whisky." $100-125; Bar stock handle advertising "Italicus Premana." $20-30.
Middle row diagonally left to right: Rasp handle. $10-15; Loop handle advertising "Made for Franco's Wines & Liquors. $60-80; Heavy Art Deco handle. $40-60; Aluminum barrel handle with pinned worm. $10-15.
Bottom row diagonally left to right: Bright chrome plated handle marked E. B. ITALY. $10-15; Marked ENGLAND on the shank. $10-15; Rasp handle marked MADE IN ENGLAND on the shank. $12-15; Two wire worms wrapped on aluminum handle. One advertising "Duncan Liquors." $5-8.

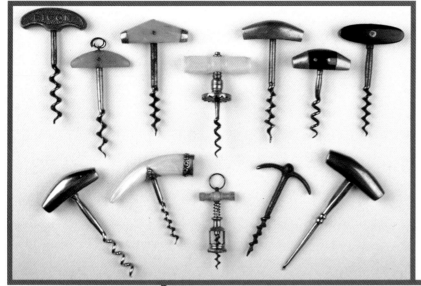

Mid-Size

Mid-size corkscrews are in the 3" to 4 1/2" overall length range with 2" to 3" handle widths. Most were used for drawing small corks from bottles containing liquids other than wine, beer, or liquor. The photographs contain a miniature spring barrel corkscrew for size comparison. They are seldom found with marks. Horn, bone, and ivory handles are usually French.

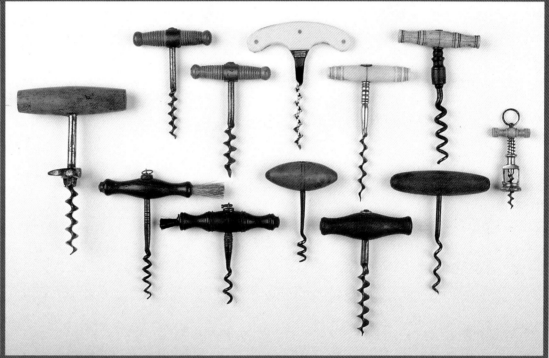

Above left: *Top row left to right:* Iron handle marked PICON. $50-60; Horn. $30-40; Horn with brass fittings. $80-100; Ivory with serrated button. $150-200; Machined brass. $60-70; Thin horn covers mounted on solid brass handle. $100-150; Ebony. $60-70.
Bottom row left to right: Machined steel handle. $60-70; Mother-of-pearl with sterling mount. $250-300; Iron for two small fingers. $30-40; Marked GUINOT. $60-70.

Above: *Top row left to right:* Wood handle with narrow worm. $15-25; Wood handle with wide worm. $15-25; Celluloid covers on two finger formed steel handle marked JOHN WATTS SHEFFIELD ENGLAND $125-150; Turned ivory handle. $125-150; Bone handle crudely mounted on early iron shaft. $80-100.
Bottom row left to right: American wood handle with wire breaker. $20-30; Wood handle T with brush. $50-60; Turned wood handle with brush. $60-75; Wood egg. $20-30; Wood T with shank penetrating handle and peened over brass washer. $40-50; Wood cigar. $20-30.

Left: *Top row left to right:* Horn handle marked FRANCE. $70-80; Ivory covers fitted on two finger steel handle. $80-100; Oreo cookie. $100-150; Horn with shaft peened over washer at top *and* secured by pin on side. $100-120; Horn handle. $40-50; Bone covers on steel handle. $50-60.
Second row left to right: 1 3/4" wide horn secured at top and on the side. $60-70; Black horn. $40-50; Horn. $60-70; Black two finger shaped horn. $70-80.
Third row left to right: Gold horn. $30-40; Green horn. $30-40; Mottled brown/black celluloid. $30-40; Celluloid ivory. $50-60.
Bottom row left to right: Wood two finger handle with shank flat marked FRANCE. $50-60; Horn $30-40; Bone with fancy shank. $60-75; Horn with brass fittings. $80-100; Wood handle with green paint. $40-60.

Miniatures

In the "Health & Home" category are many corkscrews used for advertising purposes. These were based upon patents of American inventors Clough, Crabb, and Williamson. A wide variety of miniature corkscrews without advertising have been manufactured. These replicate their parents and were used as perfume corkscrews, charms, and salesman's samples. A 1928 German catalog from Bolte & Anschütz lists a mini T-handle, a mini frame, and a mini bow as "Flacon-Korkenzieher" (corkscrews for small bottles). Additional perfume corkscrews can be found in the "Perfumes" category. The photographs contain a regular size corkscrew for size comparison.

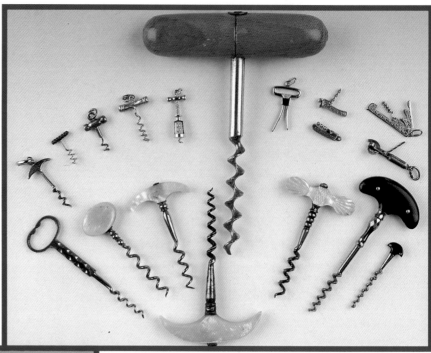

The assortment of charms in the *top row* are *from left to right:* Four T-handles on the *left* are sterling and gold. $60-80; Gold frame and gold prong puller. Sold by mail-order in 1996 for $130 each; Two small waiter's friends imprinted "To your health." $75-100; Gold waiter's friend. $150-200; Can opener combination. $50-75.
In the *bottom row* are perfume corkscrews in all steel, with mother-of-pearl handles and with tortoise shell handles. The small tortoise shell handle on the *right* is 1 1/2" long. Its "mother" is 3". $75-150.

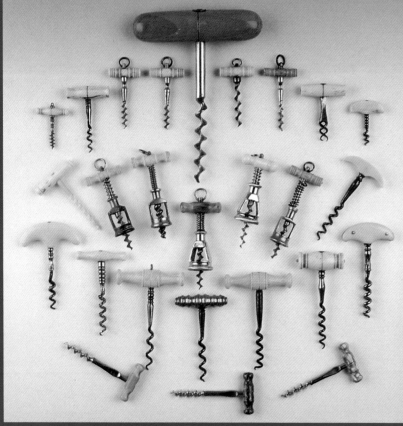

Above: Miniatures from one inch to 2 3/4" with handles of ivory, bone, brass, celluloid, and plastic. *Top row left to right:* The smallest is a one inch charm. $30-50; Ivory handle. $50-75; Four similar with varying handles, shanks, and worms. $50-75. A double helix marked SPAT and bell trademark of Brookes and Crookes of Sheffield, England. The double helix is James Wilson's 1877 English patent. $150-200; Ivory handle perfume. $40-60.
Second row left to right: All ivory (including worm) novelty. $75-100; Frame marked G & S GERMANY (Graef & Schmidt). $150-250; Unmarked brass frame. $125-175; Tapered frame marked MIGNON D.R.G.M. GERMANY. $200-300; Unmarked tapered frame. $175-225; Unmarked frame. $125-175; Ivory handle perfume. $100-125.
Third row left to right: Ivory two small finger pull. $100-125; Ivory T-handle. $75-100; 2" wide turned ivory handle. $125-175; Machined brass handle. $100-150; 2" wide fake ivory handle. $75-125; 1 1/2" wide ivory handle. $125-175; Ivory covers sandwiched on one piece metal T. $175-225.
Bottom: Three plastic handles with colorful patterns. Each was supplied on an individual card reading "Vest Pocket Corkscrew, Extra heavy plated, will not rust. Made in Germany, a G & J Product." $75-100.

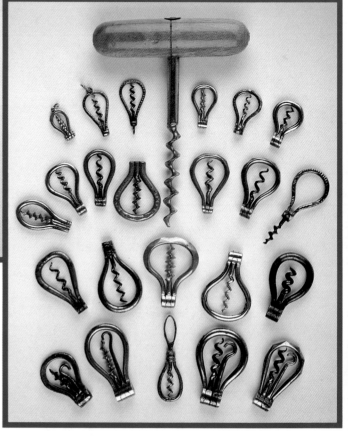

Folding bows from 3/4" - 1 3/4" (closed). Values of plain, unmarked examples with worm only will range from $20-40. Faceted, unmarked examples range from $40-70. Exceptional bows are:
Second row center: Faceted bow marked GERMANY. D.R.G.M. $75-100.
Third row center: Faceted bow marked on either side of bottom hinge GERMANY and G & S 72 (for Graef & Schmidt). $75-100.
Bottom row center: A very rare bow with one piece worm/glove hook rotating in frame. $200-300.
Bottom row: Four with worm and glove or button hook. $75-100.

Needle

In needle cork lifters air is pumped manually or gas is injected into the area between the liquid and the cork. A needle with holes near the point is pushed through the cork. The pressure of the air will either break the bottle or, hopefully, push the cork out.

What are needle lifter values?

Needle lifters can be found at flea markets as "distressed" or "close out" merchandise at prices ranging from $1 to $25. New needle lifters are sold in retail stores and through mail order catalogs. For example, *The Wine Enthusiast* currently offers a black "Corkette" for $14.95.

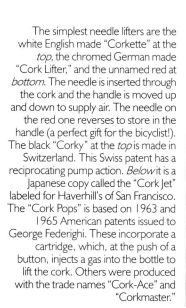

The simplest needle lifters are the white English made "Corkette" at the *top*, the chromed German made "Cork Lifter," and the unnamed red at *bottom*. The needle is inserted through the cork and the handle is moved up and down to supply air. The needle on the red one reverses to store in the handle (a perfect gift for the bicyclist!). The black "Corky" at the *top* is made in Switzerland. This Swiss patent has a reciprocating pump action. *Below* it is a Japanese copy called the "Cork Jet" labeled for Haverhill's of San Francisco. The "Cork Pops" is based on 1963 and 1965 American patents issued to George Federighi. These incorporate a cartridge, which, at the push of a button, injects a gas into the bottle to lift the cork. Others were produced with the trade names "Cork-Ace" and "Corkmaster."

Are needle lifters safe?

"Cork jet" cautions: "Do not use Cork Jet on champagne or any other 'bubbly.' It might create excessive pressure in the bottle."

"Corkette" advises: "The Corkette should not be used on fancy or flagon shaped bottles, nor on bottles which are partly empty, damaged or faulty, but only on cylindrical bottles with normal corks that are driven right into the neck. It is best to hold the bottle in a cloth."

"Cork Lifter" suggests: "Open bottle only when wrapped in a napkin" and "Do not use cork lifter for bottles containing alcoholic drinks."

"Cork Pops" cautions: "Do not use to open hand-blown bottles or Italian straw covered wine flasks. These bottles are too fragile to stand any pressure."

"Corkmaster" warns: "The Corkmaster must only be used to open full bottles of still wine which are of the standard shape."

Does needle extraction adversely affect the flavor of the wine?

"Corkette" assures: "All that is used is air, which can have no affect on the wine."

"Cork Pops" says: "Can't impair the wine flavor in any way."

"Corkmaster" claims: "Corkmaster has been thoroughly tested and approved by leading wine merchants and producers and has been found to have no effect [sic] whatsoever on the quality of the wine."

Here is some of the packaging to look for at flea markets when shopping for cheap close out merchandise.

Haverhill's "Cork Jet" instructions include some rather humorous commentary: "Remove the Seal. Sometimes you'll find that there is no cork under the seal, just a screw cap. In that case put the Cork Jet back in the drawer, forget about the points that follow, and enjoy your wine."

After piercing the cork, instructions continue with "Now the fun part starts (your family will clamor to be allowed to take turns)...This is an impressive and awe inspiring sight. You will enjoy it anew with every bottle."

And finally "Now sniff the cork...Pour some wine...fill everybody's glass, and enjoy."

Peg & Worm

Worm = the part that is turned into the cork. Peg = a peg that is stored in the center of the worm and removed and inserted into a hole at the top of the worm for use. They come in many shapes and sizes and date back to the late 18th century. They are made of steel and were brass, chrome, nickel, silver, or gold plated. The worms were usually wire or fluted.

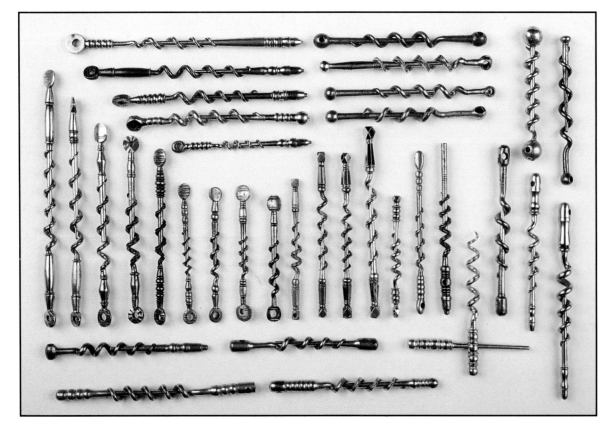

The *second in the right row of four* has a very unusual cut worm. The *third* is unusual in that it has advertising on the peg: "Crumpsall Cream Crackers." There are six corkscrews in this photo with left-hand worms. Can you find them? (answer below). Values: $75-200.

Left-hand worm corkscrews in photo: 1. Bottom in right hand row of four. 2. Third from right in middle row. 3. Top right. 4. Above bottom left. 5. Bottom middle. 6. Above bottom middle.

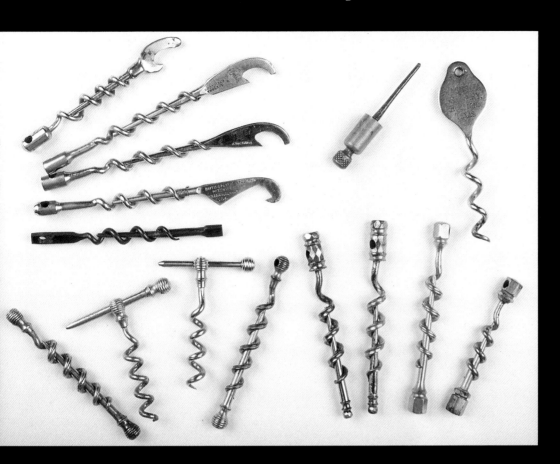

Edwin Walker was granted an American patent for the peg and worm shown at *top right*. The peg securely threads into the top of the handle, which was an ideal place for advertising. This one is for "Magnolia Brewery, Houston, Texas." Most of these were produced with a left-hand worm. $150-250.

A cap lifter was added to the peg in the four variations to the *left*. The *first* is shown in a 1946 Williamson catalog as a "novelty corkscrew and cap lifter." The *second* is marked OTIS MADE IN SHEFFIELD ENGLAND, PATENT APPLIED FOR, REGD NO 708279 (1924). The *third* is marked only PROV. PAT. (Provisional Patent). These three have the conventional under the lip cap lifter whereas the *fourth* has the over-the-top downward pressure type. The *fourth* is well-marked A. W. FLINT & CO. MADE IN SHEFFIELD, ENG., BRITISH PATENT NO. 227628, PATENTED ALSO FRANCE, GERMANY, U. S. A. Flint's American patent was granted in 1925. $100-150.

A matched set of left and right hand pegs and worms is at *lower left center*. $200-250 per set. *Third and fourth from lower right* are brass and nickel plated pegs and worms with faceted ends and unusually wide fluted worms. $125-150.

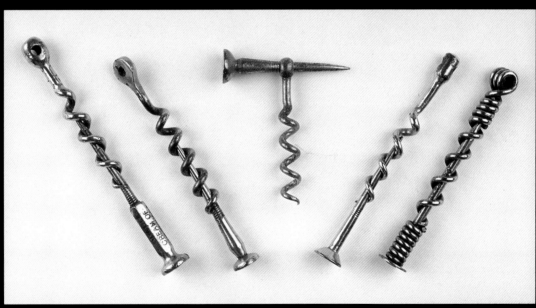

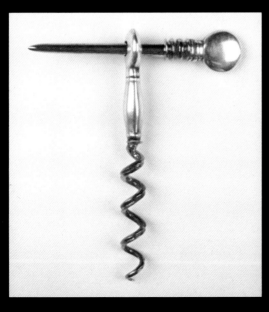

Above: These pegs and worms have pipe tampers on the peg. The *top and two outside* have left-hand worms. The peg of the corkscrew on the *left* advertises "Dundee Cream of the Barley Scotch Whisky" on the hexagonal shank. The bottom of the tamper is marked STEWART'S JOKE. $100-200

Left: Early 19th century silver peg and worm. $250-300.

Perfume

Why would a lady have a corkscrew in an implement set in her dressing or sitting room? She needed it to open perfumes, ink bottles, and medicines.

This velvet case with mother-of-pearl handle tools includes a corkscrew, tweezers, files, punches, a stiletto, a thimble, and other necessaries. $80-100.

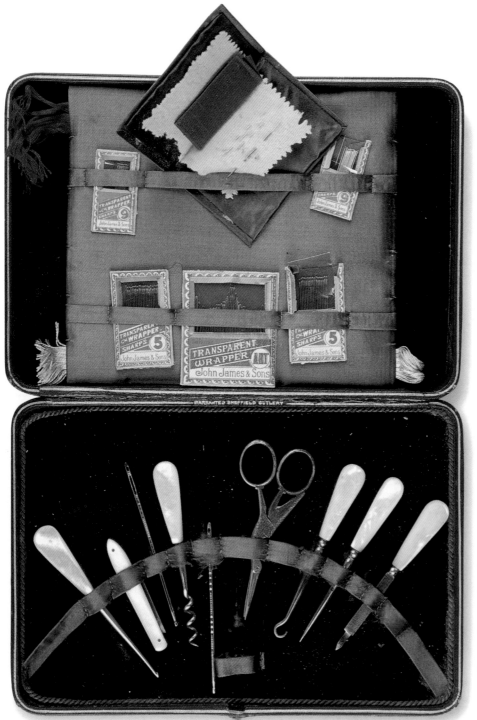

This is the most versatile case I have seen and it is marked WARRANTED SHEFFIELD CUTLERY. The handles are mother-of-pearl and, in addition to many of the usual tools, this case includes packages of needles in several sizes and threads of various colors. $400-600.

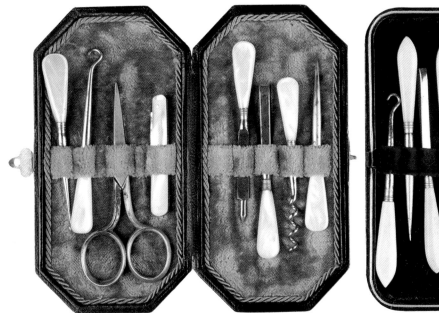
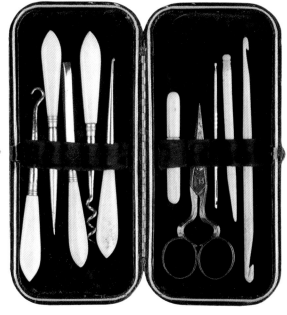

The tools in the case at *left* have bone handles. This set includes scissors, a button or glove hook, tweezers, a needle case, a crochet hook, and a corkscrew. Made by Christopher Johnson & Co. of Sheffield, England. $80-100. The case on the *right* includes mother-of-pearl handle button or glove hook, tweezers, file, penknife, punch, crochet hook, corkscrew, and scissors. $80-100.

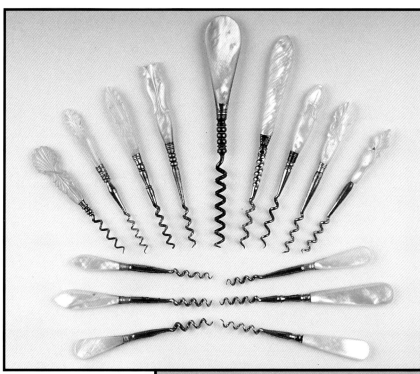

The most popular perfume corkscrews were the mother-of-pearl handle. At *left* are a few of the decorative styles and sizes. In most cases there are three pieces - the shank and worm, the mother-of-pearl, and a mounting piece between the two. Some of the cheaper versions had a point ground on the shaft, a hole drilled into the pearl, and the two pieces mated. The corkscrew to the *right of center* is an example of excellent craftsmanship in perfume corkscrews - note the ornate workmanship on the pearl, the fitting, and the shank. $30-50.

Bone and ivory handles were also very popular. The five on the *left* are all mounted using the fitting similar to the pearls. In the rest, the shaft goes all the way up the handle and the covers are mounted with two rivets. Examples with initials applied (*fifth and sixth*) are difficult to find. $20-40.

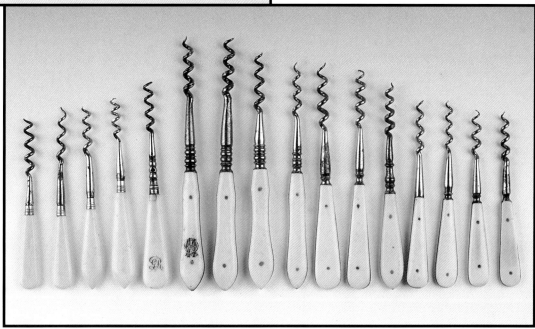

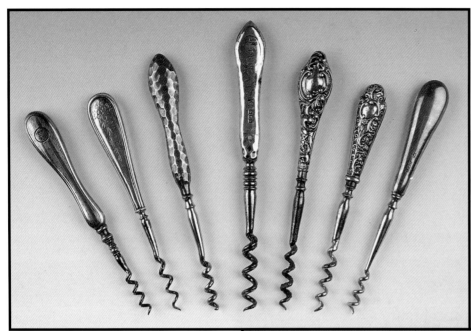

The most desired perfumes have silver handles. These usually have intricate engravings and are quite often personalized with initials. Most are marked such as these (*left to right*): Curtis trademark, North Attleboro, Massachusetts; 1920 Birmingham, England hallmark; 1883 London hallmark; 1903 London hallmark; Birmingham 1903; Birmingham 1905; Birmingham 1919. $100-150.

Two exceptionally fine perfumes. A tiger head (Birmingham 1896). $300-400. A finger loop shown in a 1900 catalog of Daniel Low & Co. of Salem, Massachusetts. $125-150.

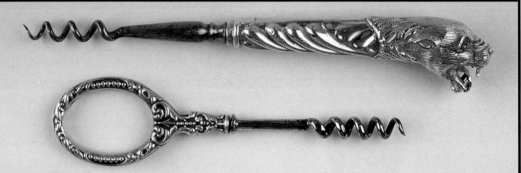

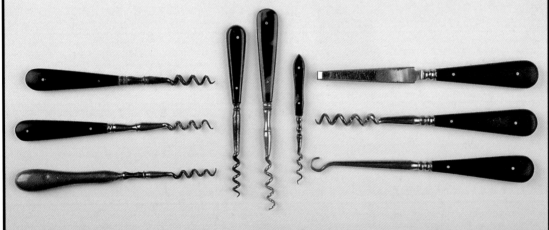

Additional materials are tortoise shell, ebony, and gold plated metal. On the *right* is a set including corkscrew, tweezers, and button hook. $40-80.

Now here is the sad part. In my bouquet are nearly 100 orphan corkscrews - all apparently taken from sets over the years by collectors who only wanted the corkscrews. There are handles of bone, ivory, ebony, mother-of-pearl, and silver. We can console ourselves in the knowledge that there are collectors of thimbles, button hooks, stilettos, needle cases, penknives, crochet hooks, scissors, bodkins, and tweezers who have also been able to satisfy their "needs."

Picnic

A picnic corkscrew has a worm with a short shaft with a ring in the top. The worm is protected by a sheath, which is inserted in the ring in the top to form the handle. It is a very convenient stowaway corkscrew for the picnic basket.

Le Dejeuner sur l'herbe

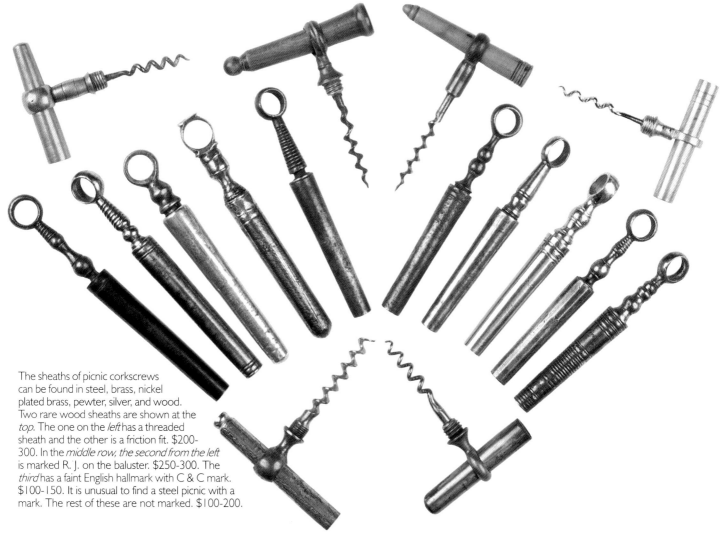

The sheaths of picnic corkscrews can be found in steel, brass, nickel plated brass, pewter, silver, and wood. Two rare wood sheaths are shown at the *top*. The one on the *left* has a threaded sheath and the other is a friction fit. $200-300. In the *middle row, the second from the left* is marked R. J. on the baluster. $250-300. The *third* has a faint English hallmark with C & C mark. $100-150. It is unusual to find a steel picnic with a mark. The rest of these are not marked. $100-200.

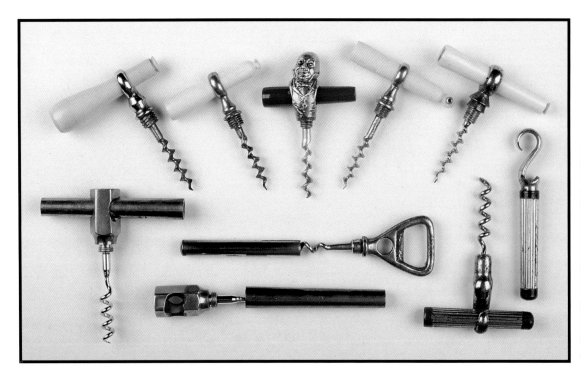

Top row left to right: Bulbous ivory sheath. $100-125; Celluloid sheath. $60-80; Pickwick figure with red bakelite sheath. $150-200; Celluloid sheath with stanhope. *$250-300; Celluloid sheath. $60-80. *Bottom row left to right:* Unmarked brass hex head with machined in cap lifter. Shown assembled and with top pulled partially out. $25-35; An unusual design with cap lifter above sheath insertion hole. Marked J H & S LD. and REG.º Nº 702970 (England 1924). $80-100; Knud Knudsen's 1939 American patent. $40-60.

*The round part at the tip contains a stanhope. A religious shrine is pictured with the words: *Nᴬ Sᴬ DE NURIA* (Our Lady of Nuria), the patroness of the shepherds of the Pyrenees mountains. Nuria is located in the mountains of Catalunya, Spain. A cogwheel train constructed in 1917 leads to the sanctuary located at 2,001 meters at the foot of Puigmal. It is said that Saint Gil of Nimes did penance in the valley in the 7th century and left behind a statue of the Virgin Mary. A pilgrim found the statue in the 10th century and the shrine shone. Today, Nuria is more popular as a ski resort than a pilgrimage. How a souvenir corkscrew ended up in such a remote location leaves a lot to the imagination. Were these Stanhoped picnics sold with different images at tourist locations throughout Europe? I have seen one other like this. It was a souvenir of Bürgenstock, Switzerland.

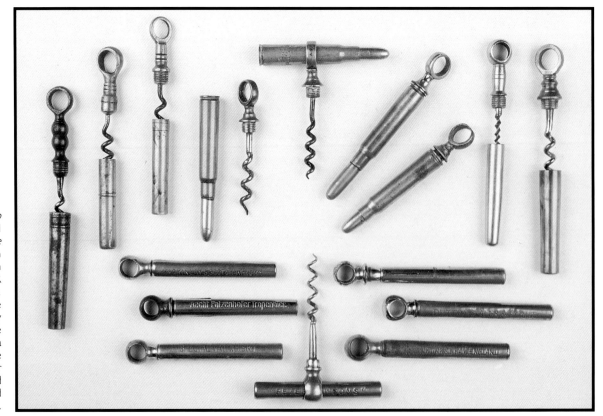

Upright picnics across the *top* are mostly German unmarked brass. $30-40. The *middle group of four* are 7mm German Mannlicher cartridge cases with one marked HENRY BOKER on a flattened top. $40-50. The seven at the *bottom* are various advertising picnics. Many collectors think these are damaged because there is a 3/4" cut in each side of the top of the sheath. This poor design was so the bulbed shank above the worm would snap into place. $20-25.

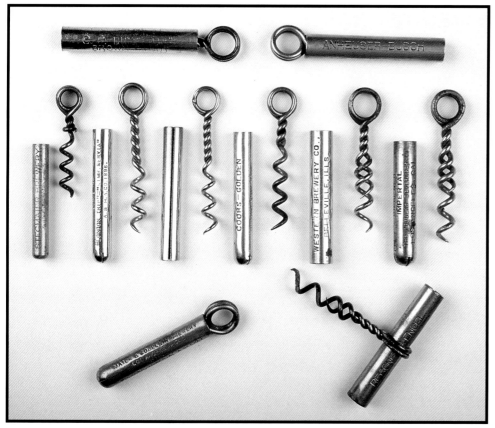

The pairs *top, bottom and at right* have various advertising on the sheaths enclosing a double helix corkscrew. *$50-75.

The first four in the center row left to right are: A small 5/16" diameter case housing a single wire formed corkscrew which makes a three loop hole. Advertises "Stegmaier Brewery, Wilkes-Barre, Pa." $70-80; A left-hand worm with case reading "Souvenir 'London Trip' - 'Servia' A & H A. Co. 1896." $75-100; Plain case with open end. $30-40; Coors - Golden. $40-50.

*In an 1891 issue of the *Western Brewer*, the C. T. Williamson Wire Novelty Company of Newark, New Jersey, advertises their power pocket corkscrew as "Made for advertising, costs less than a dime" with directions for use: "When the second or short screw enters the cork, the pressure on the cork becomes so great as to turn it in the bottle. By continuing to turn the screw and pulling slightly, the cork will be as easily extracted as by the most expensive power screw."

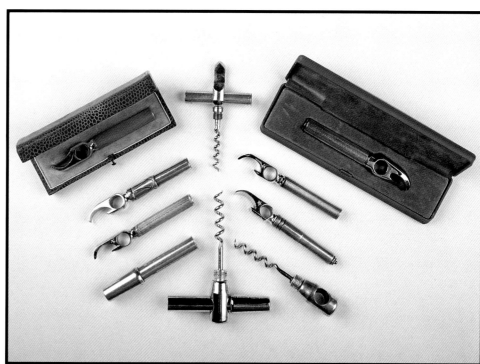

Sterling case picnics. The two at the *bottom* are from Reed and Barton silversmiths in Taunton, Massachusetts. $30-40. The others with cap lifters from Müller & Schmidt in Solingen, Germany, vary in case designs and source. $75-125.
First row: Case marked STERLING in box from Spritzer & Furhmann Juweilers; Web helix - others have wire helix; Marked 935; Unmarked case.
Second row: Case marked DENMARK STERLING designed for the Georg Jensen firm c.1933; Case marked Ax.H 9255.
Third row: Case marked TIFFANY & CO., STERLING, GERMANY; Another Jensen c.1933 design marked DENMARK STERLING.

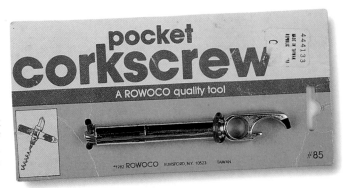

Packaged picnic, copy reads "Pocket Corkscrew. A ROWOCO quality tool. ©1982 ROWOCO, Elmsford, N. Y. 10523. Taiwan." $20-25.

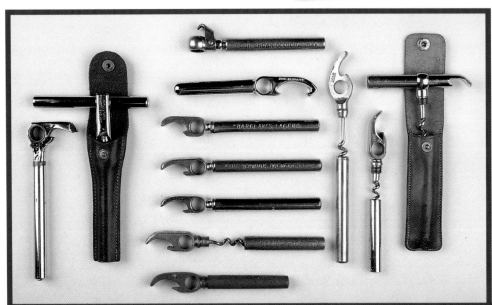

Upright left to right: English picnic with sheet metal swiveling cap lifter marked PAT. NO. 679301 MADE IN ENGLAND. A 1952 patent by Frank Wilkins. $20-25; Same in leather case. $25-30; Flat cap lifter head marked D.R.G.M. GERMANY. Slotted sheath. $30-40; By Müller & Schmidt, Germany. $20-25; Cap lifter machined in sheath marked D.R.G.M. GERMANY. Leather case. $30-35.

Middle top to bottom: Folding sheet metal cap lifter marked R^D 731702 (1927 English registered design). $40-50; Elongated cap lifter that will open by lifting from near side or far side. $25-30; Marked on cap lifter head REG^D IN ENGLAND 717886, REG^D CANADA 37-7826, MADE IN ENGLAND. 1925 registration. Advertises "Barclay's Lager." $30-40; Same without Canada mark advertising "The Berwick Breweries Ltd." $30-40; Both registrations with plain case. $20-25; Aluminum "Holman Bros. Ltd." $20-25; Zinc plated advertising "Marwood & Co. (Blackburn) L^{td}., Crown Corks & Corks." Zinc plated. Cap lifter marked MADE IN ENGLAND. $50-60.

The seven across the top have various color plastic cases that screw on. The *first two* are marked on the underside of the cap lifter head A. JORDAN CO. D.R.G.M. GERMANY. $25-35. The remaining five are unmarked. $15-20. The mottled off white advertising case reads "Drink Camel soda, All flavors, Riverside 1201 - 616 Blow St., St. Louis" (1917-1920). The head has a very unusual octagonal like head and is tapered to fit case. The case has a brass ring molded in to keep receiving end from expanding or breaking. $40-50. The other three at *bottom* are marked MADE IN ENGLAND R^D 762004 (1931 registration). $25-30.

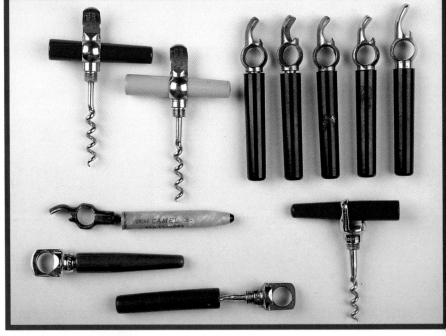

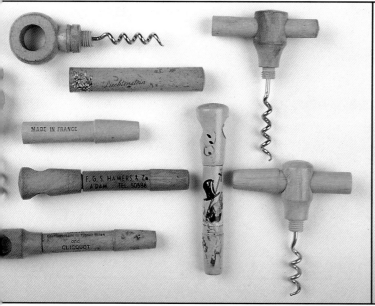

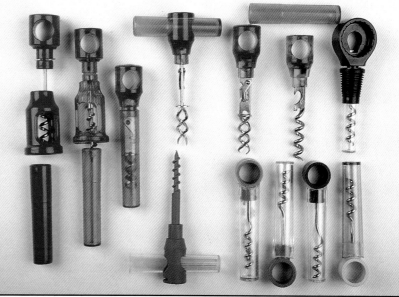

A group of French boxwood picnic corkscrews. The sheaths are threaded for secure storage of the worm. The picnic at the top is a bit unusual in design and difficult to find. This one is a souvenir of Liechtenstein. $20-30. Another is marked MADE IN FRANCE. $3-4. Two have advertising. $6-8. Two are unmarked $1-2. The last is hand painted with champagne bottle, top hat, glass, and party favors. $20-25.

Top row left to right: Red sheath with frame marked PICNIC TIME. The addition of the self pulling frame makes this picnic a much more practical tool. $8-10; Clear orange with frame marked MADE IN ITALY. $5-6; Two double helix picnics with folding cap lifter marked P. P. L. ITALY and MAXRAM SWISS MADE, SCHWEIZ PAT. ANG. $6-8; Green picnic with cap lifter in shank marked MADE IN ITALY. $4-5; Black handle picnic corkscrew also removes twist off caps. Gary Henshaw was issued both an American mechanical patent (1986) and a design patent (1987). Marked PATENT ITALY. $8-10.
Bottom row left to right: Gray plastic worm. $3-4; Four various colors with three clear sheaths and a "how can you live without it" floral motif sheath. $1-2.

How to collect plastic picnic corkscrews:
1. Check into a hotel and ask room service to send a corkscrew to your room.
2. Visit your local wine seller and ask for a corkscrew.
3. Order your own imprinted from an advertising specialty sales company. In a 1991 catalog, Best Impressions of LaSalle, Illinois, offered 5000 imprinted corkscrews for $0.46 each.

You will end up with colorful advertisements such as: Treasure Island at the Mirage; Hotel San Maartén, Laguna Beach; Marines' Memorial Club, San Francisco; Atascadero Inn, California; Yellowstone Park; Hotel Coronado; Marriott's Desert Springs; Noland Paper; Gourmet Wines & Spirits.

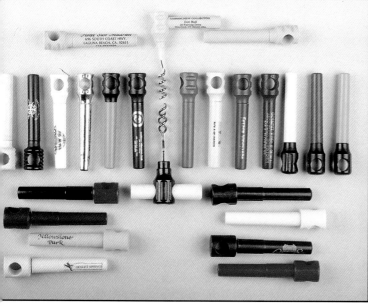

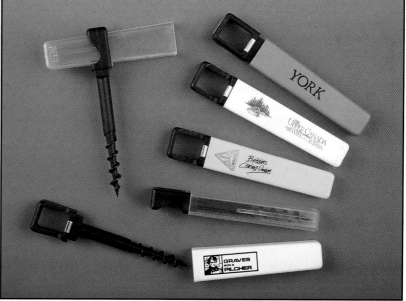

An accumulation of picnics to add a little color to a corkscrew collection. Marks noted: LEWTAN, U. S. A.; MADE IN FRANCE. All have a wire worm with the exception of the black and white picnic at *bottom center*. It was made in Russia and has a double helix with a cap lifter. This is a 1978 American design patent by Robert Marceca.

A rectangular sheath picnic patented by David Johnson in England in 1984 and in America in 1988. The flat surface is ideally suited for easy advertising imprint. Except for the metal cap lifter tab, this picnic is all plastic including the worm. Four are marked MADE IN ENGLAND. Two are marked STAR LINE ASI 89320 MADE IN CANADA. $1-4.

Plastic

Corkscrews have been manufactured using man made materials for well over a century. Goodyear's 1851 patent dealt with hard rubber. Hard rubber was used in the production of some roundlets. Celluloid was developed in 1856 and was used in corkscrew legs, mermaids, alligators, roundlets, and numerous others found throughout this book. In 1909, Bakelite appeared and corkscrews were produced using that material. In a 1946 catalog, the Williamson Company advertises corkscrews with red and green catalin sheaths and handles.

Plastics are any synthetic organic material molded under heat and pressure. If you already own celluloid, bakelite, or catalin corkscrews, you do own plastic corkscrews. They add bright colors to your collection. You can't avoid them, they are everywhere. In the late 1960s, the plastics revolution in corkscrews began to move forward by leaps and bounds. In 30 years, plastic corkscrews in hundreds of sizes, shapes, and colors have been produced. Here is a sampling of what can be found.

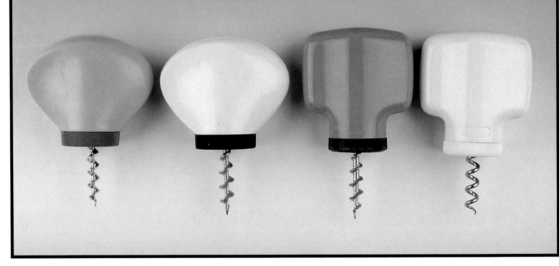

A mid 1980s full grip corkscrew invented by Gunther Pracht in Germany. By continuously turning the handle, the cork is extracted with little effort. The *first two* are German made with the white one marked SIEGER 600. The other two are made in Spain with web helix or wire helix and marked VALIA. $5-10.

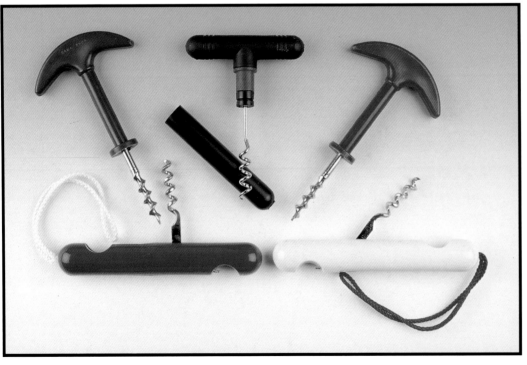

The red and brown two finger pulls with "button" are made in Hong Kong. $2-3. The black T with sheath is a rather sleek design. $3-4; The red and white folders are marked under the worm PATENT NO: 1035330, MADE IN HONG KONG. The cap lifter, corkscrew, and nylon hanging rope are sandwiched between two molded halves. $4-5.

Left to right: The "Grand Prix" has instructions on the top: "Place on bottle in position shown (handle up). Hold firmly in place. Press down on handle to start and turn clockwise until cork is drawn. Crossbow Inc., Cincinnati 45226." $10-15; Marked MADE IN TAIWAN. Flimsy foil cutter on the side. The threaded center shaft floats freely in the frame and serves no purpose. $1-2; Red marked KUHN NIKON, MADE IN SWITZERLAND. Very similar to the popular "Screwpull." $10-15; The "Corkmate" has a small wheel next to the handle to cut foil. $10-15; Red barrel with handle marked PROTEC, MADE IN ITALY. $8-10; The "EZPULL" marked U. S. PATENT PENDING. $15-20.

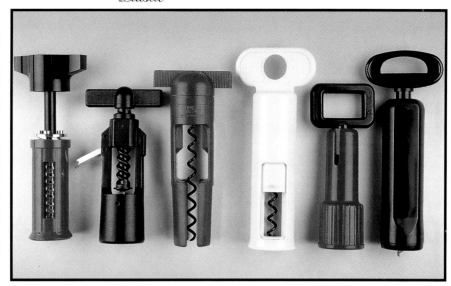

Left to right: The bottom collar is a sheath to protect the worm and a stand for the corkscrew. Marked HOAN, MADE IN ITALY. $15-20; Double action with clear barrel advertising "The Christian Brothers" wines. Marked MADE IN ENGLAND. $20-25; The two telescopes are marked KARIBA, LE SAUTE BOUCHON, PAT. PEND., MADE IN FRANCE. A 1983 patent covered the rope and pulley mechanics of this corkscrew and a 1990 patent was for the design. $15-20.

In 1953, Michael J. LaForte was granted a U. S. design patent for his "Bar Tool." The tool was manufactured by Vaughan Company of Chicago under the name "Tap Boy." The combination can piercer, cap lifter, and corkscrew at the *top left* is marked VAUGHAN'S TAP BOY, PAT. NO. 170,999 (design patent), CHICAGO 24, U. S. A. The plastic separating the metal slabs came in various colors. The Tap Boy was sold extensively for advertising purposes. The top five corkscrews are Tap Boys. $2-40 depending on brand advertised.

The two corkscrews in the *middle row* were produced by EKCO housewares and also sold extensively for advertising purposes. $2-25.

In the *bottom row* the four corkscrews on the *left* are by EKCO. $2-6. The next two are marked HONG KONG. $1-3. The last is unmarked and has a tin can opener in the formed top stamping. $2-4.

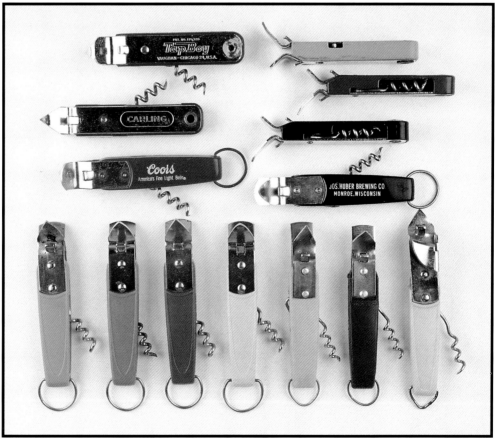

Decorated plastic corkscrews with cap lifter and can piercer. The *middle* six are like the drawings in Fred Steiner's 1969 American design patent. The worm is shaped so that a bit of the top is exposed on the right-hand side of the handle. By pushing it, the corkscrew slides out. *Left to right:* Green marked HONG KONG, Green marked STAINLESS, Green marked BONNY, Orange marked STAINLESS, White with mushrooms marked BONNY, Yellow unmarked, Yellow marked STAINLESS, Tan souvenir from Jamaica. $1-20 depending upon your enthusiasm.

"Super Quality" is the headline claim on the front of the box for this "3 in 1 Waiter Type Bottle Opener." Slide the protective cover back to expose the stainless steel can opener that is apt to reek havoc on any can lid. Close the cover and, with average size fingers, try desperately to lift the worm from the center, then give up, bend a paper clip to grab the end, and lift it. Alas, the cap lifter must be the "Super Quality" part. It will remove a bottle cap. Made in Taiwan of ABS plastic. Box marked R. O. C. PAT NO:29751. Sells for 33 Baht in the street markets of Bangkok.

Top row left to right: Combination cap lifter, bottle resealer, and plastic corkscrew. Marked MADE IN W. GERMANY. $5-10; Winged plastic corkscrew with cap lifter and twist off top remover in handle. $2-4; A simple 2 1/8" square with a rubber stopper in the center for sealing a bottle. Plastic cap lifter and corkscrew fold out of the side. When the worm is folded out, it is fixed in a position at the bottom of a diamond shape handle for better two finger grip. $8-12.
Bottom row left to right: A Korean made "3-in-one type opener" called "Triple Seven" with cap lifter, paring knife blade, and metal folding worm. Advertising Herforder Pils, a German beer. $10-12; Plastic coated 2" square with two knives, cap lifter, and metal folding worm. Marked CHINA. $4-6; Same as on *left* but with a magnet added. $10-12.

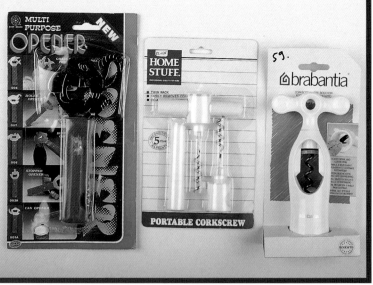

The elephant multi-purpose opener is made in China and according to the blister pack card it is an orange peeler, a holes [*sic*] opener, a bottle opener, a stopper opener (corkscrew), and a can opener. It comes with the stamped figure as an elephant, a dolphin, two fish, a hand, or a hippopotamus. The perfect gift for your corkscrew collecting friends!
The "Home Stuff" package contains two white "portable" (picnic) corkscrews. They are made in Taiwan and come with a 5 year unconditional warranty. If you break it, Home Stuff in Milwaukee, Wisconsin, will replace it for a $1 handling charge. Buy them in Korea for a song.
The "Brabantia" is a good quality plastic corkscrew with a "coated spiral and center ring." The corkscrew was introduced at the 1985 Frankfurt Spring fair by the Dutch firm Brabantia. This one was purchased in 1997 in Avignon, France, for 59 Francs.

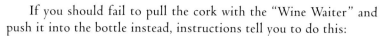

If you should fail to pull the cork with the "Wine Waiter" and push it into the bottle instead, instructions tell you to do this:

1. Remove the sleeve.
2. Tighten the cork screw in the retriever.
3. Pull the ring firmly down to extend the fingers. You will hear two clicks. Slowly insert your Wine Waiter while keeping the ring on the mouth of the bottle.
4. The fingers will spring open and the cork will float into the middle of them.
5. Carefully and firmly, pull straight up - do not twist the handle!

Here's an Italian marvel that incorporates features of several corkscrews. It has a sheath to protect the worm, a large handle for plenty of gripping power, a barrel, a rack and pinion, and a leaf spring loaded ratcheting lever. To remove a cork: Pull the handle up and place the collar over the bottle. Exert downward pressure on handle to penetrate the cork and keep turning. Grasp the side handle and push the top lever down. The lever will spring back at each movement of the internal gears. Continue to pump the lever until the cork is extracted. Marked BREVETTO W A F. $50-75.

The U. S. made "Wine Waiter" from Wine Waiter Products, Inc. of Petaluma, California, is a combination corkscrew and cork retriever. The corkscrew is a simple frame type extractor. $10-15.

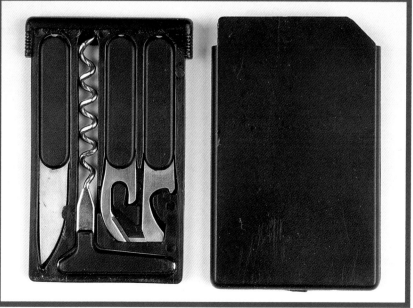

In 1981, Herbert Allen of Houston, Texas, patented his first "Screwpull." By 1989, seven mechanical and one design patent had been issued to Allen for variations and improvements of the "Screwpull." There are tabletop models, picnic or pocket types, and a lever type. Some of the frames have the added advantage of a folding foil cutter knife. The table top and picnic versions are currently sold by the French company Le Creuset in a variety of colors. Prices range from $14.95 to $29.95. The Leverpull is sold at prices ranging from $79.95 to $139.95.

A 2" x 3" x 1/4" black case with sliding drawer. The drawer contains a knife, a can opener, a bottle cap lifter, and a corkscrew. Ideal for pocket, purse, or glove box but not very good for opening a bottle of wine! $5-10.

Pocket - Collapsing

In 1891, Carl Hollweg was granted an American patent for a collapsing corkscrew that protected the pocket from the worm. Hinges in four places allow the user to fully close the corkscrew for storage or fully open to use the case as the handle. They have been produced in several sizes and shapes. Some have been used for advertising purposes. A 1913 catalog from Lewis Brothers of Montreal, a hardware wholesaler, offered this corkscrew as the "Telescope." They sold them for $2.70 per dozen.

Take a close look and you will see a Hollweg corkscrew in the bottle cork.

The Hollweg at *top* and the one to its *right* are silver with a gold plated worm. Both are marked NAPIER STERLING (from Meriden, Connecticut) and PAT. APPLIED FOR. The *first* has a decorated case and the *second* a plain case. The *second* has a cap lifter on the worm shank. $300-500.

At *top left* are two small versions measuring 2 1/4" collapsed. One is marked MADE ABROAD, PATENT APPLIED FOR, PATENT ANGEMELDET. The other has the same marks plus MADE IN GERMANY. $100-125.

At *lower left* is a 2 5/8" Swedish version marked HEDENGRAN & SONS, ESKILSTUNA with trademarks. Note the single scallop on the inside of each link. This one was produced with left-hand and right-hand worms. Others in this size with three scallops on each link have been found marked:

HENRY BOKER; WORTHINGTON'S ALES and MADE ABROAD - PATENT APPLIED FOR - MADE IN GERMANY. $75-125.

The most common size is 3 1/4". The example on the *right* has no marks on the outside of the links but is marked on the inside of the channel PATENTED FEBRUARY 24, 1891. $75-85. The *bottom* one has advertising for "Pabst, Milwaukee" on the links. $80-100. Another with beer advertising reads "The American Brewing Co., St. Louis A.B.C. Bohemian." $100-125. And another has the manufacturer's name Henry Boker. $80-100. The rarest in this size is the one in the *center* with one scallop on the inside of the links and a square shank on the worm. It is marked MADE ABROAD, PATENT APPLIED FOR, PATENT ANGEMELDET, MADE IN GERMANY. $200-250.

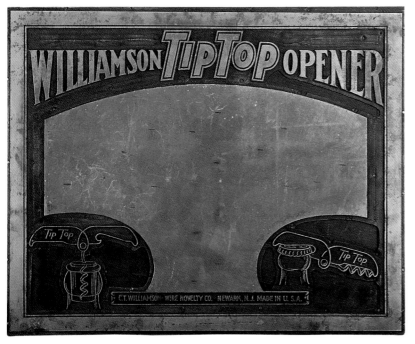

Pocket - Folding

Folding corkscrews were designed primarily to be kept in one's vest pocket or purse. As cork extractors, most are not very practical. The worm folded to a position on its metal host where it would protect the owner from being stabbed when reaching in a pocket or purse for it and would eliminate poking holes. Many of them were also used for advertising purposes. Although convenient, most of them would not easily remove a stubborn cork.

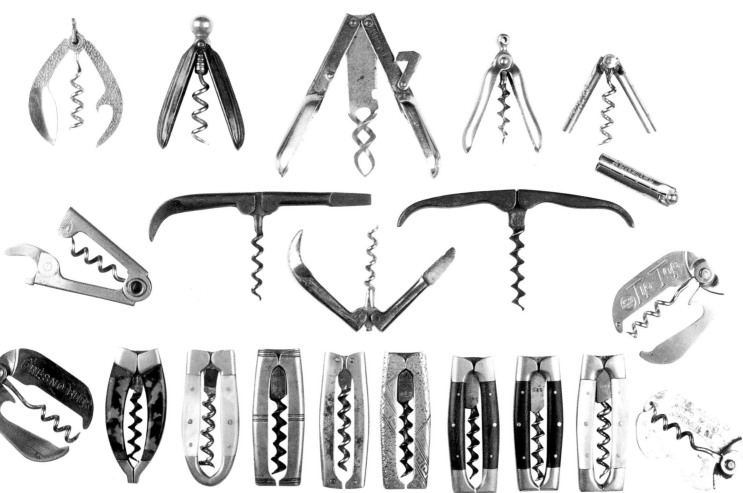

Top row left to right: The "Turkey Foot" with cap lifter and small spoon is unmarked. $125-150; The "Clam Shell" has a spring clip on the bottom to secure the sides when not in use. $200-300; The handle of the large double helix is secured by a bottle cap lifter that folds to a raised portion on the opposite side. $500-600; The "Pea Pod" was made by Perille in Paris. $200-300; The "Dainty" was made by Vaughan in Chicago and is marked PAT'D APPL'D. Apparently no patent was issued. It is shown open and closed. The Dainty was also used as an advertising giveaway. $125-150.

Middle row left to right: The "Chief" has an Indian head with headdress and is marked CHIEF, MADE IN U. S. A. $75-100; Two German folders with carriage key and foil cutter. $100-150; A simple unmarked German Folder. $75-100; The "Tip Top" (so marked) by Williamson of Newark, New Jersey. $40-60; A packaging card for the Tip Top proclaims "Lies flat in your vest pocket." The Tip Top was

also sold for advertising purposes. *Left bottom* advertises Fresno Beer and *right* reads "Compliments of Roy B. Sewell, Bremen, CA, When you think of clothing, think of Sewell." $75-80.

Bottom right beginning with second: Tortoise Shell handles marked GESETZLICH GESCHÜUTZ on shank (German for Legally Registered). $300-400; Mother-of-pearl handles marked GERMANY. $350-450; nickel silver handles marked WILSON CO. $175-200; Fancy nickel silver handles marked WILSON CO. $250-300; Unmarked steel handles. $100-125; Wood grain handles marked L. WEYERSBURG & SON, GERMANY. $250-300; Wood grain handles and mother-of-pearl handles marked G & S (for Graef & Schmidt) on one side of the shank and the Henckel's Twin trademark on the other. Graef & Schmidt were the New York City based importers of Henckel's Twin Brand cutlery. $250-325. The last six all have a mating lock at the base.

The three folders with cap lifter at the *top center* have the longest arms of the lot for a full grip and the longest worm for greatest cork purchase. $75-100. The one on the *right* is marked DREKO and it was made in East Germany. The one on the *left* has advertising for Molson Ale of Canada. The powderhorn on the *left* advertises the Vendome Hotel in Evansville, Indiana. It is marked PAT'D 4-28-14, which was a cap lifter design patent by John Sommer. $75-100. Under the powderhorn is Thomas Harding's 1928 patent for the *Nifty* cap lifter/corkscrew. This one is quite unusual in that it has a three inch rule on one side and a file on the other. It is marked DESIGNED BY AMERICAN PLATE GLASS CO., BOTTLE DIVISION N.Y., U.S. PATENT 1680291. $60-80. Next is marked D.R.G.M. Germany. It is fashioned after the *Nifty* style and has an added can opener in the military P-38 style. $75-100. Another heavier German made piece advertises "Melchers Distilleries Limited, St. Lawrence Bourbon Whiskey." $80-90.

In the *center* is an unmarked version of Robert McLean's 1926 American patent for a combination corkscrew, cigar box opener, bottle opener, and key. $200-300.

At *left* is a formed metal cap lifter with worm on the underside and advertising for "Ye Tavern Brew." $80-100. On the *right side* is Augustus Stephen's 1901 design patent for a cap lifter, which is frequently found with brewery advertising. It is unusual to see this design with a corkscrew. $75-85. Next is an unmarked simple cap lifter with flimsy worm. $50-60. The pointing hand is a spinner used at a bar to determine who pays. This one advertises the manufacturer Brown & Bigelow of St. Paul, Minnesota. $100-125. The combination tool with button hook and Prestolite key (to open the acetylene valves for gas lamps on running boards of early cars) is marked PAT. PENDING with advertising for "Metal States Novelty Co., Salt Lake City." $150-200. On the *far right* is a caplifter/corkscrew marked only MADE IN U. S. A. $75-85.

The brass cap lifter with corkscrew folding into elongated hole is unmarked. $80-90. The other with elongated hole is marked BESTEVER PAT. APPLIED FOR. This is Harry Chippendale's 1910 American patent for the addition of a cigar cutter. $800-1000. On the *bottom* are three combination cap lifter, can opener, corkscrew folders with marks MADE IN ENGLAND, U.C.-50 and D.B.G.M GERMANY. $50-75.

Left to right: The "Bonsa" marked REGISTERED. 1899 German registered design by Julius Everts. The trade name "Bonsa" was used by German firm Böntgen & Sabin. $500-750; A folding bell cap marked KUPPER LAGER. 1894 German registered design by Wilhelm Von zur Gathen. $600-800; A combination corkscrew, cap lifter, bottle stopper marked EMIDE. The worm folds out by turning the serrated disk to back off a securing set screw. When the worm is folded out, it is secured for use by turning the disk clockwise. $20-30.

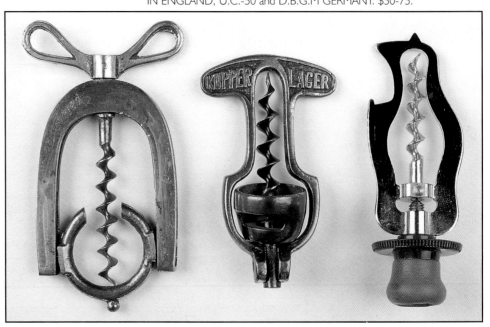

Above: These folders all have cap lifters. Many were used for advertising purposes and the corkscrew simply folds or swivels out. When in use, the cap lifter handle is the direct pull handle for the corkscrew.

At *top middle* is a product of Vaughan, Chicago. The bottle shape cap lifter without corkscrew has been cataloged with a wide variety of brewery advertisements. This example has a worm riveted to the backside ready to swivel out for cork removal. Advertising on the other side is "Broadway Sports Palace, Management, Schork & Schaffer." $40-50. One without the worm advertising "Black Horse Ale" is marked REGD. 1935.

Left side top to bottom: Two cap lifters with a pin holding the worm between two shoulders. One is marked HOFFRITZ NY GERMANY and the other has advertising "Suze Aperitif." $30-40; A waiter's style (without neckstand) advertises "Suze Aperitif Ala Gentiane." $50-60.

Right side top to bottom: Marked "SO-EZY" MADE IN U. S. A. PAT. PEND. $40-50; Two cap lifters with a slot in the handle. The backspring and worm retaining shoulder assembly passes through the slot and is riveted to the handle. When the worm is turned out for

use, it is locked by the backspring. $40-60; The cap lifter/corkscrew advertises "Compliments of Bishop's Liquor Store, 217 S. Akard, Phone 2-8523." $80-100.

Below: At *left* are three views of the "Over the Top" cap lifter patented by Harry Vaughan in Chicago in 1924. The opener is "formed by stamping out of a strip of metal a blank of proper conformation and then bending into final form by means of suitable dies." This was a very popular advertising piece and is unusual with a corkscrew. These three advertise Star Beer of Lancaster, Pennsylvania, Riedle's Beer of Winnipeg, Manitoba, and Old Scotch Ginger Ale. $30-50.

At *top right* are two views of a sturdier version of Vaughan's Over the Top opener. One has advertising reading "Enjoy Prima Beer" and the other "Drink Prima Special." $25-40.

The cap lifters with corkscrew and bottle stopper were manufactured by Ryede Specialty Works of Rochester, New York. A patent was issued to Adolph Rydquist for the "uncapping tool" in 1909. These two have advertising for New England Brewing Co. and Moerlbach Brau. $60-90.

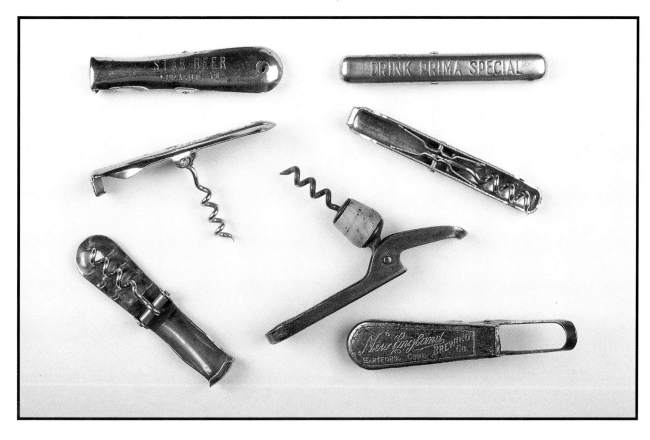

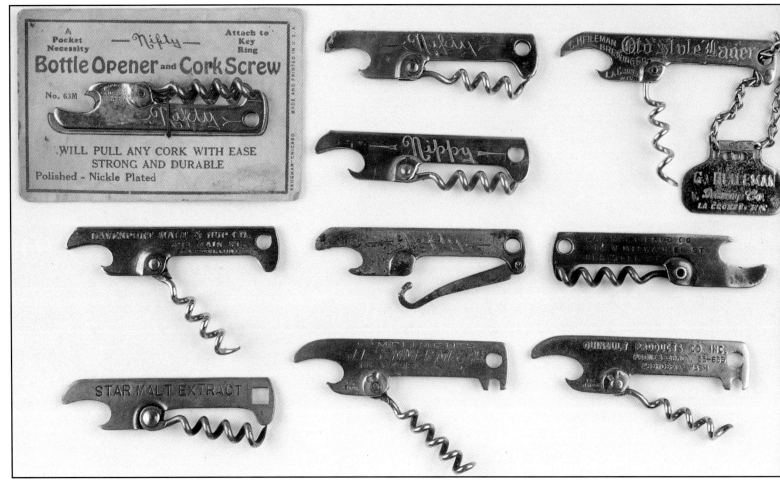

A corkscrew frequently found at flea markets is the "Nifty" type. Millions were produced for advertising purposes. And by the huge numbers that turn up, those sold as the "Nifty" and marketed as such must have been made in even greater numbers! The "Nifty" was invented in 1916 by Harry L. Vaughan and produced by his Chicago firm. A less common version was patented by Thomas Harding in 1928 and manufactured by the J. L. Sommer Manufacturing Company of Newark, New Jersey. This improved design was a single stamping with worm riveted to it. It was easier, faster, and less expensive to manufacture than the Vaughan type, which was a double stamping folded over the pivoting worm.

Nifty style corkscrews can be found with a variety of marks, opener, and worm variations and with hundreds of different advertisements. Prices can be seen as low as a quarter to $50.
Left side from top to bottom: Nifty packaging. $30-40; Vaughan type advertising "Davenport Malt & Hop Co., Stamford, Conn." $10-15; Harding type advertising "Star Malt Extract" with prestolite key. $15-20.
Middle from top to bottom: The "Nifty." $0.25-2; An English knock-off that says "Nippy." $5-10; A button hook that says "Nifty" (a screwdriver was also made like this). $5-10; A Harding type advertising "Compliments J. L. Sommer Mfg. Co., Newark, N. J., DENVER, JULY 10 to 13TH 1928." This one has a left-hand worm. $30-40.
Right side from top to bottom: Advertising on both the corkscrew and the plate for "G. Heileman Brewing Co., La Crosse, Wis." Both are marked C. T. & O. & CO., CHICAGO. The corkscrew is additionally marked PAT. ALLD. (patent allowed) and the plate PAT. APL'D FOR. Harry Vaughan's Crown Throat and Opener Co. (C. T. & O) later became Vaughan Mfg. Co. $30-40; An "upside down" Harding type advertising "Atlas Malt Prod Co." $20-30; Harding type with right-hand worm. $25-30.

Steel handles with folding wire worm marked D. PERES, GERMANY and REBE. The worm folds down and then slides in a slot in the handle to a pulling position. A backspring keeps it in a tight locked position. Similar to Eduard Becker's 1898 German patent. $200-250.

Pocket - Slide Out

In 1892, Edmund Jansen in Germany received a patent (#6145) for a corkscrew that slides out of a channel formed by folding sheet metal into a rectangle. One end and half of the underside are left open for the sliding mechanism. A backspring is located in the top of the handle and attached to it is a worm with sliding mechanism. The worm slides out the end and is turned perpendicular to the handle locking with the backspring.

Sixty years later (1952), Albert Andrews of Fort Collins, Colorado, was granted an American patent for a "Resilient casing with slidable tool." He encased a sliding mechanism in a folded sheet metal casing. The sliding mechanism had a button on it, which would then slide in a channel in the middle of the backside. His patent indicates that the slide could have a bottle or cap opener, a knife, a nail file, screwdriver head, or other suitable tool on the end of it. Although Andrews had applied for his patent in 1948, it is interesting to note that a souvenir example of this design with corkscrew was around for the 1934 Chicago Century of Progress exhibition! In addition, 1930s advertisements for the slide out from the Electro-Chemical Engraving Co. of New York proclaim "If you want to put an army of walking ads to work, this unique, disappearing bottle opener, etched and enameled in color, will serve you loyally. No owner can help playing with it and showing it off, when he is not actually using it. And whenever he pushes the button, he also pushes your brand!"

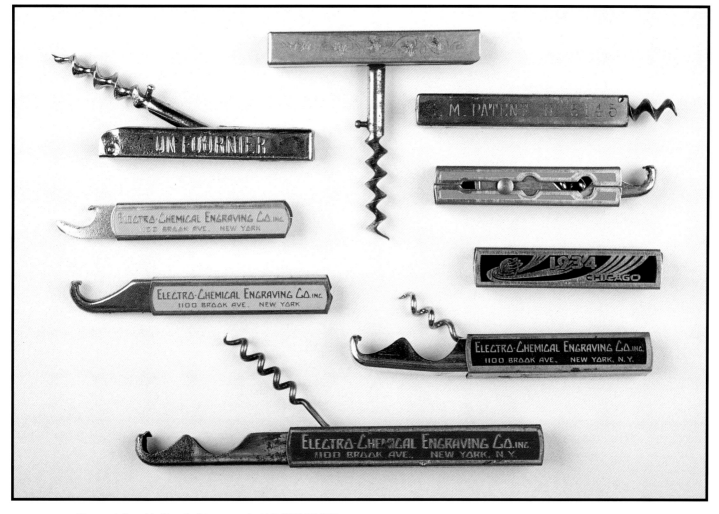

Top row left to right: French slide out marked UN FOURNIER IMPERATOR SEVE FOURNIER. $150-200; Marked GRAEF & SCHMIDT. The firm was a New York City importer of German cutlery. $200-250; Marked G. M. PATENT 6145. $200-250. *Orange and two yellow caplifters:* Marked PAT. PEND. These were used extensively for advertising and have been found in red, blue, black, green, and yellow enamels. They were products of the Electro-Chemical Engraving Co., Inc. of 1100 Brook Ave., New York. Their own advertising states "Manufacturers of metal trays, coasters, signs, displays, bottle openers." The yellow examples show the over the top and under-lift style cap lifters; the orange has the opener retracted and shows the backside. $30-100.
Blue handles: 1934 Chicago Century of Progress* with retracted corkscrew. $75-100. Electro-Chemical Engraving shown with corkscrew out. $75-125.
Bottom: Rare slide out with 3 1/2" long case to accommodate a longer worm. $250-400.

*In 1933-34, Chicago was the site of an international centennial exposition. The central theme of the exposition was "the dramatization of the progress of civilization during the hundred years of Chicago's existence." It focused on the great scientific, technological, and engineering developments of the century. In the final accounting of the fair, A Century of Progress was recognized as the only major world's fair to pay all its debts and have a surplus in cash at its closing.

Prong Pullers & Retrievers

A very common advertising giveaway today is a cork puller with two prongs sometimes referred to as a "screwless extractor." The advertising is usually on a plastic case and they can be found with the names of a host of wineries. The prong puller is not a recent invention!

Do they work? With a little practice, you will be surprised at how easily you can extract a cork without damaging it. Simply start sliding the longer of the prongs down one side of the cork. Then, using a rocking motion, work both down as far as you can. Turn the handle to break the seal between the cork and the bottle and then lift.

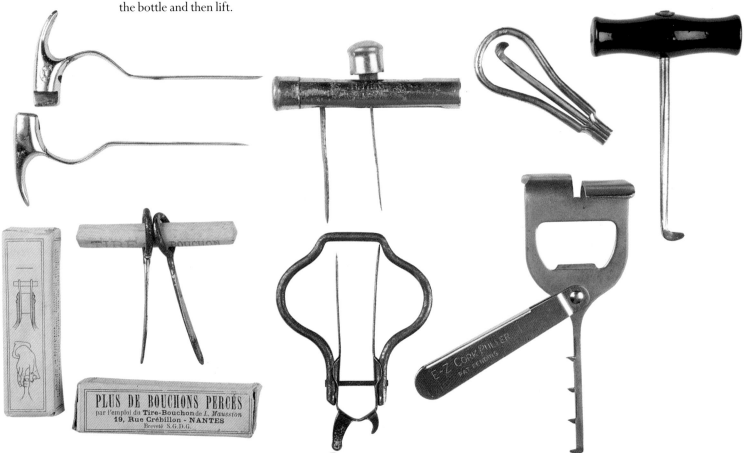

Top row left to right: A two piece prong stored by putting the prong tips into slots in the handles of the opposing pieces. An 1886 French patent by Dugert and Lafittau. $800-1000; Two prong cylinder used by pulling one prong out of the end of the cylinder allowing the second to drop down. The first is then inserted in a slot in the top and can move freely from side to side. It is marked B. LEW PATENT and has a picture of a half man/half lion extracting a cork from a bottle. This is Fred. Mann's 1881 American patent. $500-800; The folding bow and wood handle puller with hook are Benjamin Greely's 1888 American patent. As the hook is inserted by the cork, a groove in the shaft allows air to escape and when the hook is below the cork, it is turned, and the cork can be "lifted" out. $300-350.

Bottom row left to right: A 1904 French patented puller composed of a wood dowel and two prongs of equal length that fit over the dowel. A true pocket puller! Several years ago, a French collector found a hoard of them in original boxes. The instructions on the box tell the user to insert the blades first using "a small hammer or any object;" then place the dowel through the holes. $25-35; Folding bow type double prong puller with cap lifter and paper cutter. Patented in France in 1934 by Serre. $500-700; Puller with folding cover for the toothed shaft. Marked E-Z CORK PULLER PAT. PENDING.* $65-75.

Instructions for using the E-Z cork puller were:

1. Push barbed blade straight down between cork and inside of bottle neck, until end barb reaches bottom of cork. Be sure curves of barb conform to curves of inside bottle neck.

2. Turn left, forcing barbs into cork.

3. Remove cork by pulling straight up, using finger grip. Sure! Don't try this at home!

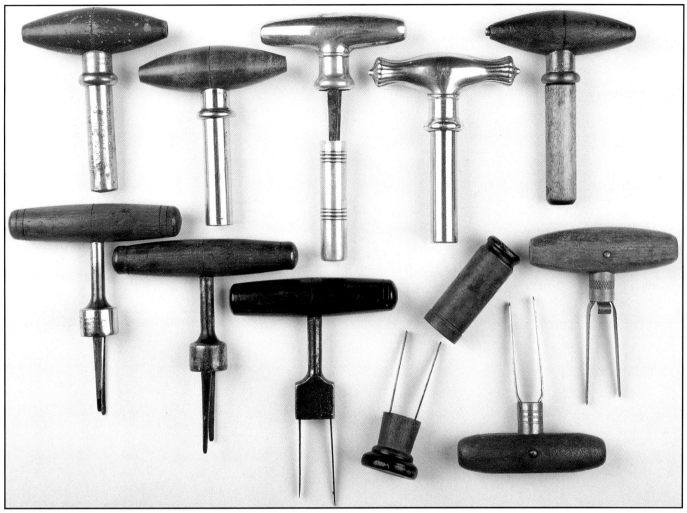

The pullers in the top row are Machil Converse's 1899 American patent. The patent is called "Cork Extractor;" yet packaging for it says "Cork Puller." All of the Converse pullers came with sheaths. Most are marked just below the handle with the patent date. An unmarked nickel plated brass sheath was most commonly used. $35-50. They can also be found with advertising. The wood handle example on the *left* reads "Holihan Bros. - Wholesalers to the People, Lawrence, Mass." $75-100. The wooden sheath at *right* is difficult to find. $100-125. The two rare silver handles also have the patent date and the *first* is engraved "Geo. R. E. Gilchrist, Wheeling, W. Va." $300-400.
In 1879 and 1892, Lucian Mumford received patents for his cork puller pictured at *lower left*. The *first two* are marked on the prong

retaining ring MAGIC CORK EXTRACTOR PAT. MARCH 4-79, MAY 10-92. $500-700. The *third* is a rarer version with flat prong retainer. $900-1100. The Mumford was not supplied with a protective sheath for the prongs.
The puller with cylindrical wood case in the *bottom row* has equal length prongs with rounded ends stored in the case. The puller is from Argentina and the base is marked IN VINO VERITAS. $100-150.
The two wood handle pullers at *right* are modern versions of the Converse. The *first* is marked on the top GOURMET. $20-25. The other one incorporates a cap lifter at the base of the prong retainer. $20-25.

At *left* are three cork pullers marked IDEAL. They have cap removers in the handle. The one on the *left* is marked IDEAL CORKDRAWER MADE IN ITALY PATENTED. $75-90. On the top one, a large cap lifter marked FOR CROWN CAPS swings away from the top handle marked IDEAL CORK DRAWER BRITISH MADE, REG NO. 708714 (1924). $100-150. The *third* has a cap lifter that swings out from inside the handle. It is marked FOR CROWN CORKS, W.U.F. IDEAL CORKPULLER, BRITISH MADE. $90-100. All three appear to be from a very similar mold as well as the one without cap lifter which is marked MARO, D.R.P. $65-80.
At *top center* is a puller with a spare set of prongs stored in the sheath. To replace the prongs, simply remove the screw in the handle. This French puller is marked SAN BRI Bᵀᴱ S.G.D.G. $125-150. *Below* this and to the *right* are two additional French pullers marked A. S. MADE IN FRANCE and LE PRATIQUE PARIS. The latter has a cap lifter in the formed sheet metal handle. $75-100.
The winged puller is marked AH-HA, D.R.G.M. GERMANY. $35-40. To its *right* is a puller marked simply J T R. $35-40. The last two with red and green handles are marked VAUGHAN'S QUICK AND EASY CORK PULLER AND BOTTLE OPENER, PAT. APL'D FOR, CHICAGO. $30-50.

The yellow "Easi-Pull" box is labeled "Made in England by 'Easi-Pull' Co., Hove, Sussex." $30-40 with box.

The puller with red plastic handle is the German AH-HA. The prongs are molded into the handle. Made by Monopol. $35-50 with box.

The "Vintage '73 Cork Puller" was marketed by AN/CO Merchandising Co., of San Gabriel, California. $15-20.

The "Wine Country Cork Puller" is currently available from Franmara Company of Italy. It is sold for advertising purposes. This one says "Do it the Goodway," an advertising slogan of Goodway Technologies Corporation, Stamford, Connecticut.

The Wiggle 'n Twist Cork Extractor comes in a leather case with instructions.

To Extract Cork:

1. Insert both blades fractionally between cork and bottle, longer blade first.

2. Don't push, but gently rock blades one by one into bottle neck to 3/4 length.

3. Gently twist handle upwards to remove cork.

To Cork Bottle:

1. Place cork full length between blades up to handle and clamp extruding blades into bottle neck.

2. Twist handle downward until cork in position.

3. Rock blades upwards out.

The instruction sheet gives the following information: Gateway Sole Distributor, Gifts Ltd., London, A Heibo Product, Wiggle 'n Twist Cork Extractor and Corker, Made in UK Pat. No. 1525876, Design Regist. 990943 (1979).

With it being so simple to cork and recork a bottle, how can one live without a Wiggle 'n Twist?

A few modern prong pullers. *Top left to right:* 1989 American patent by Wolfgang Tischler, manufactured in Germany. The equal length prongs can be inserted one at a time by moving one side handle up. $20-30; The chrome puller is the "Ah-So" by Monopol in Germany. This one has been noted with advertising such as this "Robert Mondavi Winery" engraving just below the cap lifter. $10-15; The yellow puller is marked EASI PULL and was made in England by the Easi-Pull Co. Hove, Sussex. $15-20; A recent puller with plastic sheath proclaims "Uncork New York." $5-10; The steer horns are from Scovill Manufacturing of Waterbury, Connecticut. $20-25.

Bottom left to right: The sheath and handle look plastic but only the sheath is. The puller is a well made piece marked SAN BRI MADE IN FRANCE. $30-40; Grapevine roots with worm are quite common - here is a rare genuine example with prongs. $75-100; The chrome puller with black plastic sheath is marked FGB ITALY. $8-10; The Burgundy plastic puller is marked TWISTUP. $8-10; Wiggle 'n Twist Cork Extractor. $35-

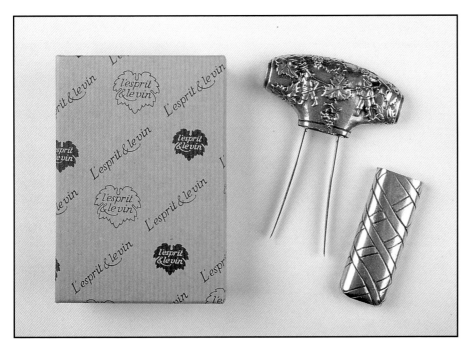

Left: A heavy cast puller currently produced in France as part of the "l'esprit & le vin" collection. Handle decorated with grapes, grapevines, and grape pickers. Sells at the corkscrew museum in Menerbes for 230 French Francs.

Below: *Top row left to right:* A French single blade cork lifter marked B^{TE} S.G.D.G. $400-500; A puller with brass handle marked MESTRE. In this 1873 French patent by Eugene Mestre, the puller is pushed down between the cork and the bottle. When the hook is below the cork, it can be turned to grab the cork and pull it up. $500-700; American made hooked cork lifter with advertising for Wacker's Liquid Malt. $125-150; A modern cork lifter marked ITALY. $10-15.
Bottom: Wood handle Bernard Bonin's 1977 American design patent for a cork retriever. Marked on shank U. S. PAT. NO. D-244,002. $15-25; A wire cork retriever. The thumb is placed in the upper hole, and two fingers are placed in the lower holes, which slide up and down to open and close the cork grips. $15-20.

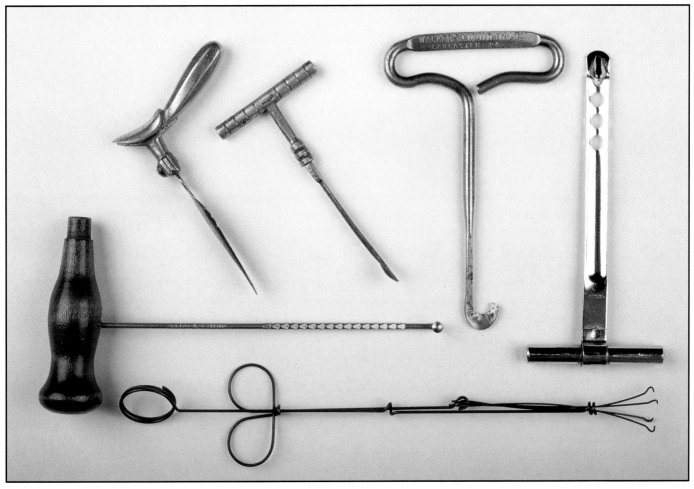

Rack & Pinion

In a rack and pinion gear arrangement, the pinion meshes with a rack with teeth, which converts rotary motion to reciprocating motion. In rack and pinion automobile steering, for example, the steering wheel column leads to a pinion gear and engages with a rack, which eventually leads to the steering arms and wheels. When the steering wheel is turned to the right or left, the pinion rotates on the rack moving it right or left.

Long before Henry Ford began mass producing Model T's, corkscrews had been produced with racks and pinions. T-handles with toothed racks on shafts with barrels or frames and engaging side handle gears were the first "rack and pinion" corkscrews. The rack and pinion design was also used in single lever and double lever corkscrews.

A highly desired corkscrew is the "King's Screw," which is constructed as follows:

A handle with worm attached to a threaded shaft
A four post frame with collar to fit a bottle neck
A toothed rack with centering button
A side handle with pinion gear

The shaft runs through the top of the handle and is secured with a nut. The toothed rack is secured within the frame with the shaft running through it. The rack tube is hollow with a thread to mate with the shaft at the inside top. The side handle shaft goes through the top of the frame with the pinion engaging with the rack.

To operate:
1. Thread handle up leaving rack entirely within the frame.
2. Rest collar on bottle neck.
3. Screw worm into cork by turning to handle.
4. Turn side handle clockwise to raise rack with frame and extract cork.

Je̦n go̦ûterai

The two "four poster" King's Screws have bone handles at top. $800-1200. One has a bone side handle and the other steel. The rack and pinion was in production in the 18th century before patents were issued.
In 1855, William Lund and William Hipkins were granted a patent for the rack and pinion corkscrew. They simplified the earlier designs by making the rack a part of the handle and worm, thus eliminating the separate rack. The patent drawing shows a two post frame like the one on the *right*. This rosewood handle corkscrew is marked LUND'S LONDON RACK at the top of the frame and LUND'S PATENT on the bottom collar. The tempered steel springs attached to the bottom of the frame are Thomas Lund's 1838 patent for a bottle-holding device. The bottle grips are marked LUND PATENTEE LONDON. The grips are also found on the Thomason Barrel and the London Rack. Lund Bottle Grips corkscrew. *$Rare.*

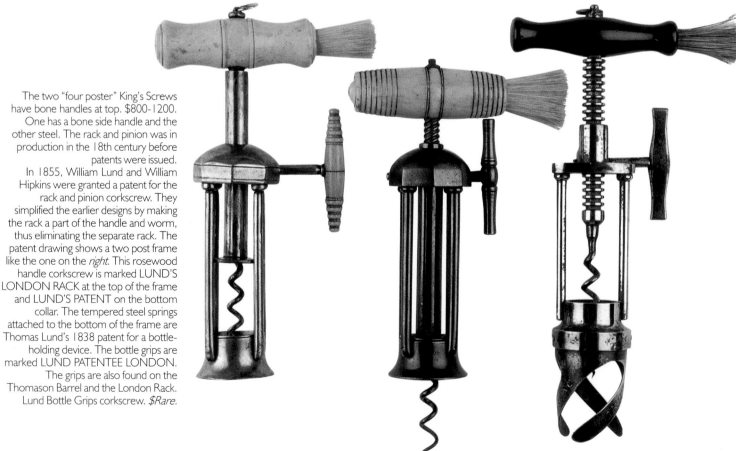

T126

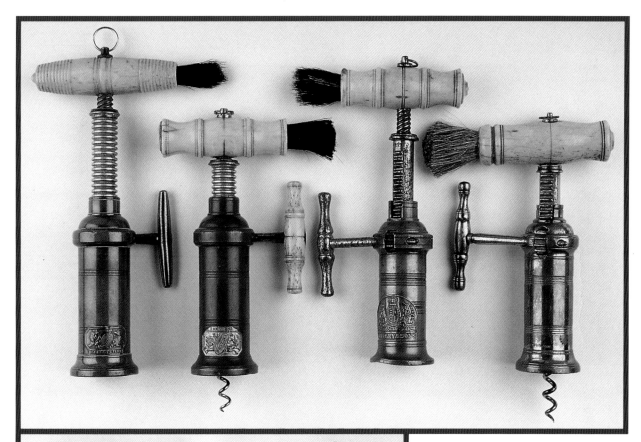

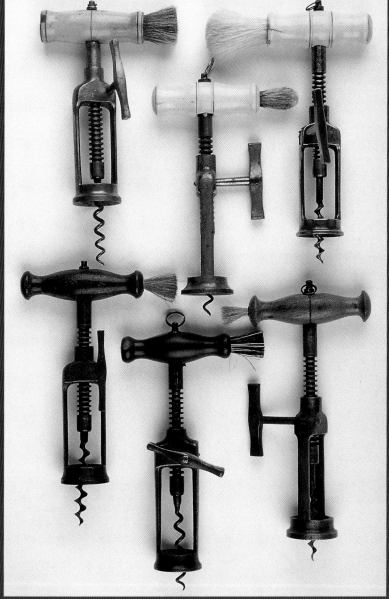

Above: Although the rack and pinion was not patented in its early version, many companies produced it in barrel form with a patent plate added. The examples on the *left* have patent plates marked COPE & CUTLER and DOWLER. The *third* has a plate marked HEELEY & SONS and the *fourth* is engraved J. MORTON. $500-1500.

Left: Here are six examples of Lund's simplified rack and pinion design.
Top left to right: Marked CASEY. $200-250; Unmarked with a small notch at the top of the frame and a pin just below the handle. When the worm is fully inserted into the cork, the pin engages with the notch to prevent further turning. $350-400; Unmarked. $200-250.
Bottom left to right: Unmarked. $175-200; Marked below handle LUND'S PATENT RACK and marked on frame sides LUND MAKER CORNHILL AND FLEET ST. LONDON. This has the same notch and pin as the bone handle version above it. In this example the pinion gear teeth are only exposed on the side of the frame (the others are exposed on the top corner of the frame). $350-400; Unmarked. $175-200.

Further examples of rack and pinions are *from left to right:*
Unmarked German version. $125-200; French marked
MODELE DEPOSE with initials JB in 12 point star. $125-
175; French marked DEPOSE PARIS with initials JP
(Jacques Perille). $150-200; Another French marked
MODELE DEPOSE with initials JB in 12 point star. $125-
175; Two unmarked. $100-150.
Note: The French versions have a narrow rack with gears
placed inside the frame on either side of the rack. The two
gear version is a 1930 patent by Georges-Pierre Creuse.

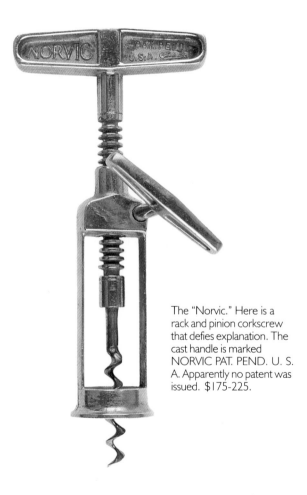

The "Norvic." Here is a
rack and pinion corkscrew
that defies explanation. The
cast handle is marked
NORVIC PAT. PEND. U. S.
A. Apparently no patent was
issued. $175-225.

Roundlets

Roundlets originated in the 18th century with the hinged barrel type containing a double hinged worm. Later versions had cases that either unscrewed or pulled apart with the worm stored in one end. After one side is removed, the worm is pulled out and turned perpendicular to the case. Then the empty side is threaded or pushed back on to form the handle. A third type is the roundlet that contains several loose tools with one or two slots in their shafts to mate with one or two slots in the case. Lighters, hammers, rasps, spoons, cap lifters, and whistles have also been attached in various ways. Roundlets can be found in brass, steel, wood, gold, silver, celluloid, rubber, and plastic. The roundlet specialist can build a rather extensive collection by looking at the great number of variations in design, size, and material.

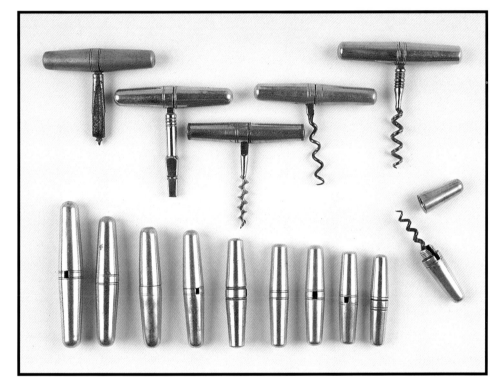

Nickel plated brass roundlets with pivoting worm are the most commonly found. However, when the collector sees them at markets, he should examine these closely. Instead of a worm, it may have a carriage key or other folding tool inside. It might have advertising engraved on it. Or it may be Benoit Thinet's 1873 French patent with loose worm fitting slot in the handle. The ex-numismatist corkscrew collector might want to carry a ruler to check the many sizes! They will range in value from $30-60.

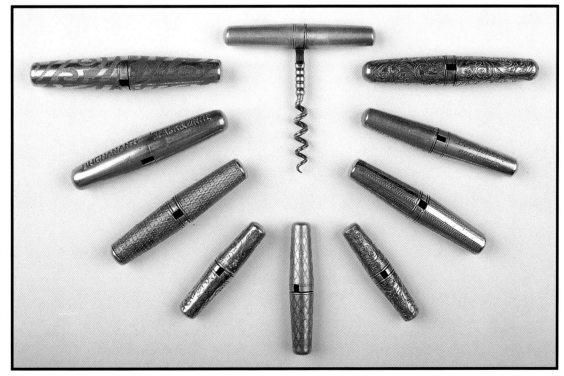

Not all nickel plated roundlets are dull and boring. Here is a lot of finely machined and engraved examples plus two with advertising. $150-250. Note: The corkscrew at the *top* has the appearance a of roundlet, but it is actually an unusual T-handle corkscrew. $75-100.

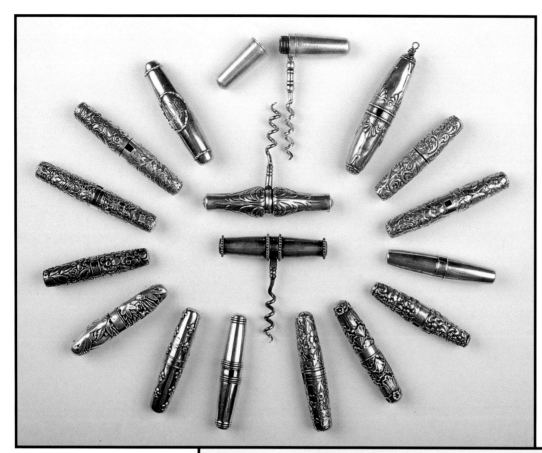

A group of ornate Sterling roundlets with marks, including "L" trademark of La Pierre (New York and Connecticut), Gorham trademark (Providence, Rhode Island), and H & H (Providence). $200-400.
The roundlet to *left of top center* is from Tiffany & Co., New York. $500-600.
The one in the *bottom row* with the fleurs de lis is from La Pierre. $300-350.

More ornate Sterling roundlets, including trademarks of American companies Whiting (Providence, Rhode Island), La Pierre, Gorham, and Simons (Philadelphia). $200-400. There are three English examples, including one with a 1902 Chester hallmark $300-400. The 3 1/2" Sterling roundlet in the *center* has a Birmingham, England 1904 hallmark. It was engraved three years later with "F. H. B. from H. H. S. Xmas, 1907." $350-400.

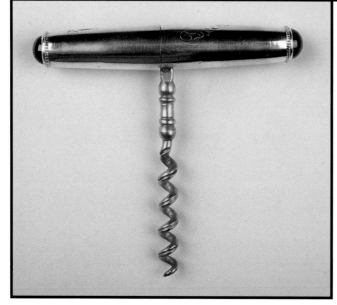

A very elegant 3 1/2" sterling roundlet with garnets mounted on each end. Engraved for a 1901 Christmas gift with initials "W. D. C." and "Dec. 25 - 01." Worm has a gold wash. $600-700.

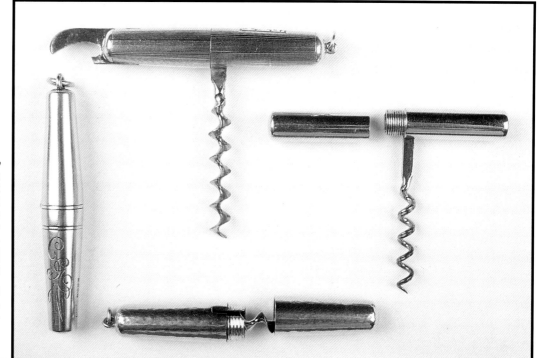

Four gold roundlets *from top center clockwise:* Worm shank marked GERMANY. Cap lifter at end. Marked 14K and engraved with initials "S M H." $800-1000; American plain, sleek, simply elegant case marked 14K. $600-700; Worm shank marked GERMANY. Case marked 14K and engraved with initials "J J S." $800-900; English 18ct hallmarked for Chester 1899. $1200-1500.

The two sterling roundlets at the *top* are Le Roy Haff's 1887 American patent. The worm is housed in a cylinder and slides out and is turned in a slot perpendicular to the case for use. The cylinder has a small projection that rotates into a slot in the blank portion of the case. $250-300.

The two corkscrews on the *left* and the one with chain are Le Roy Fairchild's 1888 American patent. Fairchild refined Haff's idea by adding a slot in the top of the cylinder so the shaft would be secured top *and* bottom. This eliminated any play in the worm when assembled for use. In some the case threads together and in others the Haff method is employed. All three have ornate sterling cases. $300-400.

The roundlets at *bottom right and above* the chain have sliding worms with friction fit cases. $150-200.

At *middle left and bottom center* are two small silver roundlets with the "standard" threaded case. $150-200.

A roundlet mixture.

Top five left to right: German version of Le Roy Haff patent with bejeweled crown end. $300-350; Figural roundlet advertising "Boyer Hammer, Consolidated Pneumatic Tool Cº Lᴰ." $250-300; Christopher Columbus figure marked COLUMBUS SCREW 1492 CHICAGO 1892 PAT APPLD FOR. $500-600; A double slotted shank on the worm is gripped by an inside collar marked G. F. HIPKINS & SON BIRMINGHAM PATENTED, PIC-NIC PATENT. A 1903 English patent by S. R. G. Vaughan. $200-250; Cheaply made case with one end sliding off to expose flimsy folding worm. $75-100;

Middle top pair left to right: 1855 patent of Lund and Hipkins marked LUND'S PATENT SPHERICAL JOINT LONDON. $125-150; Marked FARROW & JACKSON on the middle band. $100-125.

Middle bottom pair left to right: Marked VERINDER Sᵀ PAULS. $75-100; An English Registered designed by George Wright and Charles Bailey marked REGD JANY 16th, 1873. $60-80.

Bottom: A simple nickel plated roundlet and three examples of Thinet's 1873 French patent. $40-50.

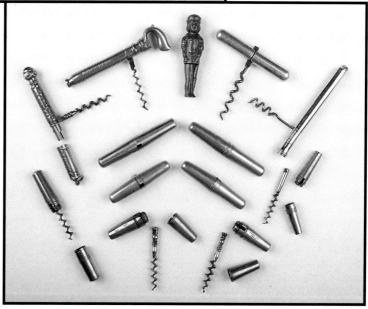

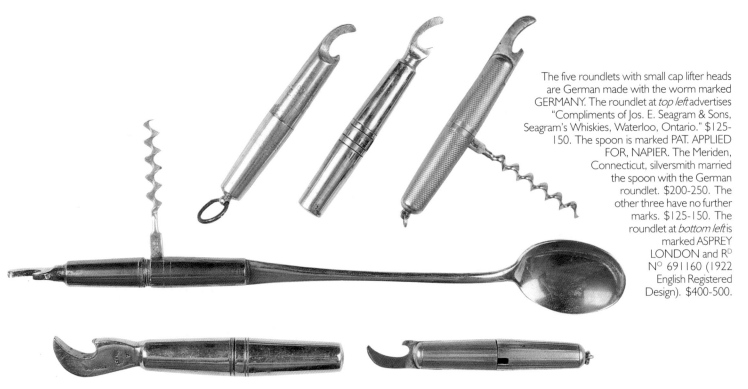

The five roundlets with small cap lifter heads are German made with the worm marked GERMANY. The roundlet at *top left* advertises "Compliments of Jos. E. Seagram & Sons, Seagram's Whiskies, Waterloo, Ontario." $125-150. The spoon is marked PAT. APPLIED FOR, NAPIER. The Meriden, Connecticut, silversmith married the spoon with the German roundlet. $200-250. The other three have no further marks. $125-150. The roundlet at *bottom left* is marked ASPREY LONDON and R^D N° 691160 (1922 English Registered Design). $400-500.

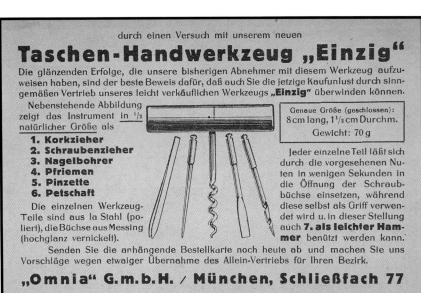

Roundlets with separate tools in the case come in a variety of sizes, shapes, and tool attachment methods. In most, the case threads together and the worm tools have a slot on the top, which is inserted into a matching slot in the case. At *top left* is one for the smoker with a lighter in the end exposed by removing only the small cap. $200-300. The roundlet with the saw has a ferrule on the end for locking the blade in place. It is marked D.R.G.M. $150-250. The kit *second down on the left* has slots in the center and at the end. The small threaded piece on the end secures the tool when placed in the slot. Marked UNIPA D R P & D R G M. $150-250. The kit at *middle left* has a bayonet fit case. $100-150. The kit in the *center* has two notches on the top of the worm. It slides through two holes in the case and is locked in place by the other side. Marked D. R. G. M. $200-250. The outside of the tool case at *lower left* has a file and rasp cut into the outside of the case. It is marked MONOPOL. $75-100. The *right lower* four are all German made containing multiple tools. $15-25. The disappointment in this batch is the roundlet with button hook. All tools thread into the end of the case but, alas, there was never a corkscrew in this one.

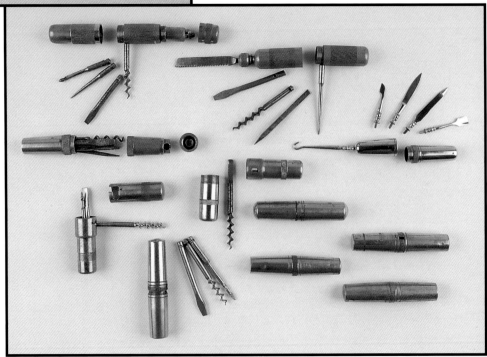

There are four small 2 1/4" celluloid roundlets at the *top*. $50-75.
The others *starting at right and working clockwise* are: Black painted wood with metal fittings. Middle band marked LB PARIS DEPOSE. $125-150; Lacquered natural wood. Brass fitting marked LB PARIS DEPOSE. $125-150; 3 1/4" black celluloid. $70-80; Marked GOODYEAR PATENT 1851. The patent was for an "Improvement in the manufacture of Indian-Rubber" and not the corkscrew. $175-200; Mottled green celluloid. $100-125; Butterscotch with silver caps impressed in ends. $200-250; Butterscotch with silver floral design wrapped at ends. $200-250. Plain butterscotch celluloid. $150-200; Boxwood case. $175-225; Walnut case with stanhope. In the stanhope it says "In Memory of Mount St. Bernard Abbey, Dublin." There are eight photo views. $300-400.

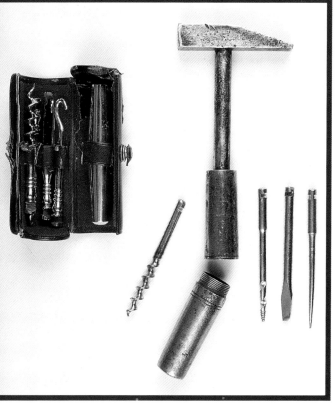

Above: Imitation horn with silver mounts marked only STERLING. The maker did not lay claim to his superior work of art. $500-600.

Right: The leather case contains a barrel marked BREVETE S.G.D.G., PARIS T. D and tools to fit in the handle barrel slot, including worm, button hook screwdriver, and awl. The loose tool in the barrel is Benoit Thinet's 1873 French patent. $300-400. The hammer threads into the tool case containing corkscrew, screwdriver, awl, and punch. $800-1000.

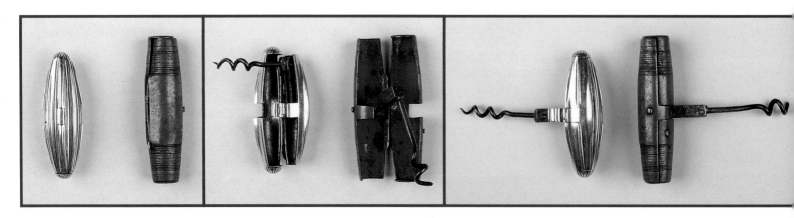

These two barrels are hinged and open like a clam to expose a double hinged worm. The upper part of the worm is held in place by a pin passing through one half of the clamshell. It is opened to unfold the worm and closed to use the barrel as the handle. On the *left* is an 18th century silver version. *$Rare.* On the *right* is a brass version. $800-1000.

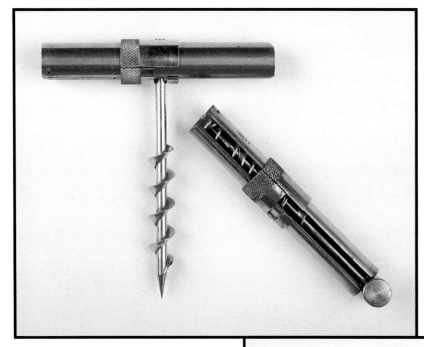

A rather ingenious Swiss made corkscrew. The worm threads into a spring in the handle for storage. The top of the worm has a cylinder that slides into a groove in the handle. The spring is pushed back with the cylinder until the shank is in the middle; the notched collar is then turned to engage it. $100-125.

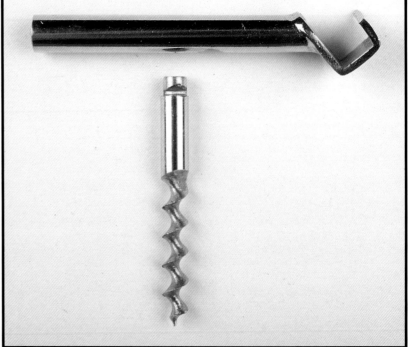

Two piece "roundlet" with cap lifter. The end of the handle is open for storage of the worm. The worm has a slot at the top that mates with a slot in the handle. $40-50.

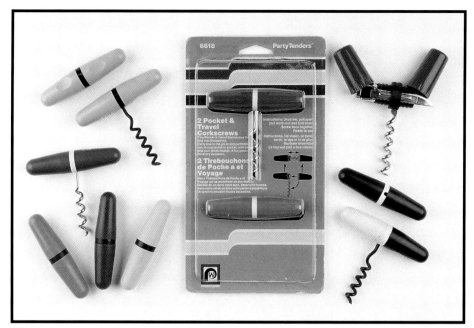

Adding a little color to a collection of corkscrew roundlets are the plastic versions. The gray, black (advertising Corona Data Systems), and black/white all have bayonet fit handles and are marked HONG KONG. $4-7. The green, orange, red, and yellow have threaded handles. They were made in Germany. $4-7.

The red roundlet at *top right* is marked MOD. DEP. MADE IN ITALY. It is made up of five pieces: Two handle ends that come off completely, a metal knife/cap lifter molded into the center hub, and the worm with ball. To use as a corkscrew, the end that exposes the knife is removed, the worm is pulled out of the hub and turned perpendicular to it, and the handle is screwed back on. It is a rather ingenious invention and done right - corkscrew and knife used by removing one end and opener by removing the other. You just don't know which end is which until you remove an end! $10-25.

The two blister packed roundlets are part of the Phoenixware Party Tender line, which included prong pullers, double levers, waiters' friends, and other bar accessories. The card says "2 Pocket & Travel Corkscrews that fold into themselves. Carry one in the glove compartment, one in your purse or pocket, suitcase and your picnic basket. A fun product for every occasion." $10-20.

In 1897, William A. Williamson was granted a U.S. patent for his invention of a corkscrew concealed inside a small bottle or bullet shape roundlet. The ends thread together and when unscrewed, a helix pivots at an angle to the base. The two pieces are then screwed back together to form the handle. Advertising plaques were applied to some bottles and bullets.

In 1900, Ralph W. Jorres was granted a U.S. Patent #657,421 for his version of this corkscrew. Jorres attached the helix to the top of the bottle instead of the base.

The 2 3/4" tall bottles at the *top* are marked on the bottom STERLING, PAT. JUN. 1.97 (Williamson Patent). $150-300. There are two oversized bullets in the *bottom row*. The *first* is silver ($175-225) and the *second* is nickel plated brass with most of the plating worn off ($60-80). Other bullets were produced with either copper or nickel plating on the end of the bullet with the rest left exposed brass. A 1906 catalog from Wood, Vallance & Co. of Ontario, Canada, describes the bullet as "Cartridge or Dewey slugs, full-plated body, nickeled tip and wire screw." $30-40. A few have been found with advertising plates ($50-100). A rare bullet is engraved "Compliments of Pittsburg Bridge Co., Pittsburg, PA" - Yes, that is the early spelling of Pittsburgh ($100-120).

Above: An army of mini bottle roundlets. Bottles were produced in nickel plated brass and were sold primarily with advertising plates attached ($50-150). Bottles have also been found with stanhopes in the top. The top is held up to the light and a small magnifier (stanhope) contains a photograph. Unfortunately, the photo was delicate and finding one complete is rare ($250-300).

Right: The two roundlets at *bottom left* are the Williamson 1897 patent. The case ends are marked PATENTED JUN 1 97, WILLIAMSON CO., NEWARK, N. J. The worm is stored in the end with the slot in it. $30-50.
The other four roundlets are the Jorres 1900 patent in which the worm stores in the opposite end of the case. These are marked PAT. SEP. 4 1900, WILLIAMSON CO., NEWARK, N.J. Note that there is a cylindrical shaped version. $30-50.
All of these roundlets are nickel plated brass. The nickel plating is worn off the example at *top right*. The roundlet on the *lower right* advertises "Compliments of Flood & Conklin Co., Varnish Makers, Newark, N.J."

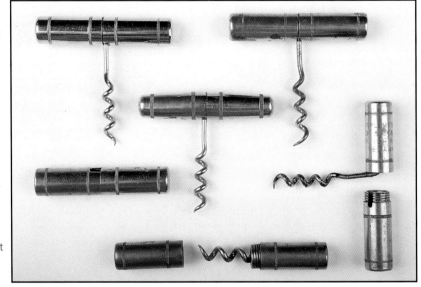

Bottle/Bullet Check List. Here is a list of bottles and bullets (*) cataloged to date. Variations in advertising copy, bottle bottom patent copy, and plate size/shape exist.

o Abbott & Co.	o Eliston Distilling Co.	o McCarthy's	o Rueckeisens Cafe*
o Anderson Distillery	o Frisch & Co.	o Melchers & Effler	o Schoenhofen Brewing
o Anheuser Busch (Closed Wing Eagle)	o Greil & Co.	o Metropolitan Dist.	o Seifert, San Diego
o Anheuser Busch (Spread Wing Eagle)	o Habich & Co.	o Miller, Newark	o Smith Drug Co.
o Anheuser Busch Malt	o Harp Lager	o Molter, Providence	o Stagg Co., Frankfort
o Barney 1899	o Hays, Sweet Briar	o Monahan's, Boston	o Standard Brewery
o Bauer & Co.	o Hicks	o Moorman & Co.	o Straus Gunshole
o Bohemian Brewing	o Home Brewing	o Napa Soda Springs	o Stroh Brewing
o Brotherhood Wine	o Indiana Brewing	o O'Keefe & Co.	o Sunstein
o Brown Forman	o Indianapolis Brewing	o Old "76" Distilling	o Terre Haute Brewing
o Brown Forman*	o Joliet Bottling	o Peebles	o Texas Brewing
o Buffalo Co-op	o Jones Ltd., St. John	o Pepper Distillery	o Turner Looker*
o Cape Brewery and Ice	o Kelly's Private Stock	o Person's Sons	o White, Hentz & Co.
o Cerveceria Cuauh.	o Kolb Bros.	o Pfeffer	o Whitney Glass Works
o Columbian Souvenir	o Lemp St. Louis*	o Pierce Co., Boston*	o Wilkinson
o Cunninghams & Co.	o Liquor Trades Gazette	o Pittsburg Bridge*	o Wilson & Co.
o Devil Caricature	o Live Oak Distl'y	o Produce Exchange	o Wilson's
o Dewar & Sons	o Mahan Supply	o Riebel Cafe	o Windisch-Muhl.
o Eastern Liquor Co.	o Martin & Co., S. F.	o Ross & Co.	o Wise & Co.
o Eldredge Brewing	o McAvoy Brewing	o Rowley's Cafe	o Wolcott & Co.

Sardine Keys

A combination tool with a corkscrew *and* a sardine tin key? One would think that would be an unlikely contrivance and, if found, a unique find. Although they are not an ordinary find, they are by no means unique. Here are several variations on the theme:

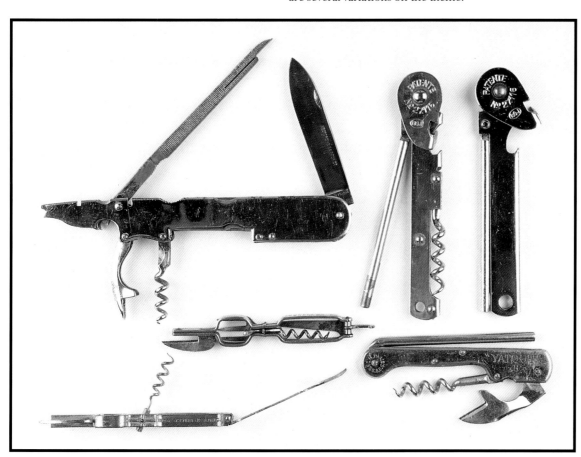

Top: The seven inch long tool at *upper left* is marked on the knife blade ABERCROMBIE & FITCH CO., MADE IN PARIS. It *is* something one would expect to find at the outfitters Abercrombie & Fitch store. It can cut, remove a cork, open a tin can, remove a bottle cap, crack a nut, cut wire, cut cigars, remove cigar box lid nails, punch leather, drive screws, file metal, and even open a sardine can. The user just inserts the sardine can lid tab in the slot at the end of the rasp and turns until the lid is curled to the opposite end of the can. As a corkscrew, it has a neckstand to perform like the normal waiter's friend. $250-350. Others have been found marked LE FAVORI NOGENT, BREVETE DEPOSE.

The two tools at *top right* are marked PATENTE NO. 27116 with a BOJ trademark (a trademark of B. Olanta y Juaristi in Spain). The one on the *right* is lacking the corkscrew but will open a tin can, remove a cap, and open a sardine can. $30-40. At *lower right* is another "waiter's friend" complete with sardine key. This is marked "YATOUT" JHP, C. M. PARIS, BᵀᴱS.G.D.G. "Yatout" is French for "All is there." The manufacturer was Perille of Paris and the inventor Charles Martinaud patented the tool in 1919. $400-500.

The two at *bottom left* have a folding fork added for eating the sardines once the lid is opened. The *upper* one has a swiveling cap lifter on the back end. Both have advertising: "Chr. Bjelland & Co., Stavanger, Norway, Bjelland's Canned Goods, King Oscar Sardines" and "B. M. Shipman Importer New York, Bon Accord Herring, Bon Accord Mackerel." This tool is illustrated in William Moore's 1918 American "Can Opener" patent. $150-200.

Bottom: The tool in the *middle* looks like a sardine key was substituted for a worm in a part of a corkscrew assembly but it was, indeed, sold as is. An advertisement for this Sardine Key states "Clear the lid from the key by screwing the wing-nut down." $25-35.

The combination tool at *left* is yet another "waiter's friend." It is marked with a letter "G" logo. $50-60. To the *right* of the chrome key is a tool marked DEPOSE FRANCE. $40-50. The *bottom* tool is marked MODELE DEPOSE. $50-60. At *right* is a tool marked SILA WESTERN GERMANY. The separate worm has a slot at the top that slides over the end of the key, which serves as the corkscrew handle. The "Sila Open-All" comes with instructions stating that it opens "Beer-Milk-Oil-Fruit Juice Cans, Caps of Jars, Screw-in Bottle Stoppers, Crown Corks, Fruit-Vegetable-Meat Cans, Sardine Cans with tongue, Fish and Seafood Cans, Vacuum sealed Cans for Coffee etc., and Bottles with Cork Stoppers." Can you live without it? $20-25.

Scissors, Grippers & Snippers

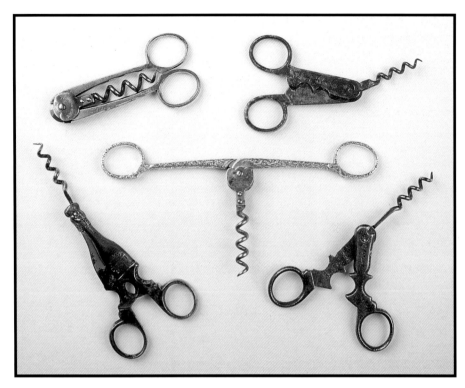

The rare scissors style corkscrew in the *center* has an ornate design on German silver handles. This is German corkscrew/ champagne wire cutter registration (D.R.G.M.) No.10985 of January 19, 1893, by Thill and Küll. The cutlery manufacturer was founded in Solingen, Germany, in 1885. When not in use, the handles are folded with finger holes together protecting the worm. $800-1000. The *upper left* corkscrew is a plain version marked G. M. S. NO. 10985 and GERMANY. $300-350.

The other three are French. These all cut cigar tips. The rarest is the figural champagne bottle at *lower left*. It is marked DEPOSE and engraved "Ch. Gardet Champagne Epernay." The handles are folded so that they form a handle with finger holes at opposite ends. The worm is then turned perpendicular to the handle for use. $800-1200. Another version of this patent is at *lower right*. It is marked DEPOSE with advertising "Gerard de Reconde." $500-600. The *upper right* model unfolds with the worm swiveling into position. It has an advertisement reading "Auguste Bar Avize." $300-400.

In 1950, Joseph Amigone of Buffalo, New York, patented his "Gripper Type Cork Extractor." Design patents were granted to him in 1951, 1954, and 1967. The 1967 patent was the first to include a corkscrew (*center of photo*). $80-100. The box containing the "AMI" reads "Ami open-all and champagne cork extractor. Perfect for cocktails and dining. Smart and handy for a host of uses." The tool is marked AMI OPEN-ALL, PAT. 163,785, BUFFALO 14, N.Y. (1954 patent). Although the AMI with corkscrew is marked the same, it is the 1967 patent. Later productions changed the number and date. $25-35. At *left* is a copy marked CMI JAPAN. $10-15.

The combination tool at *bottom* is marked HARRISON FISHER & CO. LTD., SHEFFIELD, ENGLAND. One scissors blade reads "Especially made for Carl Forslund in Sheffield, England." $40-60. The two cork grippers at *right* have advertising: "AY - France, Champagne Bollinger" and "Champagne Pommery & Greno, Reims." $20-30.

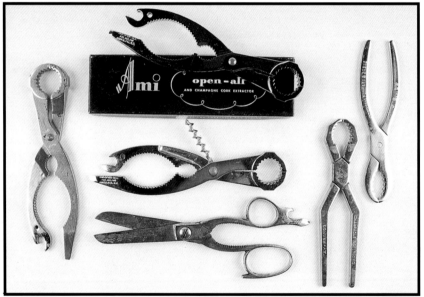

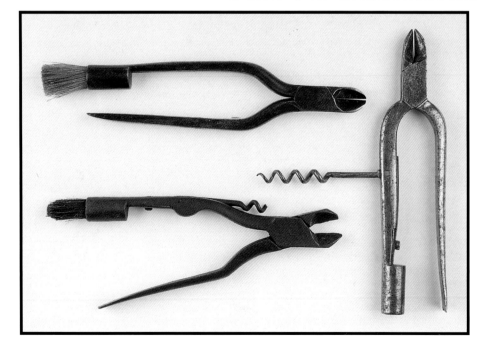

These three steel wire cutter tools are unmarked. At *top left* is the most common version having no corkscrew. $50-75. Like the one at *top*, the cutter at *right* has a serrated ice crusher on one handle. The other handle is missing the brush. A backspring in the handle keeps the worm in place when folded out for use. $250-350. The *bottom* cutter is an earlier example without the ice crusher. Several turns of the worm are missing. $200-300.

138

Sheath

Throughout this book there are many corkscrews with sheaths. They all fit better in their assigned categories with their related corkscrews. Examples shown here are more appropriately placed in the general "Sheath" category.

Above: These Figural sheath cap lifter/corkscrew combinations were produced in the 1920s and 1930s. Additional examples are shown in the "Horses," "Fish," "Anchors," and "A Few More Figurals" (pelican and alligator) categories.
Boots in background: Marked STERLING PAT. APD. FOR with trademark of R. Blackinton & Co., of Attleboro, Massachusetts. Engraved E. C. H. JR., FEB. 9TH 1928. $150-200; Cast iron and painted red. $30-40; Cast brass. $40-50.
Boots in foreground: Small cast boot. Height of boot is 2" whereas other boots are 2 1/2." $50-60; Another marked STERLING PAT. APD. FOR with trademark of R. Blackinton & Co., of Attleboro, Massachusetts, but this one has a left-hand worm. $150-200.
Right figures in background: 2 3/4" owl silver plated and marked on bottom J. B. 3572. $60-75; Pitcher marked J. B. 310 on bottom. $75-100; 2 1/4" brass jug. $50-60; 2 1/2" silver jug with Blackinton marks says "Little Brown Jug." $125-150.
In the foreground: A barrel tap. $60-75.

At first glance these two corkscrews appear to fit the "Picnic" category. However, the sheath does not fit snugly into the top hole to serve as a handle. The corkscrew on the *left* has a brass handle with two serpents. The brass sheath threads onto the handle. $800-1000; On the *right* is a steel faceted handle with decorative shank and threaded steel sheath. $125-175.

English 19th century corkscrew with top threaded sheath. The one finger pull is also a split ring key chain with swivel. $150-200.

Magnifying glass with corkscrew in the end of the handle. Top of corkscrew has United States Army insignia. $60-80.

A 1922 Norwegian patent by Paul Skarsten. The ring in the middle of the sheath fits the inside of the top of the cap lifter to serve as the handle. The handle is marked PAT. 38579. Handles can be found in several interesting designs. The fairly plain example has the patent number marked whereas the more decorative versions usually have only silver marks. $100-150.

Two well made corkscrews with cherry and dark walnut stain. Shanks on both penetrate the handle and are secured by a brass fastener flush with the top of the handle. Shanks and the knife on the dark walnut version are marked F. BOYD S. F. The worm is protected by a friction fit sheath. $40-60.

Silver

Silver corkscrews have been produced for a couple of hundred years. They are sought after not only by the corkscrew collector but by those decorators who want an accent for the dining room table or the owner of the wine cellar who wants a prize for his cellar. Prices on silver and other precious metal corkscrews continue to escalate as the competition for them grows.

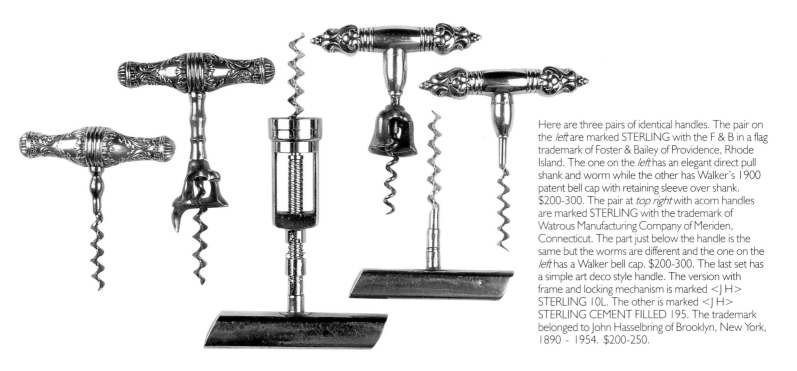

Here are three pairs of identical handles. The pair on the *left* are marked STERLING with the F & B in a flag trademark of Foster & Bailey of Providence, Rhode Island. The one on the *left* has an elegant direct pull shank and worm while the other has Walker's 1900 patent bell cap with retaining sleeve over shank. $200-300. The pair at *top right* with acorn handles are marked STERLING with the trademark of Watrous Manufacturing Company of Meriden, Connecticut. The part just below the handle is the same but the worms are different and the one on the *left* has a Walker bell cap. $200-300. The last set has a simple art deco style handle. The version with frame and locking mechanism is marked <J H> STERLING 10L. The other is marked <J H> STERLING CEMENT FILLED 195. The trademark belonged to John Hasselbring of Brooklyn, New York, 1890 - 1954. $200-250.

The two corkscrews at *top right* in the above photo have the trademark of Watrous Manufacturing of Meriden, Connecticut. Another example of the corkscrew with bell is in this silver bar set in leather presentation case. This one, however, has the mark of Simpson, Hall & Miller of neighboring Wallingford. Watrous and Simpson were two of several companies to become part of International Silver in 1898. International continued to use the marks of these firms, apparently indiscriminately. The International Silver trademark was introduced in 1928. $700-1000 per set.

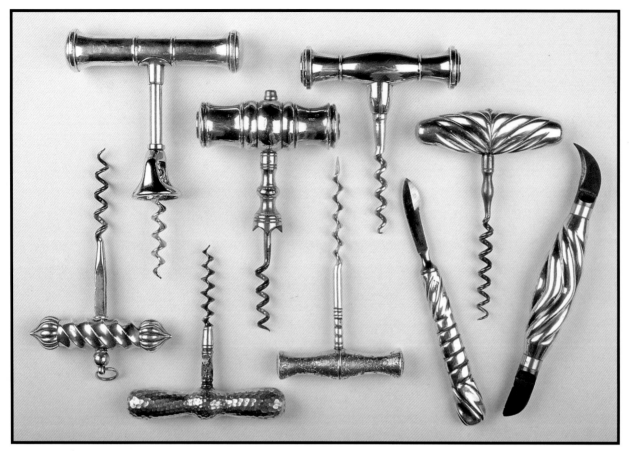

Top row left to right: Williamson's 1897 patented bell cap with handle by John Hasselbring. $500-600: Marked E S B with a 1900 Birmingham, England, hallmark. There are cork grips at the bottom of the shank and the worm is fluted. $800-1000; Marked BIRKS STERLING on one of the end rings. $500-600; Art Nouveau style three piece set by Gorham of Providence, Rhode Island. The Gorham trademark is on the champagne knife. The implement on the *left* has an ink remover blade. $700-800. *Bottom row left to right:* An English silver corkscrew with onion fluted caps, square shank, and fluted worm. 1890 Birmingham hallmark. $500-600; Unmarked Peanut shaped handle ends. $400-500; Nicely engraved nickel silver handle with grapes, grapevines, and leaves. $500-600.

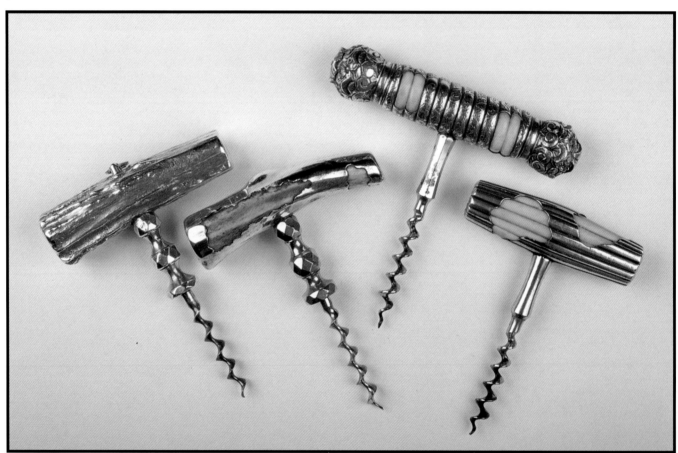

In 1886, Edward Thiéry and Charles Croselmire were granted an American patent for their "Article of jewelry and method of ornamenting the same." Designs were cut into the silver after it was electroplated to an object. The corkscrew on the *left* appears to have had the silver applied but no cuts done and there are no marks. $500-600. The *second* has the silver cut away revealing sections of the bone handle. The initials J. B. L. are engraved ornately on the end. It has the same diamond cut design shank as the first. $600-800.

The *third* corkscrew is a magnificently decorated example of this art. The silver has been applied to an ivory handle with ornate floral design caps added to the end. There is fine detailing on all sections wrapping the handle and the silver is embossed with "Compliments Rochester Brewery" and a hand holding a glass of beer. It is from Rochester Brewery in Kansas City, Missouri. It is marked STERLING 5827 without a maker's mark. c.1900. $1000-1500. The corkscrew on the *right* has the silver cut away and, again, no maker's mark. $600-800. It is surprising that the makers of these four corkscrews did not claim their fine work by adding their mark.

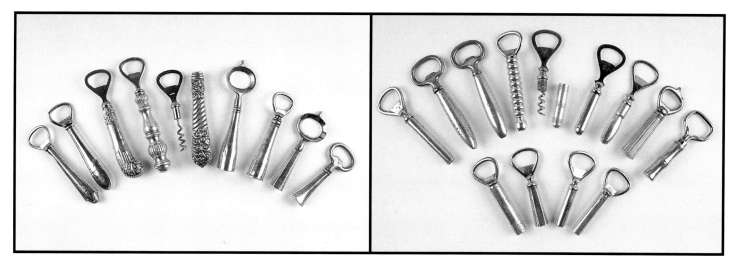

One frequently sees cap lifters with ornate silver handles in antique shows and shops. Picking them up and pulling or twisting the cap lifter can have its rewards. There may be a corkscrew hiding in that silver handle. All of these pieces have corkscrews. Some have friction fit sheaths and others threaded. The sheaths were frequently engraved with initials as gifts.

In 1906, John Hasselbring was granted a design patent for a "Bottle Opener," which had a prong for lifting a bottle stopper ring. The *sixth and eighth* corkscrews in the *left photo* have the patent date on the opener base. In the *right photo*, the cap lifter to the *right of top center* is marked PAT'D FEB. 6. 94, which was William Painter's patent for the cap lifter. Painter had patented the bottle cap in 1892 while working for Crown

Cork and Seal Company in Baltimore, Maryland. The corkscrew on the *right top* is marked PEWTER on the sheath.

Manufacturers' marks that appear on the corkscrews in these photos are James E. Blake of Attleboro, Massachusetts; Hallmark Silversmiths and Wilcox and Wagoner of New York City; John Hasselbring of Brooklyn, New York; R. Blackinton & Co. and William Webster Company of North Attleboro, Massachusetts; Meriden Silver Plate Co. and Watrous Manufacturing Company of Meriden, Connecticut; and William B. Kerr & Co. of Newark, New Jersey.

Various cap lifter/corkscrews: $75-125.

A group of late 18th century/ early 19th century English and Dutch pocket corkscrews with silver fittings and sheaths. Various handles of ivory, silver, and mother-of pearl. $750-1500.

Top row left to right: Early 19th century Dutch silver. Figure of man on horse. Unengraved seal at bottom of sheath. $1500-2500; Early 19th century Dutch lion handle. $1500-2000; Dutch silver figural. Man with two horses. Bottom of sheath has initials "M. K. O." seal. $1800-2200. *Bottom row:* Two early 19th century silver folding bows with protective sheath for the worm. $2000-3000.

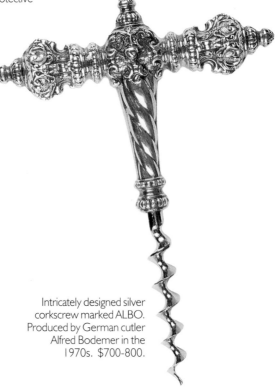

Intricately designed silver corkscrew marked ALBO. Produced by German cutler Alfred Bodemer in the 1970s. $700-800.

Wood handle with silver design tacked on by Gorham. "J. P. Wiser" engraved on one end cap, Gorham trademark on the other. $600-700.

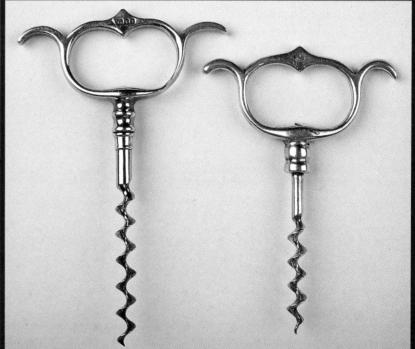

Above: Two silver four finger pulls. *Left* has a London, England, 1981 hallmark. $100-150. The pull on the *right* is marked 925 with an unreadable mark. $75-100.

Left: Current production four finger silver pull in velvet lined case.

Smokers' Tools

Here is yet another category where the corkscrew collector will find stiff competition for his heart's desire. The interest in smoking collectibles (tobacciana) has been fueled by a number of books on the subject. Books have been published on cigar cutters, lighters, chewing tobacco tin tags, camel cigarettes, and smoking collectibles in general. The interests run from worn out old cigarette packs to cigar store Indians. The smoking collector's search includes ashtrays, cigar box openers and cutters, lighters, matchsafes, pipe prickers and tampers, snuff boxes, and tobacco advertising. All of these have been found in combination with a corkscrew. Although the majority are knives, I have opted to include all in the eclectic corkscrews part of this book rather than the knife part.

The Batchelor [*sic*] is holding a *Spirit of the Times* newspaper headlined "War - 10,000 Recruits for Mexico." The American print refers to the 1898 Spanish-American war. There is a corkscrew on the table next to the smoker.

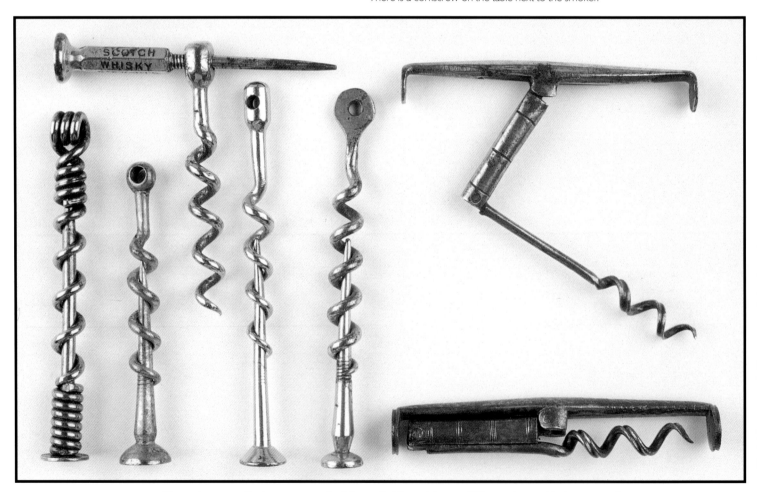

The corkscrews with pipe tamper on the *left* are called "peg and worm." The peg is stored in the center of the worm and removed and inserted into a hole at the top of the worm for use. Two of the five have left-hand worms. The peg of the corkscrew on the *top left* advertises "Dundee Cream of the Barley Scotch Whisky" on the hexagonal shank. The bottom of the tamper is marked STEWART'S JOKE. $100-200. The two corkscrews on the *right* are late 18th/early 19th century steel double end pipe tampers with double-hinged worms. $300-500.

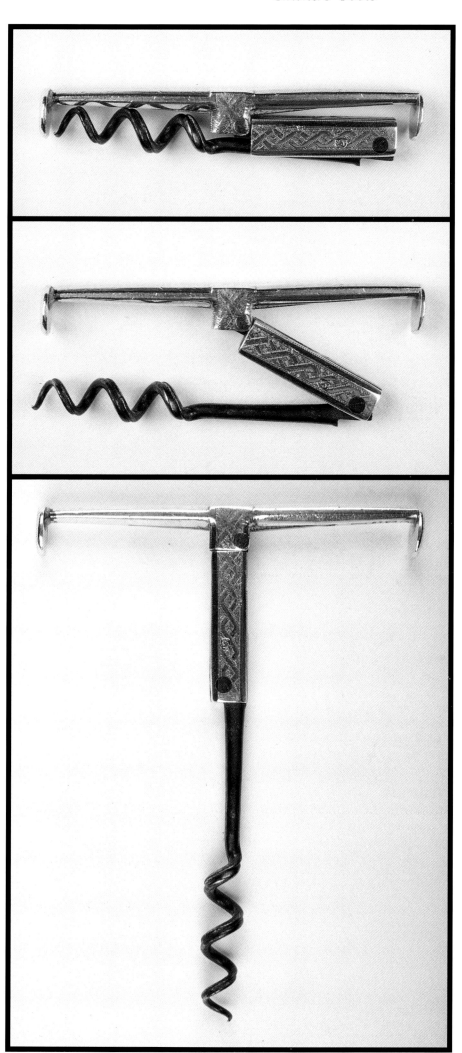

Sterling silver double-hinged folding pocket corkscrew/pipe tamper made by William Tweede in London in 1808. The hallmark is on the underside of the handle. *$Rare.*

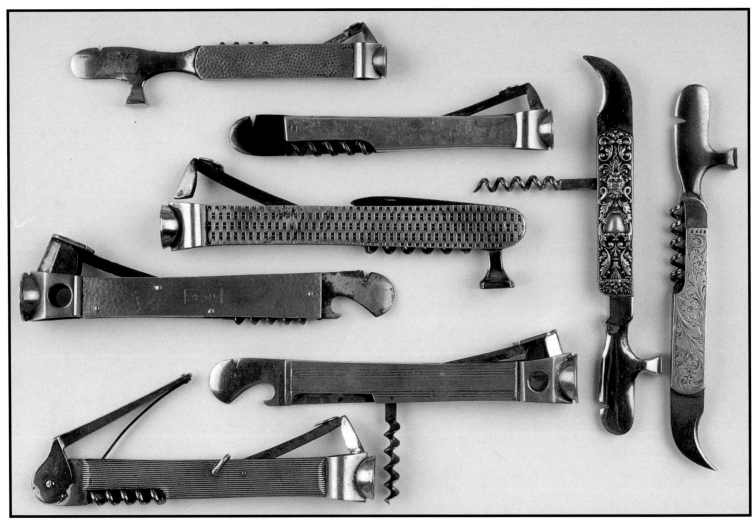

Finding cigar clipper combination tools at Antique shows is not a difficult task. The collector will see a wide variety of handles, including very plain, monogrammed, intricately decorated, and figural. The cigar clippers are found in combination with knives, pipe tampers, and cigar box openers. For the corkscrew collector, finding one with a corkscrew such as those on the *left* is a difficult assignment. Lengths of these range from 5 1/2" to 6 1/2".
Left side from top to bottom: Handles marked SILVER. Cutter marked with S S S logo. $125-150; Plain silver handles marked 900. $100-125; The only example in this group with a knife blade. Trademark of Müller & Schmidt, Solingen, Germany. $250-300; Initials "A. S. H." on handles marked SILVER. $125-150; Nickel silver Art Deco handles by Henckels, Germany. $150-200; Another by Müller & Schmidt with a wire cutter locked by a bail in the center. $250-300.
Right: Two cigar box openers with pipe tamper, corkscrew, and foil cutter. Both have silver handles with the trademark of William Kerr of Newark, New Jersey. $200-300.

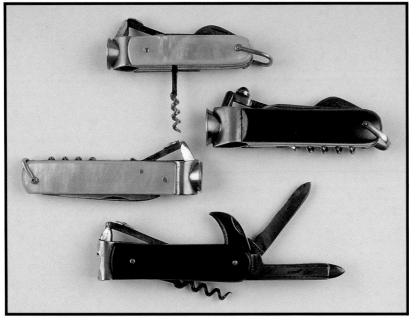

Smaller cigar clippers ranging in size from 2 3/4" to 3 1/4".
From top to bottom: Mother-of-pearl handles with cigar clipper, corkscrew, foil cutter, pen blade, and file blade marked GERMANY. $200-250; Bakelite handles with same tools as first. Gold plated clipper. $150-200: Mother-of-pearl with single knife blade. $150-200; Horn handles with five tools marked H. SCHULDER, SOLINGEN. $150-200.

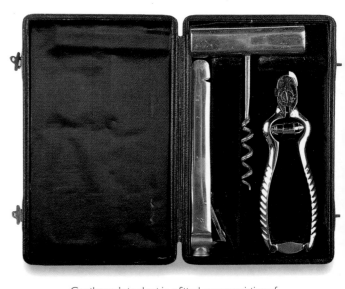

Gentleman's tool set in a fitted case consisting of combination cigar box opener and cigar clipper, corkscrew, and wire nippers. $150-200.

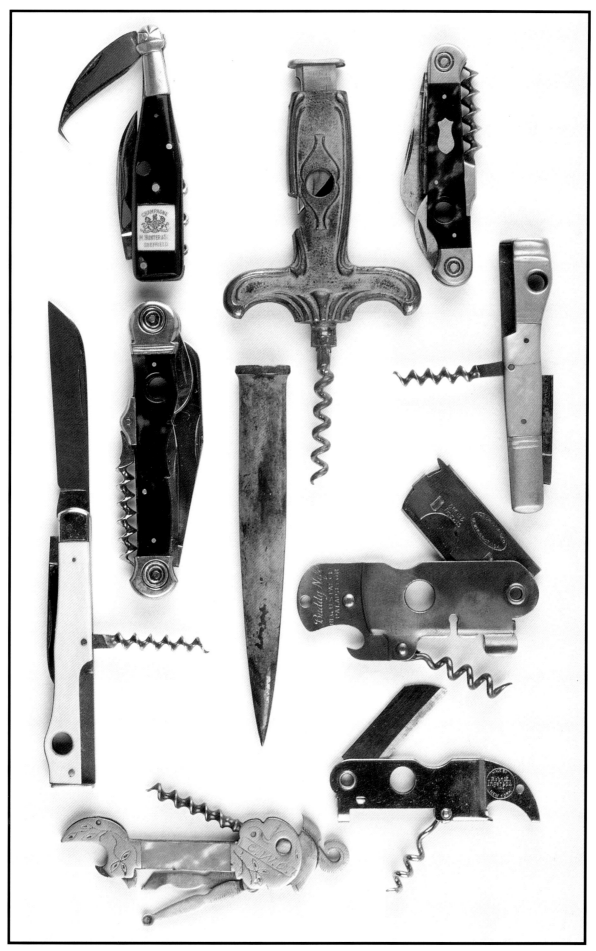

Left side from top to bottom: Champagne bottle shape cigar cutter and piercer. Bottle label reads "Champagne, M. Hunter & Son, Sheffield." A fine fluted wire worm folds out from the back. $500-600; Top quality 4" knife with tortoise shell handles. Spring activated master blade to cut cigar tip, foil cutter, pen blade, and corkscrew. Marked J. A. HENCKELS. $250-300; Two bladed ivory handle knife, cigar cutter, and corkscrew marked F. HERDER A S<u>N</u> SOLINGEN. c.1930. $250-300; Mother-of-pearl handles on combination tool engraved "C. W. C." $250-300.
Middle: A bayonet fit sword/letter opener with cigar cutter. Marked ROSTFREI D. B. P. 887711.

Right side from top to bottom: Tortoise shell handles with two blades marked KRUSIUS BROTHERS, GERMANY. $125-150; Mother-of-pearl handles marked REMINGTON U M C. $125-150; A cigar cutter that employs a disposable razor blade to tip the cigar. Marked THE GREIST MFG. CO., NEW HAVEN, CONN., BUDDY-NIFE, REG. U. S. PAT. OFF. PAT. APL'D FOR. A 1929 American patent by Carl Horix. $75-100; Another using a permanently mounted razor blade is marked PAL, FOUR IN ONE MADE IN U. S. A., MADE BY ROBT H INGERSOLL INC., NEW YORK. $75-100.

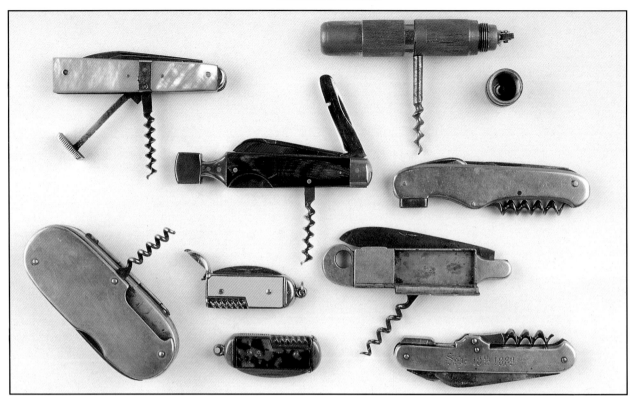

Left side from top to bottom: Two bladed knife with mother-of-pearl handles marked C. W. ENGELS, SOLINGEN, GR. The worm is buried between the handles with no easily apparent means of raising it into position. Fiddling around with it reveals that the monogrammed pipe tamper end swivels on the same pin as the worm and its arm is under the worm. Lifting the tamper puts the worm in position. $800-1000; Unusual pipe tamper with horn handle and containing a single knife blade, corkscrew, and a cigar box opener blade. Marked GEBR. DITTMAR, HEILBRONN (Germany - Dittmar Brothers). $300-400; Swedish made snuff box with single blade knife and corkscrew. Marked C. A. ERIKSSON & CO., ESKILSTUNA. c.1907. $400-600; Two match safes with match striker. The worm and the knife are not real. $200-250.

Right side from top to bottom: A German roundlet tool case containing the usual screwdriver, awl, punch, and corkscrew. The end unscrews to reveal a lighter. $200-250; A steel handle knife with match striker marked GRAEF & SCHMIDT. Contains foil cutter, corkscrew, master blade, pen blade, and cigar box opener blade. $250-300; A rare knife with single blade that cuts the cigar tip, a hinged match holder, a hinged ashtray, a match striker, a pipe pricker that pulls out (opposite side - not shown), and a fluted worm. Marked F. WEST, NO. 1, ST. JAMES (London). *$Rare*; Three blade corkscrew knife with match striker. Marked CLINTON CUTLERY CO. Engraved "Charles C. Chase, Sept. 18, 1889." $300-350.

Outside of corkscrew circles, John Watts is best known for his patent for a safety razor issued ten years before Gillette's. In corkscrew circles, he is best known for his 1892 and 1901 British patents. In his 1892 patent, a sliding pin secures a blade that is the pivoting arm of a wire cutter. The arm ends in a button hook in the 1901 patent. Watt's 1892 English patent drawing does not show a corkscrew, but his American 1897 patent does. Several of Watts' knives are marked PLA TIN OID. His 1895 catalog refers to the knives as having "Platinoid Covers." Here are seven examples of Watts' patent.

Left side from top to bottom: Marked MESSER KÖNIG. $75-100; Marked BRIT. PAT. NO. 416767, WATT'S PATENT, MADE IN SHEFFIELD ENGLAND. $50-70; Marked WATT'S PATENT plus descriptive and locale marks. $75-100; 1901 patent with button hook cutting arm marked WATTS'S PATENT (note preceding have "T'S" and TS'S is on this). $70-90.

Right side from top to bottom: Marked WATT'S PATENT. 3" ruler on back handle. The cutting arm is the 1892 patent style and has the additional feature of a shell extractor. The button hook is a separate blade. $100-120; Marked WATT'S PATENT with advertising for "Dry Monopole, Heidsieck & Co." This is the most common example of Watts' patent. $30-50; Marked WATT'S PATENT. $75-100.

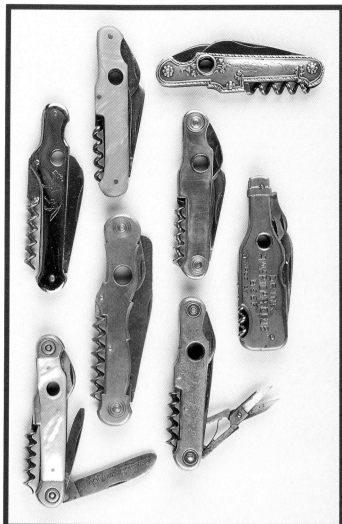

Left: An assortment of knives with spring loaded master blade cutting cigar tip in hole. The knife at *top right* has ornate sterling engraved handles. $150-200. The knife at *lower left* with mother-of-pearl handles is marked VOM CLEFF & CO., GERMANY, LION CUTLERY, WARRANTED. This knife is quite unusual in that the inconspicuous advertising "Genesee Brewing Co." is on the knife blade instead of the handle. $200-250.
Top diagonal row left to right: Marked UNION CUT. CO., OLEAN, N.Y. $100-120; Marked PAULS BRO'S CUTLERY, a New York importing firm (1887-1905). $100-125; Bottle shape marked GRIFFON CUTLERY WORKS GERMANY with advertising "Drink American Club Beer, made by Lembeck & Betz, Eagle Brewing Co., Jersey City, N. J." $150-200.
Second diagonal row left to right: Marked H. KESCHNER, SOLINGEN, GERMANY with advertising "Wolf's Monogram Whiskey, Kansas City, Mo." $100-125; Marked HENOK. $125-150; A cigar cutter knife with master blade, pen blade, foil cutter, scissors, and corkscrew marked E. HERDER A. S^{N}, SOLINGEN, GERMANY, CONSTANT. Handles are decorated with grapes and grapevines. $150-175.

Right: Here are several different cigar cutter patterns.
Left side top to bottom: Two blades and corkscrew marked DOLPHIN CUT. CO., NEW YORK, GERMANY. Stamped "John Jahr, Albert Lea, Minn." $100-120; Three blades and a corkscrew stamped "Manuf. by Joseph J. Walton, N.Y." $150-170; Three blade advertising "Indianapolis Brew'g Co." $150-200; Cheap tin handles with glass cutter. Marked CELEBRATED CUTLERY CO., GERMANY. $10-20.
Right side top to bottom: Top quality three blade advertising "Greenlees Brothers Rare Old Whiskies." Well marked J. NOVILL & SONS, SHEFFIELD. $150-200; An unusual pattern with a cigar box opener on the nose. Marked WILLIAM RODGERS, SHEFFIELD and REG^{D} 750382 (1929). $200-250; Single blade advertising "Hauck's Red Monogram Beer." Marked H. KESCHNER, GERMANY. $100-125; Another cheap knife with tin handles and glass cutter. Marked BERK CUTLERY C^{O}., NEW YORK, MADE IN GERMANY. $10-20.

A box of safety matches depicting a most unusual corkscrew, which any collector would cherish.

Springs

By incorporating a spring in a corkscrew design, the handle is given more pulling power. After the worm is turned into the cork far enough for the frame to come in contact with the bottle neck, the spring begins to exert force against the handle as the user continues to turn it. This action then causes the cork to be lifted from the bottle.

In this uncommon design the spring is inside the upper part of the frame. $150-250.

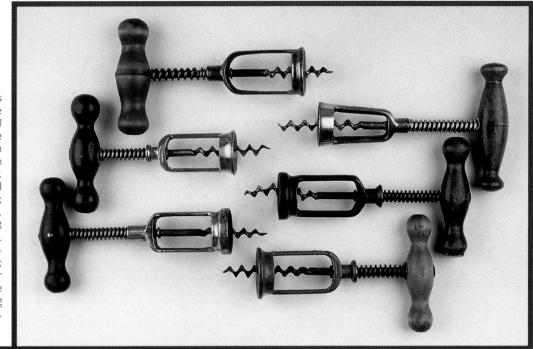

More commonly the spring is placed between a frame and the handle. Here are several variations of the "Hercules" type corkscrew. Derived from an 1883 German patent by Dunisch and Schöler.
Left side top to bottom: Thin wall unmarked frame. $15-25; Marked HERCULES at top frame. $20-30; Marked GERMANY at top of frame. $15-25.
Right side top to bottom: Hard-to-find tapered frame. $40-60; Unmarked with a handmade Star of David impressed on the handle end. $20-40; Rough casting marked HERCULES. $15-25.

More examples with spring between frame and handle. *Left to right:* All steel unmarked. $60-100; Cast frame. $10-15; A rare marked (D.R.P. 27175) version of Dunisch & Schöler's 1883 patent. A brass plate on the ribbed handle reads "The Dorking District Supply Stores." Another example reads "Weymouth Xmas 1889, Presented by C. K. Cottmin with compliments." $100-150; In very small print on either side of the frame it says "The Christian Brothers" with the mark GERMANY. $40-60; Conical spring (as pictured in the Dunisch & Schöler patent). $50-75; Triangular bell. $30-50.

On the *left* is a Walker handle with "Pabst Milwaukee" advertising. Instead of the usual cotter pin above the bell, a spring assists the self-pulling bell in removing the cork. $50-60. Another Walker handle is on the *right*. This one has "Home Brewing Co." advertising. $100-150.

The *first and third* spring barrels have a cotter pin in the shank above the worm. When the cork is extracted in this impractical design, there is no way to move the spring barrel out of the way to remove the cork from the worm. $80-100. The *second* has a pin on the shaft, which stops the spring when in use. To remove the cork, the spring is rotated upward around the pin. A 1914 German patent by Gotlieb Gießler. $100-125. The *fourth* spring barrel is Richard Recknagel's 1899 German patent. The mechanism above the spring has a slot with a diagonal guide and lock that slides up and down over a pin through the shank. The mechanism is marked D.R.G.M. 109374. $250-300. The spring barrel on the *right* has a swiveling clip that swings out of the way to raise the spring after the cork is extracted. $125-150.

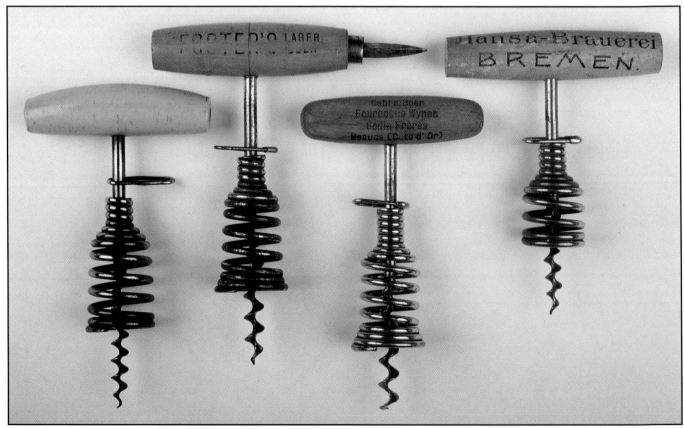

German spring barrels with "paper clip" stop, an 1895 patent by W. Sommers. The oval paper clip has a pin in the center that is inserted in a hole in the shank to stop the spring when removing the cork from the bottle. To remove the cork from the worm, pull the pin out, raise the clip and spring barrel, and unscrew the cork. Various handle types are shown. $90-120. The corkscrew with spike advertises "Foster's Lager Beer" and across the top is stamped CORKSEREW MADE IN GERMANY. Yes, corkscrew is spelled corkserew!

Stoppers & Toppers

We often see wood carvings resting atop a cork that is used to reseal a bottle. There are also some very delicate porcelain stoppers and a number of silver, gold, and pewter. Stoppers and toppers with corkscrews are much more difficult to find, and it never hurts to give an unusual stopper a twist to see if there is a worm in the cork.

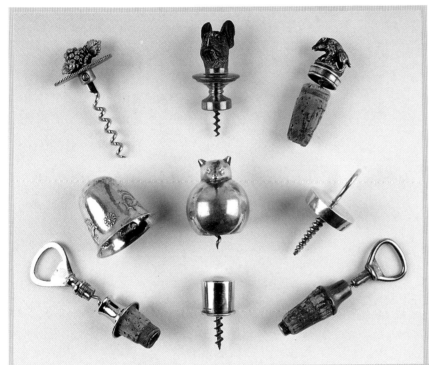

Top row left to right: A bunch of pewter grapes with grape leaf on a platform that simply rests on top of the bottle. $60-70; Dog head resting on brass base. $75-85; Silver plate wild boar with Christofle trademark. $300-400.

Second row left to right: Bell shape with worm inside. When the cork is removed, it would be replaced with this bell on top. It is marked only with the trademark of La Pierre Mfg. Co. of New York and New Jersey. $100-150; Fox head marked W 10 E. $150-200; Single ring puller/stopper with maker's mark IW and Sheffield hallmark. $125-150.

Third row left to right: Cap lifter/corkscrew threads into the fixture atop the cork. English patents issued in 1913 to Robert Edwards and Charles Barret show similar combinations. $80-100; Hat style topper marked A. KRUPP BERNDORF with a standing bear trademark. Austria c.1910. $80-100; Friction fit cap lifter/corkscrew. $80-100.

Clockwise from left: Unmarked Silver corkscrew/bottle stopper. $75-100; Hallmarked silver, 1" diameter. $125-150; Marked BERNDORF. Austria c.1910. $125-150; Gorham trademark. Pictured in a 1920 Gorham catalog as a sterling silver cheese knob. It was used to hold a ball of cheese securely while cutting. $80-100.

Above: In front of the bottle on the *right* is a knife with corkscrew, cap lifter, and stopper remover. The blade is marked WILHELM MEYER SOLINGEN. The obverse of the handle is marked GEROLSTEINER SPRUDEL and the reverse NUR ECHT MIT DEM STERN, D.R.G.M. It is a German patent for the rectangular cutout used as the stopper remover. The bottle shown has an internal thread at the top that matches the thread on the stopper. The stopper is marked H. G. $125-150.

The tool in front of the other bottle is a cheap imitation of the Meyer tool. This one has a corkscrew, cap lifter, stopper remover, and a tin can opener. It is marked CREDO. $20-30.

The black tool on the *left* is a can opener/cap lifter marked CREDO. There is no corkscrew. On the *right* is a tool marked SESAM with can opener/cap lifter/stopper remover and no corkscrew.

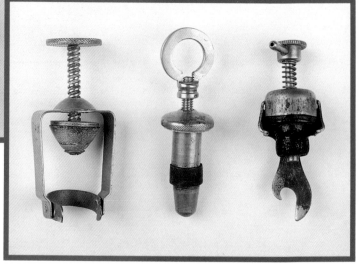

Above: None of these are corkscrews but two show a corkscrew in use. The porcelain baby is pulling a cork from a bottle. $75-100. The hobo is flat painted wood and he is also pulling a cork from a bottle. $30-40.

Right: Metal bottle stoppers with rubber seals. *Left to right:* Spring steel collar snaps on bottle neck. Rotate top button to screw stopper in tight. $8-12; Marked MADE IN ENGLAND. $5-10; Button marked SYFO. Push button down to pour off liquids through spout. $10-15.

Tableware

H ere's what every dining table needs - a corkscrew to match the knives, forks, and spoons!

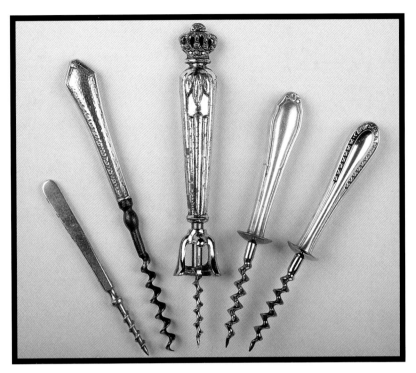

Left to right: Unmarked machined steel. This is not for removing a cork. It is used with a partner to hold a corn cob. $15-20; Handle marked STERLING HANDLE with the trademark of Webster Company of North Attleboro, Massachusetts. $40-50; An impractical corkscrew with self-puller bell cast with cap lifter. The handle is a poorly plated casting. The shank is marked JAPAN and it is possibly a fake. $20-25; The shanks of the last two are marked INOX (stainless) and the handles EBERLE. $40-50.

The table also needs some accessories:

A cheese taster with folding corkscrew. $200-300.

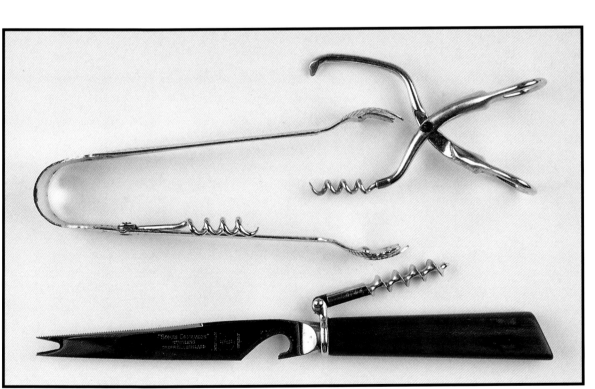

Ice tongs with a corkscrew and cap lifter. $50-75.
And another set of tongs. The "tongs" are also cap lifters. The tong handles are a corkscrew and a foil cutter. They are marked PAT. PEND. D. ARNOF, NYC. This is David Arnof's 1933 American patent simply called "Tongs." $200-250. At first glance, the knife on the *bottom* looks like modern Asian barware. Closer examination shows that it is a piece of fine Sheffield cutlery. The blade is marked "SOIRE COMPANION" STAINLESS, SHEFFIELD, ENGLAND, MONOGRAM CUTLERY. Normally it would be used at the bar, but because it looks so good, we'll keep it by the dining table. $20-25.

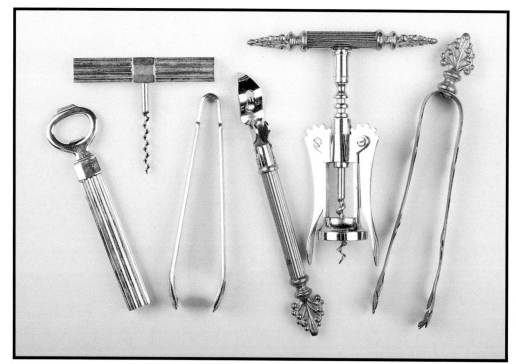

Left: Silver plated barset, including corkscrew, cap lifter, and ice tongs. $30-40.
Right: Brass and chrome barset consisting of corkscrew, cap lifter, and ice tongs with ornate handles. $15-25.

A dozen cocktail spoons with corkscrews. They have been found with coast to coast advertising. Advertisers include hotels, breweries, distilleries, retail stores, special events, museums, laundries, and funeral homes. Values are apt to be driven up by collectors of advertising from particular businesses or of local interest material.

Left to right: A pair of 7" spoons with under the lip cap lifter and riveted folding worm. "Drink Walter's Beer, Midwest Distributing Co., Salt Lake City, Utah" and "William H. Avery Musical Instruments, 18 Pleasant St., Concord, N. H." Marked B & B ST. PAUL DES PAT PDG. $10-15.

A 7 3/4" pair of spoons with the same manufacturer's marks. William Avery used this size for advertising as well as the above 7" spoon. The other says "Yale 1929, Triennial Reunion, New Haven, June 18-22, 1932." $15-30.

Unmarked 7 3/4" pair of spoons with serrated ice-chopping spoon. No advertising. $15-20.

An 8" pair with over-the-top style cap lifter and folding corkscrew. "The Penn Harris Hotel, Harrisburg, Pennsylvania" and "Barbara Fritchie House & Museum, Frederick, Md." Marked PAT APL'D FOR. Normally one would expect to fold the worm out perpendicularly to use the spoon as a corkscrew handle. However, when the worm is swiveled 180 degrees, the upper wire meets with a notch in the bottle opener end. It appears that the maker intended the cork to be pulled with the spoon in the vertical upside down position. $10-20.

A pair like the above but with slotted spoon. "John Mielcarek Wines and Liquors, 1889 Clinton St., TR-9828" and "Giroux Grenadine best mixer since 1871." $20-30.

8" spoon with round bowl. "Two Rivers Beverage Co., Golden Drops, Bobbie Ale." Marked B & B ST. PAUL DES PAT PDG. $25-30.

10" spoon with 2" diameter bowl. No marks. No advertising.

Williamson's "Pal" cap lifter/corkscrew is housed in the sheath. $30-40.

Thomason

One of the most important inventions of the 19th century was that of Sir Edward Thomason. His design was granted English patent number 2617 on May 7, 1802. He produced his corkscrews in Birmingham and was one of the first major producers of corkscrews. His mechanism was produced by several manufacturers well into the 20th century. Thomason's motto on his corkscrew was "Ne plus ultra," meaning "no more beyond." He had the ultimate corkscrew invention!

Thomason's invention allowed the user to remove a cork in one continuous motion. The five basic working components of the design are the handle, the worm right-hand thread inner shaft, the worm, the barrel or frame, and hollow shaft. The hollow shaft has an internal thread to mate with the worm shaft and an outer left-hand thread.

To remove the cork:
1. With hollow shaft fully inside barrel, extend handle upward by turning the handle counter clockwise.
2. Place flared end of barrel over bottle neck.
3. Turn handle clockwise until cork is removed.

When the worm shaft is fully threaded into the hollow shaft (handle contacts top), the hollow shaft will extract the cork by rising within the barrel as the user continues to turn the handle.

Two of the rarest Thomason barrels - Gothic Windows on the *left* and Grapes and Vines on the *right*. $1000-2000.
The *middle* corkscrew is a Thomason Variant. In this design an extra handle is added to the hollow shaft. After the worm is turned into the cork by using the top brass loop handle, the wooden handle is turned to lift the hollow shaft and extract the cork. The shield on the barrel reads "Thomason's Patent Ne Plus Ultra." $750-1500.

Thomason corkscrews seem to be cropping up all over the place. Recent sales in London have seen quite a few of them come under the auction hammer. In his memoirs, Thomason states that he made more than 130,000 in fourteen years and "a larger number has since annually been called for." It is quite evident that many of his and other manufacturers have survived! Here are seven of them. $500-800.
The three at *left* have tablets showing the Royal Coat of Arms with "Ne Plus Ultra Patent" in place of "Dieu et Nom Droit." The *center* corkscrew tablet is inscribed "Dowler Patent Ne Plus Ultra" and it has an archimedean worm. The two on the *right* have a tablet inscribed with only "Patent." The corkscrew at *lower right* has no badge or marks. Note: Plates were often marked "Patent" by the manufacturer as a marketing trick to promote sales and not to designate a new patent. Names on Thomasons that have sold in London recently include Wilmot, Roberts & Co.; Rodgers, Sheffield; R. Jones; Dowler; J. F. Lee; Barton; and W. Brooks & Sons, Sheffield.

Although most of the Thomason corkscrews seen have a closed brass barrel, the patent shows a two pillar open frame. At *left* is a late 19th century version with four column brass frame. $1000-1200.

Modern Thomason type with grape and grapevine decoration. $125-150.

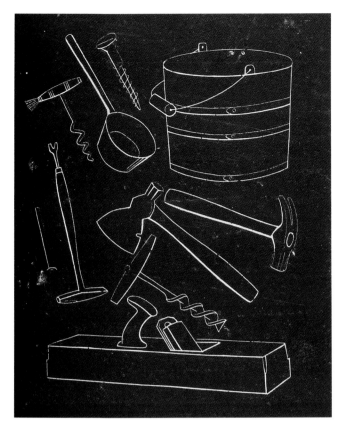

Tools

Hammers, picks, wrenches, screwdrivers, hatchets, pliers, glass cutters, and nuts and bolts have all been used in combination corkscrew designs. The reason for the hammer was not as a tool for the carpentry trade, rather as a tool for breaking ice. Wrenches on the other hand were, indeed, designed for turning bolts and a multi-tool with pliers is for gripping or squeezing that which needs to be gripped or squeezed. "Things" that look more like a tool than a corkscrew are included in this category. A close examination of the contents of an old tool box or fisherman's tackle box may very well reward the collector with one of these tools.

The "Goberg." Each of the tools in the fitted tool box is secured in the handle by a locking clip. The tool goes through the handle and a 1 1/2" slotted bar slides into a recess in the top and engages the groove on the tool. Tools are hammer, pliers, screwdriver, awl, punch, and corkscrew. Marked D.R.G.M. 1903 German design registration number 208010. Produced by Hugo Berger. $200-250.

A tool set with each tool marked HOFFRITZ FOR CUTLERY MADE IN GERMANY. All tools (except the pliers) will fit into the end or the side of the wood cover handle. One slot on the tool is inserted over a pin and turned. A lock then engages the other slot keeping the tool in a fixed, solid position. To unlock and remove, a button on the back of the handle is held down. There are many variations on this type of tool set. A 1900 catalog from Hugo Linder Deltawerk in Solingen, Germany, shows tool sets with from six up to twenty-one pieces. $100-200.

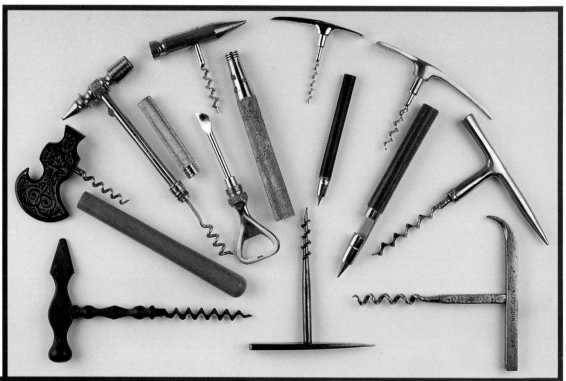

Here are a few ice breaking hammers and picks *beginning at bottom left and going right around the arc:* An early unmarked steel hammer with chopper. $60-70; Hatchet with hammer head, cap lifter, and wood sheath. $30-40; A hammer with rasp sheath for the worm marked BAR GIZMO G. M. CO., L.I.C., N.Y. TRADEMARK - DESIGN PAT. PEND. This is George Iskyan's 1950 American Design Patent No. D-160605. $50-60; Marked GERMANY. The worm with hammer handle and the cap lifter with unusual end tool both thread out of the rasp sheath. $60-70; Small pick with a hard rubber coated sheath. $25-30; Larger version of the pick incorporating a cap lifter and having a leather wrapped sheath. $30-40; Unmarked steel pick. $20-25; Square shank and handle with advertising reading "Dogshead 'Guinness.'" $80-100.

The pick at *bottom center* has a flat unmarked ironing board shape handle and archimedean worm. $60-70.

Above: *Top left:* Marked FISHERMAN'S FRIEND. $60-75.
Top right: Marked SPORTMAN'S PAL. $60-75
The Fisherman's Friend and Sportman's Pal were marketed in the 1950s by the Pyramid Sales Company of St. Louis, Mo. They were supplied with a leather holster with snap down flap. The leather holster is stamped with the same name as the tool. The twelve uses outlined in Pyramid's advertisement were: Scaler, Degorger, Gripper, Knife, Scorer, Cutters, Pincers, Splitter, Hone, Screwdriver, Bottle Opener, and Corkscrew. Regarding the corkscrew it said only "Often needed."
Bottom row: Two wood cased tool kits. The corkscrew and other accessories are affixed to the chuck on the end. $200-300.

Right: The identical hammer heads at *top* are marked GERMANY. They have cap lifters on the back end. The hammer head on the *left* has a wire worm pressed into the handle. $15-20. The other has a web helix pinned to the handle and has a thread to mate with the thread in the wood standard hammer handle. $40-50.
The hammer on the *right* with wood friction fit handle is marked MADE ITALY. $20-30.
The other three hammers have the same wedge shaped head but vary from *left to right* as follows: Hammer head with worm and cap lifter thread into the ends of the center sheath. The bottom of the cap lifter is marked JAPAN. $20-30; Threaded sheath open only on one end for the worm. The hammer head is marked MADE ITALY [*sic*]. $25-35; Fancy threaded sheath. The hammer head has a tag marked SILVER PLATED and an archimedean worm. $50-75.

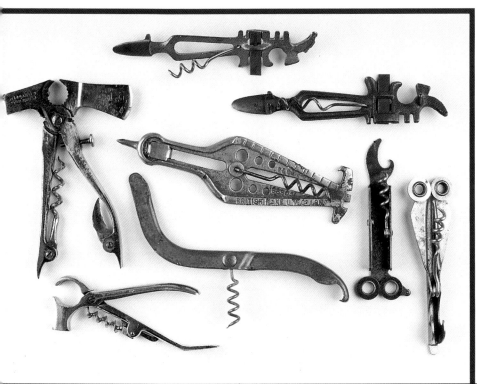

The tool at *top left* is marked WARRANTED FORGED STEEL. This is a 1899 German design registration by Julius Bader. $800-1000. Another forged steel multi-tool is at *lower left*. $800-1000.

The two tools at the *top* have an odd combination of a glass cutter and a corkscrew. The *second* one is marked THE WOODWARD TOOL PAT. AUG. 24 75. Frank Woodward was the owner of the 1875 patent. Similar tools were patented by Monce (1869), Barrett (1873), Brooks (1874), and Adams (1880). Because more of them turn up, Woodward was apparently the most successful. $5-20.

The English went much further than Woodward and the others with the "Utility" combination tool in the *center*. This is a 1922 registered design and includes tin opener, corkscrew, bottle cap lifter, bottle stopper wrench, measure, hammer, paper pattern and stencil cutter, coin tester, glass breaker and, finally, the glass cutter. $65-75. To the *right* of the "Utility" is another tool with glass cutter and, in addition, a knife sharpener. This one carries the advertisement "H. Brooks & Co. (Bishopgate) for all your glass requirements." A worm and a screwdriver are riveted to the inside of the bottom channel. $75-100.

Further right is a tool for sharpening knives, lifting lids and bottle caps, and removing corks. Alas, there is no glass cutter. It is labeled "The Wizard Knife Sharpener." Manufactured by Williamson. $75-100. The odd tool at *bottom center* is marked STEWART WARNER. It has a crown cap lifter, a wire helix, and the curved part is to lift and break free ice trays from early mechanical refrigerators. Stewart Warner was a manufacturer of refrigerators. $20-30.

The crescent wrench knife on the *top* is marked L'HALTERE DEPOSE. In 1931, Jean Soustre was granted an American patent for a "Knife adapted for multiple uses and comprising a monkey wrench." This French version includes the wrench, master knife blade, corkscrew, leather punch, and a blade consisting of cap lifter, ruler, and wire cutter. $200-300. An unmarked version without the cap lifter is shown next to it. $150-200.

The black multi-tool at the *left* is Erik Nylin's 1909 American patent. It is marked PAT 09. It includes corkscrew, can opener, pipe wrench, tack lifter, hammer, scissors sharpener, knife sharpener, wire stripper, tongs, nut cracker, wrench holes, and file. $300-600.

In 1930, Nathan Jenkins was granted his American patent for the marvel at *right* marked 15 TOOLS IN ONE and PAT DEC 9, 1930. $150-200. The double nut and bolt that these tools can be used on is marked MADE ITALY [*sic*]. The bottom bolt unthreads to reveal the worm and the top, the cap lifter. $30-40.

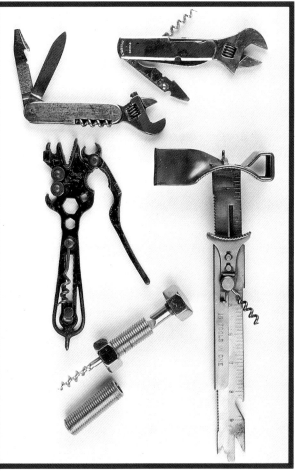

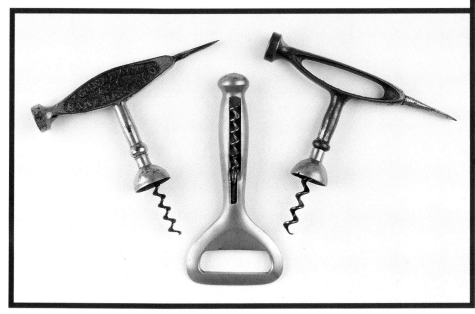

The "hammer"/spike corkscrews have cork pulling bells on the shank. The *first* has advertising for "Gundlach & Co., San Francisco." $200-300. The *second* is unmarked. $200-300.

The tool in the *middle* was patented by Marshall Neal in 1940 as a bottle opener. The other end is a muddler. The bottle openers are frequently seen with advertising on the handle without a corkscrew. They are seldom seen with folding corkscrews in the handle. $200-300.

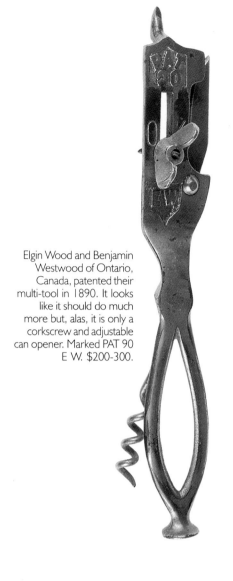

Elgin Wood and Benjamin Westwood of Ontario, Canada, patented their multi-tool in 1890. It looks like it should do much more but, alas, it is only a corkscrew and adjustable can opener. Marked PAT 90 E W. $200-300.

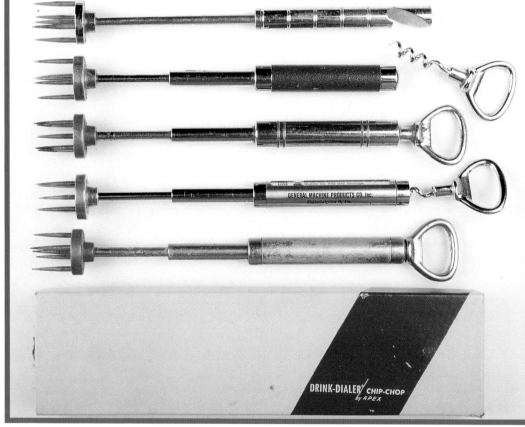

Above: The bar tool on the *left* is called the "Drink Master." Directions for use from Metal Specialties, Inc., Philadelphia, Pennsylvania, say that it "is molde and cut from solid brass and has an exceptionally heavy quadruple plate to insure lasting beauty and years of service." It is a bottle opener, an ice breake a drink muddler for crushing fruit, and corkscrew. The handle is the sheath for the worm. The *first* on has the "quadruple plate" worn off. Apparently the lasting beauty was not insured enough. $40-50. The hammer is a combination icebreaker, cap lifter, can opener, and corkscrew. The one on the *left* is a zinc die casting. The worm tucks nicely out of the way in the center of the casting. The other is plated and has a "Souvenir of Florida" tag. $15-20.

Left: The box is marked DRINK-DIALER*/ CHIP-CHOP BY APEX, *TRADEMARK, COPYRIGHT 1946. It contains a combination tool with advertising on it "General Machine Products Co., Inc., Philadelphia 6, Pa." An inse describes the tool functions as "Cocktail recipes right at your fingertips, crush ice right in glass, stir drinks, spear olives from bottle, cork screw, bottle opener." The Chip Chop at the *top* is unmarked and it has only a cap lifter built int the handle. In the other four, the corkscrew is the handle and all are marked CHIP CHOP PAT. PEND. on top of the lower button. Only th *fourth and fifth* Chip Chops have the recipes, which are read by rotating the top sleeve. The bottom part of the Chip Chop has five ice crushing points and it is spring loaded to cushion the blow when crushing ice "right in th glass." $10-30.

Tusk, Bone & Horn

Tusks, horns, antlers, and bones were all "found in nature" articles ready to be used as handles or sheaths for corkscrews. Some artists' fine carvings can be found on the very finest of these corkscrews (see "Tusk, Bone & Horn - Carvings" category). Other artifacts were simply shaped into a handle and polished. Some had silver decorative fittings added to the ends and others were hollowed out to serve as the sheaths for worms.

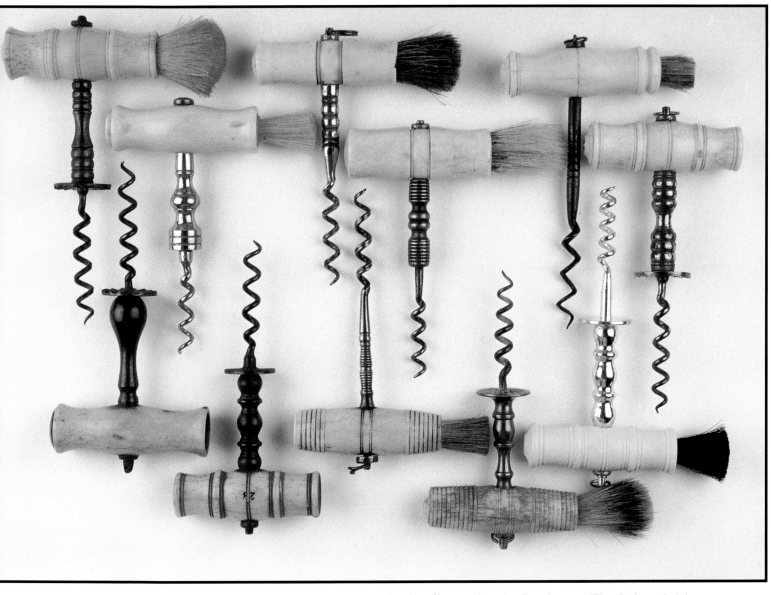

A variety of ivory and bone handle corkscrews. All handles have a hole in one end for a brush. Examples include direct pull, serrated button, and plain button. All handles are secured by a nut on the threaded end of the shaft, which protrudes through the top of the handle. $125-250. The corkscrew at *lower right* is a modern plastic imitation. $40-60.

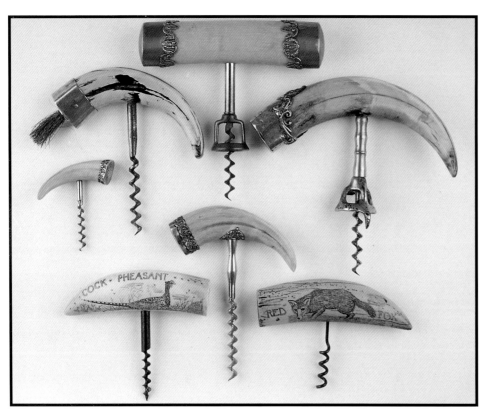

Top center: A heavy ivory handle with silver mounts marked STERLING. At the base of each silver mount is a decorative silver grapevine design. One cap has a monogram and the other is engraved Jan. 11, 1903. The self-pulling bell is Williamson's 1897 American patent. $200-300.

Second row: At *left* is a very unusual example with a brush. The silver cap is formed with a provision for the brush. Marked WW STERLING. Produced by Wilcox & Wagoner of New York City. c.1904. $200-250; At *right* is a boar's tusk with Edwin Walker's 1900 American patent bell. The silver cap is engraved "Indian Harbor Yacht Club, Club Handicap, Sept. 7th, 1903, Third Prize won by Verona." (It makes one wonder what 1st and 2nd prize were!). $250-300.

The small tusk corkscrew on the *left* would have been used for medicine or perfume. The silver cap is engraved with the monogram A.V.N.F. It has the pre-1900 trademark of silversmiths R. Blackinton & Co., of North Attleboro, Massachusetts. $75-100.

The direct pull at *bottom center* not only has a decorative mount on the end, it has one above the nicely formed shank. Monogrammed on cap. $100-150.

The two corkscrews at *bottom* are recent scrimshaw. Both have "Red Fox" on one side and "Cock Pheasant" on the other. Only the worms are different. $75-100.

Gottfried Piel's Corkscrew was made by Wilcox & Evertsen of New York City between 1892 and 1896. The large silver mount is engraved with his initials. In 1883, Gottfried with his brothers Michael and Wilhelm purchased the Landzer Brewery in Brooklyn. Piel Brothers grew to be one of the largest brewers in Brooklyn. It closed its doors in 1973 and the brand name was purchased by Schaefer Brewing Company. *$Rare.*

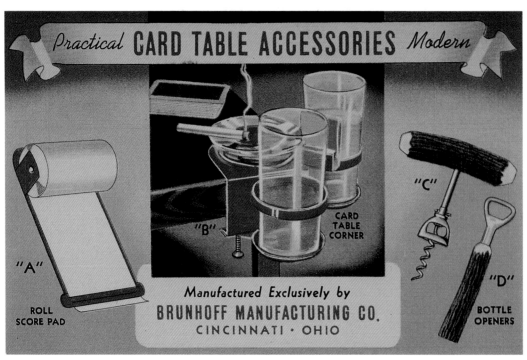

Antler or stag horn handle corkscrews with all sorts of ornamentation were produced as monogrammed gift presentations and as awards for special functions. A group of various colors and treatments can add a little spice to any corkscrew collection.

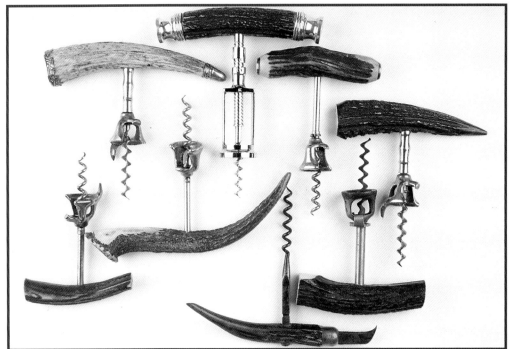

Top row left to right: Bleached stag horn with silver mounts and Walker 1900 bell. End of large cap is engraved with name J. A. Olmsted. Usually these have a monogram and very seldom is a complete name engraved. $100-150; Stag handle with large silver mounts. The top of the frame is marked J. A. HENCKELS GERMANY with the Henckels Twins Trademark. Henckels produced cutlery in Solingen. The jaw clutch on the threaded shaft is spun to the top to ready for use. The worm is turned into the cork and the jaw clutch engages the mating piece at the top of the frame. Continuing to turn the handle in the same direction will extract the cork. $150-200; Simple bell cap stag handle with sterling caps pressed into the ends. $75-100; Dark stag with Walker bell and cap marked STERLING pressed into end of handle. $60-75. *Bottom row left to right:* Stag without ornamentation and Walker bell. $15-25; Simple bell with large partially polished stag. $30-50; Stag handle with foil cutter. 5" Square shank and worm. $30-50; Antler handle with Williamson bell and cap lifter/foil cutter blade. Ends of handle are imprinted "Wallace Supply Company, Chicago." $75-125.

More stag handle examples.
Top row left to right: Stag with nickel plated brass mounts, speed worm. $30-40; 4" handle with silver mounts marked STERLING 1312, decorative ring. $25-30; Small with silver mount one end only. $25-30; 4 1/2" handle with silver mounts with initial "W" on each decorative ring. $30-40; An English example with pressed in hallmarked silver end cap. Hallmark has initials G H and was produced in Sheffield 1930-1931. Twisted shank. $60-75; Simple T-handle marked J. A. HENCKELS, GERMANY with twins trademark. (Another marked Henckels is under the *3rd from top left*). $50-70; The unusual design on the *right* has a silver mount between the handle and the shank. A decorative silver inlay is on the top. Trademark of Meriden Britannia Company of Meriden, Connecticut, on the mount. $70-90. *Bottom row left to right:* Six simple unmarked direct pull and formed button types. $10-30.

The lesson in all of these corkscrews is to always check to see if there is a corkscrew attached to the opener. The corkscrew collector will often be disappointed to find that a firm pull or twist yields no worm. Some bar sets were produced including a corkscrew with antler handle and a separate cap lifter with antler handle (no corkscrew). All of these in the photo have a worm in the hollowed out horn. With little grip, they are not very practical corkscrews. The four on the *left* are all John Hasselbring's 1906 American design patent for a bottle opener. Hasselbring's company was founded in Brooklyn, New York. c.1890. All have a "Baltimore Loop Seal" (stopper) remover at the top. They are all marked PAT. 1906. The delicate worm is fitted inside a male thread at the bottom and threaded into the silver mount. $75-125. The next three have a loose fitting cap lifter/worm. It is secured by turning the worm into the handle until it twists around a small nail that has been driven into the cavity from the side. $30-40. Next is a polished ivory example with threaded silver mount. A simple vine design has been carved into each side. $200-300. *Second from right* is a 7" example with silver mounts on both ends. The bottom mount is monogrammed. The top mount is cone shaped and the worm is threaded into the top of the cone for storage and to secure it. Both mounts have the trademark of J. F. Fradley & Co. of New York City. $100-125. On the *right* is a foil cutter without corkscrew. $15-30.

167

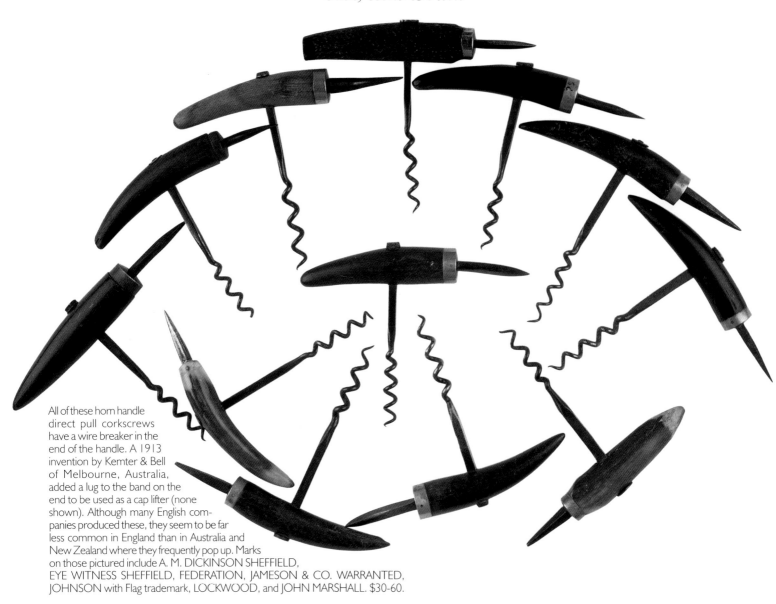

All of these horn handle direct pull corkscrews have a wire breaker in the end of the handle. A 1913 invention by Kemter & Bell of Melbourne, Australia, added a lug to the band on the end to be used as a cap lifter (none shown). Although many English companies produced these, they seem to be far less common in England than in Australia and New Zealand where they frequently pop up. Marks on those pictured include A. M. DICKINSON SHEFFIELD, EYE WITNESS SHEFFIELD, FEDERATION, JAMESON & CO. WARRANTED, JOHNSON with Flag trademark, LOCKWOOD, and JOHN MARSHALL. $30-60.

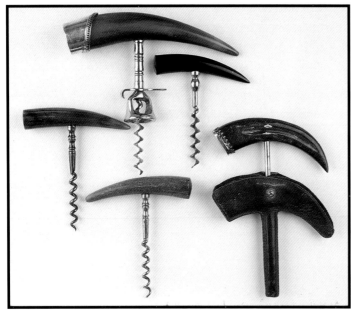

A bit more difficult to find than stag handle corkscrews are those made with horn. The polished horn at *top left* with Williamson bell and opener/foil cutter plate has a very elegant look. It has only the letter "G" ornately displayed on the end and the trademark of J. F. Fradley & Co. of New York City. $75-125. To the *lower left and upper right* of the Williamson are polished and unpolished versions of the same corkscrew marked J. A. HENCKELS, GERMANY with twins trademark. $40-50. The black handle is polished goat horn. $30-50. Simple horns are at *right and lower left*. $15-25. At *lower right* is a rare example of a horn handle direct pull corkscrew with a fitted leather case. The silver cap is engraved with initials "R. P. L." $150-200.

Miscellaneous horn handles *from left to right:* Standup counter type. $20-25; Frame with jaw clutch and silver tip by Hasselbring, Brooklyn, New York. $70-90; Crosshatch design on T-handle. $20-25; Crosshatch design on direct pull. $8-10.

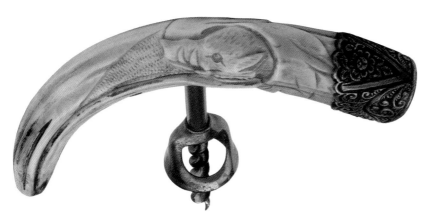

A boar's head. The silver end cap is marked STERLING and has an intricate scrollwork design. The Walker 1893 patent bell is held in place by a plain hollow tube over the shank. $400-500.

Tusk, Bone & Horn - Carvings

A very popular artistic endeavor in America was the carving of tusks, antlers, wood, or pieces of ivory as handles for corkscrews. Most incorporate a bell cap on the shank for self pulling of the cork and most of the shanks are threaded into or pinned to the handle. Any that are simply pressed and glued in a hole in the handle might well be suspected to be fake. The carvings normally had silver fittings on one or both ends. Here are a few examples.

A bird with long beak grasping a plant branch. The floral decorated end cap is marked STERLING. The square shoulder bell is held in place by a plain hollow tube over the shank. $450-600.

A floral and berry design. The STERLING marked end cap has a tapering scallop design and is engraved with ornate initials. Walker 1893 bell with plain separator tube. $400-500.

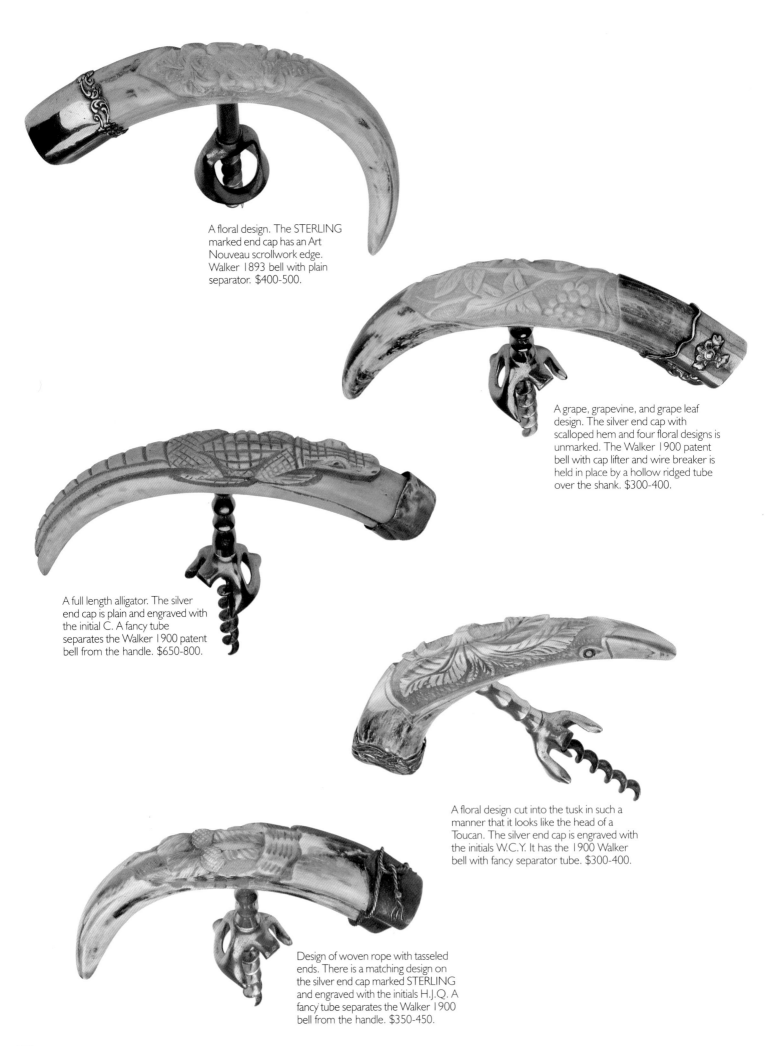

A floral design. The STERLING marked end cap has an Art Nouveau scrollwork edge. Walker 1893 bell with plain separator. $400-500.

A grape, grapevine, and grape leaf design. The silver end cap with scalloped hem and four floral designs is unmarked. The Walker 1900 patent bell with cap lifter and wire breaker is held in place by a hollow ridged tube over the shank. $300-400.

A full length alligator. The silver end cap is plain and engraved with the initial C. A fancy tube separates the Walker 1900 patent bell from the handle. $650-800.

A floral design cut into the tusk in such a manner that it looks like the head of a Toucan. The silver end cap is engraved with the initials W.C.Y. It has the 1900 Walker bell with fancy separator tube. $300-400.

Design of woven rope with tasseled ends. There is a matching design on the silver end cap marked STERLING and engraved with the initials H.J.Q. A fancy tube separates the Walker 1900 bell from the handle. $350-450.

A rose design in an imitation ivory celluloid handle. It is unmarked and has the 1900 Walker bell. $500-650.

A grapevine, bunch of grapes, and leaves intricately carved on a genuine ivory handle. It is a direct pull corkscrew. $450-550.

Two flying ducks carved into an imitation antler handle. Opener bell with wire worm. $85-100.

Top right: Antler carving of a wild boar. The diamond pattern shank is pinned to a handle, which has an ornate silver saddle in the middle engraved with the initials C.P.L. $550-700.
Top left: A dog's head carved into the antler, which has a simple shank with wire worm pinned in place. The dog has a silver collar. $300-400.
Bottom: The large dog head is 11" from end to end. The shaft is marked WILLIAMSON and is pinned to the handle. The bell has Williamson's 1898 patent entitled "Cap Lift" above it. $450-550.

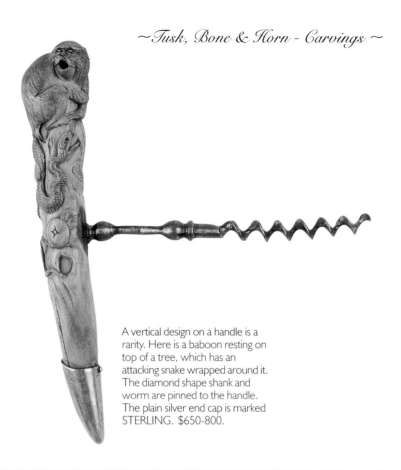

A vertical design on a handle is a rarity. Here is a baboon resting on top of a tree, which has an attacking snake wrapped around it. The diamond shape shank and worm are pinned to the handle. The plain silver end cap is marked STERLING. $650-800.

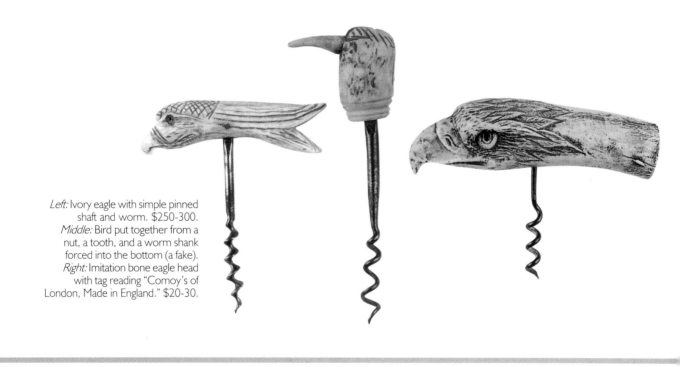

Left: Ivory eagle with simple pinned shaft and worm. $250-300.
Middle: Bird put together from a nut, a tooth, and a worm shank forced into the bottom (a fake).
Right: Imitation bone eagle head with tag reading "Comoy's of London, Made in England." $20-30.

Possibly a homemade lion corkscrew. $?

Waiters' Friends

When waiters open bottles of wine, the overwhelming majority will use one of these simple lever devices. Because these devices fold up nicely with worm protected in the pocket, they are a waiter's best friend. They can be quickly armed and ready for use by simply folding the worm and the neckstand out. In patents the neckstand is given the technical term "fulcrum plate." As stated in David Davis's 1891 patent, the point on early version neckstands was "a means for cutting the wire on bottles...as all malt liquors and many grades of wines are provided with wires to better secure the corks from involuntary ejections." Some waiters' friends have knives on the backside for cutting the foil on the bottle. The worm is inserted into the cork, the neckstand is placed on the bottle rim, the handle is raised and the cork is extracted.

An 1877 French patent by Remy Bechon-Morel. Both the worm and the neckstand pivot completely into and out of the handle. $600-750.

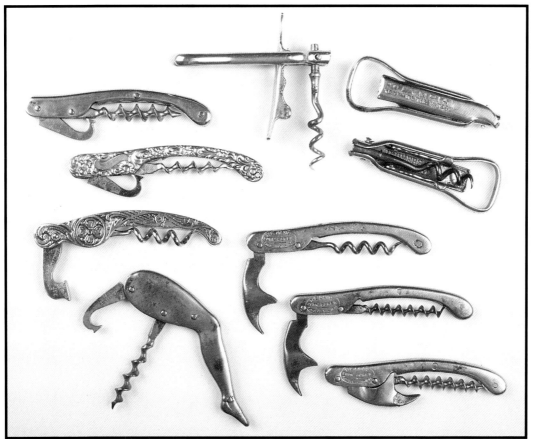

An 1892 advertisement in the *Ladies Home Journal* for the Davis Corkscrew says: "The Davis Pocket Cork Screw. No more bother about uncorking bottles! A child can open any bottle with this cork screw. It is adjustable, and fits all sizes. The sharp point cuts the wire and the most stubborn cork is easily forced out by simply lifting the handle. Combines pocket knife, wire cutter and lever cork screw; a perfect pocket piece that everybody needs. For sale everywhere. Manufactured by Davis Cork Screw Co., Detroit, Mich."

Three examples of Davis's American patent No. 455, 826 of July 14, 1891 are shown at *lower right*. Each has a different worm. All are marked THE DAVIS CORK-SCREW with a patent date. An early Montgomery Ward's catalog says of the Davis "...will fit any bottle and any woman or child can operate it." This style was frequently sold to breweries as a giveaway with an engraved advertising message. $75-100. A rare example (not shown) had a folding knife blade on the back. $125-175. Charles Puddefoot who worked with Davis at the Detroit Corkscrew Company was issued a patent a year later for his changes that incorporated a cap lifter into the neckstand. The Puddefoot was produced with a number of interesting and ornate designs. The four Puddefoots *on left from top to bottom* are: Neckstand marked THE DETROIT PAT'D JULY 10 94 with "Minneapolis Brewing Co." on the handle. $250-300; Same mark on

neckstand. Handle marked STERLING with trademark of Meriden Sterling Co. (1896-1904). $500-600; Neckstand marked "DAVIS IMPROVED" PAT'D JULY 14-91, FURTHER PATS PND'G (referring to the Puddefoot patent, which this is) and with advertising on the backside of the neckstand: "Compliments of Charles Staebler, 257 Beaubien St., Detroit, Mich." Staebler operated a saloon at that address. $700-800; Leg marked THE DETROIT PAT'D JULY 10 94. $600-700. In 1906, Harry Noyes patented a lever where the handle was pushed down rather than pulled up to extract the cork. His "UNIVERSAL" is shown at *top center*. It is found most often with advertising for Green River Whiskey. Less common are a plain version and one with advertising for Olympia Brewing Company of Washington. Three views of the Noyes patent are shown at *upper right*. $50-100.

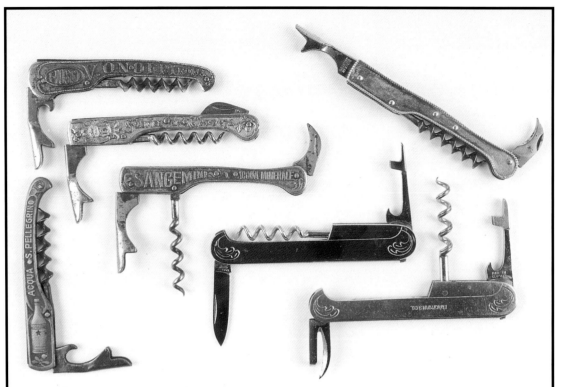

Factories in Germany's Cutlery Capital Solingen turned out many well made waiters' friends. Some of the ornate designs made these very attractive advertising giveaways. Four early examples shown here are from Fiuggi, Rome; El Aquila (Brewery), Madrid; Sangemini Mineral Water; and Pellegrino. $80-150.

The corkscrew at *top right* has Sterling Silver handles and the neckstand is marked D.R.PATENT NO. 20815. This is a German patent issued to Karl Wienke in 1882 (An American patent was issued to him in 1883). Wienke is often considered to be the father of the waiter's friend. Stamped with the name C. D. PEACOCK, a Chicago retailer. $400-500. Nickel plated versions of the Wienke are valued at $100-200.

Another Solingen product by Eduard Becker was supplied with a knife or a can opener. The one with can opener in *bottom right* has advertising for the New York City department store B. Altman & Co. $50-60.

Waiter's friends with a single knife blade and a foil cutter. In the *top two* the blades are on the same side. The *bottom* four have the foil cutter on the worm side with a slot in the neckstand to accommodate it.

Top row: Well marked on neckstand J. A. HENCKELS, SOLINGEN, ZWILLINGSWERK. $25-30; Neckstand marked COLUMBUS. Advertising "135 Jahre Joh. Koch. Westerstede ¹/₀. Spirituosen - Weine - Hefe." Trademark says founded in 1813 so this corkscrew is from 1948. $50-60.

Middle row: Marked MADE IN FRANCE and advertising "Champagne Taittinger." $15-20; German marked on neckstand MERCATOR № 7, PAT. ANG. $40-50.

Bottom: Neckstand marked ED. WÜSTHOF, SOLINGEN-GERMANY. $20-30.

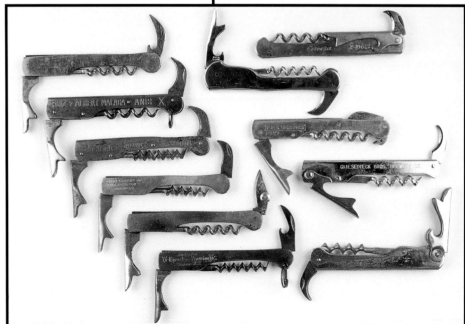

An assortment of advertising waiter's friends with foil cutter only except for *lower left*, which has a cap lifter. All have the foil cutter mounted on the side opposite the corkscrew except *top right*, which fits under the slotted neckstand. $15-25.

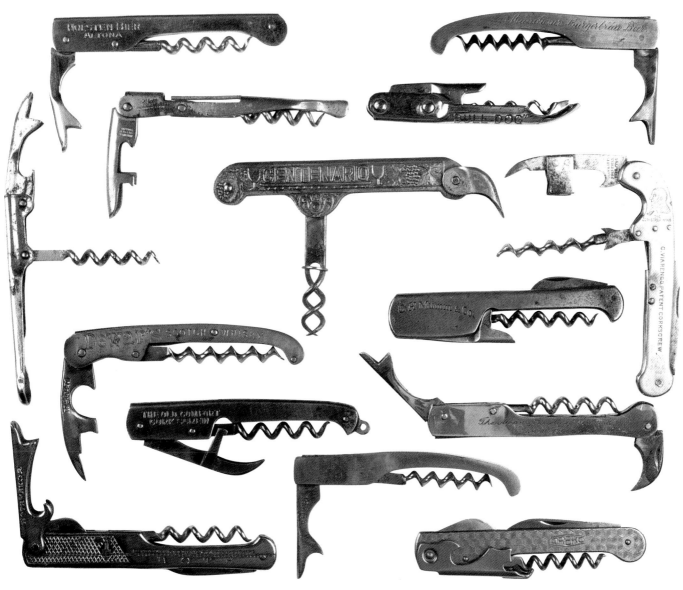

Which one is not a "Waiter's Friend Lever?" Note the one marked CENTENARIO. Unlike waiter's friends, the worm of this one folds with point toward the swivel piece on the end. The only function of the swivel piece is to protect the end of the worm, which is a double helix! The handle sports ornate grape, grapevine, and wine glass designs. The reverse side says GRAFFIGNA. *$Rare.*

The rest of the corkscrews in this photograph all use the neckstand and lifting handle method of cork extraction. The variations produced and additional patents applied for and issued are enough to confuse any collector. Modern day pieces even went to further extremes with the use of plastics and the incorporation of various can and bottle openers. A collector accumulating variations in design and the many different advertisements could amass an enormous collection. Some early examples are:

Top left and right: Holsten Bier Altona advertising and Münchener Bürgerbräu Beer advertising. $50-75.

Next two left and right: An unmarked example of the right one but the left includes a backspring to help hold the worm in place. The *right* has

advertising for "'Bull Dog Guinness" marked PAT NO. 177694. The neckstand is marked CROWN CAP OPENER. $75-100.

Left outside center: Produced by John Watts of Sheffield, England, (so marked) with advertising "Creese's for Something Good." The body is made of nickel plated stamped steel with a cantilever spring cut in the spine, which is the backspring for the wire helix. $60-80.

Right outside center: Watts' production marked C. VIARENGO PATENT CORKSCREW, (man's head) THE CORKSCREW KING, RD. NO. 581553 (1911). $250-500.

The Dewar's Scotch Whiskey has registered design No. 568470 from 1910. $50-75.

Third up from bottom right is an extremely well made corkscrew produced by J. A. Henckels Zwillingswerk of Solingen. This one is engraved "The Albany Society of New York, Jan. 10, 1906." $80-100.

The corkscrew at *lower left* was made by Heinrich Kaufmann of Solingen and says "Ein Korkenzieher Der Tut Not Zum Öffnen Einer Flasche." $50-60. The Dreko corkscrew at *lower right* was made in East Germany. $20-30.

An assortment of advertising waiter's friends with single knife blade only. In addition to variations in design, corkscrews from eight countries are in this group. $15-25. *Left side top to bottom:* Italy; Germany; United States, Spain, Italy. *Right side top to bottom:* Germany; Portugal (note the left-hand worm); France; France; Switzerland; United States.

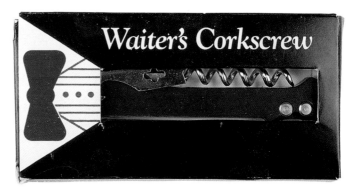

Well dressed packaging for Ferdinando Cellini's 1994 patent for a waiter's corkscrew, which has cutting wheels in the handle for cutting foil. Franmara's instructions on the box for extracting a cork are:
1. Raise the lever, pull out the worm and insert into center of cork.
2. Screw in the worm using a light pressure.
3. Place the lever (neckstand) on the neck of the bottle holding it firmly with your left index finger and pulling up on lever (handle). The sliding axis automatically changes the leverage for maximum advantage. You will use less strength to extract the cork.

The corkscrew with knife at *top* is a well made German waiter's friend with advertising: "Compliments of American Cork and Seal Co., Phila. PA." The back side is marked F. P. NOBIS MFG. CO., ADVERTISING SOUVENIRS, PHILADELPHIA, PA, PAT. 7.17.06. $200-250.
Others top to bottom: Horn marked C. KAYSER, SOLINGEN. $40-50; Steel advertising "Dressler Beer Bremen" marked JULANCO, SOLINGEN. $30-40; Tortoise shell handles. $80-100; Steel advertising "Ancre, Biere D'Alsace." marked PRADEL (French). $30-40; Steel advertising "Dow Old Stock Ale" marked MADE IN FRANCE. $40-50 At *lower left* is a cheaply made waiter's friend advertising Grandin products. The cast aluminum handles depict a bottle and list several products. $10-15.

Thousands of waiter's friends have been produced with bright color plastic handles. The use of plastics allows manufacturers to hot stamp or silk screen advertising on the handles that is quite visible. It is not difficult for a collector to build a colorful worldwide collection of this type of corkscrew. The gift shop of any present day winery is apt to have one with their name emblazoned on it. A few examples in a variety of styles, advertising, and colors are shown here. Each one has a single knife blade. $5-20.

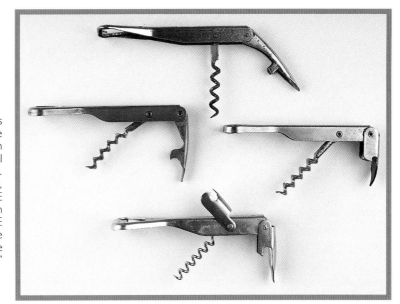

In this group of waiter's friends, the worm folds up into a channel formed by the handle. The handle stamping also has a cap lifter in line with the flat of the channel top. Four of several variations are shown here. $10-15. *From top and clockwise:* Marked CASINO, DEPOSE, RTF; Marked SKY-LINE BEVERAGE BOY, MADE IN ENGLAND; Russian made with tin can opener riveted on side; Marked SKY-LINE BOTTLE BOY, MADE IN ENGLAND. Note the differences on the neckstands on the "Beverage Boy" and "Bottle Boy."

Two groups of waiter's friends with bottle cap lifters. They all have slight variations in construction and color. The group *below* has a single knife blade added to the tool. If one collected all the different advertising and promotions found on these, the hunt would be frequently rewarding but endless. $5-25.

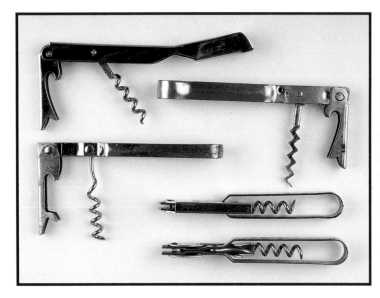

At first glance these appear to be common style can opener combinations. Look closer. The can opener is absent. These are only waiter's friends for cork or cap lifter removal. The "friend" at the *top* is marked MELVIN PATENT MADE IN ITALY inside the channel of the handle. The extra length and curvature of the handle adds leverage. $20-30.
Top right is marked D.R.G.M. MADE IN GERMANY. A backspring has been placed in the handle to secure the worm tightly in position when in use. $25-40.
Three views of a simple unmarked waiter's friend are at *bottom*. $10-20.

Modern waiter's friends.
Left side top to bottom: Two colors of the "Puigpull." A 1988 Spanish patent by Ralon Brucart Puig. $10-20; The "Maxos." A very good quality corkscrew from Japan. $15-25; The "Liftmaster" with white body. $15-25.
Right side from top to bottom: A French Laguiole knife. $100-200; Tagged "The Hugh Johnson Collection." Advertised as "Hugh Johnson's Personal Corkscrew...subtly sculpted...molded of ivory-like resin." Currently sold in fitted case by the *Wine Enthusiast* for $39.95; The "Pulltaps" from Spain. $18-30; The "Liftmaster" with nickel plated body. $15-25.

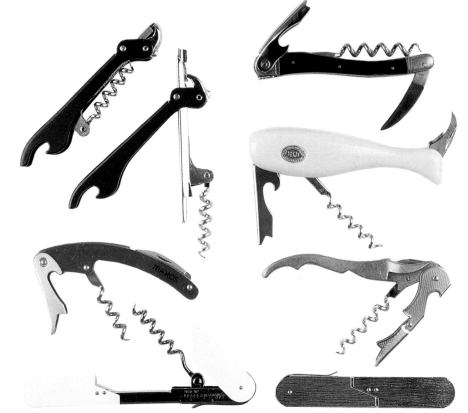

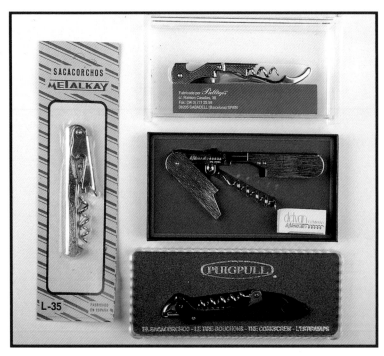

On the *left* is a waiter's friend currently sold in department stores in Spain. Blister packaging reads "Sacacorchos, Metalkay, Fabricado en España."
At *top right* is a rather remarkable current Spanish corkscrew called "Pulltaps." It has a knife for cutting foil, a cap lifter in the neckstand, and a nicely contoured handle. The neckstand is hinged. With the upper portion of the neckstand in position on the bottle top, the cork is removed halfway. The second section is folded down to the bottle neck to remove the rest.
In the *middle right* is the "Liftmaster" by the Devlan Company, Providence, Rhode Island. A corkscrew with a sliding sheath patented by Bernard DeLisle. A story from a 1993 adventure: There was a closed antique shop in the Adirondack town of Westport, New York. It was part of The Inn on the Library Lawn. I went in the Inn and asked the proprietor if there were any corkscrews in the shop. His response was the usual "I had some but they were sold." And then he said "But I invented one." It was Bernie who had invented his "Liftmaster" while living in New England, met with fair success, and by 1993 was running a hotel in the boondocks. He found white and nickel plated examples for me.
At the *bottom right* is the "Puigpull." The Spanish corkscrew extracts the cork by a ratcheting mechanism. It is produced in many colors and sold for advertising purposes.

Walker & Williamson

Edwin Walker's Erie Specialty Company was located in Erie, Pennsylvania. The C. T. Williamson Company was founded in Newark, New Jersey, in 1876. For over 40 years the two companies were seriously competing for their share of the North American corkscrew market. Walker was certainly the most inventive with over twenty corkscrew patents to his credit. Although they manufactured some patents of others by agreement, Cornelius and William Williamson secured only seven corkscrews patents themselves. Walker's earliest inventions were barscrews (1888 and 1891). Williamson's were wire and folding bow corkscrews. These and other Walker and Williamson corkscrews can be found in other categories.

This category deals with the wood handle bell cap types. This was where the two companies competed most heavily not only in inventiveness but in the battle to win orders from advertisers.

Walker had the first bell cap invention in 1893. He had taken Chinnock's 1862 idea of a long frame or barrel and shortened it. The bell is secured by a cotter pin. By continuously turning the worm into the cork, the bell would cause the cork to be lifted. Interestingly enough, Williamson was producing a frame in the 1880s using Clough's wire corkscrew patent. Walker refined his designs by adding a stopper extractor to the bell in 1897 and a cap lifter in 1900. Meanwhile Williamson worked on the mechanics of the bell cap by adding a washer above the bell for smoother action in 1897. He beat Walker to the cap

lifter by placing it above the bell in an 1898 design.

Who was the most successful in selling wood handle bell caps? In *The 1994 Handbook of Beer Advertising Openers and Corkscrews* by Stanley, Kaye, and Bull, there are 300 Walker corkscrews cataloged and only 60 for Williamson. Walker won more advertisers.

Which company was the most successful overall? Edwin Walker died in 1917. Williamson took over the production of Erie Specialty Company corkscrew in 1918 and continued to produce them for many years. A 1946 Williamson catalog shows both the Walker and Williamson bells. Williamson won the longevity battle.

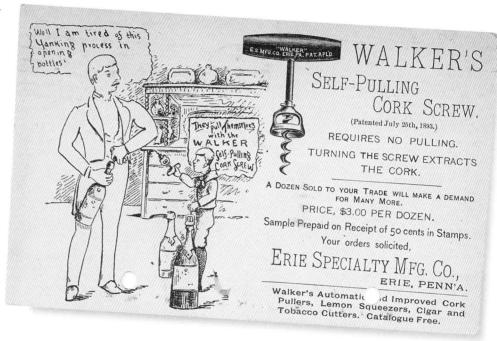

In an advertisement showing the bell with cap lifter and wire breaker, Erie Specialty Co. says "No more tugging, straining or pulling, no grasping a slippery bottle with both knees. A few twists of the wrist and the cork draws itself only. Not only draws the cork out whole every time without a miss, or agitating the contents, but it also cuts wires, removes seals, crown caps and aluminum stoppers...Don't get side-tracked, for there is nothing 'Just as good'."

Walker corkscrews with various handles and worms. The *first four* are Walker's 1897 patent. The two on the *right* are his 1900 patent. $20-40. Walker handles were usually attached by driving a nail in the end of the handle and through a hole in the top of the shank. Williamson used a pin driven through the center of the handle. The corkscrew on the *left* has the Walker bell but was manufactured by Williamson after acquiring Erie Specialty Company in 1918.

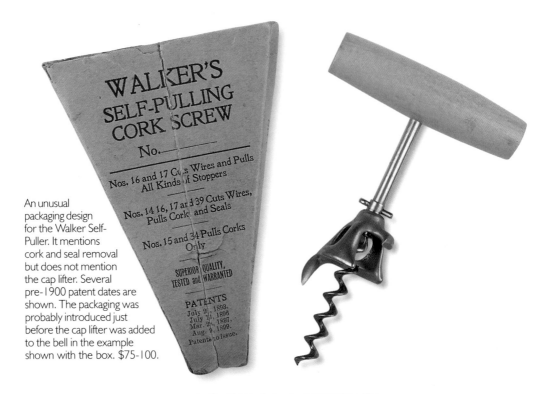

An unusual packaging design for the Walker Self-Puller. It mentions cork and seal removal but does not mention the cap lifter. Several pre-1900 patent dates are shown. The packaging was probably introduced just before the cap lifter was added to the bell in the example shown with the box. $75-100.

Left: Various corkscrews based on the 1898 Williamson design patent. *Left to right:* Cast cap lifter/wire breaker above nickel plated bell. $20-40; Cast cap lifter/wire breaker above copper plated bell. $30-50; Cast foil cutter only with square shoulder bell. $40-50; Steel stamping cap lifter/foil cutter with nickel plated bell. $30-40.

Below: Walker and Williamson bell caps with various handles, worms, bells, and advertising. $20-30. The cylindrical handle at *top right* is also a World's Fair collectible with this advertising: "D. H. Russell's Old Times, Louisville, Ky., First Prize, Old Times Whisky, World's Fair."

Easy lessons for using the self-puller.

On the underside of the handle, Walker included instructions: "Don't pull, turn until cork is out" or "Do not pull, turn cork out." On the underside of the Williamson handle, instructions are "Need not pull, keep turning" or "Self turning, do not pull." Williamson made the Old Times Whisky corkscrew with instructions on the top of the handle: "Don't pull to extract the cork, keep turning."

Above: *Top row left to right:* Walker 1893 patent with foil cutter in handle. $50-60; Williamson 1897 patent with foil cutter in handle. $50-60.
Bottom row left to right: 1893 Walker with cast iron cap lifter in handle. $50-70; 1893 Walker with cap lifter rotated 90 degrees. $50-70; 1897 Walker with cap lifter in handle. $50-70; A Walker direct pull with cap lifter and plain handle. $30-40.

Left: A Walker corkscrew with elegant bronze handle marked GORHAM CO. $300-400.

Below: A 3 1/4" cup depicting a Walker's Self-Puller. Produced in 1994 by Dennis China Works, England.

Wallmount

For the convenience of guests, motel rooms often had a bottle opener attached to the wall with two screws. Although pull tab cans and twist off tops are making them obsolete, one can still occasionally find them in roadside motels. I have, however, never seen one with a corkscrew attachment in a motel or hotel.

In 1925, Thomas Hamilton of Boston, Massachusetts, was granted a patent for his wall mounted "Bottle Cap Puller." This patent appears on many of the cap lifters made by Brown Manufacturing Company of Newport News, Virginia. They were marketed under the "Starr" bottle opener name and were an ideal advertising medium for brewers and soda bottlers.

The corkscrew appears with the opener in Raymond Brown's patent issued almost three years later. He added a worm that attached at the top of the cap lifter. It folded up for storage and down for use. Brown re-invented his corkscrew several years later by attaching the worm near the top screw as seen on the Samuel Lewis Company postcard advertisement.

Other wallmount variations were "invented" by Hoegger, Thompson, and Topping.

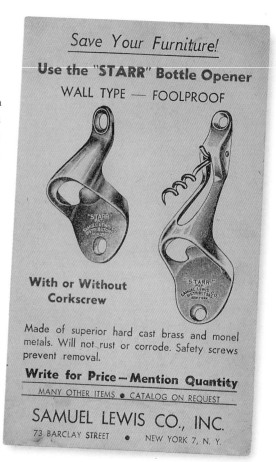

Save Your Furniture!
Use the "STARR" Bottle Opener
WALL TYPE — FOOLPROOF

With or Without Corkscrew

Made of superior hard cast brass and monel metals. Will not rust or corrode. Safety screws prevent removal.

Write for Price — Mention Quantity
MANY OTHER ITEMS • CATALOG ON REQUEST

SAMUEL LEWIS CO., INC.
73 BARCLAY STREET • NEW YORK 7, N. Y.

The most reproduced wall-mounted bottle opener advertises Coca Cola. Reproductions do not have a corkscrew. An original with corkscrew by Brown Company is at *top left*. $40-50. At *top right* is a "Starr" bottle opener without corkscrew with Hamilton's 1925 patent date. $15-20.
The *first three from left* in the *bottom row* are variations of Hamilton's patent produced by the Brown Company. The *first* without the "Starr" brand name is the earliest. The *second* has the "Starr" name added. The *third* shows both Brown Mfg. Co. and Wilcox Mfg. Co. of Chicago. In the last two, the worm hangs from the top as in Brown's 1935 patent. Oddly the *fourth* is marked with patent #2,333,088, which was issued to Brown in 1943 for a bottle opener only. $20-25.
The yellow wallmount is unmarked, but an example was found in a box labeled "Corbin Bottle Opener." $30-40. The green wallmount is marked WHAT CHEER on the front and C. S. RIPLEY & CO., CLEVELAND, O., U. S. A. PAT. PEND. on the back. It is Henry Thompson's 1935 American patent. $50-60. The wallmount at *top* is marked PAT. APP FOR, BOSTON, MASS., ROBERTS. SPEC. MFG. CO. $40-50.

A French wallmounted lever puller. A T-handle corkscrew is inserted into a bottle and then rests on two hooks with the bottle neck below the engaging collar. Pulling the lever down will extract the cork. $150-200.

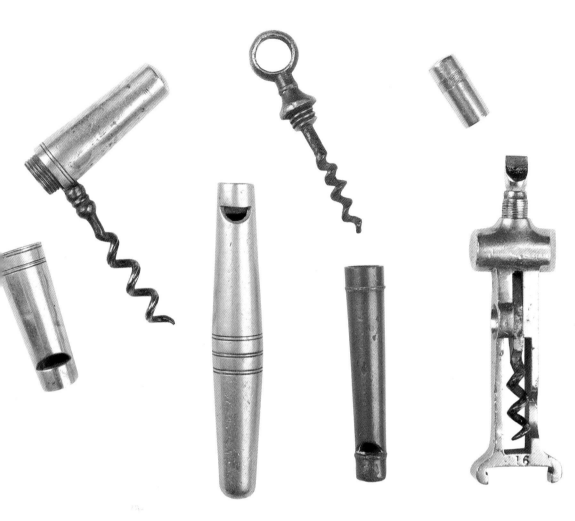

Whistles

When it is time to call friends to the wine cellar to open a bottle of wine, why not use a corkscrew with built-in whistle? A number of corkscrews have been produced to fulfill this need.

Use the roundlet to whistle, then unscrew the two parts, pull out the worm, turn the worm perpendicular to the barrel, screw the parts back together, and open the wine. $300-350. The picnic style corkscrew has a pewter sheath with whistle. When the sheath is removed from the top, it is inserted into the top ring as the handle. $250-300.

The early whistle corkscrew at *right* has several functions. The worm folds into the center chamber with the shank acting to as a cigar cutter. The top cover comes off to expose a screwdriver blade. The bottom part is used to remove shotgun shells. The grips are tapered so one side is used for 12 gauge and the other side for 16 gauge. The numbers 12 and 16 are stamped on either side. $750-1000.

The polished goat horn handle corkscrew has a whistle on the small end. Two brass pins hold the worm shank in place. The leather strap is for hanging. $100-125.

The small French horn handle is marked DEPOSE on the worm shank. $100-150.

The plate on the modern whistle with cap lifter reads "If you want me whistle." The whistle part is the sheath for the worm. $20-25.

Williamson's Opens Everything

T he activities of the Williamson Company of Newark, New Jersey, are best viewed through their own comments in an 1883 catalog: "We beg to call the attention of our patrons, and all who are interested in the progress of American Manufactures, to the flattering reception our goods have met with during the past few years in this country and in Europe. Notwithstanding the established reputation of English, French and German productions of Iron and Steel Goods, we are pleased to announce that the introduction of our Wire products into all these countries has been attended with unusual success. The Universal Exposition, Paris, 1878, gave them a high Award, and the press throughout Europe unhesitatingly and emphatically accorded us credit for showing them how to make the *best* and *cheapest* Cork Screws in the world, which in the *'Land of Bottles and Corks'* - as expressed by one journal - 'must be considered a boon of no small magnitude.'" They must have done something right because they stayed in business for 106 years, from 1876 to 1982.

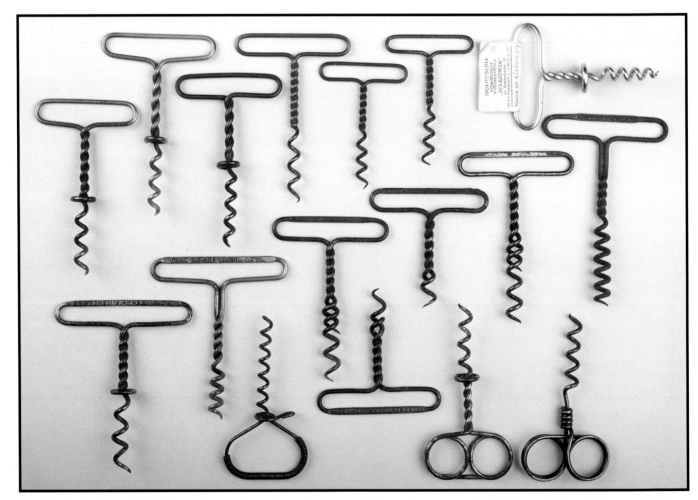

William Rockwell Clough's 1876 patent for a corkscrew formed from one or two pieces of wire was manufactured by the Williamson Company. The corkscrews were promoted extensively in their catalogs of the 1880s and their advertisements in publications for brewers. Even the Anheuser-Busch Brewing Association had its own advertising targeting distributors for an "Anheuser-Busch" marked example.
Top row left to right: Three sizes of Williamson Catalog # 19 (tinned) and #19 1/2 (nickel) "Power Cork Screw." $15-20; Two unmarked sizes of Catalog # 15 and # 16 "Double and Twisted Shank" corkscrews. $10-15; A small # 15 marked CLOUGH'S PATENT on the handle. $30-40;

An Eastern European version of Williamson's Power Corkscrew. $25-30. Various advertising wire corkscrews *in diagonal row of six left to right:* "A.B.C. Bohemian, St. Louis, U. S. A." $30-40; "Drink the Gray Mineral Water." $25-35; "Strohs Export Beer Detroit U. S. A." $30-40; "Anheuser-Busch." $40-50; "Wm. J. Lemp St. Louis Mo." $25-35; "Anheuser-Busch." $20-30.
Bottom row left to right: A wire type with button finishing in a hanger hook. Wire is wrapped on handle. Origin unknown. $75-100; Advertising "Toledo Brewing & Malting Co." $50-60; Two finger "eyeglass." $100-125; Two finger loop "eyeglass" with wire button. $125-150.

The Williamson "Power Cork Screw" directions for use state "Enter the Screw *carefully* and turn till the button reaches the cork, then *continue to turn, pulling slightly,* and the hardest cork is extracted with greater ease than with the most expensive." The version with two points, short and long, is also referred to as a "Power Cork Screw" and its use is "When the second or short screw enters the cork, the pressure on the cork becomes so great as to turn it in the bottle. By continuing to turn the screw and pulling slightly, the cork will be easily extracted as by the most expensive Power Screw."

In 1897, Williamson was granted a patent for a bell cap corkscrew with a plain washer or flat stamped steel wire breaker above the bell. The sleeve between the washer and the handle is stamped WILLIAMSON'S. Although the barrel shaped handle is the most often found, this is the handle shown in the patent drawing. $25-35.

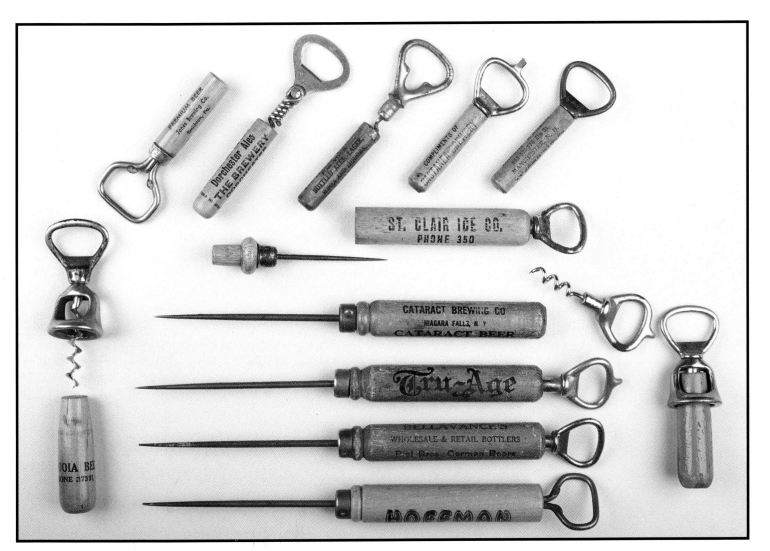

Top row left to right: Williamson's "Flash" corkscrew and bottle opener per their 1946 catalog. Found in colors and with and without advertising. $5-20; For comparison, an English sheath type advertising "Eldridge Pope & Co. Ltd. Dorchester Ales." The cap lifter is flat with wire wrapped worm. $20-30; Unusual cap lifter head on corkscrew (not Williamson) advertising "When dry, go to Burke Bros. for your bottled ales, lager, wines and liquors." $20-30; The "Pal" corkscrew and cap lifter with cast in wire breaker advertising "Castanea Brewery, Lock Haven, Pa." $25-30; Another with advertising. $5-20.

Lower left and right: Described in the 1946 Williamson catalog as "Power Corkscrew, Self pulling corkscrew with cap remover. Nickel plated. Red, green, or clear lacquered wood tube. Overall length 4 1/4." $20-30 without advertising, $30-50 with advertising. *Bottom center from top to bottom:* A rare combination corkscrew, cap lifter, and ice pick in which the ice pick reverses to fit in the handle. $75-100; Various ice-pick, corkscrew, cap lifter combinations with advertising. $30-50.

The wood sheath "Pal" cork-screws have decorative cast souvenir plates attached - "Marriage Place of Ramona, San Diego, Cal.," and "St. Paul's Church, Norfolk, Va." $30-35. At *top center* are four metal sheath "Pals" with various advertisements. $40-60. The rest are German and English versions for comparison. $15-25.

A printing plate reading "Don't Swear. To the DEALERS - To make counter display, tuck the flap behind merchandise and increase your sales."

The corkscrew on the *left* has Williamson's "Flash" design. Plastic case reads "Casali Brothers" and is marked PULL OUT FOR CORK PULLER (with arrow pointing to cap lifter). $20-25. The others in varied colors are Williamson's "Don't Swear" corkscrew and bottle opener. The sheath is made of Catalin, a plastic composition material. The large chocolate and caramel color sheaths have a pin through them to secure the corkscrew. The worm needs to be turned in and out rather than pulled or pushed. $25-50.

Wood

One of the first corkscrews a new collector finds is a wood handle T-type. To open a bottle of wine, the worm is turned into the cork and is pulled out by grasping the handle and using a little effort. Sometimes brute force needs to be used to extract a very tight cork. The collector soon learns that more interesting handles and more interesting shanks and makers' marks are more desirable. He can also expect them to be more expensive! However, a close examination of what appears to be a common corkscrew purchased at a low price may turn out to be a fabulous find. A close look at the corkscrews shown here reveals some surprises!

A comment about brushes: Many of the wood handles have a hole in the end into which a brush was glued. The brush is used for cleaning off the top of the bottle before removing the cork. It is quite difficult to tell if a corkscrew has the original brush. More often than not, they have been replaced. That seems to be quite an acceptable practice. A collector who finds corkscrews with missing brushes should consider purchasing a suitably colored clothes dusting brush for replacing the brushes. The bristles are stiff enough and are the same as the brushes originally fitted. Early ladies' and infants' hair brushes often work as well.

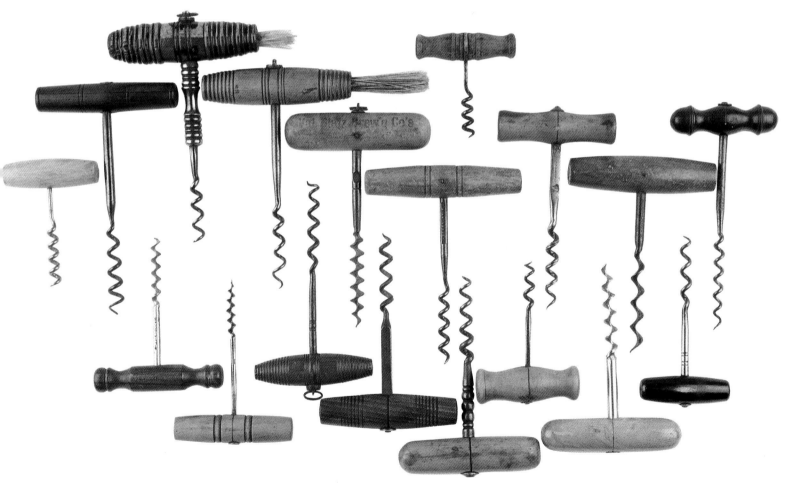

Simple wooden T-handles. *Top row left to right:* 3 1/8" pine handle. $5-10; Walnut handle with long shank/worm. $10-20; Wood handle with brush, decoratively turned shank. $20-40; Wine barrel design with brush. $20-30; Hot dog handle with advertising (Val Blatz Brewing Co.). $40-60; Small wire wrap. $3-5; Cigar shape marked WILLIAMSON vertically on shank. $20-30; Bow shape marked A. KNOX & CO. LONDON on shank. $40-50; Wood with speed worm marked WILLIAMSON vertically on shank $30-40; Narrow bulbous handle with long shank and fine worm. $30-50.

Bottom row left to right: Two finger marked WILLIAMSON on shank. $10-20; Delicate boxwood. $15-20; 3" Cigar shape with hanging ring. $20-30; Wine barrel design with square shank marked BERKELEY & CO. LTD 1941. This is a rare instance of the manufacturing year included on a corkscrew. $75-100; Hot dog handle with turned shank. $30-40; 2 5/8" bow shape handle with flat shank marked J****SH MITCHELL ST. SHEFFIELD. $40-60; Hot dog with simple chromed worm. $4-7; 2 1/4" wide handle, simple. $5-10.

More simple wooden T-handles. *Top row left to right:* Small bulbous with twisted shank. $30-40; Large (6 3/4") with simple pinned worm marked MADE IN FRANCE. $15-25; Dark hot dog handle marked J & W HARDIE, EDINBURG, THE ANTIQUARY CORKSCREW, square shank. $75-100; Log handle marked EDENBOROUGH'S CORKS, square shank, pointed worm. $75-100; Large French handle marked VINOTHEQUE BORDEAUX, flat shank. $35-50; Wine barrel handle marked on four sides of the shank A. SORBY, SHEFFIELD, 1904, PORTER & AYNSLEY, Lᴰᵈ (Another rare date mark), fluted worm. $125-150. *Bottom row left to right:* Rosewood handle, with brush, fine shank. $40-60; Red varnished handle with simple pinned worm marked MADE IN FRANCE. $10-15; Finely turned spindle handle. $40-50; Tapered handle, flat shank, fine wire worm. $20-30; Tapered handle, flat shank, speed worm. $30-40; Tapered handle, pointed worm. $20-25.

More simple wooden T-handles. *Top row left to right:* Bowtie marked J. GAMBLE on square shank, fluted worm. $50-60; Bow marked B. W. S. GERMANY on square shank. $45-55; Two unmarked barrels with brushes, square shank. $25-35; Concentric groove handle with brush. $40-50; Handle marked KHAWRI 1943, unusually long twisted steel worm. $60-75. *Bottom row left to right:* Ebony handle with fine fluted worm. $40-50; Two finger handle with large turned ends. $25-35; Small boxwood handle, flat shank. $30-40; Small handle with securing washers both top and bottom. $50-60; 3" handle with small securing washer at top. $20-30; Simple unmarked with reddish varnish. $10-15.

Manufacturers of T-handles often went the extra mile by adding elegance and grace to their handles and worms. By shaping the handles for comfort, a direct pull of a stubborn cork becomes a little less agonizing. Surprisingly, few of them put their names on them. *Top row left to right:* 4 3/4" handle with brush, shaped for a large grip. $60-70; Two with tapered ends, shanks penetrate handle with ring at top but they are pinned instead of affixed with washer. $50-60; Cherry handle, diamond pattern shank. $40-50; Marked WINGFIELD on the shank and with only the numeral 2 on the handle. $75-100. *Bottom row left to right:* Walnut handle, long (7") shank and worm. Shank is threaded at top and secured with hexagonal nut. In addition, shank is pinned. $75-90; Finely turned handle with matching turnings on shank. $100-125; Barrel handle with brush, square shank. $50-60; Wood with brush and bulbous plated shank. $30-50; Two sideways "pots" handle with speed worm. $40-50.

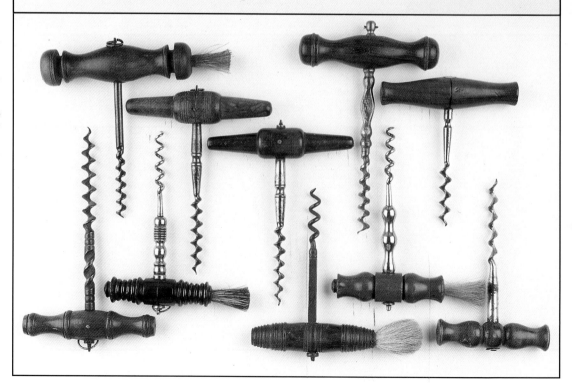

In 1795, the Reverend Samuel Henshall of Birmingham, England, was granted the first English patent for a corkscrew. By adding a button above the worm on a T-handle corkscrew, he revolutionized cork extraction. Instead of tugging and tugging at a tight cork, the user turns the worm into the cork until the "button" engages the top of the cork. By continuing to turn the handle, the seal between the cork and the bottle gives way and the cork can be easily lifted out of the bottle neck. Together with corkscrew manufacturer Matthew Boulton, he produced a corkscrew incorporating a concave button "by which construction the screw has much more power over the cork." Henshall buttons were marked on the top OBSTANDO PROMOVES, SOHO PATENT (by standing firm, one advances). Original marked "Henshall" value ranges from $1000-2500 with condition being a very important factor.

Top: The Henshall idea was further refined by a number of manufacturers by adding serration on the bottom of the button for better gripping power. The shanks are usually very fancy turnings. They are seldom marked; but when they are, it is nicely done on top of the button. *Top row left to right:* Unmarked with long worm (3 1/2"), steel shank. $75-100; Brass button marked J. RODGERS & SONS SHEFFIELD. $150-200; Caterpillar handle with steel shank and worm. $75-125; Two finger handle with bulbs, flat unmarked button. $75-100; Plated shank and worm. $75-100; Ebony handle, steel shank. $100-125; High quality handle with fine filed shank ending with plain button and worm. $125-150.
Bottom row left to right: Seven varied handles with brass shank and button. Only the *second from the right* is marked - J. RODGERS & SONS, SHEFFIELD. $100-200.

Bottom: Another innovation was the addition of gripping teeth just above the worm. *Top row left to right:* Steel shank, cut worm. $100-125; Extended handle to accommodate brush holder, brass shaft and teeth, fluted worm. $125-175; Two varied. $75-100; Marked ROBT JONES on collar above teeth. $150-200.
Bottom row left to right: Four bulbous shanks end in gripping teeth and cut worm. *First one* has extended handled. $100-175; Another marked ROBT JONES on collar above teeth. $150-200.

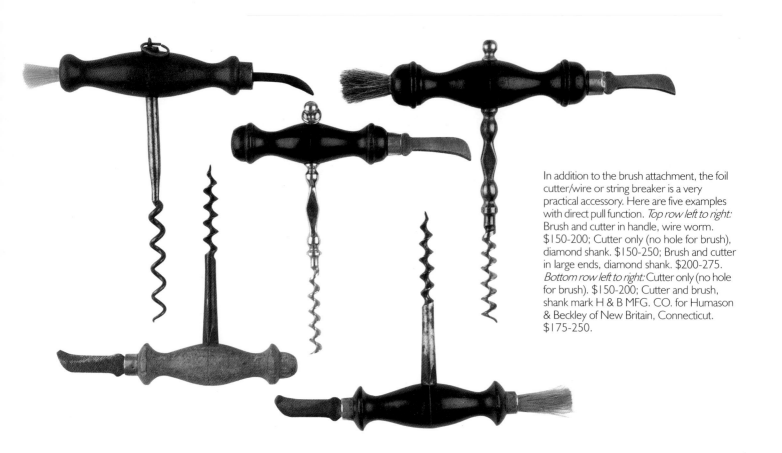

In addition to the brush attachment, the foil cutter/wire or string breaker is a very practical accessory. Here are five examples with direct pull function. *Top row left to right:* Brush and cutter in handle, wire worm. $150-200; Cutter only (no hole for brush), diamond shank. $150-250; Brush and cutter in large ends, diamond shank. $200-275. *Bottom row left to right:* Cutter only (no hole for brush). $150-200; Cutter and brush, shank mark H & B MFG. CO. for Humason & Beckley of New Britain, Connecticut. $175-250.

In 1876, Edwin Wolverson registered his corkscrew in England for a design that added a hole in the shank for the middle finger when grasping the corkscrew. Here are seven examples of Wolverson's design. The *second from top left* is marked R. JONES. The two on the *top right* are marked HOLBORN SIGNET with the last one having an English 1877 registration mark. At *bottom right* is an unusual example with speed worm. $150-300. See the "Champagne Taps & Tools" category for more of this Wolverson design.

This truly generic postcard has an inviting 1912 message to William: "Be sure & be over Sat. The hills are swell, the chicken is tender & strawberry wine is good. There are millions of daisies looking on but they won't tell. Love, Bootsie."

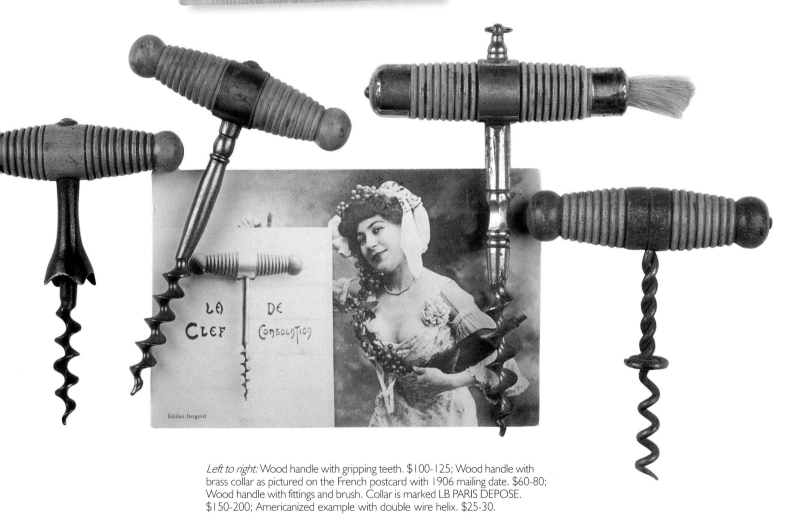

Left to right: Wood handle with gripping teeth. $100-125; Wood handle with brass collar as pictured on the French postcard with 1906 mailing date. $60-80; Wood handle with fittings and brush. Collar is marked LB PARIS DEPOSE. $150-200; Americanized example with double wire helix. $25-30.

Read's Coaxer. Marked
READ'S COAXER 4
PARLIAMENT ST. Wood
handle mounted on brass.
Ivory plaque with crest
inlaid in handle. Thomas
Read was a cutler in
Dublin in the 18th
century. c.1790. *$Rare.*

Three finger pull 1878
English design registration
by Edwin Wolverson of
Birmingham. $75-100.

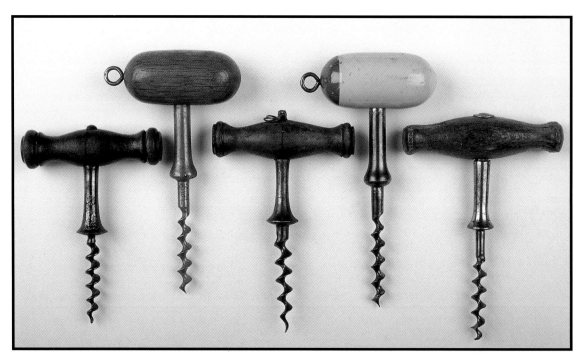

Above: Classic Swedish designs from Eskilstuna. $20-30.

Right: A cheap corkscrew with copper plated wire worm
around wood handle on card reading "Pull-Ezee Corkscrew,
A Gene Fenton Design, E. S. Klauber and Co., Los Angeles,
California, U. S. A." It sure makes you wonder what else
Gene Fenton designed, doesn't it?

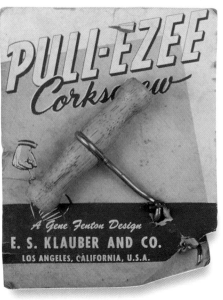

Wood & Other Double Action

These double action corkscrews have been produced for many years and are still being produced today. Plain versions can be found in housewares sections of department stores and marked varieties in souvenir shops. With the exception of the "Club," many collectors shun them. A well rounded collection should, however, have a sampling of some of the better examples. Today's examples are often called the "Bistro."

Top row left to right: Wood marked COPEX MADE IN FRANCE in original box. $30-40; Imprinted "La Maison Jacquin En France." $10-15; Black plastic imprinted "1977 The Queen's Silver Jubilee." Jubilee collectors might give the corkscrew collector some stiff competition for this one. $20-100; An unusual figural design. $10-20. *Bottom:* Barrel and wings carved from horn. Threaded shaft is plastic molded to look like wood. $30-50.

The Copex was imported and distributed in the United States by the Copex Corkscrew Company of Algonquin, Illinois. On the instruction sheet they claim that in 1946 "the Wine Institute on behalf of the Wine Advisory Board proved the Copex superior in every respect. In competition with eighteen other corkscrews of domestic and foreign manufacture, the Copex outperformed all others, receiving the highest recommendation."

Instructions were easy: "Simply place the Copex over any bottle. Grip corkscrew and bottle with one hand...a Copex automatically centers over the cork. Screw top handle in usual manner until worm penetrates through cork. Then give the large handle a few turns in the same direction and 'presto' the cork slips out intact. So unbelievably simple to operate, a child can free cork without exerting undue pressure. Moreover, the Copex does not weaken the cork, does not affect its texture. Leaves no cork dust. The rounded wire helix (worm) bores in clean and holds with a tenacious grip as cork is 'pulled without pulling'."

Now who wouldn't want one?

Top row left to right: 19th century made of olive wood. Marked THE CLUB MADE IN FRANCE. Quality construction with smooth action unlike modern versions. $100-200; Unmarked early model with large wings and barrel. Diameter of collar on barrel is 1 3/4". $40-60; Stenciling of grape leaves, grapes, and Chianti bottle. $15-30.
Bottom row left to right: Marked CAM MADE IN FRANCE. $10-20; Fancy barrel. $15-25; Unmarked. $5-10.

Just a few more...

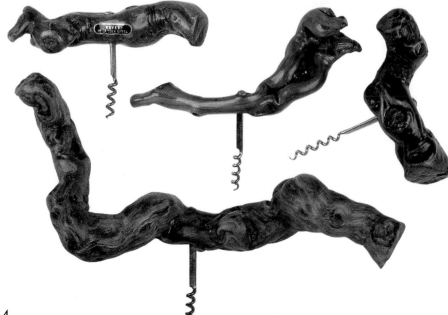

Driftwood. Old unusual carving. Burlwood. Those are three of the wrong descriptions for the handles on these corkscrews, which I have seen on price tags at antique shows. What are they? Brother Timothy of Christian Brothers described them best as "Grape Vine Heaven, Grape vines that have died and gone to Heaven, where there are corkscrews and a glass of wine. All are from the 20th century." And each is unique! They come in innumerable twists and turns. And they are still being produced today. Every collection deserves a few examples. You will find them in many sizes even as large as the one shown here with a 16" handle. $10-30.

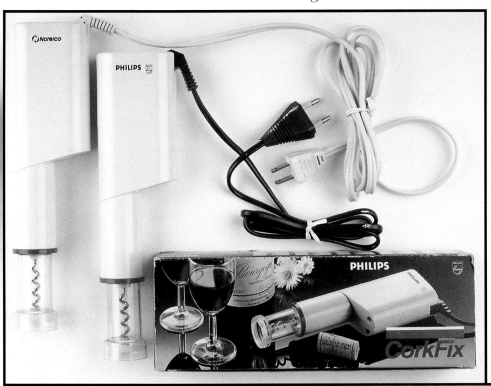

When checking in at American Airlines in Paris for a flight, the attendant asked my wife and I if we had any electrical appliances in our luggage. My wife replied that she had a hair dryer. I replied to an incredulous attendant that I had an electric corkscrew. Disbelieving she said "Sure you do!" and hastily gave us our boarding passes without further comment.

Above: Electric corkscrews called "CorkFix" marked NORELCO (110V) and PHILIPS (220V). Both are marked MADE IN AUSTRIA. The CorkFix was patented in Austria in 1984. A review in a 1986 issue of the *New York Daily News* quoted the retail price as $37.95. A notation in the operating instructions suggests that "bottles which are under pressure (champagne, sparkling wine, etc.) should always be opened carefully by hand. This will prevent the wine spurting from the bottle." $50-70.
A similar rechargeable battery operated version called the "Meyer Wine Key" also exists.

Right: *Left to right:* Unmarked brass barrel with cap lifter handle. $20-30; Chromed barrel with handle marked ITALY. $30-40; A superb perpetual (criss cross grooves for continuous rotation) type corkscrew marked DICO, WAKEFIELD, MASS., PAT. PEND. (DICO = Diamond Instrument Company). $350-500; Barrel marked NEUE HERKULES MIT KORK AUSTOSSER, D.R.G.M. GERMANY. 1932 German design registration by Georg Usbeck. After the cork is extracted, the barrel is "unlocked" to slide it out of the way to remove the cork. $100-125; Unmarked brass barrel. $20-30.

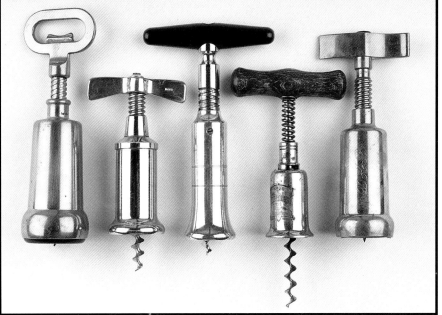

Left to right: The "Pet" two finger self puller. $75-100; German bell with mustache handle. 1892 German design registration by Eduard Müller. $150-200; William Plant's 1905 English "Magic" patent. $75-100.

A direct pull corkscrew with a handle made up of brass and celluloid rings, brass end caps, and wood cylinders. $80-100.

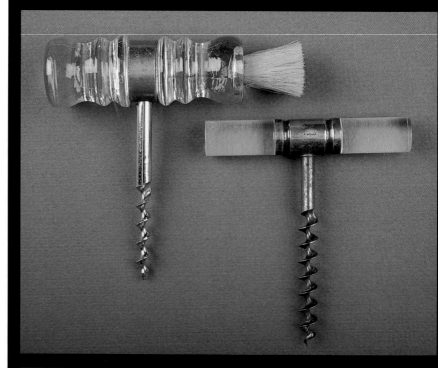

Left: Glass handle corkscrew with brush from Lindshammar Glass Factory, Sweden. c.1960. $60-70.
Right: Lucite and Sterling handle. $80-100.

An assortment of modern agate handle corkscrews. The boxed example is from Brazil. A wide variety of colors is available to spice up a collection. $10-20.

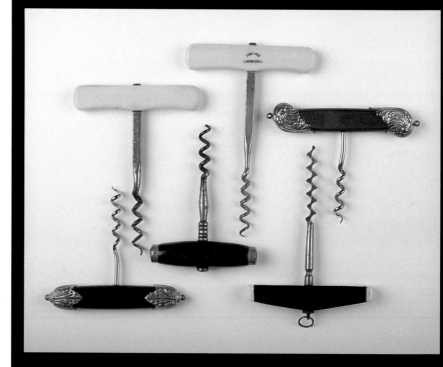

Top row left to right: Celluloid with advertising on shank "Fletcher Humphreys & Co. L™, Wine Merchants, Christchurch" (New Zealand). $40-60; Celluloid with advertising on handle "Puritan Leather Shoes." $40-60; Red celluloid handle with fancy mounts. $10-12.
Bottom row left to right: Green celluloid handle with fancy mounts. $10-12; Horn handle with brass mounts holding agate rounds. $30-40; Horn handle with ivory mounts. $40-50.

Left: Two multi-purpose tools marked COLUM-BUS and GES. GESCH. This German tool is a can opener, cap lifter, champagne cork remover, nut cracker, and corkscrew. Produced with smooth and stippled handles. $40-50.
Right: Two combination cap lifter, can opener, and corkscrew tools with the trademark of Müller & Schmidt, Solingen, Germany. The *left* version has covers with intricate raised copper design. $40-50. The other has an etched intricate design on the handles. $30-40.
Bottom: Combination cap lifter, can opener, and corkscrew marked A S ITALY. Mountain scene on handles. $25-30.

Left: Two finger silver plated pull with the number "21." Marked REG Nº 865704 (1951) and P.H.V. & CO., MADE IN ENGLAND. $75-100.
Right: A chrome plated key with the number "21" and the same marks. $60-80.

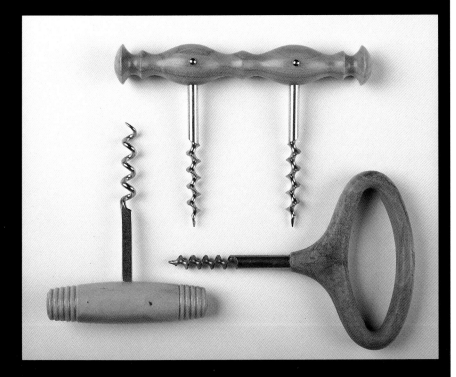

Look closely and you will see that this unusual corkscrew has worms for both left-handers and right-handers! Klaus Pumpenmeier had this corkscrew produced by corkscrew maker Norbert Holland-Cunz of Steinbach-Hallenberg, Germany. The handle is from cherry wood and was turned by August Huhn in South Thuringia. Production was limited to 22 corkscrews. The other two left-handed corkscrews have maple and composition handles. $10-15.

Part II

Figural Corkscrews

Anchors

It's a natural. Turn an anchor upside down and it is the perfect corkscrew handle! Anchor corkscrews are most frequently found in brass with a friction fit sheath with a cap lifter on one end. In the best "T-handle" design, the anchor base pulls out with worm attached. The sheath then serves as the handle for a cap lifter. The less desirable types have a worm attached to the cap lifter, which is exposed when the cap lifter is pulled from the sheath.

Above: All of these anchors have a cap lifter and a friction fit sheath. In the *three top left* corkscrews, the manufacturers attached the worm to the cap lifter using the anchor only as a sheath. The *third* has a souvenir plate from Kennebunkport, Maine. $20-30. The next five in this photo use the cap lifter handle as the sheath for the worm taking advantage of the anchor base for the handle. $20-50. *Bottom left* is marked H.M.S. VICTORY. $20-30. The silver plated anchor is marked UK. PAT and has the initials M H engraved. $50-60.

Right: *Top left:* Anchor lashed to a piling, which is the sheath for the worm. It has a "Cape Cod" souvenir plate. $20-30. *Top right:* Anchor with can opener added to the base. $15-25. *Bottom left:* Anchor with bayonet fit sheath. Supplied in plastic case marked (in Russian) "Souvenir Anchor Opener, October 25, 1981, Cost 2 Rubles." It is from the city of Voronezh, the "cradle of the Russian fleet." Voronezh is a city of over 650,000 located on the Don River halfway between Volgograd and Moscow. $35-40. *Bottom right:* Another Russian anchor supplied in fitted plastic case marked Souvenir Anchor Berdyansk, 1991. Berdyansk is a Russian city of over 100,000 on the Black Sea. $35-40.

Anri

ANRI figures have been produced in Northern Italy since 1912. The name comes from the founder *An*tonio *Ri*ffeser. Carvings produced by ANRI include corkscrews, bottle openers, bottle stoppers, humidors, salad sets, barsets, figurines, napkin rings, nut-crackers, cigarette boxes, calendars, pipe holders, pourers, place card holders, bookmarks, letter openers, thermometers, and toothpick holders. In the hunt for ANRI corkscrews, the collector will find some pretty stiff competition from the ANRI collector.

Carvings include human and animal figures. All of the carvings are done by hand by the village people of Val Gardena, S. Cristina. The earliest human figures were caricatures of the villagers themselves.

When the collector spots a wood carved figure at a flea market or antique show, it never hurts to see if the head lifts off. The reward could be a corkscrew or a bottle cap lifter. The disappointment for the cork-screw collector will be in finding that it is only a wood carving. Corkscrews have been found in single figures, double, and triple figures on stands and benches. Bar scenes have up to six figures.

Many heads of humans and animals were sold without bodies. Examples can be found under the "People" and "Dogs" categories in this book.

Many of the heads are interchangeable on bodies, which significantly increases the number of collectible pieces. Although each hand carving is different, it is not unusual to find similar faces/heads on bodies with varying dress.

What better place to start the examination of ANRI figures than the monk in the wine cellar? This one is quite different in that the head does not lift off the monk. The worm and a bottle stopper are attached to the barrels resting on barrels. $125-150.

The monks in the cellar are one of many scenes created by ANRI with multiple figures serving as corkscrews, cap lifters, and bottle stoppers. A set of monks in a wine cellar is valued at $100-150. Bar scenes have been found with figures from three to six. Some include a dancing figure with music box. $125-350.
The choir of monks on the *left* includes corkscrew and cap lifter heads. The five in the *background* are ANRI. $30-60. The choir boy in the front is not ANRI. His head is a corkscrew and in the base is a cap lifter. Marked MADE IN FRANCE. $150-200.

The colorful monks resting on barrels have corkscrew heads. The bottles behind them are cap lifters and the mugs are cork stoppers. $40-60. The sailors with corkscrew heads on barrels are much harder to find. They have the cap lifter behind them but not the stopper. One is playing a concertina. $70-100. They are joined by a standing sailor corkscrew. $50-60. The people in barrels in the *foreground* were produced with corkscrews and cap lifters. $30-40.

A wide variety of village caricatures with corkscrews or cap lifters. $30-50. The fat man on the *right* is not ANRI. He comes from Japan and separates apart in the middle to reveal a storage area for the metal cups. $60-80.

The double standing figures attached to a base (*back left*) are a corkscrew and cap lifter. One is usually grasping the arm of the other to either hold himself up or assist his partner. $50-75. Other double figures are musicians like the pair in the *middle rear*. $75-100. The musical trio includes a cork stopper. $80-110. In the *foreground* is a very unusual double set with an ashtray. $100-150.

Some of the ANRI figures got drunk and can be found leaning on lamp posts. The head is a cap lifter and the lamp is the corkscrew. Some have a suitcase behind them, which is a wind-up music box. When the head is lifted off, the music plays. Music box drunk: $100-125. Without music box. $50-75.

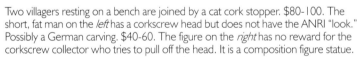

Two villagers resting on a bench are joined by a cat cork stopper. $80-100. The short, fat man on the *left* has a corkscrew head but does not have the ANRI "look." Possibly a German carving. $40-60. The figure on the *right* has no reward for the corkscrew collector who tries to pull off the head. It is a composition figure statue.

Coaster holders. Alas, when you lift the head, you find a cap lifter and not a corkscrew! A nice go-with for the ANRI corkscrew collection. $100-125 with original coasters. $75-90 without coasters.

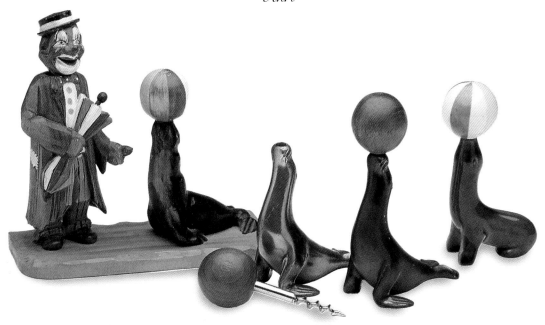

Can a seal be trained to juggle a corkscrew ball? The ANRI clown is training his to do this. The carved wood pair are mounted on a wood stand. Instead of a cap lifter, the clown has a can piercer under his head. $100-150.

The other seals are not ANRI. The two seals in the *middle* with wood ball are copper and pot metal. $75-100. The seal in the back is by Wade Pottery. $150-200.

The bartender figures *right and left* carry three foaming mugs filled with cork stoppers. These are much larger than the previous figures and have corkscrew heads. The figure on the *left* has a cap lifter towel tucked under his arm. $100-150. The gentlemen in the *middle* has a music box behind him, which plays when the corkscrew head is lifted off. $150-200.

A reunion of village carvers.

Bottles

One would certainly expect to see a corkscrew in the shape of a bottle. Many varieties have been produced and many have been used extensively for advertising purposes. Over 80 different advertising plates have been cataloged on the mini bottle roundlets alone (see "Roundlets" category).

Top left to right: A bottle marked M C L on the base. The worm is stored inside the bottle and when used, is fitted into a slot in the base with the top securing it in place. $60-75; A waiter's friend in the shape of a bottle picturing a Cointreau Liqueur label. The neckstand is marked MADE IN FRANCE, A & S. $75-100; A bottle showing a Suze Gentiane label. $50-75; The Clicquot Club bottle in finely enameled and brass versions. The worm folds into the back of the bottle and the cap lifter drops down from the bottom. $200-300.

The cast bottle on the *lower left* has a cast in label with crown and "Renat." Renat is a Swedish acquavit liqueur. The bottom is marked W & D, SV TENN. It was made by Widerholm & Dahlberg of Eskilstuna, Sweden, in the 1930s. $70-80. The wooden stubby bottle on the *right* has a pin going through the bottom of the bottle to secure the handle. $25-35.

The twin chrome and brass bottles are embossed "Korkenzieher, Kurketrekker, Tire-Bouchon, Corkscrew, Cavatappi." and decorated with vines and grapes plus a lion shield. The shank below the handle is marked MADE IN W-GERMANY, FABRIQUE EN R.F.A. and BMF N in a triangle. The cork self extracts into the barrel, which has stepped gripping teeth inside. To remove the cork, turn the handle counterclockwise. $25-35. The brass champagne bottle corkscrew has a cap lifter handle. Turn the handle clockwise to penetrate the cork and reverse to extract into the barrel. $40-50. The French champagne bottle on the *right* is marked MOD. DEP. in the hollow back. It has a folding worm, an over-the-top style cap lifter and a champagne cork puller on the backside. $75-100.

Left to right: Wood 4" bottle with Black and White Scotch Whisky label. $15-20; Copper colored pot metal corkscrew/opener set with Guinness Extra Stout label. $20-25; Wood with Guinness Extra Stout label. $15-20; Plastic bottle with "1985" neck label and bottle label reading "Qualitäts Korkenzieher mit messer." The knife is under the cap and the worm folds out from inside the bottle. $25-30; Wood bottle with Ballantine's Export Beer label. $30-40; Four "waiter's friend" plastic bottles (plus one in the *foreground*) in various colors.* All marked PAT. INT. 45751 ITALY (1986 Italian patent). $8-25.; Wood bottle with fixed worm and Bordeaux label. $5-10.

*The plastic waiter's bottle friend is an invention by Germano Farfalli. The well-engineered molding has a cavity in the back to fit each turn of the worm with a notch for lifting. The cap lifter/neckstand folds out from the bottom. The green example in the photo has an advertising label from the Danish beer Tuborg. The red has a label reading "Life's too short to drink cheap wine." The others are labeled "Vintage, Vinnie D'Corker, A DCM Industries Product."

Above: The "VAT 69" bottle is a T-handle corkscrew made in Japan. $10-15. The other two are part of current series of wine bottle refrigerator magnets. $3-6.

Left: *Collector beware.* The corkscrew in the bottle folds down for use. This bottle has been seen offered as an antique. It is currently sold in the United States at Pottery Barn stores for $10. The packaging says that it is "made in india for pottery barn" [*sic*]. A pig with folding worm is also available.

Brussel's Spout

A block away from the Grand Place in Brussels, Belgium, one can find the Mannekin Pis. It is a small statue of a little boy peeing. He's high up on his fountain pedestal and his smallness takes many visitors by surprise. A 1619 bronze statue replaced the original from 1388, which was lost. It was based on a model by Belgian sculptor François Duquesnoy. Not far from the little boy is a museum that displays the 500 plus costumes that have been presented to the city over the years for dressing the boy. He is known by the people of Brussels as their oldest citizen.

When I visited Brussels in 1985, I went to the intersection where the statue is located and kitty-corner from the statue was a souvenir shop. The display in the window was of hundreds of Mannekin Pis statuettes in all sizes and materials. The number with corkscrews was mind-boggling and, again, in all sizes.

During the past 25+ years I have been offered the Mannekin Pis corkscrew through the mail many times for prices ranging from $1 to "It is extremely rare and can you make an offer?" Descriptions given include "Naughty Boy;" "Corkscrew is his Private Part;" "I don't know how to tell you this but...;" "Made in Alaska many years ago;" "Rare - I've never seen this before;" and "Hard to find." Most I passed up for fear of getting stiffed.

Corkscrews with fixed worms. Some are marked BRUXELLES. Note that he is holding his worm with his left hand. Apparently Mannekin Pis is left-handed! $10-30.

A very early Mannekin Pis . His worm has a joint so it can be moved up and down. $75-100.

There are many imitations of the Mannekin Pis corkscrew, including these African looking variations. When the head is removed from the tall one in the back, a cap lifter is exposed. Although most of these also appear to be left-handed, some hold their worms with both hands. $10-30.

More imitations, including a fly fisherman. The figure in the *back at left* has a lighter under its head. $50-100.

A closer view of the figure with lighter.

The Mannekin Pis in Brussels pees all day long - every day. Here are some from Ron MacLean's collection. They just stand there!

Slide the barrel to the left to reveal his worm. $40.

The Flasher. $100.

Bulldogs

A bulldog is a short-haired dog of a breed with a large head. It has square, strong jaws and a stocky body. It is known to be a stubborn dog. Could one ask for better such qualities in a corkscrew?

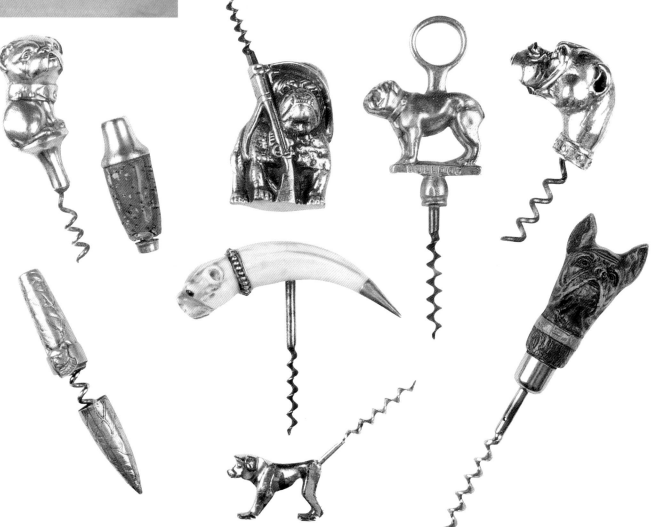

Above: The Sterling Bulldog at *top left* serves double duty as a corkscrew and cork stopper. It was made by R. Blackinton & Co., of Attleboro, Massachusetts, and sports their trademark. $250-300. Armed Bulldog is marked REGD NO 844318, which is an English Registered Design of 1945. $125-150. Brass two finger pull with hanging hole says BULLDOG on the platform the bulldog stands on. $30-50. The cast Bulldog on the *right* is unmarked. $30-50. Carved tusk Bulldog has a silver collar. $300-500. On the *lower left* is a cigar shaped Roundlet. The "cigar" holds the worm, which turns perpendicular to the case when opened. The case is screwed back together and serves as the handle. The "cigar band" around the center has a Bulldog on it. $400-600. Note that the Bulldog at *lower center* is the only Bulldog with the tail serving as the corkscrew. $30-50. The Bulldog at *lower right* was made in the 1940s by the Syracuse Ornamental Company (SYROCO) of Syracuse, New York. $30-50.

Right: A picnic type corkscrew with composition bulldog figure. The worm protecting sheath slides through a hole in the body to be used as a handle. Marked GERMANY. $100-125. A composition English bulldog head. $50-70.

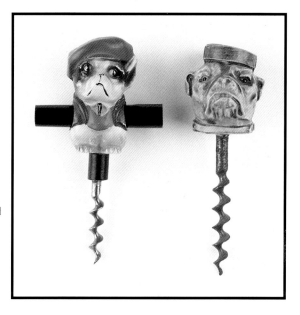

Bulls

Y ou didn't really expect to go through this book without being subjected to Bull corkscrews, did you? "Bull" is defined as an adult male bovine mammal, the uncastrated adult male of domestic cattle, and the male of certain mammals including moose and buffalo.

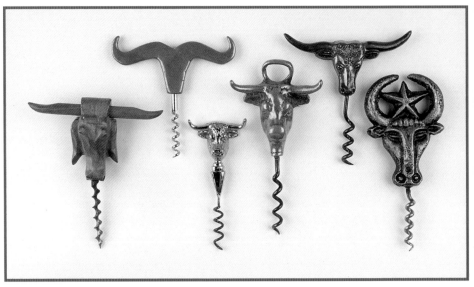

Left to right: Teak water buffalo bull head. $30-40; Stylized steer head. $40-50; Brass plated head. $30-40; Brass head with hanging ring. $40-60; Copper plated head. Face is on both sides. Part of a set including spoon and cap lifter. $60-80; Bull with star in horns. Cast aluminum. $20-30.

In front are two carved wood bulls with the horns formed into a cap lifter. $10-20. The charging bull between them has a Texas shield on it. Folding corkscrew tail. It is cheaply made pot metal. $10-20. The pot metal cows trying to look like bulls also have folding tails. One has a tag on the bottom marked DAYSUN FOREIGN. $2-6. The free standing bull head is a wood carving. $25-35. The head with stand in the *background* was offered as the "Steer Cork Pull" in a 1995 catalog from Geerlings & Wade of Massachusetts for $38.

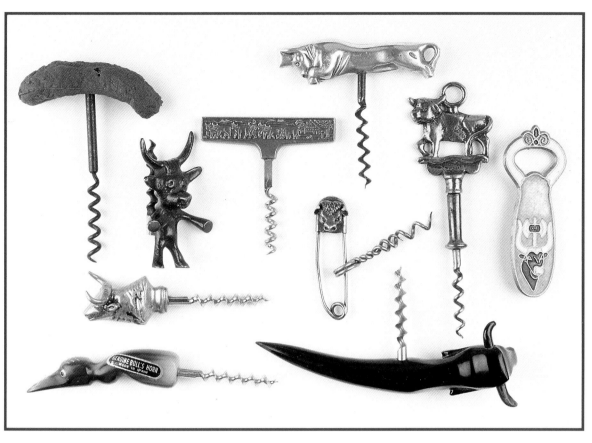

Top row left to right: Very soft spongy dark brown handle presented to Don Bull by corkscrew collector Don Morway. Quite possibly a fake. Surprisingly, it has no odor. $—; Bull with folding tail. $15-25; Pewter T-handle with scene of herder walking with five cows and a bull. Shank marked ST. GALLER PRÄGE. $20-30; Charging Bull aluminum T-handle from Peru. The same handle is found on a set of steak knives marked SPRINGFIELD, USA. It also comes with a Rhinoceros handle. $40-60; Brass two finger pull with hanging ring. $30-40;

Middle row left to right: Heavy brass bull head. $20-40; A pin with a bull head holding a wire corkscrew presented to Don Bull by corkscrew collector Paul Luchsinger. $—; An enameled cap lifter with folding worm on the back presented to Don Bull by corkscrew collector Herb Danziger. $—.

Bottom row left and right: Tag says "Genuine Bull's Horn, Made in Spain." Tag on other side says "Esuna Creacion, Euro Cado." $25-35; Part of a set including corkscrew and cap lifter. $50-75.

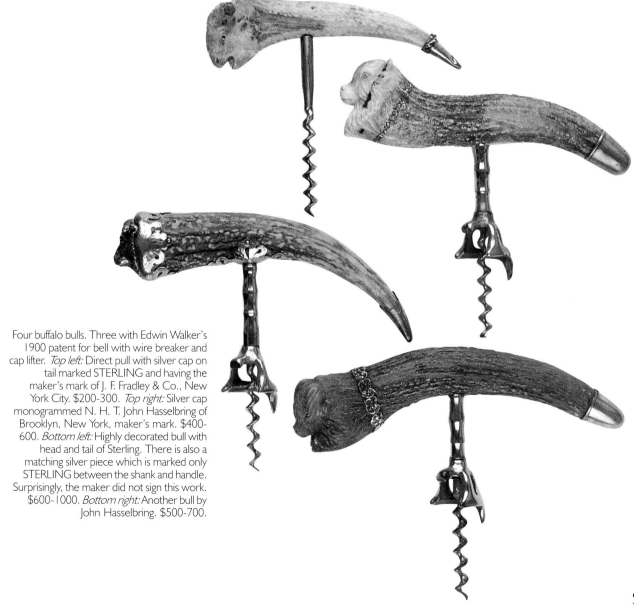

Four buffalo bulls. Three with Edwin Walker's 1900 patent for bell with wire breaker and cap lifter. *Top left:* Direct pull with silver cap on tail marked STERLING and having the maker's mark of J. F. Fradley & Co., New York City. $200-300. *Top right:* Silver cap monogrammed N. H. T. John Hasselbring of Brooklyn, New York, maker's mark. $400-600. *Bottom left:* Highly decorated bull with head and tail of Sterling. There is also a matching silver piece which is marked only STERLING between the shank and handle. Surprisingly, the maker did not sign this work. $600-1000. *Bottom right:* Another bull by John Hasselbring. $500-700.

Cats & Mice

Vite, papa est pressé

Cats were domesticated in early times to catch rats and mice. The few shown here have been equipped to extract a cork while several continue the mouse hunt.

Left to right: Copper finish cat with triangular opener base. $60-80; Cat on sheath stand. $75-100; Black cat with gold face. $50-60; Cast iron with copper finish. $60-70; Copper color with gold face. $50-60; Black cat marked MADE IN AUSTRIA with backward R/forward R trademark. $60-75; Open frame glass-eyed cat with locking handle marked MONOPOL WEST GERMANY. $75-100.

Cat with sheath stand. $75-100.

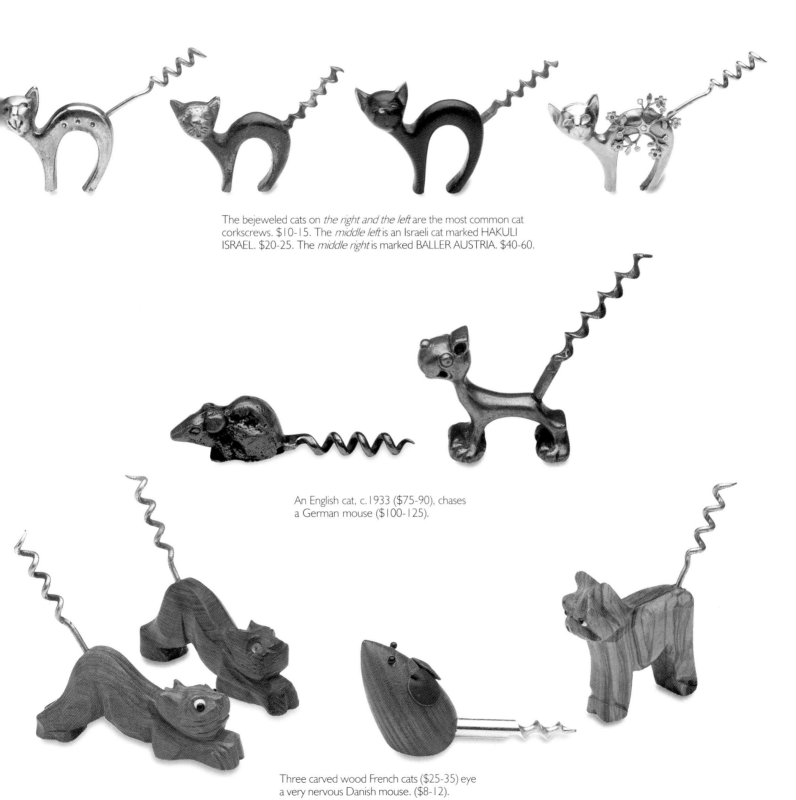

The bejeweled cats on *the right and the left* are the most common cat corkscrews. $10-15. The *middle left* is an Israeli cat marked HAKULI ISRAEL. $20-25. The *middle right* is marked BALLER AUSTRIA. $40-60.

An English cat, c.1933 ($75-90), chases a German mouse ($100-125).

Three carved wood French cats ($25-35) eye a very nervous Danish mouse. ($8-12).

Cellar Keys

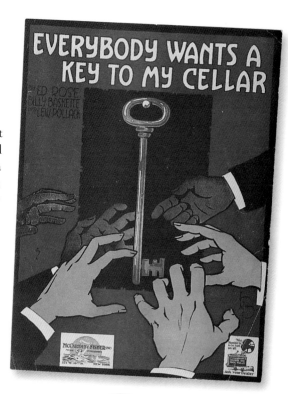

"Down in my cellar, I've been changing everything around. I've a secret hidden there. I'll guard it with my life. There's only one mistake I made. I told my wife. Now everybody wants a key to my cellar. People who wouldn't give me a tumble. Even perfect strangers are beginning to grumble 'cause I won't let them have a key to my cellar. They'll never get in just let them try. They can have my money. They can have my car. They can have my wife. If they want to go that far, but they can't have the key that opens my cellar, if the whole darn world goes dry." The 1919 Prohibition song was composed by Rose, Baskette, and Pollack. What was the secret hidden in the cellar? Why not a bunch of corkscrew cellar keys?

A 1946 advertisement from the Castle Key Corporation of New York City promotes their cellar key as "The Castle Key, the smart accessory for every home," claiming the "design inspired by an authentic castle key." The advertisement shows it lifting a bottle cap, pulling a cork, and cracking ice. Paul Wyler applied for a design patent on this key in 1946 (granted 1948).

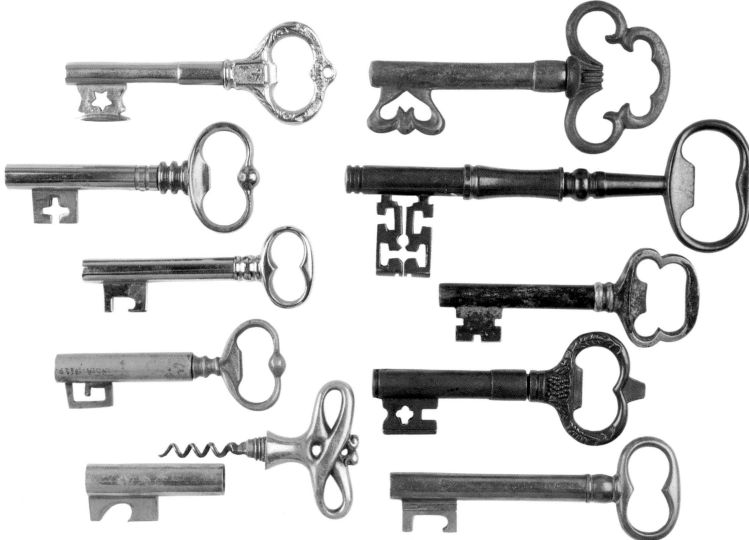

Elise Westberg was issued American patent No. 1,338,542 on April 27, 1920. Westberg, a Norwegian, was adding a cap lifter to a key. That cap lifter is present in most cellar key corkscrews.
Left side from top to bottom: A Russian bayonet fit corkscrew marked BERDYANSK, a Russian city on the Black Sea. $15; Marked MADE IN HOLLAND. $20-30; Unmarked. $10; Marked INDIA. $5-10; Marked ANBOIK. Austrian. $40-50.

Right side from top to bottom: Unmarked. $15-25; Unusual handle and bit. $40-50; Very well made corkscrew. Unusual because the corkscrew handle is much longer than on most keys. It goes into the sheath at the halfway point. $50-60; Marked W. GERMANY. $20-25; Grape and grapevine motif. $20-25; Unmarked. $15-25.

The most common key corkscrews are those with a verdigris finish and having a grape and grapevine motif. Many are marked IN VINO VERITAS and many have place name shields attached. The *second and third* keys are from Achern and Mannheim, Germany, and have the city coats of arms on them. $15-20. The key at *lower left* was found in a box marked ZZG CENTRALA PRZEMYSTOWO HANDLOWA "VERITAS" WARSZAWA. $50-75. The key at *center right* is a rare example of a key this size used for advertising purposes. This one reads on a triangular stamp "Rahr, Malt of Reputation, 1847." $80-100. The key at *lower right* has a very unusual handle design. $50-60.

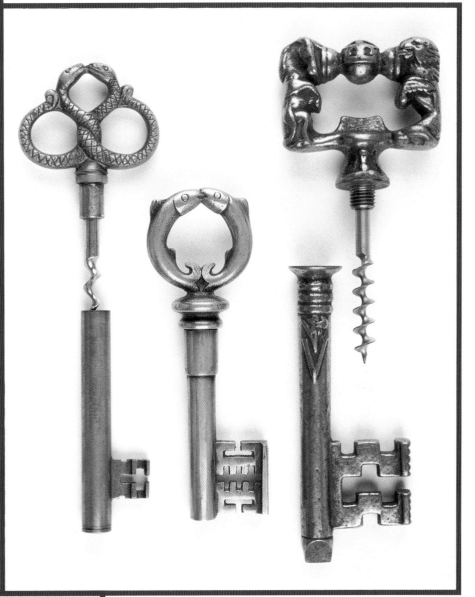

Above: The key at *left* does not have a cap lifter designed into the interwoven two snake handle. This unusual corkscrew is marked HANDARBEIT (hand made) on the corkscrew shank and GERMANY on the end of the barrel. $125-150. The key in the *center* has a nicely disguised cap lifter in a kissing fish design. This one is marked on the bottom of the bit RÖ-WI BILD GUSS. $100-125. At *right* is a very regal looking key with sitting lions. Note the screwdriver tip at the end of the sheath. $100-125.

Left: The silver keys in the *top row* are German. On top of the *first* are the four animals from the Brothers Grimm Fairytale *The Bremen Town Musicians*. When these musicians performed the donkey brayed, the hound barked, the cat mewed, and the cock crowed. $60-80. The *second* key has a spread wing eagle. $40-50. The *third* has two lions on a shield with a key on it. This is the "Bremer Schlüssel" (Bremen Key). Note that the key on the shield has the same key bit as this corkscrew and the previous two! Also, when the bit was welded to the shank, it was rotated 90 degrees. $60-70. The *fourth* has the same key in the shield but a different sheath (possibly the wrong sheath). $30-50.
The three silver keys at the *bottom* were all made by Napier (so marked) of Meriden, Connecticut. Note the difference in the bits on the two with split ring handle. The *bottom left* Napier key is less common than the other two. $50-75. The key at *top right* is only 3 7/8" long and has advertising on it: "Greetings Mankato Bottling Co., Bottlers of Key City Beverages, Hamm's Beer." The cap lifter handle is marked B & B, MADE IN U. S. A. B & B was Brown & Bigelow Company of St. Paul, Minnesota. $15-25.
A modern oddity is the all plastic (except the worm) Russian key shown at *bottom right*. $10-20.

HULLO! I SEE YOU'RE
BACK AGAIN.

Dogs

Which is man's best friend - a dog for companionship or a corkscrew for wine? Owning a few dogs with corkscrew tails will eliminate the need for a decision!

Various dog designs produced in England and Scandinavia. English dogs are sometimes marked with registration numbers from the 1930s and others are marked only ENGLAND (e.g. *fourth from left*). Many of the English dogs were produced by Pearson Page Jewsbury Co., Ltd. of Birmingham. Some of the Scandinavian pewter designs are marked SV. TENN. (Swedish pewter) including the *fourth from right*. Mixed breeds with corkscrew tails. $40-80.

Poodles.
Left to right: Brass with gray finish. 2" from base to top of head. $40-60; Brass with copper finish. $40-60; Two brass poodles from Israel. One has green patina. $30-40; Unmarked cast iron. $25-35; Pot metal poodle with a folding corkscrew leg and cap lifter halo. $50-60.

Dachshunds.
Foreground: Marked "Crosby Pup." Folding worm with backspring. 4 1/4" long. Tail and hind legs are a cap lifter. $500-700.
Middle row left to right: Dachshund from Israel. $30-40; Copper designed as a comfortable two finger pull. $50-60; Modern poor brass casting and worm. $10-15.
Back row left to right: Front legs marked BALLER AUSTRIA. $75-100; Black finish on brass. Marked MADE IN AUSTRIA with backward R/forward R trademark. There is also a cat with the same marks. $60-75; Unmarked brass example of the previous. $50-60.

A story is told in corkscrew circles that Bing Crosby had 60 of the "Crosby Pups" produced to give to his friends.

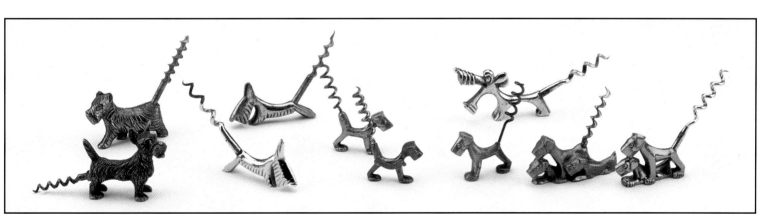

More dogs *from left to right:* Marked MADE IN ENGLAND on front right paw. $60-75; German made with folding tail. $250-300; Chromed. $25-30; Brass marked ENGLAND. $25-30; Common brass with wire worm. $10-20; Brass with "Ireland" souvenir plate. $20-30; Yelping chrome dog. $40-50; and the last three are: A brass terrier with wire worm. $10-20; A brass terrier being "pushed" by another terrier while a third terrier watches! $50-75: A brass terrier being pushed by another terrier. Marked ENGLAND. $40-50.

Various carved wood dogs with corkscrew attached to head and stored in body. $25-50.
The finest is *second from the right* and is marked MADE IN FRANCE. The two with
hooked iron cap lifter tail are also French carvings.
The worst "carving" is at *right*. This corkscrew/cap lifter combination is part of a series
that includes a lion, a horse, and a cat.

A pack of wooden dogs from Denmark, France, Germany, and Japan. All have corkscrew
tails except the French dog in the *middle* caught in the act of raising his leg. $25-50.

Top row left and right: Carved wood Dachshund and Scottish Terrier. The Terrier is marked GERMANY. $20-30.
Bottom row left to right: Cork stopper with seated dog. $4-10; Corkscrew/opener set by ANRI. $30-40; Floppy eared dog by ANRI. $20-25; Airedale by ANRI; $20-25; Syroco Terrier $20-25; Dachshund head. $30-40.

"Hootch" is the slang for inferior or bootleg alcoholic liquor. Here are two marked and one unmarked version of the "Hootch Hound." For a similar type see the "Monkey Shine" under the "Wild Kingdom" category. $50-75.

Left: A frightened dog marked on the bottom NEGBAUR N.Y. U. S. A. PAT. PEND. 220. It is pot metal and has a folding tail like the parrot produced by Negbaur. $150-200.
Right: Flat Art Deco dog, which threads into a metal female thread insert in the celluloid sheath. Not marked. $150-250.

Feathered Friends

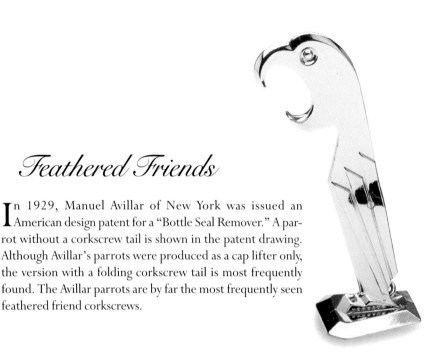

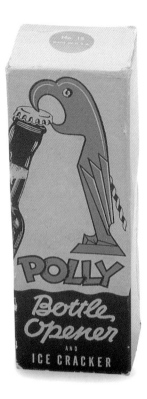

In 1929, Manuel Avillar of New York was issued an American design patent for a "Bottle Seal Remover." A parrot without a corkscrew tail is shown in the patent drawing. Although Avillar's parrots were produced as a cap lifter only, the version with a folding corkscrew tail is most frequently found. The Avillar parrots are by far the most frequently seen feathered friend corkscrews.

The packaging for the parrot pot metal corkscrew reads "Polly Bottle Opener and Ice Cracker. Practical and useful. Bill removes caps, tail pulls corks, base cracks ice. Chromium plated." The feet are marked NEGBAUR, U. S. A. PAT'D. Harry Negbaur was a tool and die maker for the Dollin Die Casting Company of Irvington, New Jersey, that cast the figures. $50-75 (in original box).

The chrome plated 5" parrot with plain Art Deco lines (*3rd from left*) is by far the most common of the parrots. $15-25.
The two at *left* are solid brass and stand 6 1/4" tall. They have a web helix tail. $75-100.
Left to right beginning with the fourth: Bronze painted marked NEGBAUR. $15-20; Chromed with feathers marked NEGBAUR. $40-50; Not plated or marked. $20-25; Green finish marked PAT'D only. $30-40; Unmarked with "jewels." $5-10; Brass with web helix. 4 3/4." $30-40; Short version with "jewels" and fixed worm. $20-25.

The parrot on the stand lifts off to reveal a web helix attached to its perch. $30-40. The crested parrot bears some similarity to the Avillar patent in the body design and cap lifter mouth. It is a solid casting with the wire helix folding between the wings protruding out the back. Unusual and rare. $125-150.

Above: *Top row left to right:* Wood parrot with Williamson bell marked WILLIAMSON on shank. Parrot is pinned to the shank on backside. $30-40; Bird carved from horn. 50-60; Bronze rooster marked DENMARK. $100-125; Ceramic cock* made in Portugal. 5-10.
Bottom row left to right: Silver plated duck head. $100-150; Penguin with bakelite sheath. A 1933 American design patent by Kurt Rettich. $30-40; Composition material rooster head with sheath that goes through the head for use when not protecting the worm. $100-150; Exotic bird. $10-20.

Right: *Left to right:* Painted 4 1/2" pot metal flamingo with a corkscrew hanging from its nose and a cap lifter in the base. $60-80; Brass pelican. $60-75; Cast cock. $50-60.

*The Cock is the revered Portuguese Cock of Barcelos. The story goes: At a banquet given by a rich landowner in Barcelos the silver was stolen and one guest was accused of the theft. He was tried by the court and found guilty. In spite of the overwhelming evidence against him, he still claimed innocence. The magistrate granted the man a final chance to prove his case. Seeing a cock in a basket nearby, he said, "If I am innocent, the cock will crow." In the morning the cock crowed and the prisoner was set free.

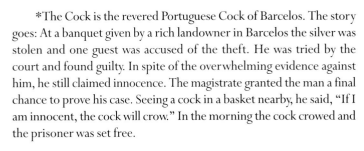

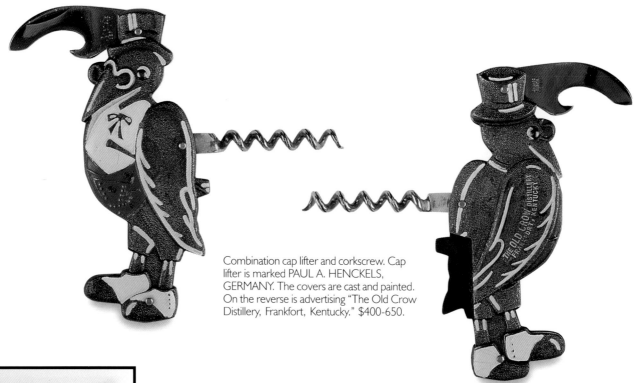

Combination cap lifter and corkscrew. Cap lifter is marked PAUL A. HENCKELS, GERMANY. The covers are cast and painted. On the reverse is advertising "The Old Crow Distillery, Frankfort, Kentucky." $400-650.

Left: Owl's head with body sheath. 3 3/4". Marked HAND-MADE IN AUSTRIA. $20-25

Below: The three birds on stands should be in the "Bernie" category in this book. The stand in all three is the corkscrew handle. The heads come off the *first two* to expose a cap lifter and the *third* has a cap lifter tail. *$Bernie*.
The duck is a nut fitted with plastic feet, head and bill. $10-15.

Fish

A fish swallowing a worm?
Now that's appropriate!

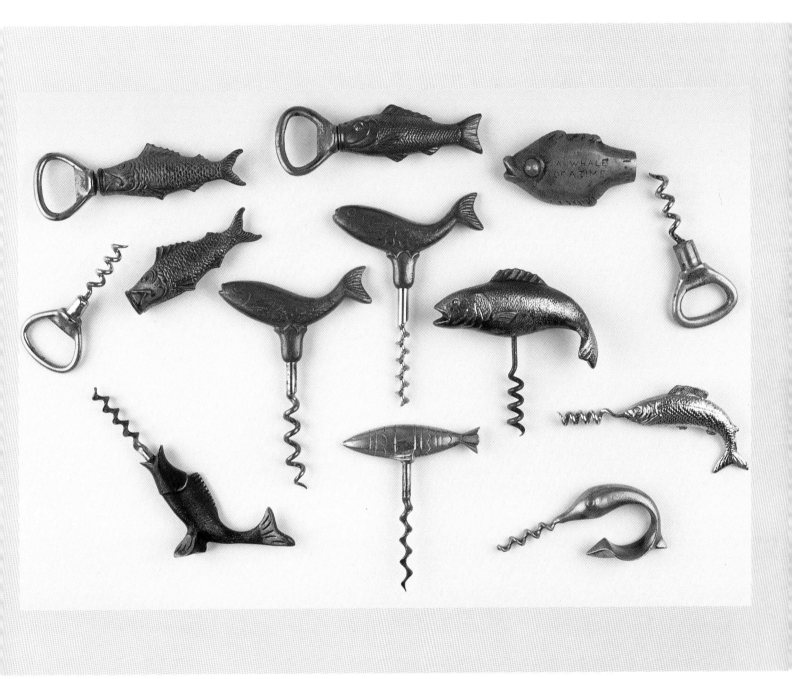

The cast fish swallowing a worm at *top left* is marked JB. $50-60. To its *right* is a copper plated slightly different fish marked MADE IN JAPAN. $40-50. A third unmarked example is at *2nd from top left*. $45-55.

At *top right* is a fish with corkscrew engraved "A Whale of a Time." $40-60. The two similar pewter designs with fish as the handle have different worms. $70-90. Large cast fish at *right center* is nicely detailed. $75-100. Deco style fish at *lower center* is nickel plated brass. $80-100. Fish at *mid right* is pot metal. $10-15. The two *bottom* fish are free standing. $75-100.

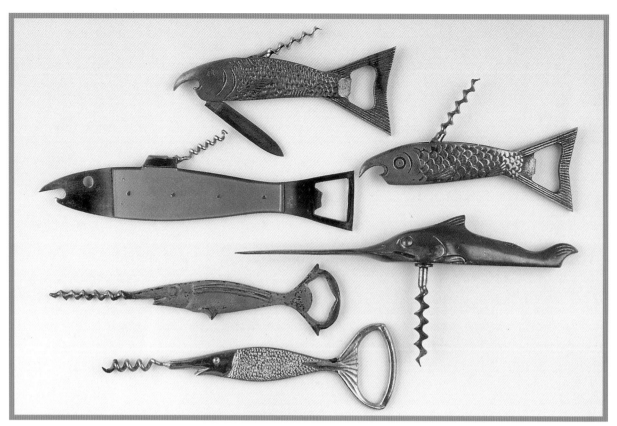

At *top* is a fish with can opener mouth, cap lifter tail, folding worm, and single knife blade marked GERMANY and SAKS FIFTH AVENUE. $100-150. *Below it to the right* is a cheap imitation without the knife. $30-40. The long fish with folding worm is marked STAINLESS STEEL JAPAN and has plastic covers. $15-25. The three swordfish are: Heavy combination letter opener and corkscrew. $125-175; Brass cap lifter/corkscrew with green finish. $20-30; Brass with cap lifter tail. $15-25.

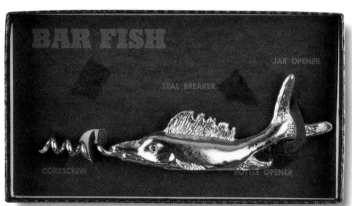

Above: *Background left to right:* Scandinavian blowfish with cap lifter tail fin marked ROSTFRI SMF STÅL. $10-15; A French mahogany wood carved whale. Tail is corkscrew handle. $20-25; A blowfish without cap lifter. $10-15. *Foreground:* An 8 3/4" split whale with corkscrew attached to front section and a cap lifter tab inside the back. $15-20.

Left: The "Bar Fish" is a corkscrew, seal breaker, bottle opener, and jar opener. Box is labeled "Artamount, Inc." $10-15.

Golf

Surprisingly, there are few corkscrews representing sports. There is a German corkscrew with a hockey stick handle. There is a series of Austrian Hagenauer corkscrews, including an equestrian and a polo player. A series of French knives show basketball players, equestrians, and other sportsmen. No sport seems to have received the attention in corkscrew production to the extent that golf has. Many were produced as novelties and some as golf awards.

The corkscrew for the golfer most commonly seen is the ball *second from the left*. This direct pull corkscrew comes in a set with the cap lifter club to its left. Both pieces are marked JAPAN. $15-25. The golf ball with frame is marked MADE IN ENGLAND on the ball. $15-25. The *third* golf ball comes complete with built-in tees! $12-15. The next club has a folding worm on the base with a cap lifter at the top. $10-15. The cap lifter putter has a protective hard plastic sheath for the worm. $10-15. At *bottom* is the best quality piece of this novelty lot. It is marked WEST GERMANY. $35-50.

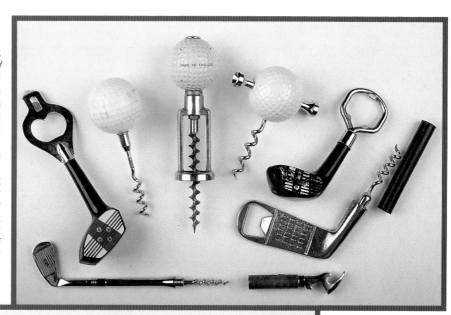

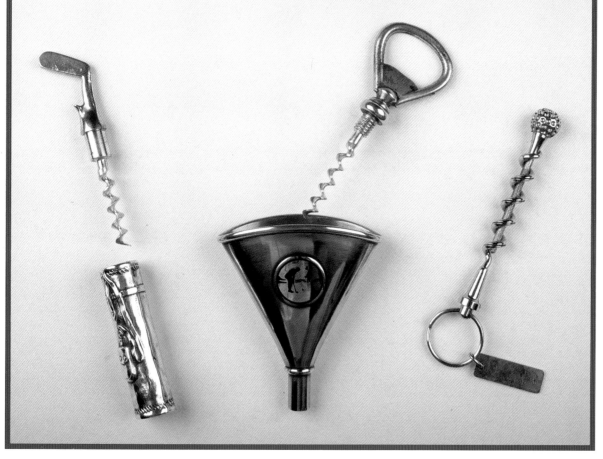

The golf bag is marked on the bottom STERLING 19, PAT APD FOR with R B Co. trademark of Blackinton Company. R. Blackinton & Co., which was founded in North Attleboro, Massachusetts, in 1862. They sold out to Wells, Inc. in 1967. This bag is engraved "Hook and Slice Club, August 9, 1928, Second Net." $400-500. The wine funnel with corkscrew is also by Blackinton and it pictures a golfer ready to putt on the green. $100-150. On the *right* is a modern peg & worm with golf ball top on the peg. It is currently produced in France as part of the "l'esprit & le vin" collection. It was priced in a 1995 catalog from Geerlings & Wade of Massachusetts at $35.

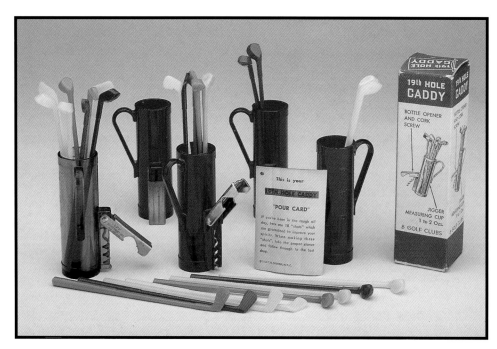

The complete "19th Hole Caddy" set includes a golf bag with measuring cup, bottle opener, corkscrew, eight golf clubs, and a "Pour Card" with 18 drink recipes. The drink recipes have such names as Sod Car, Green's Lady, Divot Sling, Partini, and Swinger. The cap lifter folds over a plastic recess, which houses the worm. The clubs are used as swizzle sticks. The bag is often seen in red and seldom seen in green. Some are marked EPP, 225 5TH AVE. N.Y. CITY PAT APP FOR. A set complete with all clubs, instructions, and box has the highest value. $10-50.

This very unusual double lever weighs in at a hefty 1 1/4 pounds. Turn the ball to thread the worm into the cork and raise the clubs. Once the worm is inserted, lower the clubs to extract the cork. It is well made, silver plated, and marked VALENTI, MADE IN SPAIN. $400-600.

This 7 1/2" high trophy would be the pride of any golfer. The golfer lifts off the base to expose the opener, which unthreads for the corkscrew. This base has not been engraved. One marked "Trenton Country Club 1928, F. Richard Cass" sold at Christie's London in November of 1996 for £552. $900-1000.

A bar set to delight any golfer! The golf bag is 6 1/2" tall and comes complete with pockets for two tees. Inside are a set of clubs with jigger, spoons, strainer, cap lifter, pick, and a golf ball corkscrew. Made in Taiwan. $5-25 depending on your handicap.

Hands & Feet

Here is a bunch of very handy corkscrews!

A fist gripping a bar is a very logical choice for a corkscrew. A handshake is used to open the bottle. *Left to right:* A carved mother-of-pearl hand gripping a gold plated ornate bar. $400-500; Brass hand and bar. $100-125; Early 19th century two pillar frame with ivory hand gripping bar. *$Rare*; Late 20th century plated cast hand and bar. $30-40.

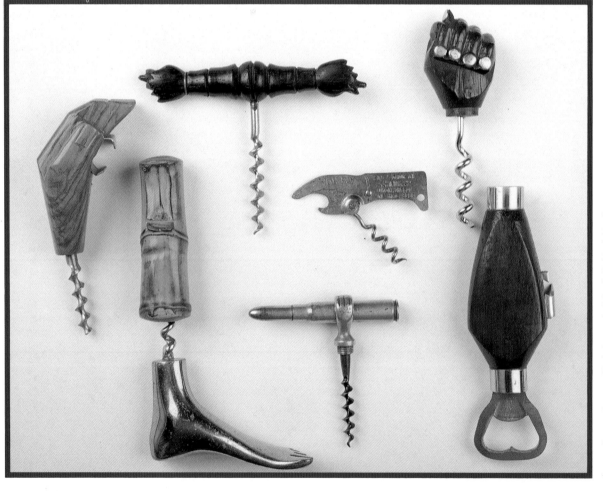

The wooden hand cups a cap lifter. $5-8. The T-handle is in the form of two joined wooden right arms. $20-25. The pointing hand is a spinner used at a bar to determine who pays. The advertisement is "Eat & Drink at Shanks' Union, Oregon, We have beer." $100-125.
The black arm on the *right* has a cap lifter at the top of its sleeve, a can opener on the side, and a hand with worm inserted in the cuffed end. $10-15. The "Scratcher." A brass hand gripping the shell casing sheath is marked D.R.G.M. 99881. It is a German 1898 design registration by Pfeffer and Weber from Steinbach-Hallenberg. $150-200.
The brass foot with leg bone sheath is marked on the sole MADE IN AUSTRIA. $20-25.

Horses

"Doing the Corkscrew.
Cheyenne Frontier
Days."

Many silver corkscrews depicting animals were made by the Dutch in the 19th century. The design rested atop the pulling handle, which threaded into an ornate sheath that often had a sealing wax stamp on the bottom of it. Here are two with horse theme. $1500-2500.

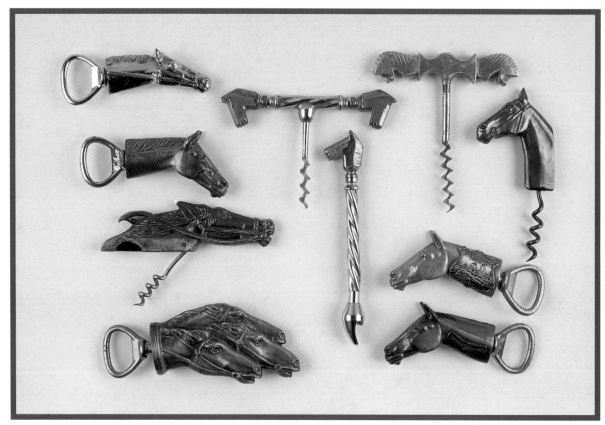

The horse head is very prevalent in corkscrew manufacture. Some of the sheath types have souvenir nameplates attached - at *upper left* is a silver plated example with a plate for Louisville, Kentucky. One might well expect to find this in the home of the Kentucky Derby. $50-75. *Below* it is a souvenir of Provincetown, Massachusetts. $40-50. The sheaths at *lower right* are from York and Maine and Boston, Massachusetts. $40-50. The unusual triple horsehead sheath is unmarked. $90-100. *Third down on the left* stands on a counter with the corkscrew folded in and hidden away. It is marked simply MADE IN U. S. A. $30-40. The bar set with double head corkscrew handle and single head cap lifter is marked PHV & CO., MADE IN ENGLAND. $30-40. At *top right* is an aluminum handle with chess piece like knights on each end. Marked on the shank WILLIAMSON'S. $65-75.

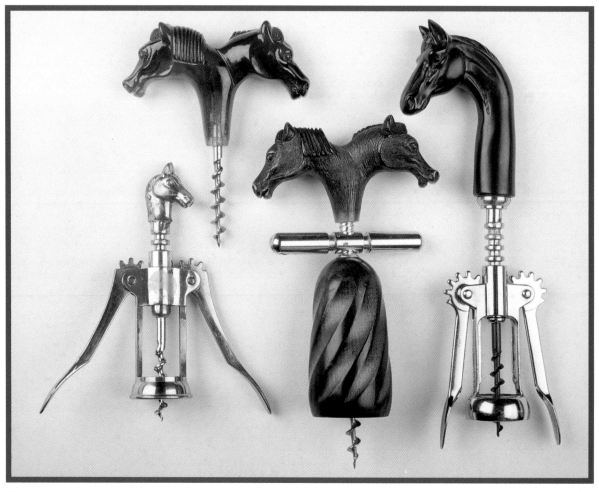

The amber color plastic handle is well molded for direct pull of the cork. $90-100. The wood double head double action corkscrew in the *center* has the same style horseheads as the plastic example. $100-125. The double levers are modern Italian productions. $30-50.

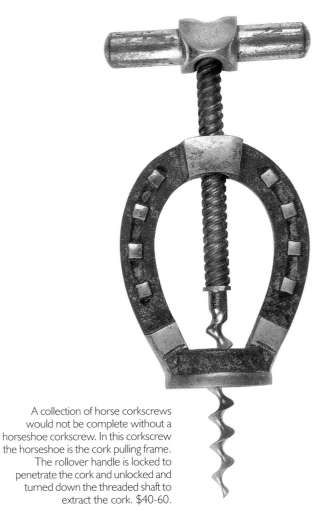

A collection of horse corkscrews would not be complete without a horseshoe corkscrew. In this corkscrew the horseshoe is the cork pulling frame. The rollover handle is locked to penetrate the cork and unlocked and turned down the threaded shaft to extract the cork. $40-60.

IMPORTED
GENUINE
WOOD

IDEAL GIFT

BOTTLE TOP
CORK SCREW

HAND PAINTED

The ultimate corkscrew? Two pieces of elastic hold the horse head corkscrew to cardboard reading "Imported Genuine Wood, Ideal Gift, Bottle Top, Cork Screw, Hand Painted." $2-3.

"Round Up. Bucking Contest. Wiley Blancett on Corkscrew."

Jolly Old Topper

The Steele and Johnson Manufacturing Company was located in Waterbury, Connecticut. It was founded in 1851 as the Waterbury Jewell Company and several years later became the Steele and Johnson Button Company. The company produced brass buttons and various metal goods until they went out of business in 1933. In addition to their Waterbury factory at 779 South Main Street, they had retail stores in Chicago and New York. A 1902 city directory lists the company as manufacturers of brass goods for the plumbing supply trade, including screws, nuts, washers, bolts, chains, and hooks; gas and electric light fixtures, including shade holders and canopies; work for electrical switches; and buttons - military, society, livery, and dress. There is no mention of corkscrews.

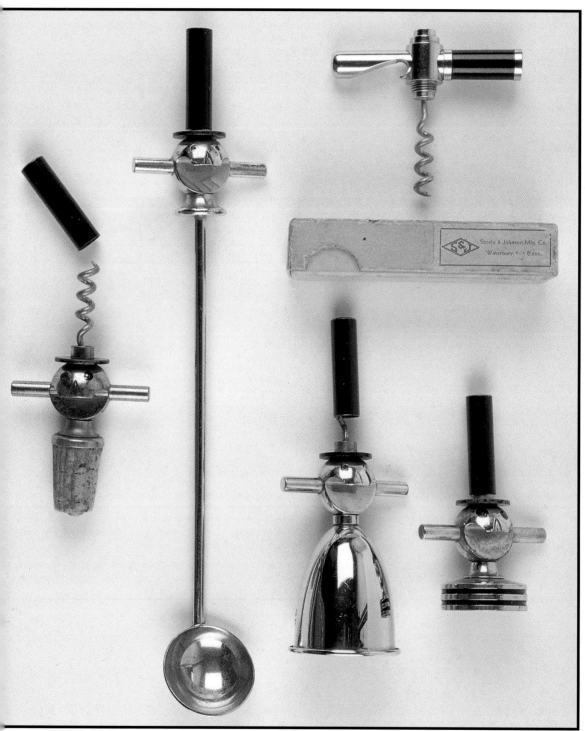

The hefty well-made corkscrew/cap lifter at *top right* came in box labeled "Steele & Johnson Mfg. Co., Waterbury, Conn., Master Bottle Opener, Made in U. S. A., No. 6264 Pol. Chromium and Black." $40-60.
All four of the "Jolly Old Topper" figures have a wire helix hidden under their stovepipe hats. The mouth is a cap lifter and the ears are handles for the corkscrew. The bar accessories are cork stopper, spoon, jigger, and bottle top. $50-100.

In advertising, these corkscrews were poetically described as:

The Jolly Old Topper

His big mouth will uncap ale and beer
He has big ears and perhaps looks queer
Pull off his hat and you will see
Just why it is that he's screw-ee

Kirby

Andrew Volstead (1859-1947) was a Republican member of the United States Congress from 1902-1922. Volstead is sometimes called the "Father of Prohibition," a title that better fits Neal Dow of Portland, Maine, who campaigned successfully for Prohibition in the early 1800s. Volstead was not even a diehard Prohibitionist ("Dry"). He was simply the person who introduced a bill to Congress that provided the means to enforce the prohibition of "the manufacture, sale, or transportation of intoxicating liquors" as called for by the 18th Amendment to the U. S. Constitution (1919).

A take-off on the sculpture *The End of the Trail*, this is a bottle opener (umbrella handle) marked COPYRIGHT 1933, PROHIBITION, THE END OF THE TRAIL.

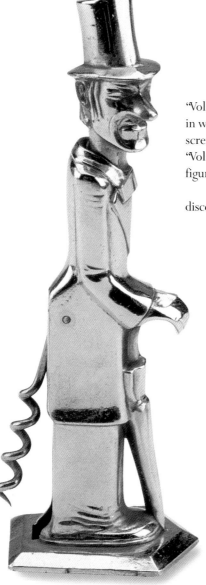

This corkscrew figure is commonly referred to as "Volstead." The earliest "Volstead" reference I can find is in a corkscrew addict's 1979 Six Best corkscrews in which six examples are pictured. The figure is subsequently shown in the corkscrew books of Perry (1980), Watney & Babbidge (1981), and Bull (1981) as "Volstead." Many auction catalogs, newsletters, and journal articles have called the figure Volstead. Is it?

In 1988, I talked to a lot of people about the "Volstead" and came up with these discoveries:

1. Part of a conversation between Don Bull and the then 92-year-old Horace Bridgewater:

> DB: What was the inspiration for your design patent of a character in a casket with corkscrew?
> HB: A popular cartoon figure of the time.
> DB: Was that a caricature of Senator Volstead?.
> HB: No!

2. Ninety-year-old Charlotte Whitney of Granite Falls, Minnesota, was a nanny to Volstead's children. She never heard him referred to as "Old Snifter." He often wore a bowtie and carried an umbrella.
3. A Charles Dickens figure, Rev. Stiggins, is pictured with top hat and umbrella.
4. In *The Wrecking of the 18th Amendment* (1943, The Alcohol Information Press), Ernest Gordon writes "the novelist Dickens took a sharp dislike to them (English nonconformist ministers) and caricatured them at every opportunity. Stiggins . . . was one [of] his creations . . . a man with threadbare black clothes, a prim-faced, red-nosed man with long thin countenance . . . he carries the inevitable umbrella of the Englishman and wears the tall hat of the Abe Lincoln period."
5. A similar figure appears in Moliere's 17th century play *Tartuffe*.
6. In *The World Encyclopedia of Cartoons* (1980), Maurice Horn says of Rollin Kirby his "most famous contribution to cartoon iconography was Mr. Dry, a figure representing Prohibition . . . which bore an almost exact resemblance to a figure employed for the same function by Joseph Keppler in 'Puck' a generation earlier."

7. While looking through "picture" books of the Prohibition era, I happened upon the figure with top hat and umbrella drawn by Rollin Kirby. It was indeed the figure corkscrew collectors have come to cherish.

8. More digging turned up an article by Rollin Kirby in a 1933 issue of *Vanity Fair* magazine in which he describes his "invention" of the figure.

9. Photos of Volstead do not resemble the corkscrew.

Are the corkscrews caricatures of Volstead?

NO! They are a direct takeoff on the "Dry" figure invented by Rollin Kirby. Kirby's figure was of his own design but, as with most works of artists, is based upon objects of the past and present. Kirby's figure is a combination of Moliere's Tartuffe, Dicken's Stiggins, Abe Lincoln, Keppler's studies, and his own vivid imagination. The figure is "Mr. Dry", "Old Snifter", "Little Snort", "Codger", "Old Codger," and "Topper." He is portrayed as the wets saw him and he carries the umbrella of the "dry" faction (I hope the meaning of this symbol is easily recognized!).

The "Volstead" corkscrews are not "Volstead." They are the "Kirby" corkscrews.

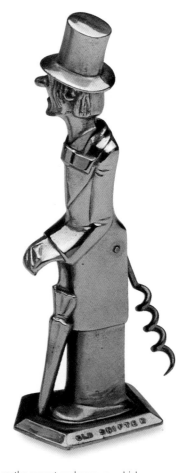

The Schuchardt patent bears the closest resemblance to the figure created by Rollin Kirby. This late comer (Prohibition had died over a year before the patent application) was invented by John R. Schuchardt of New York. On the underside of the umbrella are the marks MADE IN U. S. A. PAT'D and NEGBAUR, N. Y. Harry Negbaur was a tool and die maker for the Dollin Die Casting Company of Irvington, New Jersey, which cast the figures. $100-200.

The "Negbaur" name also appears on the parrot corkscrews, which were the design patent of M. D. Avillar of New York (#78,554 issued on May 21, 1929). Negbaur received many design patents from the 20s through the 50s for bill clips, pocket flasks, cigarette lighters, and other utensils. Many of the figures without turning head are marked DEMLEY. Schuchardt's son vaguely recalled that "Demley may have been the legal guy from Great Neck that worked with my father and the manufacturer."

Many variations of the "Kirby" corkscrew exist. On the *left* is the rarest. This 7" brass corkscrew has cap lifters cast into the front and back of the head. Note that he is carrying an umbrella like the type with turning head. *$Rare.*
The *second from left* is a cast aluminum cap lifter without corkscrew. $50-60. The rest *from left to right* are: "Old Snifter from Bermuda" cast into base. $100-125; Unmarked and with bronze paint. $80-100; "Old Snifter" cast into base with DEMLEY mark. Bronze paint. $100-125; Unmarked with a hinge for a hat which exposes a lighter when lifted. $150-200.

There are a number of variations of the "Demley" corkscrew. Most frequently seen are those marked on the base OLD SNIFTER and DEMLEY in chromed or bronzed variations and are approximately 6 1/2" high. Both come with fixed or removable hats.
Left to right: A rare silver plated example. $250-300; Chromed with black hat. $75-100; Sticker on base says "Chicago World's Fair, 1833-1933, A Century of Progress." $150-200; Black hat with Old Snifter mark only. $75-100; "Heller Chicago" sticker. $125-150; Old Snifter black hat. $75-100; Taller (7") version with OLD SNIFTER and ICEBREAKER cast into base. $150-175.
The box assures us that Old Snifter is "the life of the party."

Left to right: Four bronzed examples with slight variations in sizes and marks. $80-100; "Bishop and Babcock" cast into base. This was a brewer supply house located in Cincinnati, Ohio. Advertising on these corkscrews is rare. $150-200.
The broken corkscrew in the front is stamped "Welcome to Boston tercentenary 1630-1930."

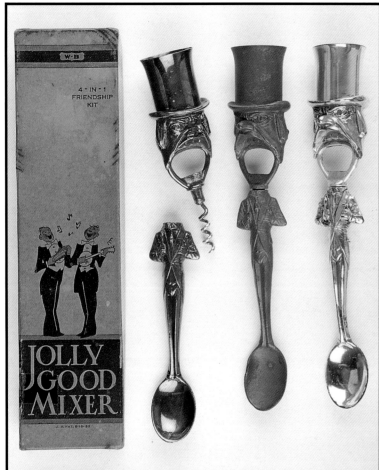

Left: The design patent of the then Trumbull, Connecticut, resident Alfred Flauder was assigned to the Weidlich Bros. Mfg. Co. of Bridgeport, Connecticut. The manufacturer's pattern number 905 appears on the back of the spoon handle. Design patent Number 87,658 was issued for a "Bottle Opener" on August 16, 1932. The combination bar tool has been noted in silver plate, nickel plate, and bronze plate. $150-200.

Below: The "Jollyfication Set" was also produced by Weidlich Brothers. The set includes a cocktail spoon and a bottle shaped sheathed corkscrew/cap lifter combination. $100-150.

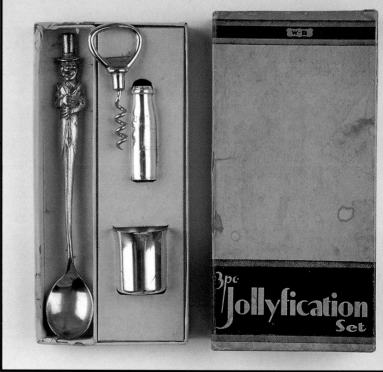

So who do corkscrew collectors really have to thank for the "Kirby" corkscrews? If it had not been for the power of organizations such as the Anti-Saloon League and the Woman's Christian Temperance Union (W.C.T.U.), Congress would not have passed the 18th Amendment. In the absence of Prohibition, Kirby would not have found his character. And Bridgewater, Schuchardt, and Flauder would have no reason for their patent designs. Prohibition was responsible for the "Kirby" corkscrews. What a price to pay!

The 18th Amendment to the U. S. Constitution was ratified on January 16, 1919. On January 16, 1920, it went into effect. The Amendment read:

Section 1: After one year from the ratification of this article the manufacture, sale, or transportation of intoxicating liquors within, the importation thereof into, or the exportation thereof from the United States and all territory subject to the jurisdiction thereof for beverage purposes is prohibited.

Section 2: The Congress and the several states shall have concurrent power to enforce this article by appropriate legislation.

Section 3: This article shall be inoperative unless it shall have been ratified as an amendment to the Constitution by the Legislatures of the several states, as provided in the Constitution, within seven years from the date of the submission hereof to the States by Congress.

The figure in the casket was a design patent of Stratford, Connecticut, resident Horace Bridgewater and was assigned to the Artistic Bronze Company of Bridgeport, Connecticut. The design patent #87,618 for a "Combination Bottle Opener and Dispensing Apparatus" was issued August 23, 1932. The coffin is 6 1/2" long and is marked inside the lid PATENT APP'D FOR COPYRIGHT 1932. $300-400.

Editor's Note: Rollin Kirby is considered the finest political cartoonist in America and was awarded the Pulitzer Prize on this score in 1921, 1924 and 1928. In the following article, he tells the story of his invention of the high-hatted figure which became the national symbol of Prohibition, a fourteen year national disaster which has now disappeared, we trust forever, from the American scene.

The Death of a Puppet
by Rollin Kirby from Vanity Fair Magazine, 1933

Back in the days when Frank Irving Cobb was editor of the *New York Morning World*, out of the seething turmoil of the period when we were giving until it hurt, hunting out pro-Germans, and bands were playing *Over There*, there arose, almost unnoticed by the press of America, a wartime measure to help win the war.

Out of the confusion of the time it eventually became the Eighteenth Amendment. Tacked onto it was an act proposed by an obscure Congressman from Minnesota named Andrew Volstead. Finally the drum-fire ceased, the boys came home and the wayfaring citizen suddenly realized that something extraordinarily unpleasant had stepped into his life. His liberty had been curtailed, for one thing. He resented that. He also saw growing up around him a sinister, hardfaced gentry: the racketeer and the bootlegger.

The tom-toms beat far into the night in the prohibitionists' camps. They were jubilant, hypocritical, smug, and, above all else, insolent. They combined what they considered to be virtue with a thin-lipped savagery. They gloated and cheered when a rum-runner was murdered by a prohibition agent. They applied insofar as they were able the methods of Torquemada. The Methodist Church seized the gonfalon from the Anti-Saloon League and, aided by the W.C.T.U. and kindred organizations, swept up onto the barricades and thumbed their noses at the bewildered but extremely sore populace who stood huddled in impotent anger in the doorways. They took the Republican party by the scruff of its aging neck and licked all the fight out of it. But at the beginning of the debacle Frank Cobb and the *World*, backed by its owners, the Pulitzers, sailed into the fight.

When the press of the country was lying supine under the hob-nailed boots of the Anti-Saloon League, that paper dared to say that the whole thing was vicious, un-American, economically unsound, and a fraud without parallel in our history.

And I, as the political cartoonist, evolved a figure upon which we could hang our displeasure - a figure tall, sour, weedy - something to express the canting hypocrisy we felt about the movement and, above all, something to catch the quasi-ecclesiastical overtones inherent in the thing.

This last element was filled with dynamite; for there is an unwritten law in the Fourth Estate that religion is a sacrosanct subject - that it is not a controversial topic and that any criticism, be it ever so oblique, must never enter into the news columns.

However, Frank Cobb approved of the symbol I had evolved and we printed him. After that, the deluge. Letters from ministers, professional drys, Y.M.C.A. secretaries, and the whole self-appointed crew of field marshals in the new dry army poured in on every point.

But the *World* was a fighting paper and I drew him again and again. Upon our unbowed heads fell the bludgeonings of the Anti-Saloon League – the Methodist Board of Temperance, Prohibition and Public Morals, Bishop Cannon, Mabel Willebrandt, and all of the hired tubthumpers of that unhappy epoch.

Undaunted, we kept on month after month and the attack never relaxed. Then one day in the exchange room of the *World* I picked up some out-of-New York paper and found a cartoon in which my figure had been used. It was not as anti-clerical as mine but the tall hat and the white tie and the long nose were there and he was labeled PROHIBITION. Some other editor had taken his courage in his hands and come out against the dragooning crowd we were fighting.

And so, as public opinion changed, the more timid papers joined in with us and my puppet became a stock figure until along toward the end of the nobly intended experiment became as standardized as Tammany's tiger or the G.O.P. elephant.

As the creator I have seen him change under my hand. He became steadily more furtive, more disreputable, crueler. And then, as the golden flood which once had nourished his veins was diminished, he became even more emaciated. No longer was he a dictator. He became sniveling and whimpering. He was broke: he, who once had browbeaten Senators, Congressmen, national conventions, and, even, stood a patched, unshaven scarecrow holding out a battered tall hat for such largess as could still be wangled from credulous supporters. No longer was he a tyrant - he was simply an exposed humbug whose fall had nothing of dignity nor anything deserving of pity. And now he is *inextremis*. He lies on a broken pallet in a forgotten attic with his long, dank hair matted over his brow; his hollow, fanatical eyes burn in their sockets; the unshaven jowl has sunk to the contours of the bones; his clothes are in tatters and on the floor lie the broken tall hat and the skeleton of his umbrella. I shall miss him. He has been a good friend. Days when news furnished little, I could always take him out of his box and he danced to my tune.

Bonus Deus faciamus graciam ingurgitare bonum vinum sine soulographiam.....
Amen !...

Collection R. G. — Nº 14.

People

The Delsam Company of Vineland, New Jersey, called their product "The Lovable Bar Bum, A handy man for your bar." He is a 1950 American design patent by Samuel Gerson. His hat is a bottle opener, his ear is an ice or nut cracker, and his pants are a jigger. Removing the bayonet fit top reveals an ice pick, muddler, and corkscrew. He was produced in painted, bronzed, and aluminum finishes. $40-50.

The cast aluminum "Man in Fez" bar set is seldom seen complete with original wood stand. $100-150. The "Black Minstrel" set is even harder to find. $150-200.

Background left to right: "Koktail Kids" are a cap lifter, cork stopper, and corkscrew. The men are 3" tall from base to top of hat. $15-25; "Mr Bartender" is a corkscrew/cap lifter surrounded by six holes to hold wooden toothpicks. $5-7; A pepper shaker with corkscrew and a salt shaker with a cap lifter. Holder and pieces marked JAPAN. $3-5. *Foreground left to right:* Man with bowler hat. 5" overall. $4-8; Man with top hat. 4 3/4" overall. $4-8; Pilgrims in stocks marked JAPAN. Corkscrew, cap lifter, and stopper. $15-25.

"Bar Flies." The boys are a cap lifter and a corkscrew. The girls are cork stoppers. Figures are larger than most of these sets. The boys are 4 1/8" tall, not including the worm and cap lifter. $15-25.

A vegetable ivory nut commonly called the "Tagua Nut" is the fruit of a 20-30 foot palm like tree growing in several tropical regions of Panama, Columbia, Ecuador, and Peru. It is close grain and very hard with a cellular structure and grain similar to elephant ivory. However, the nut is denser and more resilient. For over two centuries, vegetable ivory has been used by ivory carvers to make netsuke, umbrella handles, needle cases, dominoes, and chess pieces.
In South America, the nut is also called Anta, Pullipunta, or Homero. The English call it a Corozo Nut, the Japanese - a Bironji nut, and the Germans - Steinnuss.
These three heads are carved from the Tagua Nut. Two of them are marked MADE IN FRANCE. $200-400. Another Tagua Nut carving used as a cane handle can be seen in the "Canes & Walking Sticks" category.

Top row left to right: Composition head with real twine hair. $20-30; W. C. Fields. Frequently seen with matching cap lifter. $3-5; Woman with toothache. $50-60; Smoking sailor. $70-90; Huntsman. $70-90. *Bottom row left to right:* Ceramic head. $30-40; Footballer. $15-20; Middle Eastern lady carrying pot. $20-30; Farmers. Corkscrew and opener set. $15-20.

Bust form corkscrews produced by ANRI of Italy were sold either individually or in a set with cork stopper and cap lifter resting in a stand. Head only corkscrews were sold with a body to conceal the worm. ANRI figures with corks, including many with mechanical actions and cap lifters, are easier to find than ANRI corkscrews. For much more on ANRI, see the "ANRI" category.
Top row left to right: Man with jockey hat. $20-30; Gapping teeth man (missing body) $10-15; Uniformed big nose. $20-30; Egyptian. $25-35. *Bottom row left to right:* Cork stopper. Push lever down in back, mouth opens and hat rises exposing another head rising. $40-60; 6" Indian. $50-75; 5 1/2" Indian. $50-75; Happy face (missing body). $10-15; Man in bowler hat with cap lifter. $10-20.

On the *left* is a cast iron corkscrew/cap lifter bar set marked MADE IN ENGLAND. The characters are Andy Capp and his wife, Flo, from the *Andy Capp* comic strip created in 1957 by Reg Smythe. $40-50. The "Bar Openers" in the *middle* are wooden. Such a gift for the "World's Greatest Bartender!" $20-25. On the *right* is a cast set for the Great White Hunter returning from an African safari. Corkscrew and cap lifter marked MADE IN ENGLAND. $40-50.

More corkscrews from an African safari. *Left to right:* Marked in hollow back MADE IN ENGLAND. $10-15; Marked on spear sheath NAPIER SILVERPLATE. The head, for no apparent reason, threads up and down the shaft of the spear. $15-20; A pot metal puller with a generous size grip. $2-4.

Really tacky stuff. Were they given as gifts? Did someone actually bring them home as souvenirs? *Left to right:* They're called "Adam & Eve" and they've mated. Adam has his worm on top and Eve has her opener on top. $2-5; Folk art wood carving with worm shank glued in. $2-5; The Viking. Lift off his head to expose a cap lifter; pull out the base for the corkscrew. $2-5.

Top row left to right: Chrome Scotsman. $15-20; Austrian man with bowler hat. $30-50; Brass Scotsman. $15-20.

Middle row left to right: Carved Ivory Monk. $80-100; Bellhop combination corkscrew/cap lifter in sheath. Plate on sheath says "New York World's Fair 1939, The Theme Bldg." $125-150; Atlas lifting a cap lifter. Worm folds out of back. Copenhagen, Denmark, twin tower trademark. $150-175; Man on motorcycle. Bottom of base has English registration number 873,699 (1954). $75-100.

Bottom row left to right: Soldier designed after the Mannekin Pis (see "Brussel's Spout" category). Marked GOLDEN WHEEL. $10-15; South American T-handle with carved and painted figures. $40-50; Peruvian silver figure. $30-50; Pewter long tressed nude with corkscrew folding out of back.* $150-200.

*The bottom of the base on the nude is marked "Miss America, Chicago, 1934." The Miss America pageant was started in Atlantic City, New Jersey, in 1921. The contest was suspended from 1928 through 1932. It was revived in 1933 and Marian Bergeron, Miss Connecticut, was crowned Miss America. The contest was again suspended for the year 1934. The World's Fair (Century of Progress) was held in Chicago in 1933-1934. Marian was the reigning Miss America for the fair.

Real men.
Left to right: Danish hobo carrying his sack of clothes on a pole over his shoulder mounted on a marble base. The sack is the corkscrew handle. He has a cap lifter in his back pocket. $100-125; One of a limited edition of 300 corkscrews from the 1994 annual meeting of the ICCA in Portugal. Presented at a dinner with the Confraria dos Enófilos da Bairrada. $—; Popeye. A 1937 Swedish corkscrew patented in France by Bulls Pressjänst AB of Stockholm. $400-600.

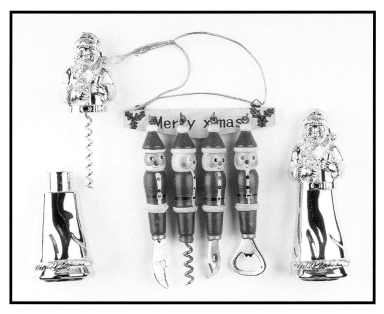

Above: Corkscrews for the holidays. The Santa Claus figures at *right and left* were sold at The Bombay Company stores during the 1996 and 1997 Christmas seasons for $19.95 each. They are made in China and marked GODINGER©.
The Santa Claus bar set includes corkscrew, cap lifter, can opener, and can piercer. A 1950s decoration. $20-30.

Right: A bronze of Socrates with two finger pull molded into the shoulders. The stand with center hole is an interesting combination of marble, wood, silver, and leather. $100-125.

Bonne Année

Pigs

Who could resist the temptation to make a corkscrew using a pig's tail as the worm? It's a natural!

The four pigs are Howard Ross's American design patent #D-154,880 of August 16, 1949. They are made of composition material and stand 2" tall. The snout is a cap lifter. $75-100.

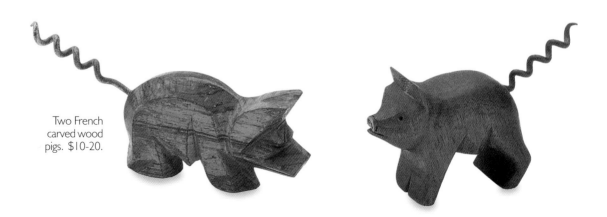

Two French carved wood pigs. $10-20.

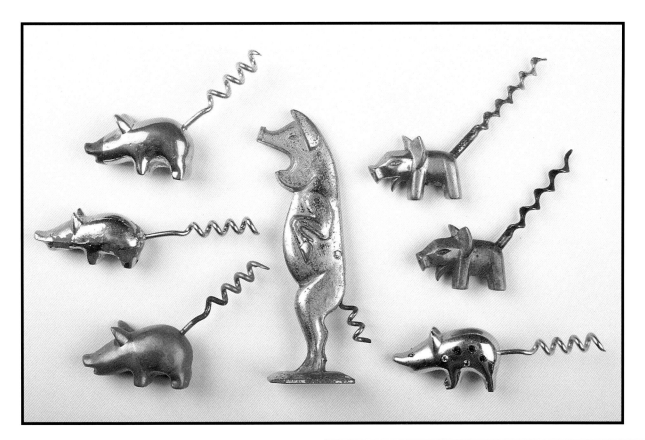

Above: The standing pig in the *center* with folding corkscrew tail was produced by Negbaur of New York. He also produced Avillar's 1929 Parrot design and Schuchardt's 1935 Old Snifter design. $100-125.

The two pigs on the *top right* are marked RD NO 779326, which is a 1933 English Registered Design. $50-60. These and other animal figure registered designs were produced by the Birmingham, England, firm of Pearson Page Jewsbury Limited. The other cast pigs have been found in brass plate, chrome plate, and cheaply bejeweled. $20-40.

Right: The pig on the *left* does not have the usual corkscrew tail. It is a cast iron two finger pull marked GOBERG GESGESCH on the shank. Produced in Germany by Hugo Berger. $200-300.

The pig's rear end on the *right* has a bottle cap lifter on the other flat side marked COLONIAL CRAFTS PAT. PENDING. $50-75.

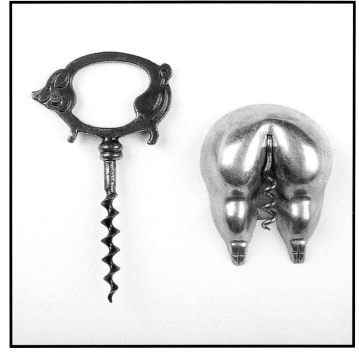

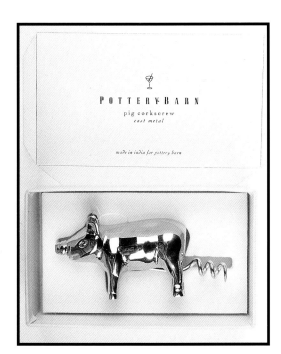

Collector beware. The pig's corkscrew tail folds down for use. This pig has been seen offered as an antique. It is currently sold in the United States at Pottery Barn stores for $10. The packaging says that it is "made in india for pottery barn." A bottle with folding worm is also available.

Here's how a pig opens a bottle of champagne. There are five cards in the set. The first shows two pigs with a bottle of champagne. The second shows one pig trying to pull the cork with teeth while the second pig offers another solution. The pig threads the cork onto the pig's tail and pulls. In the last card, the cork is out of the bottle and clinging to the pig's tail. Life is so simple for pigs.

Pistols

A pistol with a corkscrew trigger? Yes, they were produced in the 19th century in Austria, Belgium, England, France, Germany, and the United States. The Sheffield, England, cutlery manufacturer Unwin & Rodgers showed one in an 1849 advertisement and claimed a stock of 20,000 - 30,000 various cutlery items. Other manufacturers included Berthod and Marti, France; Cromwell, England; and Arnould and Boden, Belgium. Handles were made of ornate silver, mother-of-pearl, ivory, and horn slabs. Values for real corkscrew pistols range from one thousand to several thousand dollars. A weapons collector is apt to value them much higher than a corkscrew collector would.

The pistol at *top center* is a single shot rimfire pistol with knife blade. $1000-1500. At *top right and left* are nicely cast revolvers produced by Gagnepain in France. $400-500. These are currently being reproduced and when compared to the older versions, a lot of the fine detail is missing. $100-150. At *bottom right and left* are two cast pistols with the barrel serving as a protective sheath. The cheap modern pistol on the *left* has a friction fit plastic sheath. $10-20. The quality early version on the *right* has a threaded metal sheath. $80-100.

The revolver at *bottom center* is very rare. It has two knife blades one of which is marked SOLIDUS REGISTERED with a double F trademark. The covers of the barrel are black celluloid. The handle has a mother-of-pearl diamond inset in brown celluloid. The worm folds into the handle. Made by Franz Frenzel in Nixdorf, Bohemia. c.1900. *$Rare*.

"What poor an instrument can do a noble deed?" (Anthony & Cleopatra). That's what it says on the leather fitted sheath for the *middle* corkscrew. It is a two finger brass pull with a hanging ring and really isn't too poor of an instrument for a noble deed—like opening a bottle of wine! The ship is the H.M.S. Victory. It does have an indistinguishable English registration mark on the back side. $50-60.

Unlike the corkscrew in the middle, the corkscrew on the *right* is a very poor attempt at making a cast brass two finger pull in the form of a sailing ship. Indeed, a poor instrument for any deed! $5.

The two finger pull on the *left* is another version of the Victory and it is so marked. This one comes from a set of three, including cap lifter and bottle cork. $15-25.

Before passing up a Viking ship at a sale, one should examine them closely for variations. Of course, one needs to remember what the ships at home look like! A close examination of these four reveals: The two on the *left* have a head and a tail. $75-100. The other two have two heads. Two heads are better and rarer than one. $100-175. The *top right* has overlapping shields on the side. It is pewter and its sail is rectangular. The back of the sail is marked ZERO. It is the rarest of the four. The other ship with two heads is marked O.S.P. 40 on the bottom. *Bottom left* has a shield on the sail. The other head/tail ship is unmarked.

Which way does the sail go? When you see them at sales with pointed ends up, show the seller how much you know - the flat side goes up (the shield on the *lower left* one is your clue).

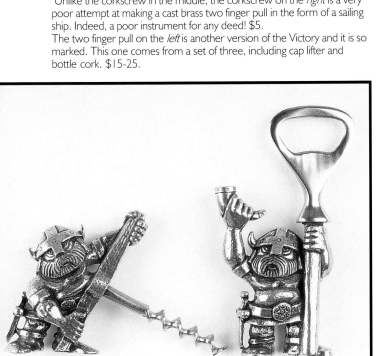

Here are a couple of Vikings ready to set sail. The Viking on the *right* brought a horn and cap lifter. The Viking on the *left* has pulled up the anchor. They are modern souvenirs marked TINN-PER NORWAY. $15-20.

Grab the ship's wheel and set a course to hunt for more corkscrews! $15-20.

Serpent

L.M

When I first saw this box several years ago, I wondered what the "L.M." meant. After opening the box, I knew. It meant "Lucky Me." Inside was a beautiful corkscrew.

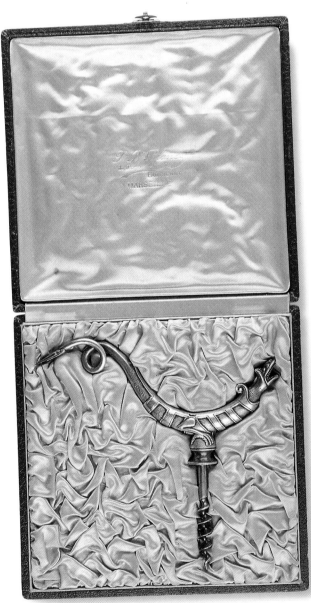

Serpent. *$Rare.*

There are no markings on the corkscrew itself. But inside the box is "Jn Bte Blanc de Juge Fabricant, Marseilles." In hopes of dating the corkscrew, I contacted corkscrew collecting friends in France, Guy and Edith Olive. Within a short time, they came back with a time frame for my "Lucky Me" corkscrew - The company listed in the red box was in business from 1900 to 1918 at 16 de la rue Longue-des-Capucins in Marseilles.

Syroco

In 1983, corkscrew collector Herbert Danziger wrote an article on corkscrews made by the Syracuse Ornamental Company (Syroco) of Syracuse, New York. Collectors had quite frequently run across the Syroco man with top hat and the waiter. A few others had been discovered, but now collectors' eyes were opened to a whole new world of Syroco corkscrews. The hunt was on and a many have been found since then.

Syroco was founded in 1890 and produced a line of decorative accessories for home and office. The corkscrews are compression molded with a composition of wood powder and thermoset resin. The worms and bells were supplied by Williamson Company of Newark, New Jersey. Syroco catalogs found by Danziger place the corkscrews to be between the years 1940 and 1950.

There are three types of Syroco corkscrews: Full figure with removable head to expose the corkscrew, head only, and a full figure (Scotty dog only) with corkscrew attachment. Some of the figures were painted while others were stained with a walnut finish. All of the detachable heads could be purchased separately. The only full figures are the man with top hat, waiter, Indian, monk, clown, and knight. The collector should be cautious of other Syroco heads placed in these bodies or mismatched!

Left to right: Painted top hat man named in various catalogs Old Codger, Codger, and Topper. $90-150; Walnut stain version. $100-175; Painted waiter. $90-150; Walnut stain version. $100-175. Heads only. $30-50 each.

Left: Three versions of the Syroco Monk. One stained and two with partial paint. $300-450. Head only: $50-80.

Below: *Left to right:* Stained clown. $350-550; Painted clown $350-550; Indian wide face/body version, yellow and green feathers. $900-1200; Narrow Indian, red and green feathers. $800-1100. Clown head only: $80-100. Indian head only: $100-200.

Left to right: The "Country Gentleman" with feathered hat, vest, and jacket. $75-125; Laughing Man. $80-130; Pickwick. $90-160. A corkscrew similar to the Pickwick was produced in a walnut stain and dubbed "David Copperfield." $75-100. Note: None of these figures was produced with a body.

Top row left to right: A dog with cap lifter only. $25-35; Two Police Dogs. $75-100; A Bulldog. $80-120 (see also "Bulldogs" category); Dog head sheath with combination corkscrew/ cap lifter. It looks very much like a Syroco figure, but it is real carved wood. $45-60.
Bottom row left to right: Black and white Scotty Dog opener/corkscrew set. $150-250 per set; Scotty on bell corkscrew. $90-120. The dogs were not produced with bodies.

Note:

A Golden Knight also exists with full body armor. The proportions of this figure are different than the other Syroco corkscrews and the Knight may have been produced during a different time period. $1000-1500.

Direct pull (no bell) corkscrews were produced with a Bulldog, a Scotty, and a Terrier. $30-50.

Beware of Syroco corkscrews that were originally produced as bottle openers. Someone may have been overcome by the temptation to convert them to a corkscrew. Syroco bottle openers include Bulldog, Laughing Man, Scotty, Terrier, Police Dog, Pickwick, Elephant, Rooster, and Horse Head.

Caution: Collecting Syroco corkscrews can lead to "Syroco Disease," which is an obsession to own everything produced by Syroco. The first symptoms are brought on by finding Old Codgers and Waiters like those shown here. These are the same figures as the corkscrews. They are solid on only the front half of the figures. They have a ring on the base for hanging a bar towel. The disease progresses when a bit shorter Waiter is found with a clock in his stomach. The disease is in full bloom when the collector recognizes other objects made from Syroco wood, including book ends, brush holders, wall plaques, ashtrays, cigarette boxes, pipe holders, tie racks, candy dishes, and napkin rings.

Wild Kingdom

Here's something to ponder: Figural bottle cap lifters cast in the form of elephants and donkeys turn up at antiques sales frequently. Donkey cap lifters seem to be more commonly found than elephants. However, in corkscrews few donkey figures have been discovered, while a number of elephants have turned up. Does this mean that Republicans drink wine and Democrats drink beer?

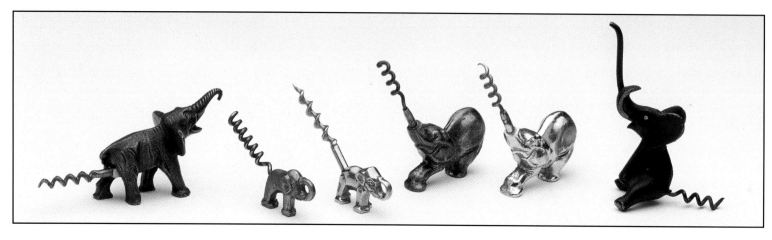

Left to right: A brass elephant with folding fluted helix. Bottom of left rear foot is marked GERMANY. 2 1/8" from base to top of trunk. $200-300; Brass elephant with wire helix. $60-80; Nickel plated elephant with web helix. Note the difference in sculpting from the previous. Rear feet marked ENGLAND. $80-100; Brass and plated elephants marked R T ENGLAND on stomach. c.1933. $100-125; Seated Austrian elephant. $125-150.

The carved elephant on the *left* with glass eyes and cap lifter mouth is marked MADE IN FRANCE. The worm is attached to the back of the head and stores in the body. $30-40. The composition material cork stopper and corkscrew were made in Germany. $75-100. The elephant in the *center* is a very simple wood carving with wire worm. $20-25. The black elephant is being stabbed in the back by a corkscrew with cap lifter handle. $40-50.

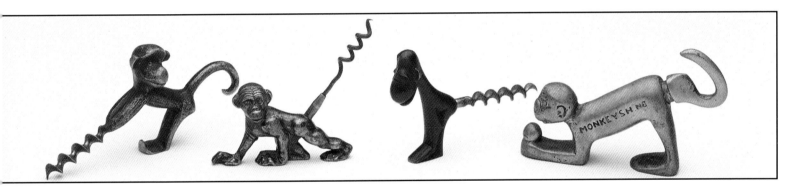

Left to right: Brass monkey with arms ending in a worm. Tail is a bottle cap lifter. $30-40; Brass running monkey. $60-75; Sad Austrian monkey. $60-80; "Monkey Shine." The cap lifter tail has a worm attached and stores where the sun doesn't shine. For a similar type see the "Hootch Hound" under "Dogs" category. $75-100.

Left to right: A prancing lion with cap lifter mouth. Base is marked MADE IN ISRAEL. 4 1/2" tall. $60-80; A flat brass lion with cap lifter mouth stamped Big 3 W E Co. $75-100; Israeli unicorn head with a corkscrew horn (just like a real unicorn!). $40-50; Hollow brass unicorn with cap lifter cast in base. $40-50; Zebra. $50-75.

The Morning After.

An unusual mechanical postcard. The lid of the stein moves up to reveal the monkey with a corkscrew.

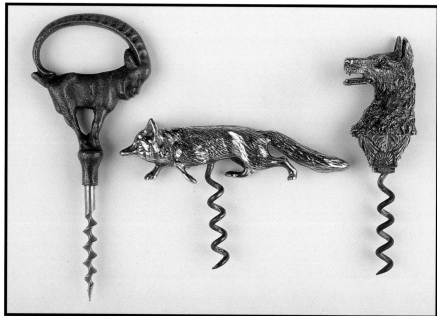

Left to right: Brass mountain goat. $100-125; Silver plated fox. Collector beware: The fox corkscrews are current productions offered as antiques at prices ranging from $50-200; Wolf head marked SILVER. $30-40.

The two monkeys on the *left* are difficult to find. $100-150. The two monkeys on the *right* are bejeweled novelties. Like their cat and pig cousins, they are fairly common. $8-15.

A Few More Figurals

What the devil are these?

The red devil on the *left* is clinging to a composition material bottle labeled "Champagne Foreign." $125-175.

The brass two finger 7 1/2" pull with hanging ring says "Dartmoor Pixie." $30-40. The reclining pixie is a three dimensional handle direct pull corkscrew. c.1933. $100-150. The seated 1 1/2" pixie is engraved "Dartmoor Pixie." $75-100.

The brass devil is seated atop a corkscrew handle ready to twist it into a cork. $800-1000.

At *lower right* is a red devil on a triangular cap lifter base. $100-125.

From top to bottom: A wood carved cap lifter and corkscrew set in the form of a pipe. $10-15; A wood pipe with corkscrew tip and salt shaker in the bowl. $8-10; A brass pipe with the stem serving as a sheath. Cap lifter in bowl. Attributed to Architect and Industrial Designer Gio Ponti. $40-50.

Left to right: Two English donkeys. c.1933. $60-80; An Israeli donkey. $50-75.

Left to right: French squirrel. $25-30; Lion with cap lifter and corkscrew. $8-10; Two French rabbits. $25-30; A French donkey with cap lifter mouth. $25-30; Bernie's donkey bearing a corkscrew and a cap lifter. $4-6.

Wouldn't all of these go over big as souvenirs in Florida? *Top to bottom:* Cast pelican eating both a fish and a worm. Tag on top says "Miami." $100-125; Cast 4 3/4" alligator eating a worm. Copper inset plate says "Florida." $80-100; 4 3/8" alligator. $80-100; 3" alligator with legs spread out. $90-110.

Top row left to right: Black skull and crossbones with folding worm on back, cap lifter at the bottom, and hanging ring. Imprinted "Name your Poison." $10-15; White skull and crossbones marked © METALART. $10-15.
Middle row left to right: Deer foot. $3-5; Gargoyle. Tag on bottom reads © Ganz Made in China. Recent. $5-10; Early wood gavel with concealed worm. Sheath is threaded. Handle is a wine barrel with a cast bust applied to it. $50-75.
Bottom row left to right: Russian made cannon. A rather interesting design - the cannon swivels perpendicular to the base forming a T-handle. The base has a built-in cap lifter. The cannon barrel pulls off to expose the worm. $20-30; Brass umbrella handle direct pull. A corkscrew for a rainy day. $30-40.

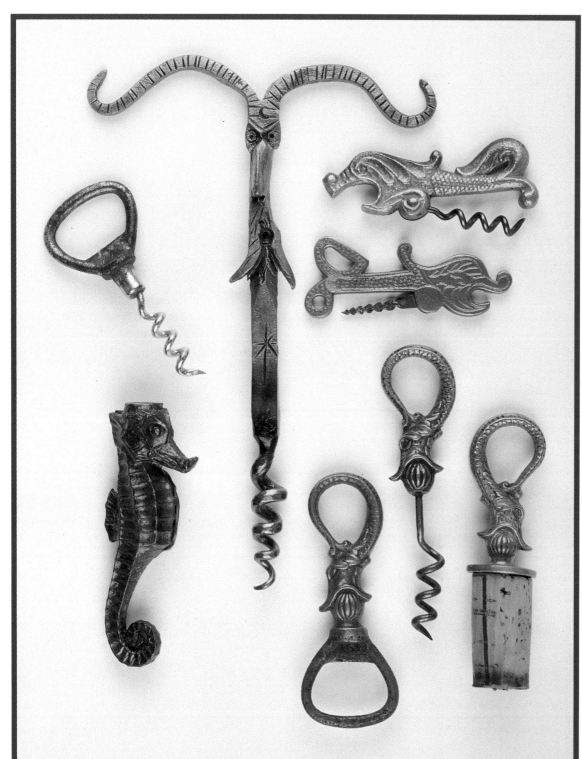

Strange sea creatures. *On the left:* A seahorse with souvenir plate from the Old Wind Mill, Cap Cod, Mass. $100-125. *In the middle:* Neptune. $40-50. *Right top to bottom:* Three dimensional sea serpent. $60-80; Flat brass sea serpent. $90-110; Set of three sea serpents, including corkscrew, cap lifter, and bottle cork. $50-75.

Left and right: Pot metal turtles with corkscrew tails. $20-25. *Middle:* A French carved wood turtle with corkscrew, cap lifter, and cork stopper. $30-35.

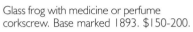

Glass frog with medicine or perfume corkscrew. Base marked 1893. $150-200.

Left: Novelty helmets with tags imprinted "Solid Brass Made In England." $15-20.

Below: The stand with dog corkscrew and two bird cork stoppers is an odd combination of the "Dog" and "Feathered Friends" categories. $30-40. An even stranger combination is the cat corkscrew and monkey stopper with coasters. $30-40.

Part ☰

Corkscrew Knives

Advertising

Knives of all sorts have been a popular means of advertising for well over one hundred years. The better the quality, the more likely the knife will be kept handy by the owner. The advertising message will be read time and time again. The corkscrew knives most sought after are the Anheuser-Busch champagne pattern pocket knives. In the late 1800s and early 1900s, over 65 varieties of these were produced to be given away by Adolphus Busch during his world travels. Lest he be forgotten, a photo of him was included in a peephole or Stanhope lens mounted in the knife. Some had a second peephole picturing the brewery. The oldest A-B knives have the "Eagle in A" trademark, showing the eagle's wings spread out. Most of the knives were produced after the trademark was changed to an eagle with wings tucked behind the letter A. Collectors of knives, breweriana, advertising, Anheuser-Busch, stanhopes, and corkscrews compete aggressively for all types of advertising knives. Knives with missing or broken stanhopes and blades lose a considerable amount of their value.

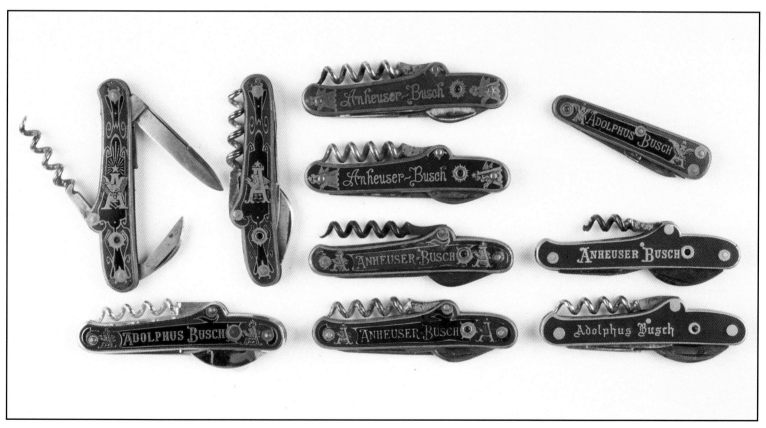

An assortment of Anheuser-Busch knives with enameled handles. All were produced in Germany and imported by Kastor & Bros. of New York City. The red and black example on the *left* shows the early spread wing eagle trademark. Note that all of these advertise "Adolphus Busch" and not the brewery. The spread wing is rare and valued at $550-650. The tucked wing to its *right* is the most common of the A-B knives. $250-350. *Below* them is a 1952 production by Schrade of Walden, New York. $200-250.

In the *second vertical row* are four knives in rarer colors. $350-500. At *top right* is a 2 1/2" spread wing eagle knife with scissors but no corkscrew. Adolphus' own name appears on this one and, perhaps, he gave this one to the ladies. $300-400. The pair at *lower right* have red enameling with a Stanhope. The *first* advertises the brewery. $200-250. The *second* promotes Adolphus and has the spread wing eagle trademark. $300-400.

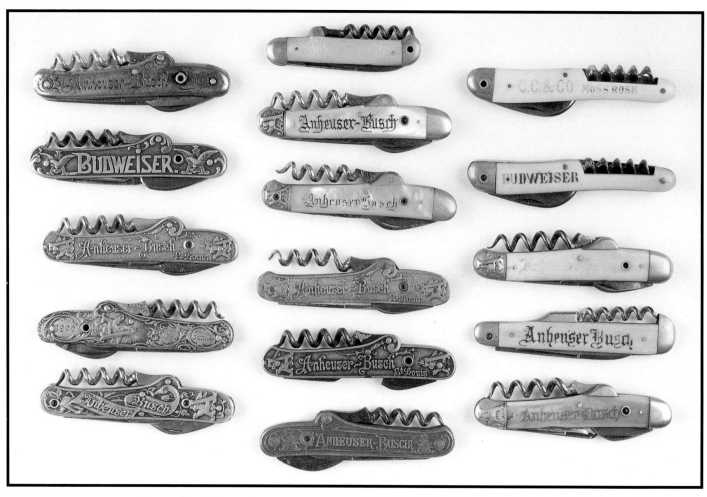

Anheuser-Busch knives with steel, nickel silver, brass, mother-of-pearl, and ivory handles. $300-600. The *second one in the first column* is a rare example of an A-B knife with only "Budweiser" on it. It is the only one in this group with the spread wing eagle. The *fourth in the first column* is dated "Jan. 1st, 1900." The two at *top left* are promotional knives from C. Conrad & Company, which distributed A-B products in the late 1800s.

For those looking for advertising corkscrew knives other than Anheuser-Busch, there are plenty to be found. Cheap high production run knives abound. Advertising specialty firms have done a good job in selling cheap knives to all sorts of businesses. Free is good; but when a firm gives a quality knife, the firm is more likely to be remembered. Here are some better quality knives.

Top row left to right: French brass. "St. Raphael Aperitif." $30-50; German steel with stamped in bottle. "Wicküler Kupper Brauerei, Wuppertal." $50-75; German brass with cast in bottle. "Reina Blanca, Cerveceria de Sonora, Hermasillo, Mex." $60-70; Brass advertising the manufacturer "Compliments Ed. Wüsthof, Solingen, Germany." $80-100.

Second row left to right: "Walter Brewing Co., Pueblo, Colo." Two blade knife by Imperial, Providence, R. I. $80-100; "In Vino Veritas." Made by Baron, Solingen. $125-150; "Singer Varrogepek" depicting woman seated at sewing machine. Made by Kaufmann, Solingen. $150-200.

Third row left to right: French champagne pattern by Sarry, Thiers. "Louis Roederer Reims/Champagne." $100-125; "Laidlaw's Premier Scotch Whisky." Made by John Watts, Sheffield, England. $100-125.

Bottom row left to right: A dated knife: "C. Sandheger 1900." Made by Henckels, Solingen. $125-150; An unusual rectangular pattern. "Plätzen - Pils." $80-100.

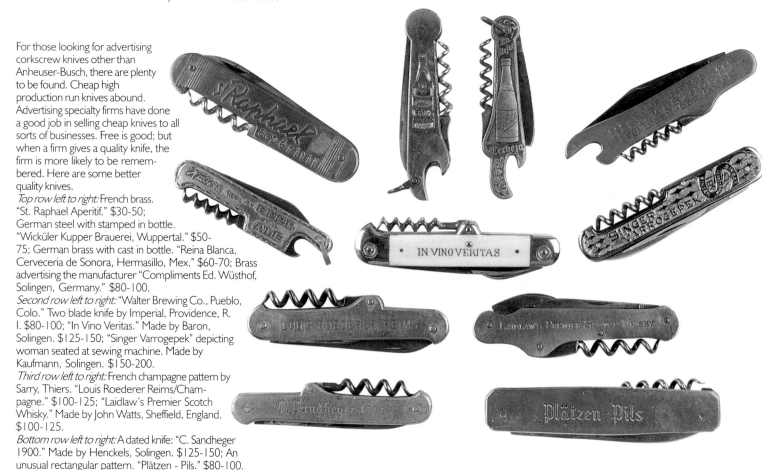

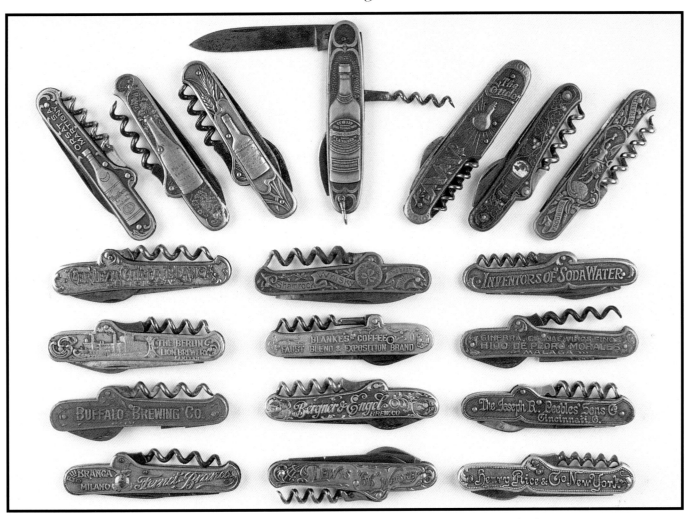

When looking at detailed embossing on an advertising knife, you do get the feeling that the advertiser probably made an excellent product to match his quality taste in advertising. Embossed knives depicting the company product such as the bottle are more highly valued. Products advertised in this group include beer, tea and coffee, soda water, whiskey, tequila, cognac, wine, champagne, light bulbs, and even the gas company. Ron MacLean has embossed knives promoting dress trimmings and eyes and voices for dolls. Manufacturers include Herberz, Herder, Kaufmann, Peres, Prager & Loge, and Reimer in Germany. Importers include Kastor and Thistle Cutlery in New York. $100-250.

Left to right: French six blade utility knife marked PRADEL. Advertising for "Chatard Vichy." Different shape bottle on opposite side. $125-150; French two blades plus corkscrew knife marked VAUZY. Advertising for "Bitter Secrestat" depicting a bottle on both sides. $125-150; Three blades plus corkscrew on an unmarked knife depicting a generic bottle of Cognac. $150-200.

Bottles

A collector would expect to find a knife with corkscrew in the shape of bottle. A collector would also expect advertising for wine on the bottle. It seems like a very logical place for a winery to advertise its products. Surprisingly, most bottle shape corkscrew knives have advertising for champagne, beer, soda, or liquors rather than wines.

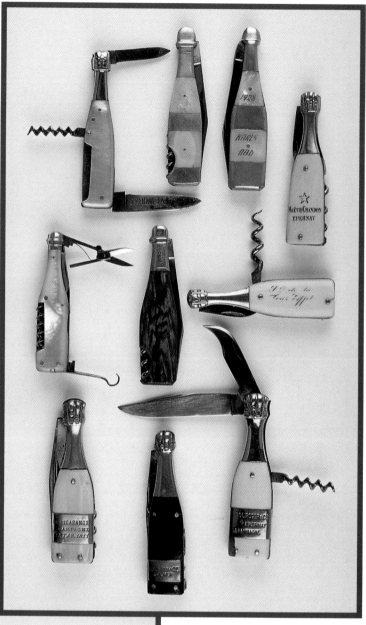

Champagne bottle knives were a very popular pocket knife and advertising/souvenir knife in the early 20th century.
Top row left to right: MOP handles with web helix, file blade, and master blade marked SCHMACTENBERG BROS. GERMANY and "Eagle Lye Works" advertising. c.1897-1916. $300-350; Four piece MOP handles with wire helix and two blades with trademark showing a boat and letters H K. $250-300; MOP handles with fluted wire helix and two blades. A 1928 souvenir from Karlsbad, Germany. $300-350; Ivory handles advertising "Moét & Chandon, Eperney" with wire helix, master blade, and foil cutter. $300-350.
Middle row left to right: A ten tool knife, including scissors and button hook, marked HENRY SEARS & SON. $300-400; Marble pattern celluloid handles with wire helix and two blades. Marked SOLIDUS on blade and stamped with anchor and forward/backward F trademark. Made by Franz Frenzel in Nixdorf, Bohemia. c.1900. $300-400; Ivory handles with wire helix, master blade, and foil cutter. An early souvenir of the Eiffel Tower. $300-400.
Bottom: Three French champagne bottle knives with advertising plates attached: "Ch. DeCazanove Champagne, Estab. 1881," "J. Bertier & Cie, Saumer," and "Pol Roger & Co Epernay Champagne." $250-350.

Left first column: A pair of knives advertising "Orangina Gazéifiée a la pulpe d'orange." The *top* one has a cap lifter stamped into the rear of the handle. $175-225. The *second* has a cap lifter at the top and a neckstand added like a waiter's friend. The neckstand is marked A S MADE IN FRANCE (A. Sarry, Thiers). $200-250.
Second column: Two French champagne bottle waiter's friends made by A. Sarry of Thiers. One is marked BIAT and has "Champagne Renversez Bernard" advertising on it. $150-200.
Third column top to bottom: An embossed bottle knife marked F. W. JORDAN, SOLINGEN with advertising for Maggi's flavoring: "Für jeden tisch, Maggi's Würze, altbewährt" and on the other side "Für Jede Küche, zum verbessern schwacher suppen und speisen." $250-300; A poorly embossed bottle advertising "Chas. A. Zahn Co., Chicago, Ill., Old Stock Bourbon, A whiskey of quality." $100-125.
Right side top to bottom: "Diehl & Stein, Inc., New York" advertising on a bottle marked DIXON CUTLERY CO. GERMANY $150-200; "Edw. F. Miller, Oelwein, Iowa, Hamm's Beer" on the same knife marked GRIFFON CUTLERY WORKS GERMANY. $150-200; Three more French waiter's friends advertising "Champagne Mercier," "Champagne Henri Abelé," and "Champagne H. Germain." $200-250.

Canteen & Picnic

The traveler who wanted to be prepared to eat as well as open a bottle of wine had many choices. He could get an entire knife, fork, and spoon set, including a glass, seasoning shaker, and don't forget the corkscrew. The combination of a knife, fork, spoon, and corkscrew fitting together as one piece made a good travel companion. The simplest form for the traveler was one tool with folding knife blade, fork, and corkscrew.

Travel or camping canteen sets. *Left to right:* 19th century leather case by George Wostenholm, Sheffield, holds cup, ivory handle knife, fork and spoon, and salt shaker. $200-250; Leather case stamped "Couvert de Voyage. Au Depart, 2S.Avenue de L'Opera, Paris" contains glass and utensil set. $300-400; German set with leather case, glass, knife, and fork/corkscrew combination. $100-125; Cylinder case with cup top, containing glass with leather pouch holding utensil set. Marked CROSS. $150-200.

The leather case on the *left* is fitted with a 3 1/2" oval glass holding a leather pouch with knife, spoon, and fork set. The corkscrew is on the knife. $100-125.
Each of the silver pieces on the *right* is marked FRANHIESS & SOHNE, WIEN (Vienna, Austria). Each utensil has a positive lock when swiveled into position. A button is depressed to release it. The corkscrew is on the fork. $175-225.

Two travel sets in velvet lined hard leather cases. The vine and bloom decorated set on the *left* has the corkscrew on the spoon. The knife blade is marked JOSEPH MAPPIN & BROTHERS, QUEEN'S CUTLERY WORKS, SHEFFIELD. c.1851. $150-200. The *second* set has the corkscrew on the fork. The covers are decorated with sailing ships and the personalization "Capt. A. W. Jenkins." The knife blade is marked RODRIGUES, PICCADILLY (London). c.1850. $200-250.

A 1914 Henckels catalog advertises the take apart utensil sets as "Army Knives" and in German: "Manöver und Touristenmesser;" in French: "Couteaux de manoeuvres;" in Spanish: "Navajas de Campo." Knife collectors sometimes call them "Hobo" or "Slot" knives. The two or three utensils are connected by interlocking slots and tabs on the brass liners. They can be found with ivory, tortoise, horn, wood, silver, or celluloid handles. The worm is attached to either the spoon or the fork. Some worms fold out to the end and others to the middle. Sets shown here are from Austria, Germany, and the United States. $150-300.

At *top left* is an eleven tool imitation stag handle camping set made in Japan. The tool does not come apart to make a table setting as in "Hobo" knives. If the camper is eating soup, he folds the spoon out. If he is eating fish, he folds the fork out of the opposite end. $8-10.

The five tool figural set at *top right* is marked MADE IN CHINA. $15-20.

At *bottom* is a Russian version of the "Hobo" knife. In this cheap version, the spoon and fork with red plastic covers are held in place by lowering the knife blade to tabs on the center liner. A cap lifter, a can opener, and a punch make it a somewhat more versatile tool. $15-20.

Top left to right: An ivory French "Hobo" knife. Knife and fork only. Worm attached to knife handle. Marked only LEU CHARS on knife blade. $150-200; A two piece ivory set with worm on the fork. The fork is hallmarked for Sheffield 1875. $200-300; A two piece ivory set marked RUSSELL & JACKSON, SHEFFIELD. $200-300. All three utensils in the set at the *bottom* are marked INOX. $50-75.

Sadly, many utensils get separated from their mates either by loss, breakage, or collectors looking for only knives, forks, spoons, or corkscrews with no interest in keeping complete sets. The horn handle spoon and fork at *top left* is missing the knife. The fork marked ALPACCA, MADE IN GERMANY with wood covers may be a stray. Two more unmarked strays are at *right*. Strays valued at $25-75. The knife with pinkish imitation mother-of-pearl covers in the *middle* is Russian made. It is complete with folding fork, knife, and worm. $10-15. At *bottom left* is the ultimate in basic, simple camping tools. Tin handles have three tools and the spoon and fork stems sandwiched between them. The spoon and fork are visible on the outside of the handles when folded. $4-6.

Two combination implements marked MADE IN CHINA. They include useless wire worm, knife, fork, spoon, can opener, bottle opener, and punch. One also has the additional feature of a finger nail clipper! $8-10.

Decorative

Corkscrew knives with richly decorated handles with varying themes make colorful additions to any collection. They are works of art in their own right.

Wine, women, song - and corkscrews! They all go together so well! Several of the beauties posing on these knives are accompanying advertising (W. Meyer & Sons; Petroleum Products Co.) or slogans ("Im Wein Liegt Wahrheit!" and "Hopfen und Maltz - Gott erhalt's!") on the reverse. Others have female companions on the reverse. Manufacturers and distributors include H. Konejung, D. Herder, Sperry & Alexander, Norvell Shapleigh Co., Western Cutlery Company, and Hermann Bierhof. All are in the Art Nouveau style except for the *lower right* Art Deco nude with sail boat on reverse. $150-250.

Workers, their factories, and shipping are depicted on these knives.
Top row left to right: Two knives (3" and 3 1/2") with advertising of the manufacturer, Carl Schlieper of Solingen, Germany. Both depict a cutler with tools of the trade. $150-200; Advertising Wilh. Sonesson & Co., Malmö (Sweden) depicting construction worker. Blade marked F. W. KLEVER JR., SOLINGEN. $175-225; A high quality knife with blades marked REMINGTON UMC, MADE IN U. S. A. The finely detailed handles depict a woman at a sewing machine and the reverse has advertising "G. M. Pfaff A-G, Nähmaschinen-Fabrik, Kaiserslautern." $250-300; Factory scene knife manufactured by Justus Bierhoff, Solingen. Reverse depicts an iron railing and staircase with advertising "Eisenwerk Joly, Wittenberg, Feuersichere Treppen, Patent Joly." $200-250.
Bottom row left to right: Three more knives by Justus Bierhoff. Ship with "Norddeutscher Lloyd Bremen." $200-250; Ship with "Wilton Engineering & Slipway Co., Rotterdam." $200-250; Factory scene with "Werkzeug-fabrik, J. Gottlieb Peiseler, Remscheid-Haddenbach." $200-250.

Decorative knives with a political theme.
Left to right: Bismarck manufactured by Gustav Felix in Solingen. $300-400; A knife by C. W. Engels of Solingen depicting Wilhelm II, V. Hindenburg, Franz Josef, Prinz Heinrich, Kronprinz Rupprecht, Kronprinz Wilhelm, V. Falkenhayn, and V. Einem. $300-350; A knife by Carl Schmidt of Solingen with ivory handles imprinted with Norwegian flag and "Fridtjof Nansen, Norges Søn, Verdens Ven." $150-200.

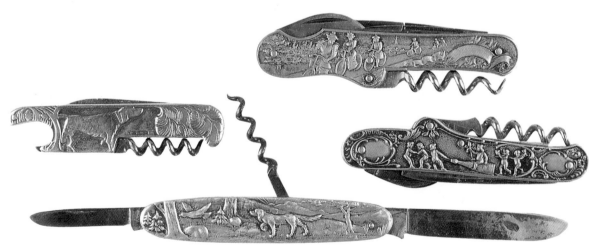

Decorative knives with hunting and playing themes.
Top: The front depicts three women on bicycles pursued by three men on bicycles. More male bicyclists are shown on the reverse. Master blade marked W. H. MORLEY & SONS, GERMANY. $250-300.
Second row left and right: A single blade knife with silver cap lifter handle. Depicts a hunting dog on the front and a wild turkey on the back. Blade marked MANDRIL OSLO (Norway). $100-150; Several cherubic figures are partying and pulling a bottle of champagne on this knife advertising "Otard Dupuy & Co. Brandies." Blades are marked MATADOR MADE IN GERMANY. $250-300.
Bottom: Nickel silver handles depict a hunting dog pointing at a flying bird on this knife made by Rich. A. Herder of Solingen, Germany. $100-125.

French brass handle knives with sports and music themes. Most are marked
PRADEL and DEPOSE. Value range is $40-80.
Figures on front and back left to right: Bagpipe player/standing woman;
Footballer running/tennis player; Climber/climber; Tennis player/footballer
catching ball; Basketball player/accordion player; Male gymnast/female gymnast.

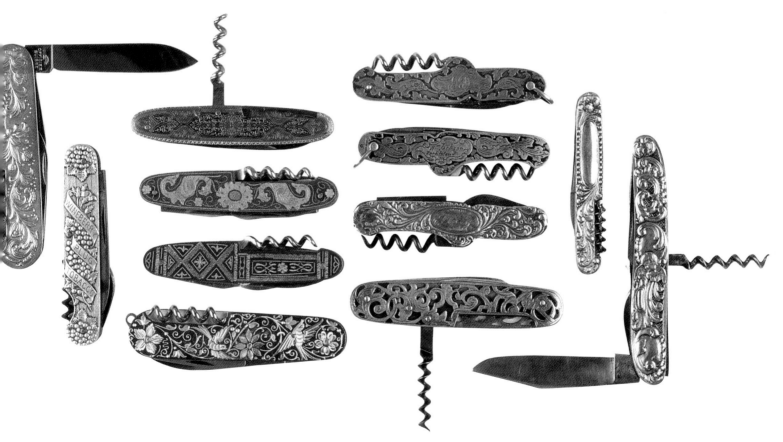

Decorative knives that make charming gifts for friends and beautiful presents to own.
Left pair: Both are decorated with grape and vine designs. The *first* with sterling handles was made by
Victorinox of Switzerland. $100-150; The *second* advertising "Wineberry Plug Tobacco" was imported from
Germany by the Chicago firm of Henry Sears & Son. $150-175.
First column from top to bottom: Hammered pattern in red, gold, and black made in Germany. $100-150;
Two Spanish damascene patterns with one blade marked PAT. 52725 and another blade TOLEDO. $50-
100; A current Spanish damascene knife marked AITOR INOX - SPAIN. Retails for $25-35.
Second column from top to bottom: Two knives with master blade, file blade, and scissors marked E T & CO.,
GERMANY. Sterling handles engraved with "J. B." and "Wm Jackson, Rock Island, Ill." $200-250; Unmarked
silver handles engraved "Stacy." $150-200; Two knife blades and a corkscrew in an open work handle so you
can see the knife action! $150-200.
Right pair: A 3" three blade knife and a 4" six blade knife. Both have ornate silver handles ready to be engraved
as gifts. $125-200.

"Men differ about politics and religion, and the girls they want to marry, but all agree that a good knife is a great blessing." That was early advertising copy by wholesaler Maher & Grosh of Toledo, Ohio. They offered elegant knives for fifty cents while stating "well worth $1.00." In advertising for direct mail order sales to the public, they suggested "Compare it with the rubbish sold in your store at 50 cents!" And, finally, in bold Madison Avenue advertising copy: "Jewelers complain because we do not ask $5.00 each for them; we would probably sell more to some soft-headed folks *if* the price was *$5.00*. But we are desirous of the trade only of people with good sense."

What better gift for a gentleman than the gift of gold? Here are four gold pocket knives. *Clockwise from top:* 1 1/4" diagonal pattern handle. $150-175; 3 1/4" with master blade and file blade marked I*XL GEORGE WOSTENHOLM, SHEFFIELD, ENGLAND. Ornate handle is marked 14K and engraved with initials "R. F. W." $600-800; A "nifty" design with web helix and one knife blade. Bail is marked 1/20-10K G. F. BATES & B, U. S. A. $250-350; Two blade knife engraved with initials "J. V. H." Blade is marked EMPIRE. Bail is marked 14K with trademark of R. Blackinton & Co., North Attleboro, Massachusetts. $250-350.

And what gentleman wouldn't enjoy a high quality stainless steel knife with several tools he can actually put to good use? This is a representative group of these fine 20th century pieces.

First row: 4" seven tool pattern finish marked INOX. $200-300; Three tool mirror finish marked PAUL A. HENCKELS. $100-150; Three tool mirror finish marked REMINGTON U M C STAINLESS. $250-300.

Second row: Six tool pattern finish marked ALTENBACH SOLINGEN. $100-150; 4" eight tool with mirror finish. Marked ELOI with letter P trademark and MADE IN FRANCE. This is from Eloi Pernet, one of highest quality cutlers in Europe. $400-500.

Third row: Six tool mirror finish marked J. A. HENCKELS, SOLINGEN. $150-200; Six tool mirror finish marked A. GERMAIN, THIERS (France). $125-175.

Fourth row: Three tool pattern finish marked J. A. HENCKELS, SOLINGEN, TRIODUR. $100-125; Six tool pattern finish marked MAKINO. $80-100; Three tool pattern finish marked PRADEL. $60-80.

Fifth row: Three tool pattern finish marked Ed Wüsthof, Solingen. $40-50; Six blade pattern finish marked MADE IN POLAND. $20-30; Five tool with sterling handles. Müller & Schmidt, Solingen trademark on master blade. $100-125.

Right side top to bottom: Five tool mirror finish with "Abercrombie and Fitch" on master blade and FRANCE on the tang. The handle has the Abercrombie and Fitch trademark on it. $200-300; Three tools depicting a man smoking and walking with a cane. "Bob" engraved on the handle. Master blade marked BATES. $50-75; Three tool pattern finish marked DUNN BROS., PROV. R. I. Handle engraved "G. H. V." $50-75.

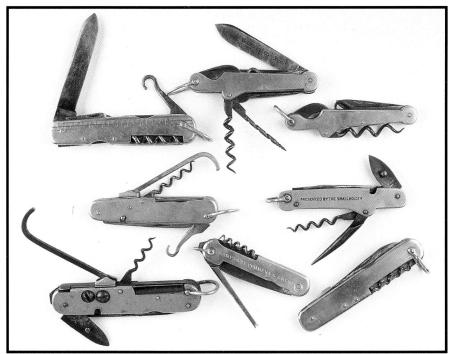

One French and seven English early gentlemen's steel knives.
Top row left to right: A 4 1/2" seven tool knife marked C. BARRETT & CO., 158 STRAND (London), a retailer for SHEFFIELD MADE knives. Handles delineated with "Metre" and "London" measures. $200-250; Seven tools marked G. BUTLER & CO., SHEFFIELD, ENGLAND. Master blade stamped "Butler's 'Park' Knife." $200-225; Four tools marked ARMY & NAVY C. S. L. (Cooperative Stores Limited). This was an English hardware retailer. $200-250.
Middle row: A steel Farrier's knife with seven tools marked CROWNSHAW, LIVERPOOL, SHEFFIELD MADE. Crownshaw was a retailer. The knife is engraved "A. W. Davie" and was, no doubt, a knife that pleased that gentleman in the late 19th century. $300-400; A six tool knife with blades marked only SHEFFIELD MADE. The handle is stamped "Presented by the smallholder." $150-200.
Bottom row: A massive 4 3/4" long x 3/4" rather ugly looking but practical knife for the fox hunt. It includes two knife blades, a tin opener, a button hook (for the riding boots), a shell extractor pivoting on one blade (for after the kill), a hoof pick, a bleeding tool, a wire cutter, a corkscrew, and, to top it off, two harness repair bolts (affixed through the handle). The master blade is marked JOSEPH RODGERS & SONS, Nº 6 NORFOLK ST., SHEFFIELD. $400-500; French five tool knife advertising "Champagne Pommery & Greno." $100-125; Six tool plain steel handle knife marked McPHERSON BROTHERS, SHEFFIELD HAND MADE on the master blade and REPEAT, NEEDHAM BROS., SHEFFIELD on the pen blade. McPherson Brothers were distributors in Glasgow. $200-250.

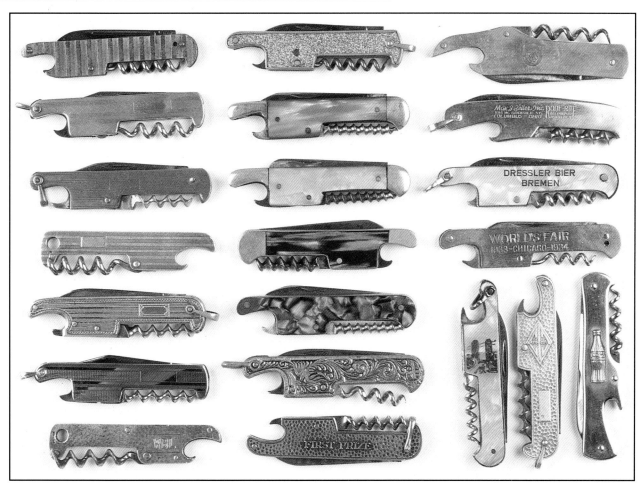

In 1916, Harry L. Vaughan of Chicago invented a pocket corkscrew that had a cap lifter in the nose and a folding worm at the bottom. His invention was marketed under the name "Nifty." Millions were sold for advertising purposes (see "Pocket - Folding" category).
The "Nifty" design can be seen in this assortment of knives. A close inspection of the lot even reveals two silver "Nifties" without knife blades (*fourth and seventh in first column*).
In the hands of knife manufacturers the "Nifty" is transformed into works of art. There are different handle materials, different worms, and slight design differences; and, yes, these too were very popular among advertisers.
Left column top to bottom: Brass with vertical line design from Fairmount Cutlery, New York City. $20-30; Gold plated with horizontal line design with monogram block. Marked S & S on the bail. $80-100; Gold plated with arrow pattern. Marked J & C N CO. on bail. $80-100; "Nifty" marked STERLING. $60-80; Two blade with plated horizontal pattern handles. Marked L F & C., U. S. A., UNIVERSAL (Landers, Frary & Clark, New Britain, Connecticut). $40-60; Plated with monogram block. Marked MERIDEN BRAND U. S. A. $30-40; "Nifty" marked STERLING and engraved "W B L." $60-80.

Middle column top to bottom: Gold sparkle celluloid handle. $20-30; Pink and yellow celluloid. Blade marked IMPERIAL, PROVIDENCE, R. I. with "Worcester Salt Co." advertising. $30-40; Cracked ice celluloid. Marked IMPERIAL, PROVIDENCE, R. I. $25-35; Dark celluloid by Imperial. $20-25; Rainbow celluloid marked ENDERES. Enderes was an Iowa wholesaler for Camllius Cutlery Co. $30-40; Ornate brass. $40-50; Hammered pattern with "First Prize" embossed on one side and monogram block on the other. Marked ROBESON SHUREDGE ROCHESTER. $100-125.
Right column top to bottom: Arched steel handle stamped with "R & J N" trademark. $50-60; Curved steel handle advertising "Rode-Rite All Purpose Asphalt." Marked REMINGTON U M C, MADE IN U. S. A. $75-100; Cracked ice celluloid with "Dressler Bier Bremen" advertising. $20-30; Souvenir stamped "World's Fair 1933 - Chicago - 1934." Marked N. SHURE CO., CHICAGO. $60-80; *(L-R)* Cracked ice celluloid marked ELOSI, MADE IN GERMANY. $25-35; Hammered pattern with "Imperial" logo and monogram block. $60-70; Plain handle with Coca Cola bottle applied. Marked SCHRADE, WALDEN, NY USA. $125-150.

Horseman's

The Norvell-Shapleigh Hardware Company of St. Louis, Missouri, (1902-1917) described knives like these in their catalog as "Farmer's Knife; Length 3 3/4 inches; Polished Steel Bolsters; One Large Spear and One Small Pen Blade; Full Polished; One Saw Blade, One Horse Fleam, One Hoof Cleaner, One Cork Screw, One Gimlet, One Square Reamer, One Screw Driver, One Pair Tweezers and One Steel Needle; Iron Lining, German Silver Shield; Weight per Dozen 4 lbs. Genuine Stag Handle. $150.00/Dozen." Other catalogs refer to the knife as a Horseman's or a Farrier's knife.

Most of the Horseman's knives have two or three blades on top. Two or three tools including the corkscrew are under the hoof cleaner. A pick and tweezers are usually inserted under the handle.

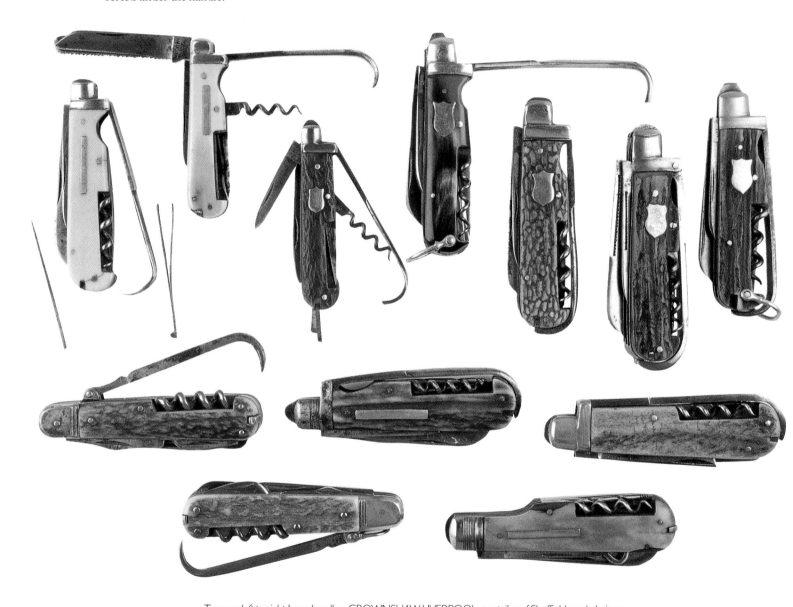

Top row left to right: Ivory handles. CROWNSHAW LIVERPOOL, a retailer of Sheffield made knives. $300-350; Ivory handles. WILKENS & SON. $300-350; Stag handles. G (crown) R RODGERS CUTLERS TO HIS MAJESTY (1820-1830). $300-400; Horn handles. Master blade marked WILLIAM RODGERS SHEFFIELD. Small blade marked I CUT IT MY WAY. $300-400; Stag handles. PATTERSON & CO., BELFAST. $400-500; Stag handles. ELMWOOD CUTLERY CO. $300-350; Stag handles. WILLIAM RODGERS SHEFFIELD/I CUT IT MY WAY. $300-350.
Middle row left to right: Ten tool stag handle knife marked on master blade DITTMAR HEILBRONN. The back of the hoof cleaner is marked DEUTSCHES ARMEE-MESSER (German Army Knife). $700-1000; Stag handles. W. S. SEARLES. $250-300; Stag handle. Tang of blade marked OLD AIKEN. Blade marked ABERCROMBIE & FITCH C°., NEW YORK. $400-500.
Bottom row left to right: Bone handles with nine tools plus tortoise shell pick and brass tweezers inserted under the handles. Marked ROBT KLAAS, SOLINGEN. $300-400; This one is the same design as a horseman's knife without the hoof cleaner. Four tools on top and four tools on the bottom plus pick and tweezers inserted under ivory handles. Marked BRITTON & SONS. $300-400.

Ivory, Bone & Horn

Tortoise shell and ivory handle corkscrew knives continue to escalate in value partially fueled by import and export restrictions on the products. The collector must be aware that export licenses are required in some countries to take these materials out. The collector bidding successfully at English auctions should secure such licenses if they intend to take the knives out of the country. Also, the knives can be confiscated at some borders if not properly declared, e.g. Canada. The hosts of the materials as well as the knives are becoming endangered species.

Tortoise shell handle knives with a variety of patterns and blade counts. The open knife has 16 blades and is marked with a backward and forward F trademark. $300-400.
Top row left to right: 2 1/2" narrow knife with single blade marked CAST STEEL. Web helix. $60-80; 2" with ten tools marked AOLLI LAUSANNE (Switzerland). $200-250; Seven tool with J shape silver decoration. Marked IXL GEORGE WOSTENHOLM, SHEFFIELD. $250-300.
Middle row left to right: Fifteen tool plus tweezers and pick under tortoise handles. $200-250; 2" twelve tool marked SCHNEIDER A GENÈVE (Switzerland). $200-250; Six tool unmarked. $60-80; Bartender's knife with two knife blades, foil cutter and web helix. Marked W. H. WEBSTER'S CELEBRATED CUTLERY. $125-150; Prime tortoise shell handles on a five tool knife with crossed keys trademark of Friedr. Herder Abr. Sohn, Solingen, Germany. $200-250.
Bottom row left to right: 3 1/2" with four knife blades and a web helix folding out from the end. $100-125; Six tool marked GEORGE WOSTENHOLM IXL CUTLERY. 175-200; Six tool marked MAPPIN & WEBB (Sheffield). $150-200.

~Ivory, Bone & Horn~

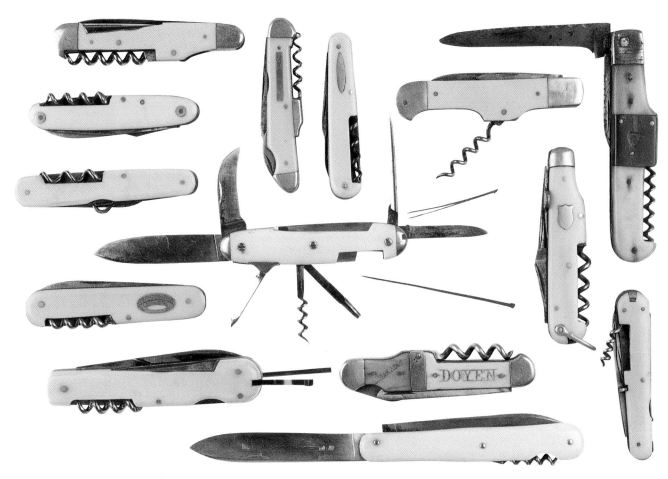

For the corkscrew collector, quality ivory handle corkscrew knives can be the hardest and dearest to find. The patterns shown here represent a number of manufacturers who took pride in prominently marking their names on the knives. The master blade of the fully open knife is marked BOUEYRE, 46 R. DAUPHINE, PARIS. There are eight additional tools, including a tweezers and pick, which slide into a slot in the bolsters. $600-800.

Left side top to bottom: Four tool with bolsters on each end. Marked D. PERES SOLINGEN. $300-400; Six tool marked D. PERES, SOLINGEN. $300-350; Six tool marked TRUSTWORTHY, MAPPIN & WEBB (Sheffield). $300-400; Two blades and a fluted wire helix. Marked ALEXANDER COPPEL, SOLINGEN. A silver tire with

"Continental" advertising is inlaid in the ivory. $200-250; 4" six tool knife with locking master blade and cigar box opener blade. A tortoise shell pick and a steel tweezers are inserted under the handles. Marked J. A. HENCKELS, ZWILLINGSWERK. $500-600.

Top center: Two three and four blade Sheffield made knives. $150-200.

Right side top to bottom: Unmarked with scalloped edges on blades. $60-80; Marked S. MOLIN, ESKILSTUNA (Sweden). $250-300; Marked CARRICK & CRAIG, GLASGOW / SHEFFIELD HAND FORGED. $250-300; Ten tools plus brass tweezers and pick inserted under handles. Marked F. HERDER, SOLINGEN. $200-250; Four panel ivory advertising "Champagne Doyen." $250-300; 4" knife with master blade and silver fruit blade marked G R. $400-500.

The who's who list of manufacturers of polished horn and bone handle corkscrews is very long. Values range from $20-$250 with high quality, older, and multi-blades at the top end. Here are the horn and bone (except as noted) handle products of a few manufacturers.

Top row left to right: Frey A Colmar; Kutmaster, Utica, N. Y. (celluloid); Rud. Buchel, Merscheid, Solingen; W. H. Morley & Sons; Herm. Konejung, Solingen; Clütters & Co., Solingen.

Second row left to right: Jowicka, Solingen; Knivbolaget, Eskilstuna, Sweden; Hartkopf & Co., Solingen.

Third row left to right: Bruckmann, Germany; Junkerwerk, Ohligs, Solingen; Robt. Klaas, Solingen.

Bottom row left to right: Ka-Bar (hard rubber); C. W. Engels, Solingen, GR; Contento, Made in Germany (wood); Gottlieb Hammesfahr, Solingen, Foche; Continental (wood); J. A. Schmidt & Soehne, Solingen; Hammer & Schlegel, Solingen, Germany; Hoffritz (wood - made in Italy); Christian's, Solingen (celluloid); IA, Solingen.

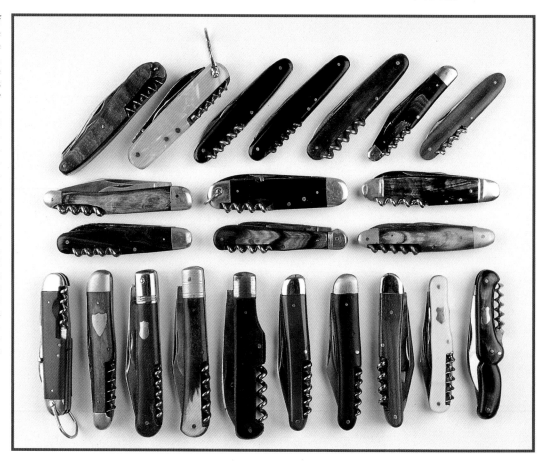

276

Korn's Patent

On February 8, 1883, George W. Korn of New York was granted German patent number 21125 for his "Korkenzieher." On August 28, 1883, Korn received U. S. Patent Number 283,900 entitled "Cork Turner." Korn's knife contains the "Cork Turner," having two "prongs." The long prong is carefully slipped in beside the cork until the cork is penetrated by the short prong. Four serrations on the long prong just below the point on the short prong engage the cork. A twist to break the cork free from the bottle wall and a long, slow pull will nicely draw out the cork.

An examination of those pictured here reveals a bit of a mystery in "Korn's Patent" knives.

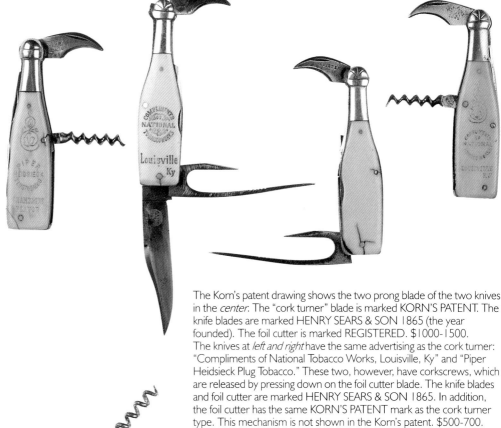

The Korn's patent drawing shows the two prong blade of the two knives in the *center*. The "cork turner" blade is marked KORN'S PATENT. The knife blades are marked HENRY SEARS & SON 1865 (the year founded). The foil cutter is marked REGISTERED. $1000-1500.
The knives at *left and right* have the same advertising as the cork turner: "Compliments of National Tobacco Works, Louisville, Ky" and "Piper Heidsieck Plug Tobacco." These two, however, have corkscrews, which are released by pressing down on the foil cutter blade. The knife blades and foil cutter are marked HENRY SEARS & SON 1865. In addition, the foil cutter has the same KORN'S PATENT mark as the cork turner type. This mechanism is not shown in the Korn's patent. $500-700.

The knife blades of the urn are marked Cattaraugus Cut. Co. and the foil cutter is marked REGISTERED like the cork turner. $600-800.
The master blade of the knife at *bottom right* is marked HALLSTROM ESKILSTUNA (Sweden). Depressing the foil cutter raises the cork in the same manner as the bottle foil cutters. $300-400.

So why are some of the bottles marked KORN'S PATENT when they don't appear to be Korn's patent at all? All of the knives with corkscrews in this category appear to be more like the Bierhoff & Wever patent than the Korn's.

My guess? The manufacturers of the Korn's patented "Cork Turner" realized that it was a rather impractical, cumbersome method of pulling a cork. The Bierhoff & Wever concept with worm was better and the bottles were changed to use this method. Leftover foil cutters with the Korn's patent mark were used in the manufacture even though the knives produced were not the patented cork turner.

The bottle with mother-of-pearl handles (*right*) has the SEARS markings and the KORN'S PATENT mark on the foil cutter. $700-900.
The extraordinary glass with mother-of-pearl handles (*middle*) has the corkscrew mechanism and all blades are marked Novelty Cutlery Co. *$Rare*.
The knife on the *top right* has one blade marked D.R. PATENT 14392. This is a German patent of December 31, 1880 issued to Bierhoff & Wever of Solingen. The worm is raised from its compartment by depressing the lever on the back of it, thus operating in a similar fashion to the foil cutters described above. $600-800.

Legs

Laguiole is a small town in south-central France famous for cattle, cheese, sausages, and cutlery. Around the town square are knife shops galore. In addition to the famous Laguiole knives, they do sell Swiss Army knives and a wide variety of other kitchen gadgets.

The Laguiole knives are produced with wood, bone, ivory, horn, and manmade materials. Blades are stainless or carbon steel. The pocket knives with corkscrew sell for $50-$350.

Pierre-Jean Calmels designed the original Laguiole knives in 1829. The knives were sturdy, good looking, and meant for farm work. The corkscrew knife was not added to the products

of the town until 1880. On the back of a genuine modern Laguiole knife is a bee. Earlier knives have a fly. In the mid-1800s, there were seven or eight manufacturers in the small mountain town. The production of cheaper, machine made knives in other parts of France gradually drove the Laguiole manufacturers out of business by the middle of the 20th century.

In 1985, a revival took place. A new Laguiole factory opened. Now there are nearly a hundred knife makers in Laguiole and their products are sold worldwide.

Many of the Laguiole knives with corkscrews have the appearance of a leg.

If you are looking for a Laguoile, don't grab and buy a leg shape too hastily. At first glance you might think they are Laguioles, but take a closer look.
Top row left to right: Imitation stag handle with two blades marked A. W. WADSWORTH & SON, AUSTRIA. $80-100; Horn handle. Marked VERITABLE LAGUIOLE. $100-120; Imitation horn handle. Blade marked G. FAYET, VERITABLE LAGUIOLE. Also has a punch. $120-140; Celluloid with punch and master blade marked G. DAVID, LAGUIOLE. $130-150.
Bottom row left to right: Horn handle with two blades marked A. W. WADSWORTH & SON, AUSTRIA. $80-100; Light stag handle with two blades marked A. W. WADSWORTH & SON, AUSTRIA. $80-100; Horn handle. Marked VERITABLE LAGUIOLE. $100-120.
The postcard pictures Mr. Robert Cognet with a 2.5 meter knife.

An assortment of knives for the leg man.
Top row left to right: Russian knife with two knife blades and a web helix. Long silver bolsters with wood handles. Dated 1899. $250-300; Celluloid handle advertising "Brown^{bilt} Shoes." $200-250; Celluloid handle advertising "Brownbilt Tread Straight Shoes." Blade marked SENECA CUTLERY CO., UTICA, N. Y. c.1930s. $200-250; Horn handle with two unmarked blades. $40-60; Red celluloid handles with Laguiole bee on the backspring. $100-125.
Bottom row left to right: Imitation stag handles. $20-25; Bone handle. Marked SOLINGEN (Germany). $60-80; Bone handle. Unmarked. $30-40; Bone handle. Marked W. HERMANNS & SOHNE, SOLINGEN. $60-80; Polished horn handle with brass bolsters. Laguiole bee on backspring. Blade marked TOLEDO. This is a current Laguiole knock-off from Spain retailing for $30-40; Large (9 1/2" open) two blade knife. The master blade is locked when extended and released by pushing down on the second blade. $125-150; Large stag handle knife. Master blade marked W. R. KIRSCHBAUM, SOLINGEN. The master blade is locked when extended and released by pushing the ring against the back of the blade. $150-200.

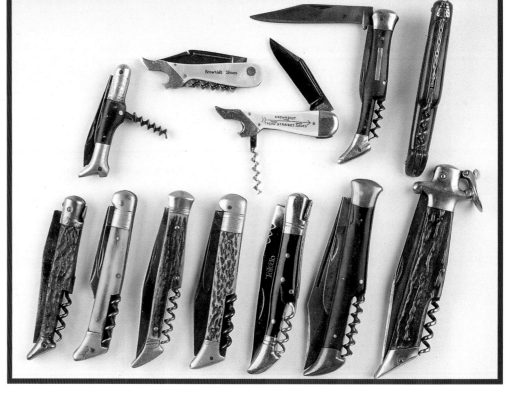

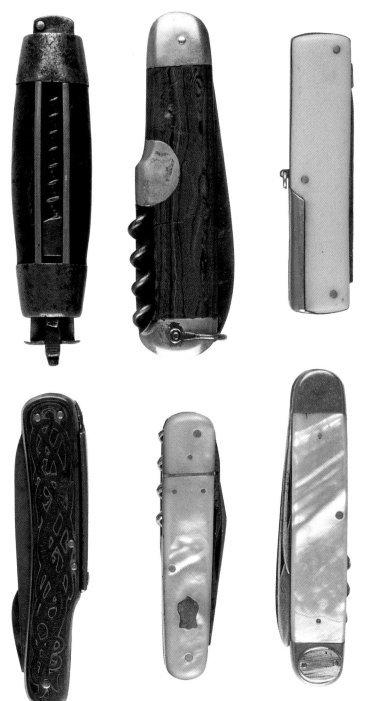

Mechanical

In 1987, the late Bob Nugent published his booklet *Knives with Corkscrews*. Bob had a great passion for corkscrews knives and spent hundreds of hours researching their history. He was fascinated with the many ingenious mechanisms employed to release the worm from the knife handle. These methods are illustrated and detailed in his booklet. Most of the inventions dealt with making the worm and shank as long as the knife handle to ensure greater purchase of the cork and gripping room for pulling the cork. The booklet includes worms on knives that slide, rotate, expand, hinge, pivot, and come out of hiding.

These six knives with unusual opening/release mechanism were owned by the late Bob Nugent. They are shown with the corkscrew closed and opened.

Top left: A Swedish "art" or "barrel" knife, which is more frequently seen without the corkscrew in a variety of sizes. In 1874, Johan Engström of Eskilstuna invented the knife that folds into a brass case and slides into the barrel handle. The corkscrew was added in the early 20th century by C. G. Segerström. It pops up by pushing a tab at the top and is then slid along a channel to the center to form a T-handle corkscrew. $800-1200.

Top middle: The corkscrew lifts up normally; but there is no fingernail notch for lifting the knife blade. When the worm is fully extended, pushing it to one side will move a spring to lift the knife blade. When the knife is fully extended, it locks and is unlocked again by moving worm. Celluloid mahogany grain handles. Blade marked SOLIDUS, FRENIX ARMY MODEL and D.R.G.M., PATENTE. Made by Franz Frenzel in Nixdorf, Bohemia. c.1900. $400-500.

Top right: 1908 German registration by Carl Windhövel and Cuno Weyer. A small ring attached at the halfway point of the corkscrew is grasped and slid down a slot to bring the worm out. It can then be turned perpendicular to the handle. The knife has two unmarked blades. $800-1000

Bottom left: A three blade knife marked HEDENGRAN & SON, ESKILSTUNA (Sweden). The worm is hidden under a nail file. When the file is moved laterally, the worm pops out of its chamber. Reverse the movement, to store the worm. File is marked PATENT. $700-900.

Bottom middle: The mother-of-pearl on one side is in two pieces affixed to a two piece brass liner. The larger piece of the liner pivots. By pushing it up, the worm is raised. Contains scissors and two knife blades with master marked S T & R GERMANY, COLUMBUS E G G. $600-800.

Bottom right: Two blade knife with mother-of-pearl handles marked CROWN CUT. Cº. GERMANY. The worm is released by grasping oval disks on the end bolsters between thumb and forefinger. Turning the disks moves a pin that locks over the last turn of the worm and a spring forces the worm upward. $600-800.

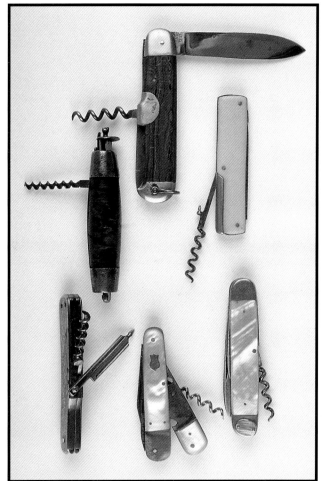

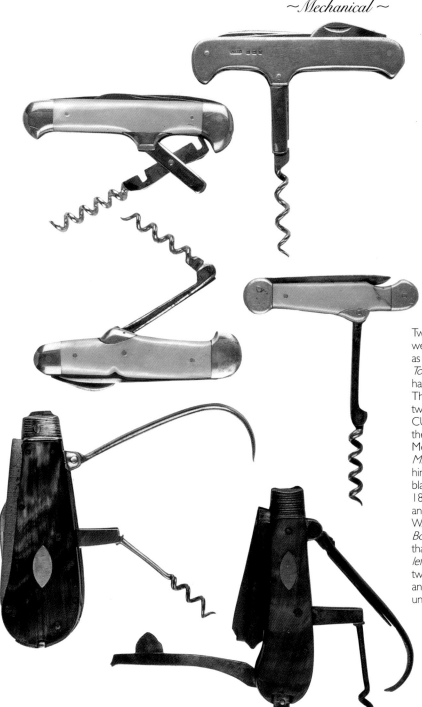

Two piece worms, hinged worms, sliding worms, and pivoting worms were various methods conceived to make the worm of a knife as long as possible for more purchase of the cork and greater pulling power.

Top row: The two piece worms of the pearl and sterling handle knives have notches in the shaft that lock onto a pin when opened or closed. This is an 1897 German design registration by Ernst Steinfeld. The two blade knife on the *left* is marked H. BOKER & CO'S IMPROVED CUTLERY. $400-500. The silver handles on the three blade knife on the *right* have a 1920 London hallmark and the trademark of S. Mordan & Co. $500-600.

Middle row: The worms on both mother-of-pearl handle knives are hinged for maximum length. The 3 1/4" knife on the *left* has three blades and is marked D. R. PATENT Nº 92116. This is Rob. Paffrath's 1896 German patent. $800-1000. The 2 3/4" knife has two blades and is marked MADE ABROAD EXELANDRA, SHEFFIELD STEEL WARRANTED. $700-900.

Bottom row: Two 18th century horn handle knives with hinged worm that folds into a chamber covered by a hoof pick. The example on the *left* has two knife blades, a saw, a hoof pick, pullout picks and tweezers, and a corkscrew. $1200-1500. *Right* is marked BUTLER and has two blades, hoof pick with a small pick in a channel on the underside, two fleams, and a pullout blade. $1300-1500.

In 1897, Gottlieb Hammesfahr of Solingen, Germany, obtained a patent for his rather ingenious method of making a knife with a long corkscrew. The worm pivots on a pin horizontally 180° on one half of the upper arm. It is then lifted into position.

The knife at *lower left* was made by Remington in the United States after Hammesfahr obtained an American patent in 1898. $400-500. The other five knives were made in Eskilstuna, Sweden. $250-300.

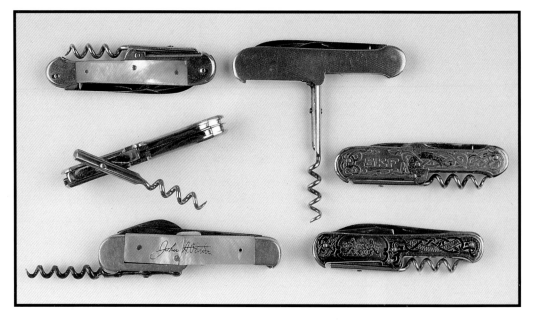

In 1896, Alfred Williams of Sheffield, England, was granted a patent for a knife in which the worm has a slotted shank traveling on a pin. It pulls out to one end of the knife, is swiveled on the pin, and locked into position. A spring on the shank keeps the worm in place when closed. The two knives at *lower right* are true to the patent and are marked ALFRED WILLIAMS, SHEFFIELD, ENGLAND, PAT. NO. 25659. One has faint marking on the handle "R. M. S. Mauretania." $300-400. The German made knife on the *left* is like William's patent and is marked A. KASTOR & BROS WARRANTED CUTLERY. Adolph Kastor, a New York City importer, was granted an American patent in 1897 for Williams' knife. $250-350. The four other mother-of-pearl knives are marked J. A. HENCKELS, GERMANY. In this version of the Williams patent, the spring is mounted on the back of the knife instead of the shank. The small knife is 2 1/4" and the others are 3 1/4" long. $250-350.

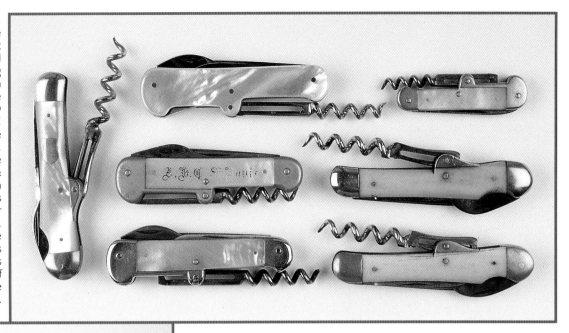

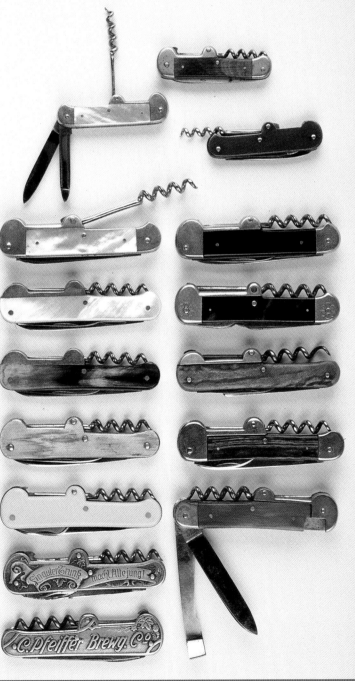

Left: Carl Müller's 1896 German patent was a much simpler idea. The worm slides horizontally in a ring until a square form on the end of the shank stops it. The ring and worm are then pivoted into position perpendicular to the handle. A spring holds the worm in place when closed. Examples of true Müller patent knives are rare. The only one in this photo is the *fourth from top right*. The bolster is marked D. R. P. 89172. $400-500.

A simplified version of the Müller patent has a pin mounted between the shoulders on the back of the knife. The shank of the worm slides under the pin and stops when its hooked end meets the pin. It is then swiveled on the pin and into position. The babies at the *top* were made by Feist and Peres in Solingen. $150-200. Manufacturers of the 3 1/4" size with various handle materials and designs include Peres, Kayser, Judson, and Wormser from Solingen. Two of these are marked D.R.G.M. for Müller's 1897 registration. $150-250.

Below: In these knives the shank of the sliding worm is housed within the handles. The knife at the *top* has hard rubber handles and the shank is totally hidden when closed. Marked J. A. HENCKELS, SOLINGEN. $250-300. In the other four the worm shank is visible by looking down between the handles. Manufacturers of these late 20th century plastic handle knives include C. Lutters, Aug. Muller, and Gust. Haker from Solingen. $150-200.

Miniature

All of the knives in this group measure in the 1 3/8" - 2 1/2" range. Miniature knives were made as charms, perfume and medicine screws, novelties, and souvenirs.

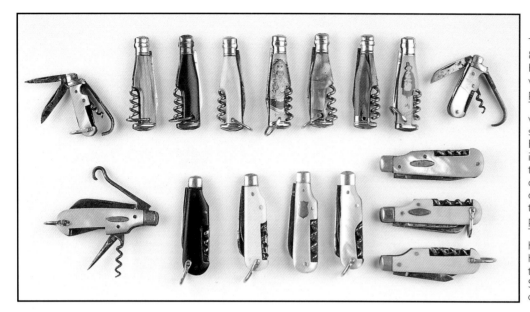

The two identical knives at *top left and right* are 1 3/8" miniature versions of the Farmer's or Horseman's knives. Each has two knife blades, a wire helix, and a hoof pick. Perhaps made for picking the hooves of a Lilliputian horse? $60-80. The seven knives with colorful celluloid handles were made by Richards of Sheffield. All have a single knife blade and wire helix. Some are marked RICHARDS, SHEFFIELD, ENGLAND. Two interesting souvenirs are the one commemorating the 1953 coronation of Queen Elizabeth II and the other picturing Jenny Jones of Wales. Richards was one of the largest 20th century Sheffield manufacturers. The firm gained success through the production of large run, cheap knives. $5-30. The knives in the *bottom row* have a variety of handle materials and designs. They have a wire helix and punch on the bottom and one, two, or three blades on the top. They were all made in Sheffield. One has an Australian distributor's name on the tang - "W. Jno. Baker, Sydney." $20-40.

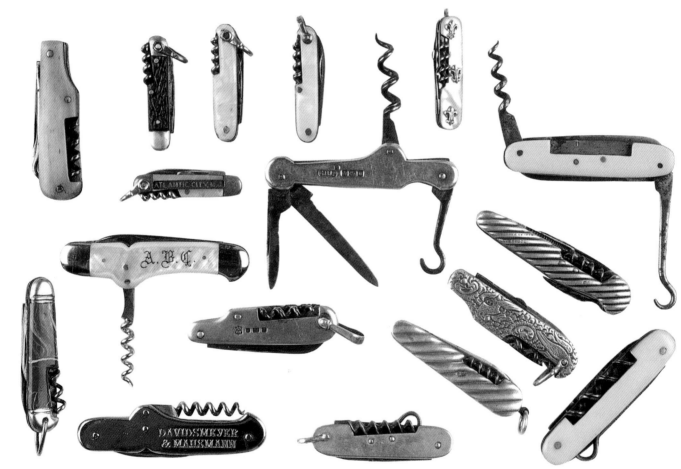

Top row left to right: Unusual SILVER STEEL mark on the blade tang. $30-40; 1 3/8" imitation stag handle. Two blades and wire helix. Made in Germany. $15-25; Two celluloid handle two blade knives made in Germany. $8-15; 1 3/8" knife with three blades, scissors, and web helix. Gold fleurs de lis applied to pearl handles. Marked GRAEF & SCHMIDT, GERMANY. $125-150.

Second row left to right: Souvenir knife marked MAUSSNER GERMANY (1900-1932). "Atlantic City, N. J." plate inlaid in handle. $80-100; Six tool knife with silver handles stamped with Sheffield 1930 hallmark. Blades marked BUTLER. $150-175; Four tool knife with ivory covers. Marked SHEFFIELD CUTLERY. $75-85.

Others: The 2 1/2" pearl handle knife is made by Henckels of Solingen. This is a good example of a pearl with advertising imprint that has survived. The advertising is for A. B. C. Brewing Co. of St. Louis. $200-300; Green celluloid handles marked FABRIQUÉ EN ALLEMAGNE.

$20-30; Steel handles advertising "Davidsmeyer & Mahsmann, White Horse Tavern, 567 Hudson St., N. Y." (*bottom left*). Marked GRIFFON, GERMANY. $100-125; Steel handles with button hook on same side as worm (*bottom center*). $60-80; Ivory handles (*lower right*). Marked ROBERTS CELEBRATED CUTLERY SHEFFIELD. $50-60.

The four silver knives are:

Plain silver handle with 1890 Sheffield hallmark and maker's mark of James Veall and Walter Tyzack. Blade marked with "Eye" trademark and WITNESS. Six tools. $250-300.

Diagonal pattern handle (*top*) marked ALEXANDER BROS. L^D, LIVERPOOL. Five tools. Blade marked SHEFFIELD. $200-250.

Ornate design with 1881 London hallmark and mark of retailer Walter Thornhill. Four tools including scissors. $250-300.

Diagonal pattern with 1906 Birmingham hallmark. Scissors, knife blade, and web helix all on top. $200-250.

Mother-of-pearl

The 1891 print was published by A. Guérinet, Editeur, Paris. It depicts a child uncorking a bottle of Bordeaux with a mother-of-pearl handle knife. Perhaps the prettiest natural material knives are the mother-of-pearl. Knife collectors often refer to these as simply "Pearls." They are designed as elegant furnishings for a lady's dressing table, with accessories for the smoker, as special occasion gifts, for point of purchase displays, and for exhibitions. They are certainly not designed for carrying in one's pocket or tossing in a tool or tackle box.

Pearls with corkscrews can be found with a single blade, two blades, three blades, etc. - look hard enough and you will find the number you want!

One of the most famous exhibition knives with mother-of-pearl is the "Year Knife." The 32" knife was made by Jonathan Crookes and exhibited in 1821 with that number of blades. Every five years, new blades are added to bring it up to date. Crookes sold the knife to Joseph Rodgers & Sons Ltd. in Sheffield. Stanley Tools purchased the knife in 1969. The "Norfolk Knife" containing 75 blades and measuring 34" high was made for the 1851 Crystal Palace Exhibition in London. A one hundred blade pearl called the "Centennial Knife" was exhibited by Boker at the 1876 Philadelphia Centennial Exposition.

The unusual shape pearl in the *center* has eight implements. Note that the worm, like the other tools, is pinned at the end giving the user very little power to pull a cork, but enough to remove a small one from a medicine or perfume bottle. 3 1/8" closed. $300-400.
The others clockwise from top right: 2" with seven tools. Marked MANZ. $150-200; 2 3/4" with five tools. Marked GERMANY. Quite unusual because it has "hidden" advertising on the blade tangs: "Lembeck & Betz, Eagle Brewing Co." (1890-1920). $250-300; 3 1/2" with master blade, pen blade, and fluted helix. Marked C. F. KAYSER, SOLINGEN. $100-150; 3 3/8" with three knife blades and fluted helix. Not marked. $75-100; 3 1/2" with two knife blades and web helix. Four panel pearl handle with decorative bolsters. Marked A. W. WADSWORTH & SON, AUSTRIA. (1905-1936). $200-250.

The 3 1/4" pearl in the *center* has five tools on the top, three on the bottom, and a tweezers and tortoise shell pick inserted in slots under the handles. Marked E. WECK, GERMANY, with ECHO in an oval trademark. Weck was a New York importer who purchased the Pauls Brothers ECHO trademark in 1904. $200-250.
The others clockwise from top right: Four blades on top marked F.A.G. Fluted helix and punch on the bottom. $150-175; 2 1/2" twelve tool knife including two worms. Marked F. A. KOCH & CO. A New York City importer. $200-250; 3" fifteen tool knife including a comb blade. Marked A. W. WADSWORTH & SON, AUSTRIA. $200-250; 3 1/8" twenty-five tool knife marked P K W. $250-300; 3 3/4" 12 tool knife marked with letters C M in a scroll trademark. $250-300; 2 7/8" five tool knife marked A. KASTOR & BROS., GERMANY. $150-175; 2 1/2" knife with five tools plus pick and tweezers in slots under the handles. Marked KRUISIUS BROTHERS, GERMANY with K B EXTRA in an oval logo. $200-225.

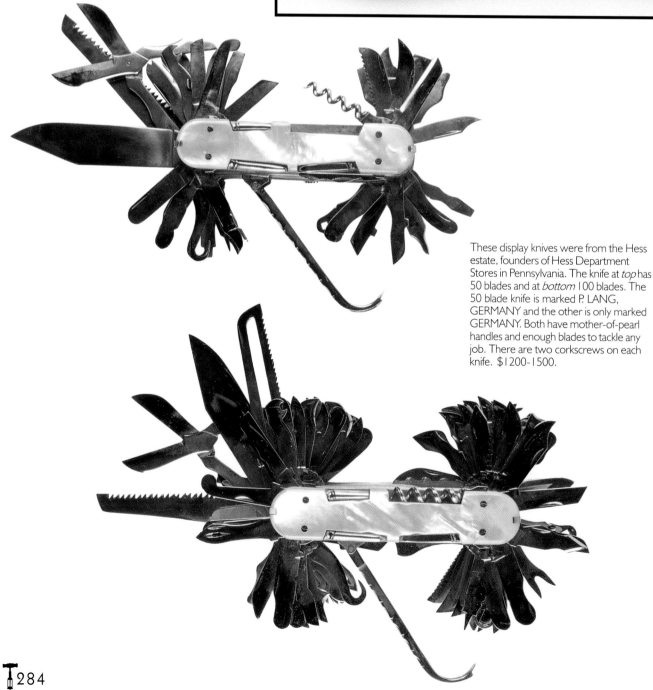

Some of the best quality pearls have four pieces of pearl pinned in four sections on the handles. Here are nine different patterns. $150-250. The knife at *lower right* shows faint traces of "Pabst, Milwaukee" imprinted on the mother-of-pearl. While that advertising did not survive its age, the master blade did. It is clearly engraved "Pabst, Milwaukee." The *second from top right* has a sensible location for advertising. It is engraved on the metal between the pieces of pearl "C. F. Schmidt & Peters, Veuve Clicquot."

These display knives were from the Hess estate, founders of Hess Department Stores in Pennsylvania. The knife at *top* has 50 blades and at *bottom* 100 blades. The 50 blade knife is marked P. LANG, GERMANY and the other is only marked GERMANY. Both have mother-of-pearl handles and enough blades to tackle any job. There are two corkscrews on each knife. $1200-1500.

Shell Extractors

A natural addition to a sportsman's knife is a cartridge or shell extractor. Most are a fixed design for 12 and 16 gauge shells at the end of the knife handle. John Watts and the team of Joseph Westby and Charles Levick of Sheffield both came up with adjustable designs in 1892. In Watts' patent, one side of the extrac-tor is fixed on the handle and a pivoting blade is used for the other side. An example of Watts' patent is shown under the "Smoker's Tools" category. Westby and Levick had a fixed 12 and 16 gauge extractor formed at the end of the handle, but added a pivoting blade for other sizes. The pivoting tool also cuts wires.

Top: Westby & Levick's 1892 English patent. Marked THORNHILL'S NEW SHOOTING KNIFE, PATENT 12/16 on the handle and GRADUATING EXTRACTOR on the foil cutter. $300-400.

Second row: A six tool knife with a shell extractor swiveling on a folding blade. The extractor is marked 12 CARTRIDGE EXTRACTOR 16. The master blade is marked RICHARTZ, SOLINGEN, GERMAN MAKE. $250-300; A seven tool knife with one end of the extractor pivoting on the other folding arm. Handle marked THE ADJUSTABLE EXTRACTOR with an 1883 registration mark. Master blade marked JAMES DIXON & SONS, SHEFFIELD, ENGLAND. $200-250.

Bottom row left to right: Orange celluloid handles. $50-60; Black plastic handles (Russian). $30-40; Bone handles. Locking master blade marked DITTERT & CO. $125-150; Imitation stag handles marked INOX. $40-60; Wood handles. Marked FOX EXTRA. $50-75; Italian made shell extractor with horn handles. Marked MANIAGO. $75-125; A steel handle shell extractor with wire cutter, button hook, three knife blades, and wire helix. Originally assembled with blades of two manufacturers marked JOHN WATTS, SHEFFIELD, ESTB. 1765 and SCOTIA, JAMES McCLORY, SHEFFIELD. $150-200.

Stag

A ntlers from deer are one of the most popular materials used for knife handles. They are commonly referred to as "stag handle knives" or in knife circles as simply "stags."

French and English stag handles. The knife in the *center* is French and marked NOGENT. $125-150. The English *clockwise from top right:* IBBERSON, SHEFFIELD, ENGLAND. $150-175; JOSEPH RODGERS & SONS, NO. 6 NORFOLK ST., SHEFFIELD, ENGLAND on the master blade and foil cutter. Button hook supplied by Wheatley Brothers $150-200; H. G. LONG & CO., SHEFFIELD. $150-175; IXL GEORGE WOSTENHOLM. Includes pick and tweezers inserted under the handles. $175-225.

American stag handles.
Top row left to right: WINCHESTER TRADEMARK, MADE IN U. S. A. 4975. $250-400; REMINGTON U M C, R3843. $200-300; EMPIRE, WINSTED, CT, 3751 S F. $200-300.
Bottom row left to right: EMPIRE, WINSTED, CT. $200-250; CATTARAUGUS CUTLERY CO., LITTLE VALLEY, N. Y. 3239H. $150-250; CHALLENGE CUTLERY CORPN. $150-200.

German stag handles.
Top row left to right: DROESCHER'S S R D BRAND. New York City importer. $125-150; HARTKOPF & CO., SOLINGEN. $125-150; MANN with bridge. Trademark of Ernst Bruckmann. $100-125; P I C 14500 GERMANY. $80-100; KRUSIUS BROTHERS GERMANY, K B EXTRA. $100-125; HENRY BOKER & CO., BAUMWERK-SOLINGEN, GERMANY-ALEMANIA. Locking master blade. $175-200; FARNY HAND HAMMERED, MADE IN GERMANY. $200-300; FRIEDR. ERN & CO., SOLINGEN, WEYER. $250-300.
Middle row left to right: J. A. HENCKELS, SOLINGEN. A lady's 2 3/4" stag with six implements, including scissors and button hook. $150-200; ANTON WINGEN J^R, SOLINGEN-GERMANY. Locking master blade. $150-200.
Bottom row left to right: NEW YORK KNIFE CO., WALDEN, HAMMER BRAND (an American knife gone astray). $150-200; A heavy dangerous looking knife that is 11" long when the locking master blade or saw blade is extended. It has a fluted wire helix and plenty of gripping power to pull a cork. $200-250; J. A. HENCKELS, GERMANY. $150-200.

Fixed blade knives.
Left: A cheap imitation stag handle. Fixed blade marked DECORA - SOLINGEN, MADE IN GERMANY, D.R.G.M. $40-50.
Right top to bottom: Marked D. ZISSU with an Aztec calendar. $60-80; A high quality German knife marked PUMA-WERK, SOLINGEN, MADE IN GERMANY, HANDARBEIT GES. GESCH. N° 5/5790, BESTELL N°. 3591 and ORIGINAL WALDME*ff*ER FÜR SCHALENWILD. $250-300; An unmarked fixed blade knife in a leather case. Corkscrew, punch, and saw lock into a pin on the end the handle. A sharpening stone is included. Note position of corkscrew when locked on and consider what would happen if your hand slipped when attempting to pull a cork! $200-300.

A knife with locking blade and folding corkscrew. The Damascene work blade is marked J. A. HENCKELS TWIN WORKS SOLINGEN GERMANY with the Henckels twin logo. $800-1000.

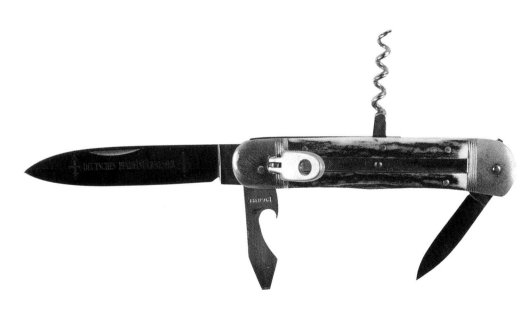

A "switchblade" knife. When holding the knife in hand, the lever on the back is depressed and the master blade flies out. The blade is stamped HUBERTUS, SOLINGEN, ROSTFREI GESCHMIEDET GERMANY and DEUTCHES PFADFINDERMESSER. $200-300. Note: In 1958, a United States law was enacted that bans "the manufacture, transportation, or distribution in interstate commerce of switchblade knives."

Just a Few More Knives

"THIS IS AN EXCELLENT KNIFE, SIR— IT
HAS A CORKSCREW AND FOUR BLADES"

"HAVE YE ONE WI' A BLADE AN'
FOUR CORKSCREWS?"

Yes, knives were made with four corkscrews.
There were even some made in Sweden with six
worms. This single blade knife with two left-hand
and two right-hand worms was made by C. O. Ryd
of Eskilstuna, Sweden, between 1900 and 1915.
The handles are tortoise shell. $700-900.

Four single blade knives with a cap lifter formed in
the handle stampings.
Top row left to right: Blade marked F. ED. OHLIGER,
REGISTERED GERMANY. Advertising "Stocksbridge
Bottling Co., Ltd., Specialties: Lime - Lemon - &
Orange - Crushes." Over the top style cap lifter.
$100-150; Blade marked G. IBBERSON & CO.
(Sheffield). Advertising "McNish's Doctor's Special
Scotch Whisky." $100-150.
Bottom row left to right: Blade marked CHAS
CLEMENTS, 17 BILLITER ST., E. C. (Sheffield). The
handle is stamped "Clements Crown Cork Opener"
and marked with three registrations: R^D N^O 610074
(England 1912), Modèle Deposé (France) and
D.R.G.M. (Germany). $200-250; Blade marked
JOHN BROOKES, SHEFFIELD. Handle stamped
REG^D 709835 (1924). $200-225.

Top: Stag handles with master blade, saw blade, and wire helix.
Marked on master blade tang A. KASTOR & BROS., SOLINGEN
and MED. DEPT. U. S. A. Supplied to the U. S. Army by New
York importer Kastor. Was the corkscrew used to open a bottle of
whiskey for the doctor or patient before using the saw? $150-
200.
Left: Six tool utility knife with mottled green celluloid handles. The
master blade is marked only MIGNON. In a very unusual fashion,
a box wrench is mounted on each side of the handle. The
wrenches are slotted in the middle to mate with a coupling
mounted on either side of the handle. By turning the wrench
180°, it can be lifted off the handle. $200-300.
Bottom middle: A fancy French horn handle sportsman's knife. The
hoof pick has a five centimeter scale and is marked BREVETE
S.G.D.G. Under the pick is a brass six kilo scale marked with D P
in an oval. The scale spring mechanism ends in a hook. The web
helix folds out to the end to use the handle in a vertical position.
At the *bottom* is a glass cutter. The master blade is stamped
"Expositions Universelle, Paris." $400-500.
Right: Six tool knife marked WATTS SHEFFIELD with unusual
addition of a finger nail clipper. The bottom handle extends 3 1/2"
to form the base of the clipper. The top ends at 2 1/2" allowing
room for the clipping top. Watts' 1895 catalog describes it as
"Improved manicure knife. The special advantage of this knife is
the combination of two exceedingly useful manicure requisites -
viz., corn knife and nail nippers. The nail nippers are readily
worked by either hand, and produce a smoothly-cut and well-
rounded edge, unobtainable by any other means." $200-250.

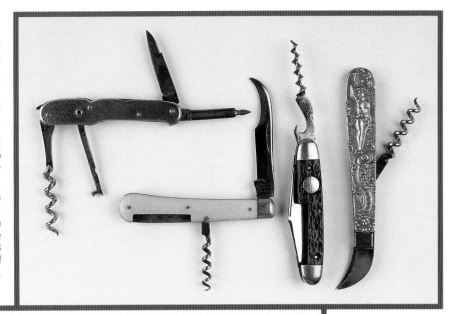

The waiter's friend with knife and file blades is an 1898 German registered design. Blades marked J. ALBERT SCHMIDT, SOLINGEN. The narrow neckstand is marked D.R.G.M. 94195. $700-900.
The ivory handle champagne knife is marked SLATER BROTHERS, SHEFFIELD. c.1858-1901. $400-500.
The shield on the stag handle knife is marked BOKER. The unusual combination cap lifter/corkscrew blade is marked PATENT APPLIED FOR. $250-350.
The fixed blade sterling champagne knife on the *right* is marked J. A. HENCKELS, SOLINGEN. The ornamental design features Bacchus and is engraved with the initials "G. R. H." The knife style is a 1908 German registration by Ed Wüsthof of Solingen. $700-900.

Left: Polished horn with a medallion stamped "The Original Jaguar." Two blades with fluted wire helix. A modern brush at end. $100-125.
Middle from top to bottom: 4 1/2" twelve blade knife marked KNIFBOLAGEI, ESKILSTUNA, SWEDEN. $200-250; Hardwood handle two blade knife with swiveling cap lifter on end. Saw blade is marked XVIII. $300-400; Early 19th century champagne knife with brush. Marked JONATHAN CROOKES CHAMPAGNE KNIFE with heart and pistol trademark. $300-350; 5" knife with eight blades plus long pick and tweezers under the hard rubber handles. Marked CLEMENTS, SHEFFIELD MADE, HAND FORGED, STAINLESS THROUGHOUT. The spike is a "marlin spike" used by sailors in tying knots. $300-400.
Right: Wood handle knife with tin can opener, heavy wire helix, and master blade marked LAUTER JUNG & CO., SOLINGEN with a tiger trademark. $200-250.

Four knives with the master blade locking in place when extended. The ring is pulled to release the lock and close the knife.
Top: The knife is 10 1/2" when opened. A stag horn has been split in two sections and mounted on full brass liners. The blade is marked HENRY BOKER'S IMPROVED CUTLERY. The web helix folds out of the curved back. $250-300.
Middle: A modern design marked HERMES PARIS on the master blade. A second blade has a cap lifter. The third tool is a punch and the fourth is a fluted wire helix fitted into the metal assembly on the back. $500-600. An early 19th century carved horn fitted with a master blade marked only A. T. and a web helix fitted into the fancy long backspring. $300-350.
Bottom: A modern bone handle with master blade marked J. M. NOGENT - INOX, FORGE MAIN. Also has a saw blade and a fluted wire helix. $250-300.

Top: Bone handles with locking master blade marked PUMA SOLINGEN, MADE IN GERMANY, ROSTFREI, HANDARBEIT, BESTELL NR. 959 (Handmade and order number). Open blade is released by depressing raised end on backspring. Two additional blades plus gutting hook and fluted wire helix. $300-400.

Bottom: Bone handles with locking master blade marked TRIODUR (Henckels trade name). The gutting hook is marked D B P 1057300. $200-250; A deer foot with locking blade marked W. M. ELLIOT & Cº., AUSTRIA. $75-100.

The cutlery center of Sweden is Eskilstuna where over 100 cutlers were working around 1900. Here are seven examples of early Swedish knives with ornate decoration. Manufacturers of these knives include Emil Olsson, L. G. Olsson, and Allström. $100-125.

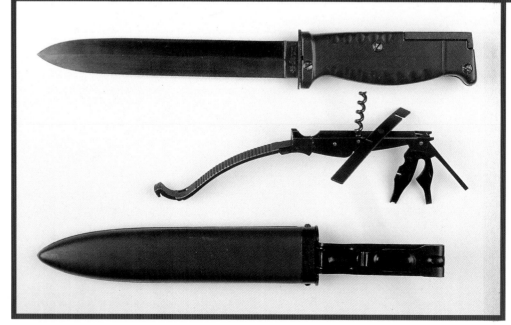

A Bayonet marked INTERARMCO REG. PAT. GERMANY. The combination tool in the *center* folds up and snaps into the handle of the bayonet. A cover swivels out of the way to expose a chamber for the worm. When the worm is pulled out, the cover is swiveled back and a notch engages with the worm to lock it in place. Five thousand of the bayonets were made for Sudanese Army AR10 assault rifles. c.1950. $300-400.

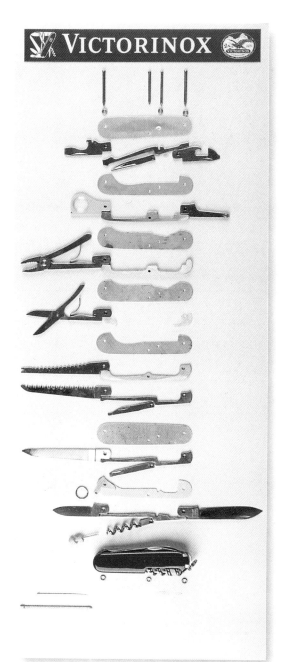

A board mounted with the parts of a Victorinox Swiss Army knife. $50-100.

A corkscrew hunt story: On a hot summer day in September 1997, Joe Paradi took Howard Luterman, Ron MacLean, and me on a hike through the streets of Avignon, Provence, France. He was hunting for a knife shop where he had window shopped when closed. After u-turning from several dead end streets and traversing some of the same streets (going around in circles), we finally happened upon the shop. We saw many knives; but the only ones with corkscrews were several Swiss Army knives and a couple of Laguioles. Then I spotted the Victorinox board. After much pleading with the shopkeeper, he finally agreed to part with it. No doubt, the manufacturer will supply him with another.

Top: Laguoile waiter's friend knife in leather case. Currently retails for $129.95. Other Laguoile knives range from $50 to $350.
Middle: Hubertus picnic knife with "Deutches Klingenmuseum Solingen" (German knife museum) on the master blade is sold at the museum for about $20.
Bottom: Swiss Army knife with watch, three blades, and a wire helix. Currently sells for $110. A two blade knife with corkscrew from Robert Klaas, Solingen. $100-125.

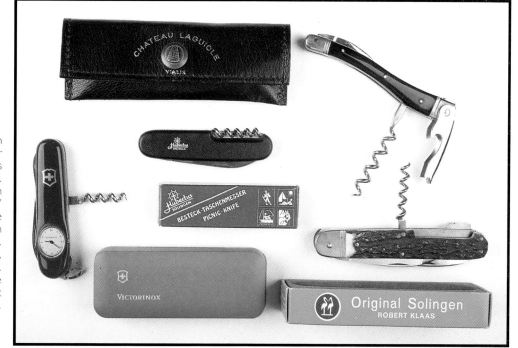

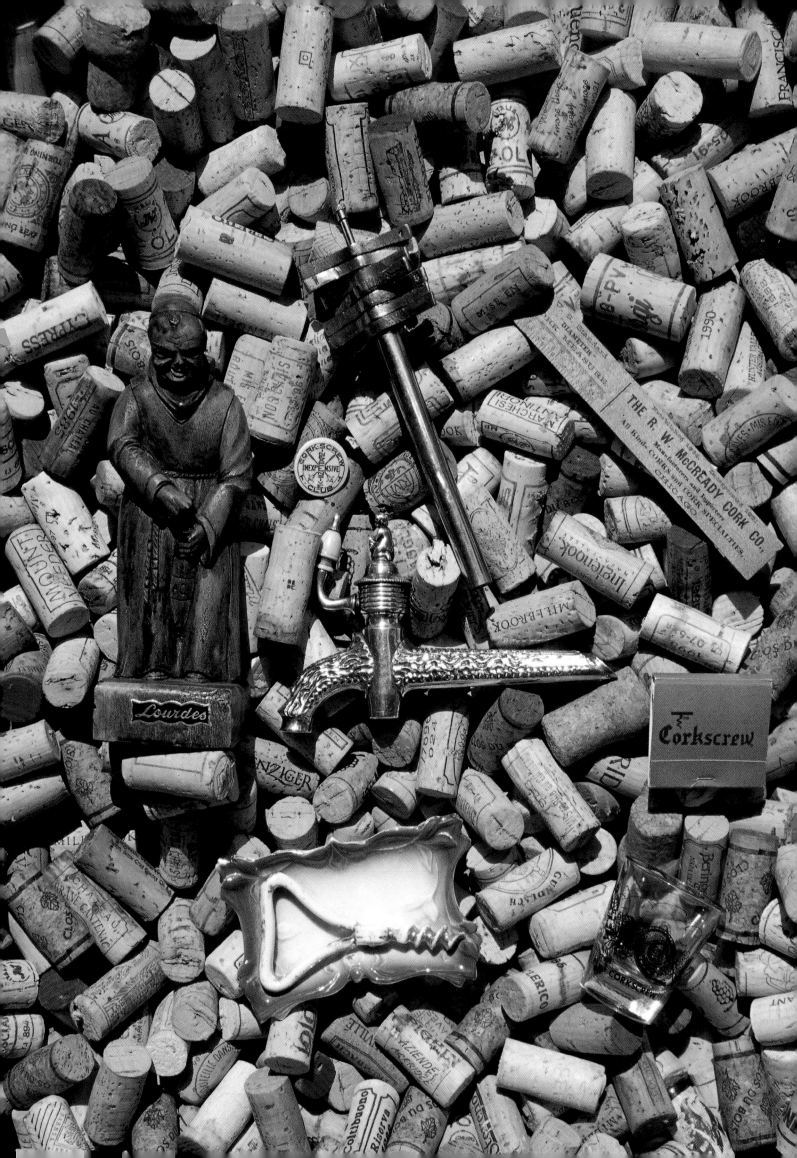

Part TTTT

Miscellaneous

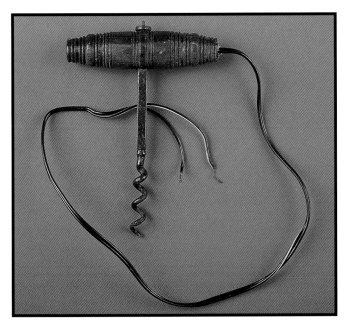

Bernie

Among the thousands of corkscrew collectors, Bernie stands out as the screwiest and most twisted. Bernie collects only corkscrews that no other collector would want. Because there is no competition for Bernie's wants, the prices are quite low. As a matter of fact, most corkscrews in his collection have been donated to him. Bernie does not collect any of the corkscrews shown in other categories of this book although some of them should be in his collection! Here are a few examples of Bernie's corkscrews.

Above: An electric corkscrew. The user grips the handle with fore and index fingers placed firmly against the square shank. The worm is turned into the cork and then the two wires are inserted into an electrical outlet. The resulting shock causes the user to yelp, dance, and shake. The movement will cause the cork to be extracted. *A gift from Ron MacLean.*

Right: *Left:* A single double lever corkscrew. *A gift from Stan Greenfield.*
Middle: A frameless double lever corkscrew. *A gift from Jack Bandy.*
Right: A twin single lever double lever corkscrew. *A gift from Don Minzenmayer.*

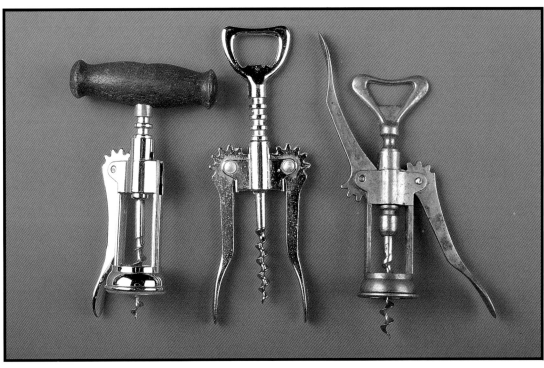

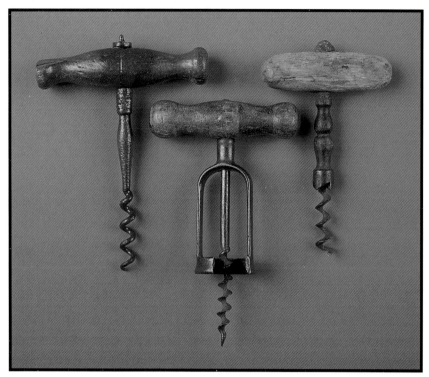

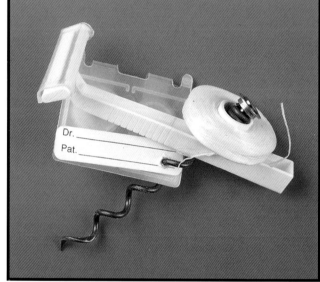

Above left: *Left:* A corkscrew specifically for opening Christmas wine. It has been meticulously painted in red and green in the true spirit of the season - even the worm was painted. *A gift from Mike Sharp who collects red and green corkscrews.*
Middle: An open frame. Not only can you see the cork rise into the frame during extraction, you can watch the entire operation through the opening in the bottle neck collar. This design also facilitates cork removal from the worm. *A gift from Howard Luterman.*
Right: A really old corkscrew found under an old railroad bridge when it was torn down. *A gift from the late Homer Babbidge.*

Above right: A travel corkscrew. This convenient corkscrew has a razor handle with rotating dental floss spool top. The razor handle is secured by a contact lens case. Apparently used by traveling business persons. *A gift from Alf Erickson.*

Left: Corkscrew with steel handle that goes over the top shank just far enough to expose a hole for placing it on your key ring. The intricate cross hatch design on the shank is to give you better grip whilst you turn the worm into the bottle. *A gift from the late Fred Andrew.*

Left: Two bone handle corkscrews. It is quite possible that both bones were found by the corkscrew maker's dog. The one on the *left* has a face burned into it and it is impossible to tell whether it is pre-Columbian art or yesterday's art. *Gifts from Ken Hark.*

Below left: A fine horn handle with nautical corkscrew theme. The combination cap lifter and worm penetrate the horn and are pinned to the handle. The shank above the worm is an interesting concentric design similar to that which would mate with something having a female thread. The realistic ship's wheel is mounted on the end with a round head slot screw and washer so that it is free to spin. This gives the user something to play with while he is drinking his wine. *A gift from Dean Walters.*

Below: At top is a Polish blunt worm waiter's friend. The blunt worm prevents injury to the user. *A gift from the late Bob Nugent.*
A screwless extractor is at *left. A gift from Joe Paradi.*
On the *right* are a boot and a blob handle richly decorated with plastic and glass pieces of junk. *Gifts from Joel Goodman.*

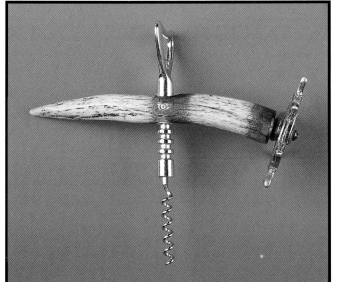

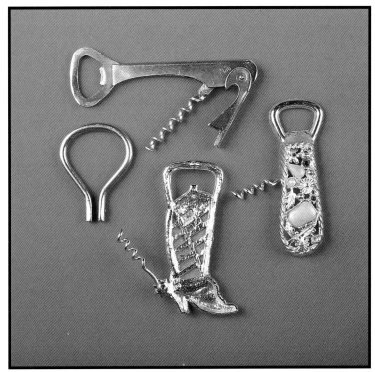

Go-Withs

The 7" wood carved monk is pulling a cork out of a bottle marked A. C. The label applied to the base says "Lourdes." $75-100.
The brass monk drinking directly from the bottle is mounted on a marble base. He is carrying a working candle with a wick. On the floor next to him are a corkscrew and a wine barrel. $150-200.

A bottle guard made of leather mounted on a cast iron base. The guard slides over the top of a bottle. The user holds it in place and the bottle down by stepping on the two pedals on the side. This assists in pulling the cork and also protects the user in case of glass breakage. c.1870. $500-700.

Left to right: Sculpture hand made and painted in Scotland by Peter Jages, 1988. A cat with bread, cheese, grapes, a bottle of wine, a corkscrew (on the grapes), and a glass filled with wine. $15-20; An original miniature (1 3/4" x 2 1/4") oil painting signed CARTIER 83. *$Rare;* A pottery Charlie Chaplin in a bath tub admires the painting. Bathtub uses a cork instead of a rubber plug to hold the water! $75-100.

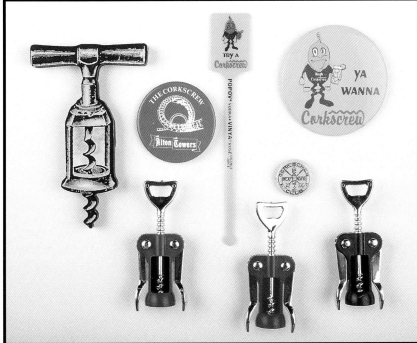

Top row: A magnet in the form of a bearing frame corkscrew from Polar Productions, Canada. Purchased new in 1998 in Norwalk, Connecticut, for $4.95; 2" Pinback button depicting a roller coaster and reading "The Corkscrew, Alton Towers." $10-15; A swizzle stick "Try a Corkscrew - Popov Vodka, Vinya Rose, Orange Juice" (the Corkscrew drink mixings). $10-15; 3" Pinback button showing advertising character "Hugh Corkscrew" saying "Ya Wanna Corkscrew." $15-20; Small button from the "Inexpensive Corkscrew Club" c.1909. $75-100. *Bottom row:* Three double lever magnets with moving parts. Currently sold in housewares stores for $1.99 - 2.49.

Left to right: Sterling tie clip with corkscrew, bottle, and two wine glasses. $75-100; A pin marked "TUS. OBERROTWEIL, VOLKSWANDERUNG 1976. Bottle labels say "Henkenberg Auslese." $50-75; A sterling crown cap lifter showing a hand grasping a corkscrew inserted into a bottle neck. Advertising "The Crown Cork and Seal Co., Baltimore 1908." Cap lifter is marked PATD FEB 6 '94, a patent by the father of the crown cap William Painter. $100-150.

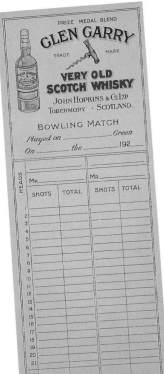

The stoneware jugs on the *left and right* are from John Hopkins & Co., Ltd., Glasgow, Scotland. The Glen Garry Scotch Whisky jugs picture Hopkins' corkscrew trademark. The matching Clough corkscrew reads "Glen Garry Scotch Whisky, S. S. Pierce Co., Agents for U. S. A." Jugs: $50-80.
The stoneware bottle in the *middle* is from Harston & Co. Limited, Leeds and Harrogate. It depicts a corkscrew screwed into a cork. $50-70.
The card is a bowling match scorecard. c.1920. $25-30.

Top: 5 1/2" saucer from Ridgway Potteries in Staffordshire, England. It is called the "Homemaker" and depicts a corkscrew, bottle opener, and other things found in the home. $50-60.
Left: A mid 19th century 7 1/2" plate. It depicts a kitchen scene with a man holding up a bottle and a glass. There is a corkscrew on the table. It reads "The Bottle. The bottle is brought out for the first time. The husband induces his wife 'just to take a drop.'" $150-200.
Right: A 9" plate made by Formasetti in Milan, Italy, in 1956. $60-75.

Matchbooks for businesses named "The Corkscrew" are unusual finds.

The two at *top left* are front and back of matchbooks from "The Corkscrew" restaurants, which had operations in the Canadian provinces Alberta, British Columbia, and Ontario. Note the corkscrew stylized letter "T" in the word "The." $10-15. The *bottom* book on the *right* does not list locations but has the same logo as those above. $10-15. The giant matchbook is from Lande's restaurant in Denver, Colorado. A corkscrew is depicted at *lower right* of the circle design. $30-40. The green matchbook is from Corkscrew I & II liquor stores in Denton, Texas. $3-5. The black and silver book is from "The Corkscrew, 2604-6 No. Kings Highway, Phone Rosedale 9385." $6-8. The postcard has a cork with wire worm threaded into it (it was mailed that way). The card was printed and manufactured by Lindenwald Novelty Co. of Kinderhook, N.Y. It says "You are a real (cork)er. Have one on me." The card was mailed to Miss Liza D. Powell in 1907 from Carrie with this great message: "This would be a great one to send to Liz but I hate to waste the postage in sending them a card. Tell Rose & Hilda I will send them tomorrow because the post is closed and I only have one stamp." How cheap can Carrie be? $30-40.

In the background left to right: A shot glass from the Cedar Point amusement park in Sandusky, Ohio. It depicts and labels two roller coasters located there - "Gemini" and "Corkscrew." $20-25; Big shot glass decorated with bottles, pitchers, cocktail shakers, fruit, glasses, *and* a corkscrew. $20-25. A Pooh Bear with corkscrew double handle cup. $30-40; An "In Loving Memory" cup showing a bottle of bass ale, a pipe, and a corkscrew. $40-50; A mug with a coat of arms depicting a corkscrew, cap lifter, bottle, and mugs with inscription "The Same Again Please." The back says "The Beer Drinker's Arms." $25-30.

In the foreground: Two ceramic 2 3/4" x 4 1/2" trays with corkscrew cast in. Stamped MADE IN GERMANY. *Left* one is imprinted "Souvenir of San Francisco." $50-75.

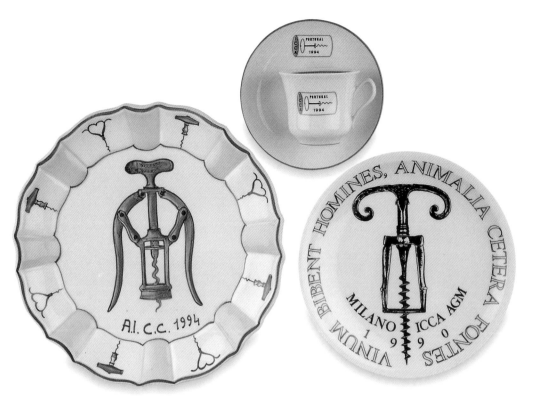

Top: A porcelain cup and 5" saucer given as souvenirs to attendees of the 1994 meeting of the International Correspondence of Corkscrew Addicts in Portugal.
Left: A 9" plate made in Italy. Souvenir of the 1994 meeting of the Italian Corkscrew Collectors Club (A.I.C.C.).
Right: A 7 1/2" plate. A souvenir of the 1990 meeting of the ICCA in Italy.

The 12" x 15" frame has a molded corkscrew and a molded barrel spigot applied. The monk is drinking beer from a glass mug and smoking a cigar.

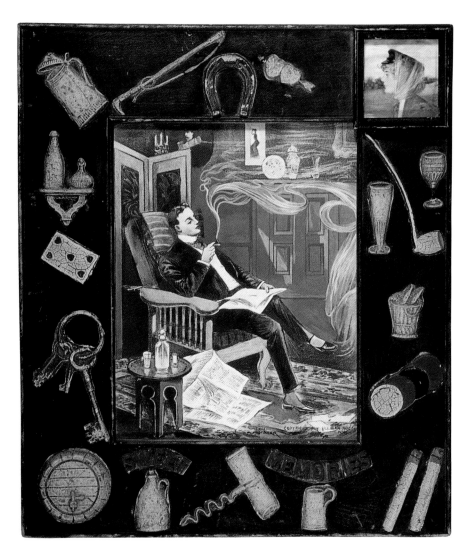

A gaudy 13 1/2" x 15 1/2" frame. The drawing by Lou Mayer has a 1904 copyright date by Ullman Mfg. Co. The print is surrounded by "Sweet Memories," including a corkscrew.

Draw to Fill is the title of the scene on this 13" porcelain enamel tray with metal rim. The waiter is drawing a cork while a poker game is in progress. Two postcards in the same drawing style by Bernhardt Wall depict pool players. In these a corkscrew is on the pool table and they are entitled *Kiss* and *Froze*. The postcards were copyrighted in 1904 and 1907 by Ullman Mfg. Co. of New York. The tray is from the same period.

In the Sad Caberet by W. Zegoni, 1986. An original 18" x 19" painting in Aquarelle
and Tempura by the Czech artist from Prague. Zegoni was born in 1958.

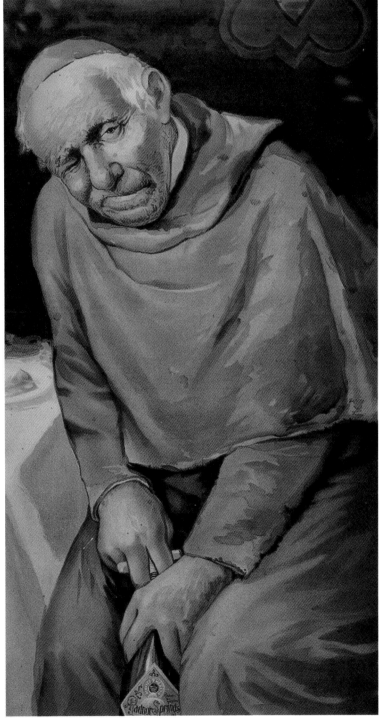

Above: *Champagne or Quite Well* is the title of this early 19th century English hand colored print. A wood handle corkscrew is on the platter on the table.

Right: A lithograph by Montreal Lithographing Co. Limited entitled *A Little for his Stomach's Sake*. It is an advertisement for Radnor Spring Mineral Co. The bottle label reads "Radnor Springs Mineral Water, Radnor, Quebec. Perfect Health. For Table Use. Refreshing Tonic and Stimulant." 17" x 22."

A 12" x 18" tin lithograph from the Silurian Mineral Spring Company, Waukesha, Wisconsin. A corkscrew with wire worm, wood handle, and foil cutter lies on the table next to the bottle of effervescent water.

Right: An assortment of printing blocks with cuts used in the production of catalogs and advertisements for Williamson Company, Newark, New Jersey.

Far right: A cork and corkscrew wreath by Bonnie Bull.

Taps, Sizers & Corkers

A silver 19th century barrel spigot. Barrel spigots are inserted into the bottom hole of the barrel to empty it. These are also called barrel taps or wine faucets. Bacchus is on top holding a bunch of grapes. Turning handle is fitted with ivory. Front lip is marked PATENT. $1200-1500.

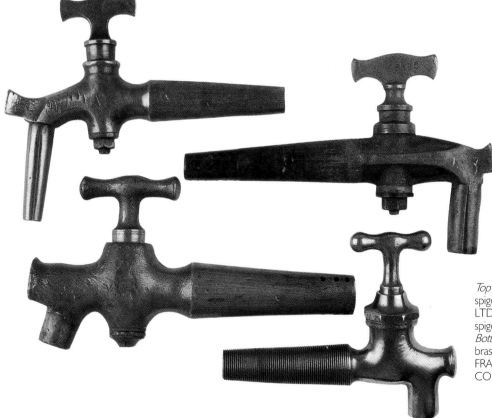

Top row left to right: Long spout barrel spigot marked FARROW & JACKSON LTD LONDON. $70-80; Brass spigot marked ANSELL'S. $50-60. *Bottom row left to right:* Unmarked brass. $20-30; Marked LANDERS FRARY & CLARK, NEW BRITAIN, CONN, U. S. A. $60-70.

Two wooden barrel spigots. $10-20.

On the *left* are cork cutters numbered from 1 through 7. They measure from 4-10 millimeter diameters. $60-100. A virgin champagne cork is at the *top center*. At *top right* is a cork measure with advertising for Armstrong Cork Co., Pittsburgh, Pa. Manufactured by Whitehead & Hoag Co., Newark, N. J. The backside has a gauge showing graduations from 1 to 10 for insertion into the bottle neck for sizing. $10-15. The ruler and cork measure advertises "Trefoil Prescription Corks" from "The R. W. McCready Cork Co., Manufacturers and Importers, All Kinds Corks and Cork Specialties, Chicago Established 1866." $20-25. At *bottom right* is virgin cork. Cork (*suberose parenchyma*) is the bark of the cork oak, a tree growing in western Mediterranean countries.

Cork presses with two, three, and four sizes. In order to make the cork easier to put in the bottle, it is wetted and squeezed in the appropriate hole in the cork press. These are all nicely decorated presses in iron and brass. A 1906 catalog from Wood, Vallance & Co. hardware wholesalers of Canada offered cork presses for $3 per dozen. $20-50.

The rotary cork press was used in apothecaries to size corks for medicine bottles. The two on the *left* have 3 1/2" wheels and are marked NO. 1. The front press has a brass tag for Elmer & Amend in New York City. The other is marked PAT. AUG. 7, 1857, ENTERPRISE MFG. CO. PHILA. $80-120. The rotary press on the *right* is marked NO. 2 and it has a 4 1/2" wheel. $60-80. Behind it is a 13" press marked YANKEE PATENT PENDING USA. $80-100. The last is a 15" cork cutter and press marked on the handle THE PRIZE CUTTER BY S. LEE. $100-125.

To insert the cork into the bottle, a corking machine is used. The cork is inserted into an opening in these wood corkers. The corker rests on the bottle neck and the plunger is used to force the cork through a tapered hole and into the bottle (largest diameter at the top!). In front is a hinged type. $30-50.

This an exceptional French rack and pinion corker. Raise the rack, insert a cork, place over bottle top, and crank the rack down. A sliding flange engages the bottle neck to keep it in place. It will easily drive the driest and tightest cork home. Marked BREVETE S. G. D. G. $400-600.

A corking "machine" marked YANKEE PAT AP'D. $100-125.

A bottle corking "machine" marked MF'D BY SOMERVILLE MACH & FDY CO., MERVILLE, MASS, LILY NO. 2, PAT PENDG. $150-200.

Not Corkscrews

The dictionary defines a corkscrew as "a device for drawing corks from bottles, consisting of a pointed metal spiral attached to a handle." The objects here have pointed metal spirals, but they are not used for drawing corks from bottles. It is not unusual to see them at antique shows and in antique shops with tags calling them corkscrews. So if they are not corkscrews, what are they?

"I HATE TO BORE YOU THUS."

On the *left* are various tools used for cleaning and removing wadding from gun barrels. At *top right* are four awls used for making holes in wood or leather. At *lower right* is a handle with removable tools. The awl is secured by inserting it into the hole and tightening a thumb screw. It is marked CROWN GERMANY REGISTERED.

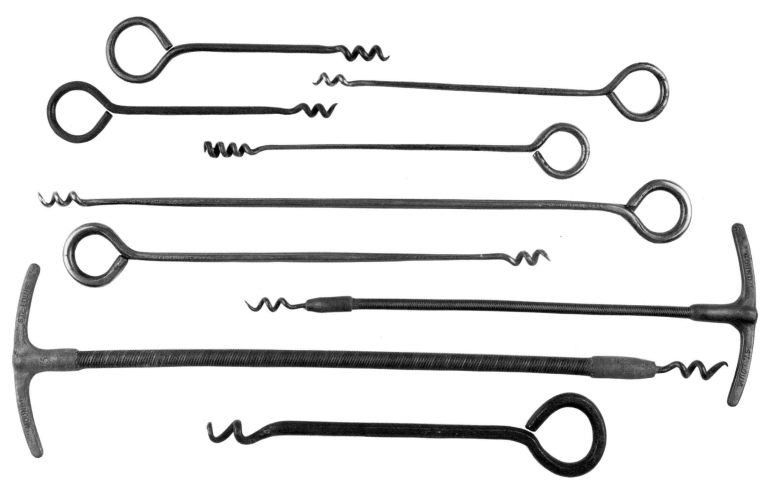

A group of "Packing Tools." Marked examples are: *Fourth from top* - SUFFUM DOI CO., LOUISI-ANA, MO.; *Fifth and sixth* - THE GARLOCK PACKING CO.; *Seventh and eighth* - MOUND ST. LOUIS. The packing screw on the *bottom* is a very early iron example.

A current catalog from industrial supply giant McMaster-Carr of Chicago devotes a page called "Packing Tools" to these devices. A 6 1/2" "Mini Flexible Packing Tool" with corkscrew (!) tip at $9.53 "makes it a cinch to remove small-size packing from valve stems and packing crates." Another "to allow easy access to stuffing boxes (of engines, pumps, etc.) for removal of packing" comes in six sizes from 6 1/4" ($5.41) to 22" ($21.48). Rigid packing tools are available from 6" ($10.58) to 20" ($22.00). And, finally they offer the tool with interchangeable corkscrew, wood screw, or brush tips.

I found a great use for the packing tool with flexible shaft. A sink trap was plugged in my kitchen. I snaked the tool into the drain, screwed into the offending material, and pulled it out. The packing screw saved the day!

A Stage Screw. Shown in a c.1950 Catalog #50 of the H. M. Sanders Co., Boston. It is screwed into the wall or floor. Theater stagehands then use it to secure ropes when opening and closing, or raising and lowering stage curtains. It is the subject of much contemplation and erroneous identification by collectors at flea markets, tools meetings, and whatsits sessions where most often it is captioned a cooper's vise. And, for the corkscrew collector, the dealer will gladly call in a corkscrew!

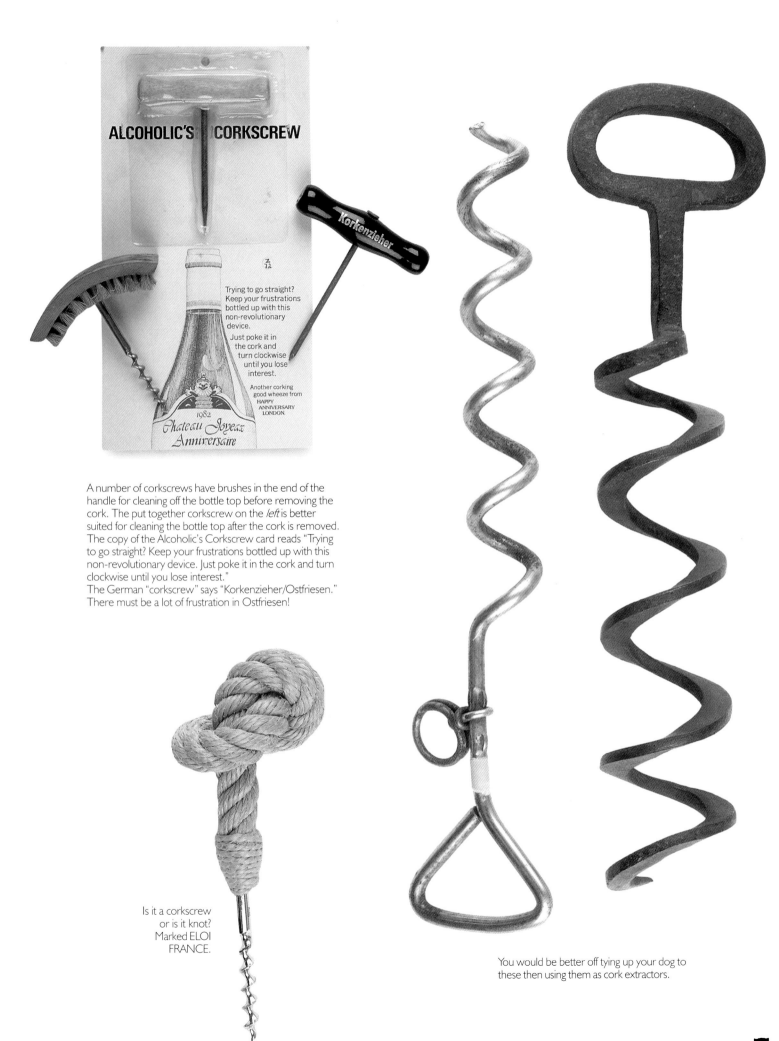

ALCOHOLIC'S CORKSCREW

Trying to go straight? Keep your frustrations bottled up with this non-revolutionary device.

Just poke it in the cork and turn clockwise until you lose interest.

Another corking good wheeze from HAPPY ANNIVERSARY LONDON.

1982 Chateau Joyeax Anniversaire

Korkenzieher

A number of corkscrews have brushes in the end of the handle for cleaning off the bottle top before removing the cork. The put together corkscrew on the *left* is better suited for cleaning the bottle top after the cork is removed. The copy of the Alcoholic's Corkscrew card reads "Trying to go straight? Keep your frustrations bottled up with this non-revolutionary device. Just poke it in the cork and turn clockwise until you lose interest."
The German "corkscrew" says "Korkenzieher/Ostfriesen." There must be a lot of frustration in Ostfriesen!

Is it a corkscrew or is it knot? Marked ELOI FRANCE.

You would be better off tying up your dog to these then using them as cork extractors.

Corkscrew Places

How about a collection of corkscrew places to go with your corkscrew collection? Many sites are named corkscrew simply because of their shape - winding stairs, winding roads, corkscrew shaped trees, etc. Tire Bouchon is quite popular as a restaurant name in Europe; however, there aren't many "Corkscrew" restaurants in America. There are plenty of liquor stores with that name though. Here's a tour of some of the corkscrew places I have found.

Corkscrew Restaurants and Bars:

Au Tire-Bouchon, 5 rue des Tailleurs-de-Pierre, Strasbourg, France

Au Tire-Bouchon, 5580 EPRAVE (en face de l'église), Rochefort, France

Bar Le Tire Bouchon, Schlosshotel Vier Jahreszeiten, Berlin, Germany

Cabaret Tire-Bouchon, 9, rue Norvins, Paris, France

Corkscrew Lounge & Rest, 8249 Sheridan Rd., Kenosha, Wisconsin, U. S. A.

Il Cavatappi Enoteca Bar, 10, V. Saluzzo, Torino, Italy

Korkenzieher Pilsbar, Türkheimer Str. 4, Amberg B Buchloe, 86854 Germany

Korkenzieher Restaurant U. Weinlokal, Bad Ems, Germany

Le Tire Bouchon, Le Pied des Gouttes, Montbéliard 25200, France

Le Tire Bouchon, Montmartre, Paris, France

Le Tire Bouchon Style Bistrot 1900, 11 cours Julien, Marseilles, France

Le Tire Bouchon, G/F, Old Bailey Street, Hong Kong

Le Tire Bouchon, 61 Upper James Street, London, England

Le Tire Bouchon, 19, rue de la préfecture, Nice, France

Le Tire-Bouchon Winstub - Restaurant, Riquewihr, Alsace, France

The Cavatappi (Italian for Corkscrew) Restaurant, San Diego Hilton Beach and Tennis Resort, San Diego, California

Corkscrew Wine and Liquor Stores:

Cavatappi Distribuzione, 1019 Westlake Ave. N., Seattle, Washington

Corkscrew Liquors, 3460 W. Carefree Circle, Colorado Springs, Colorado

Corkscrew Party Shoppe, 38256 Ford Road, Westland, Michigan

Corkscrew Party Store, 912 E. Cork Street, Kalamazoo, Michigan

Corkscrew Wine & Liquors, 100 Applegarth Road, Cranbury, New Jersey

Corkscrew Wine Emporium Ltd., 3120 Montvale Drive, Springfield, Illinois

Corkscrew Wines & Liquors, 1928 Jericho Turnpike, Elwood, New York

Corkscrew, 1235 W. Oak Street, Denton, Texas

Corkscrew, 1781 Coventry Road, Cleveland, Ohio

Corkscrew, 1s219 U. S. Highway 2, Hurley, Wisconsin

Corkscrew, 238 S Arlington Avenue, Reno, Nevada

Corkscrew, 590 Macarthur Boulevard, Pocasset, Massachusetts

Corkscrew, 66 Mountain Boulevard, Watchung, New Jersey

Corkscrew Wines, 28 King Street, Winterton Scunthorpe, DN159TP England

Korkenzieher Weinmarkt, Köstlinstr. 4, Stuttgart, 70499 Germany

Princeton Corkscrew, 4-6 Hulfish Street, Princeton, New Jersey

Corkscrew Hotels:

Hotel "Goldner Pfropfenzieher" (Golden Corkscrew Hotel) D-55430 Oberwesel am Rhein, Germany. In the Rhine Valley, near the Lorelei Rock between Bingen and Koblenz

Lodging on Corkscrew Street:

Turningpoint Farms, 864 Corkscrew, Armstrong, British Columbia, Canada

Corkscrews to the Rescue:

Big Corkscrew Island Fire Rescue, 13240 Immokalee Road, Naples, Florida

Corkscrew Worship:

Corkscrew Baptist Church, State Road 846, Immokalee, Florida

Homes for Corkscrews:

Corkscrew Woodlands Association Inc. (Mobile Home Park), 21600 Corkscrew Woodlands Blvd., Estero, Florida

Horsing Around with Corkscrews:

Corkscrew Ranch, 12593 McGregor Blvd., Fort Myers, Florida

Corkscrews for the Birds:

Corkscrew Swamp Sanctuary, Immokalee, Florida

Canoeing Corkscrews:

The movie *Deliverance* was filmed on and around the Chattooga River. One of the toughest rapids on the river to navigate is called "Corkscrew." The Chattooga River begins at the base of North Carolina's Whitesides Mountain and forms the border between South Carolina and Georgia.

The Corkscrew Entrance at Bandit Hall in the Mammoth Cave of Kentucky.

The Corkscrew Tree, a giant redwood in Prairie Creek State Park, Humboldt County, California.

Corkscrew Resort:

Corkscrew Cove is located in the resort of Sheffield Beach, South Africa. It is a 35 minute drive from Durban.

Corkscrew Climbing:

Corkscrew Peak is in Death Valley, California. It has a 3300 foot gain with a twisty appearance.

Corkscrew Hills:

Gregans Castle Hotel, Ballyvaughan, County Clare, Ireland, is located at the foot of Corkscrew Hill. It overlooks the "Burren" and Galway Bay.

Corkscrew Fountain:

In 1820, Robert Abrams designed gardens at Alton Towers in Staffordshire, England. A corkscrew fountain was built-in the gardens and is still standing today. It is an 18 foot tall solid mass of carved stone. The water makes a corkscrew like descent from the top and cascades away down into the gardens.

Corkscrew Trails:

The "Devil's Corkscrew" is part of the Bright Angel Trail at Grand Canyon National Park.

Corkscrew Manufacturers:

Monopolwerk Usbeck& Söhne, Frauenbergstrasse 33, 3350 Marburg, Germany.

Corkscrew Paintings on exhibit:

Boston Museum of Fine Arts, Corkscrew to Collage: Still Life by John Singleton Copley

The boardwalk at the National Audubon Society's Corkscrew Swamp Sanctuary near Naples, Florida.

Corkscrew Drive on Tunnel Mountain, Banff, Canadian Rockies.

Corkscrew Museums:

Musée du Tire-Bouchon, Menerbes, Provence, France. A museum of corkscrews in a winery.

Victoria and Albert Museum, London, England. A few corkscrews from the collection of the late Gianni Giachin.

Zentrum für Aussergewoehnliche Museen (The Center for Unusual Museums), Munich, Germany. Several specialty museums are located here including a corkscrew museum, a lock museum, a chamber pot museum, and a pedal car museum.

The Reinprecht Heurige (Tavern) on Cobenzglasse in Grinzing, Austria has over 3000 corkscrews on display.

Le Secq des Tournelles Museum in Rouen, France has many early French steel corkscrews on display.

Greystone Cellars in the Napa Valley, California houses the collection assembled by Brother Timothy of Christian Brothers Winery and corkscrew collecting fame.

Harveys Wine Museum, Bristol, England.

The Seagram Museum in Waterloo, Ontario, Canada had a museum which included a few corkscrews but the museum is now closed.

And finally...

At the Laguna Raceway in California, there is a "corkscrew" in the track. One racer commented, "The Corkscrew is a fun part that is important to be fast in because it can help your time a lot and because if you're not fast there, the AI guys might rearend you. When you have a full tank, you will tend to slide on the exit if you get a little gas happy."

A view of the Spiral and Corkscrew Tunnels in the Canadian Rockies.

Corkscrew Hill, Lisdoonvarna.

The "Roaring 20s Corkscrew" roller coaster at Knott's Berry Farm, Buena Park, California, was moved to Idaho in 1990.

Arrow Dynamics Inc. was founded in 1946 as Arrow Development Company in California. The company has designed rides for amusement parks worldwide. In 1975, Arrow discovered a way to reliably and safely turn a roller coaster rider upside down. They used tracks made of steel tubes in a series of corkscrew spirals. Their first "corkscrew coaster" was built for Knott's Berry Farm in California. In the 20+ years since then, a number of roller coasters named "Corkscrew" or with corkscrew designs have been built to thrill millions.

Roller Coasters named Corkscrew:

(year built)

Alton Towers, Staffordshire, England. Corkscrew. Described by Alton as "Famous for its double loop-the-loop along a hair raising half-mile track, this monster exerts a pull three times that of gravity. It's a corker!"

Athol, Silverwood, Idaho. Gravity Defying Corkscrew. In 1990, the corkscrew roller coaster from Knott's Berry Farm (1975) was moved here.

Cedar Point, Ohio. The Corkscrew (1976). A red, white, and blue machine that flips riders upside down directly over the midway.

Geuga Lake, Aurora, Ohio. The Corkscrew (1978). In 1996, plans were being made to dismantle this roller coaster.

Muskegon, Michigan: Corkscrew at Michigan's Adventure (1979).

Myrtle Beach, South Carolina. The Corkscrew at the Pavilion (1978). A steel roller coaster designed by Arrow.

Rocky Point, Rhode Island. Corkscrew Loop (1984).

Salem, New Hampshire: Canobie Corkscrew at Canobie Lake Park (1975).

Shakopee, Minnesota. The Corkscrew at Valleyfair. A roller coaster with two giant spirals with a height of 85 feet and speeds up to 50 miles per hour.

Vancouver, British Columbia, Canada: The Corkscrew at Playland (1994). A wooden coaster with a double helix including a 75 foot drop.

Corkscrew Type Roller Coasters:

(Location, Coaster Name, Type of Design, Coaster Designer, Year Built)

Calgary, Alberta, Canada: Calaway Park, Turn of the Century/Steel Corkscrew/Arrow/1982

Elysburg, Pennsylvania: Knoebel's, Whirlwind, Steel Corkscrew, Vekoma, 1984

Memphis, Tennessee: Libertyland, Revolution, Steel Corkscrew, Arrow, 1979

Montreal, Quebec, Canada: La Ronde, Le Super Menage, Steel Corkscrew, Vekoma, 1981

Nashville, Tennessee: Opryland USA, Wabash Cannonball, Steel Corkscrew, Arrow, 1975

Tampa, Florida: Busch Gardens, Tampa Python, Steel Corkscrew, Arrow, 1977

Corkscrew Trivia

Corkscrew Definitions:

Noun - A device for drawing corks from bottles, consisting of a pointed metal spiral attached to a handle.

Verb - To move or proceed on a repeatedly curving course

Adjective - Resembling a corkscrew in shape; spiral.

Corkscrew Translated:

Albanian: Hapëse e Shishes
Arabic: Minza us Sida-Da
Bulgarian: Terbuschon
Chinese: Kai Sai Zuan
Czech: Otvírák
Danish: Proptraekker
Dutch: Kurketrekker
Finnish: Korkkiruv
French: Tire Bouchon
German: Korkenzieher
Greek: Tirepouson
Hebrew: Pothan
Hungarian: Dugóhuzó
Islandic: Tappatogari
Italian: Cavatappi
Italian: Levatappi
Japanese: Sennuki
Lithuanian: Kamsciatraukis
Norwegian: Korketrekker
Polish: Korkociag
Portuguese: Saca-Rolhas
Romanian: Tirbuson
Russian: Probotschnik
Russian: Schtopor
Serbian: Otvarac za Botse
Spanish: Sacacorchos
Swahili: Kizibuo
Swedish: Korkskruv
Swiss German: Zapfenzieher
Turkish: Sise Acacagi
Turkish: Tirbuson
Vietnamese: Cai Monut Chai
Yugoslavian: Vaditschep

Corkscrew Music:

A Corkscrew and a Candlestick (or *Good Goods*) written and composed by John Stamford. Corkscrew with web helix on the sheet music cover.

Gilhooleys Supper-Party written and composed by J. F. Mitchell. On the cover a waiter is extracting a cork from a bottle.

Screw Polka composed and dedicated to the Junior Screw Association of Philadelphia by Jas. W. Porter. Corkscrew with wire helix on the sheet music cover.

In 1992, *Corkscrews!*, a New York musical comedy revue, was performed at Jerry Kravat's Club 53 at the New York City Hilton.

A corkscrew or not a corkscrew~that is the question.

According the *Los Angeles Times*, on September 26, 1989 a lifeguard at Santa Monica Beach was stabbed with a corkscrew.

Some marbles are called corkscrew because of their design. They are usually around 5/8" diameter and descriptions include Oxblood, Limeade, Triple Twist, Cornelian Agate, and Popeye.

A large slide at the 1906 Exposition Internationalle in France was called "Le Tire Bouchon."

In 1995, corkscrew collector Alf Erickson commissioned Cameron Balloons Ltd. of Bristol, England, to construct a balloon featuring six corkscrews on its panels. Erickson has since built a second balloon with corkscrew designs and is planning a third. Erickson also owns an elephant polo team in Nepal, which he calls the "Screwy Tuskers."

In 1903, the U. S. Playing Card Co. of Cincinnati, Ohio, placed an advertisement in *Munsey's Magazine*. A deck of cards depicting a seated elderly couple with the man extracting the cork is featured. The deck is called "Anticipation."

Rotini are corkscrew pasta that most sauces cling to easily.

Fusilli are corkscrew pasta.

Ficus trees are shaped into a corkscrew design.

The *Corylus Avellana Contorta* is a Corkscrew Hazelnut tree grown but dead in the backyard garden of Ron MacLean.

Corkscrew *valliseneria* is an aquatic plant.

In 1985, Ed Kaye, Editor and Publisher of *Just for Openers*, reported that a cat owned by Laura Sturza of Kensington, Maryland, had a whisker shaped like a corkscrew.

Robinia Tortuosas is a corkscrew locust tree.

Salix matsudana 'Contorta' is a corkscrew willow tree.

Keith Floyd, a BBC chef, said "A kitchen without a corkscrew is merely a room."

In 1994, The Black Crowes performed at small private parties under the pseudonyms "The Corkscrews of Renown."

In 1996, Gurcharan Singh in Kuala Lumpur, Malaysia, invented a "disposable circumcision device" resembling a corkscrew.

In skating, a Scratch Spin or Corkscrew spin is the most basic of all spins. The skater is standing up straight on the left leg and the right leg is extended in front. With arms up and out to the side, the skater spins.

The tango term "enrosque" means corkscrew. It is a circular sweeping action in the dance.

Recipe for the "Corkscrew" Drink:

Ingredients: 1 1/2 oz Light rum, 1/2 oz Peach schnapps, 1/2 oz Dry Vermouth, 1 Lemon twist

Mixing instructions: In a mixing glass half-filled with ice cubes, combine the rum, peach schnapps, and vermouth. Stir well. Strain into a cocktail glass and garnish with the lemon twist.

A Corkscrew Riddle:

The *Amusing Puzzle Book* from the early 19th century contains several riddles including this:

> Tho' I alas! a prisoner be,
> My trade is prisoners to set free,
> And when I have them by the pole,
> I drag them upwards from their hole,
> Tho' some are of a stubborn kind,
> I'm forced to leave a limb behind;
> Like polished steel I oft appear,
> The drooping soul I help to cheer,
> Tho' in myself nor drink nor food,
> Yet of great service when improved.

Do *you* know what it is?

Quotes from The complete works of Corkscrews by Mel Reichler and Jim Egan:

"A Corkscrew is a sentence....It's a sentence that bends and twists with a handle on one end and a point on the other."

"A Corkscrew is like a story. For a story to work right it's got to have some bends and twists in the plot, a story line to hold on to, and some semblance of a point at the end. But a poem can be a Corkscrew or a song. Even just a couple of words arranged properly can be a Corkscrew."

"The beauty of a good Corkscrew is that it opens ideas up but it doesn't pour the contents all over you. It lets you peek inside and smell what's there and if you want to, you can try to pour out it's meaning or put the cork back or just leave it uncorked."

"A Corkscrew shows you an idea then it shows you the pattern of the idea and then it shows you the pattern itself without the idea."

"Corkscrews are always crazy but true - they touch upon ideas that are strange but when you think about them, not so strange after all."

"Like good sex, a Corkscrew is its own context."

"There are Corkscrews for which there is no cork."

"Corkscrews are the sex of the mind."

"Corkscrews are lost point down and found point up."

"A Corkscrew is the common ground between any truth and its contradiction."

"A Corkscrew is a one person dialogue or a two person monologue."

"The meaning of a Corkscrew is always another Corkscrew."

Resources

Books

Bernston, Buster, and Per Ekman. *Scandinavian Corkscrews.* Täby, Sweden: Tryckeriförlaget, 1994.

Blake, Philos. *Guide to American Corkscrew Patents, Volume One 1860-1895.* New Castle, Delaware, USA: Bottlescrew Press, 1978.

Blake, Philos. *Guide to American Corkscrew Patents, Volume Two 1896-1920.* New Castle, Delaware, USA: Bottlescrew Press, 1981.

Bull, Donald, and Manfred Friedrich. *The Register of United States Breweries 1876-1976, Volumes I & II.* Trumbull, Connecticut, USA: Bull, 1976.

Bull, Donald, Manfred Friedrich, and Robert Gottschalk. *American Breweries.* Trumbull, Connecticut, USA: Bullworks, 1984.

Bull, Donald. *A Price Guide to Beer Advertising Openers and Corkscrews.* Trumbull, Connecticut, USA: Bull, 1981.

Bull, Donald. *Beer Advertising Openers - A Pictorial Guide.* Trumbull, Connecticut, USA: Bull, 1978.

Coldicott, Peter. *A Guide to Corkscrew Collecting.* Stockbridge, Hants., England: Coldicott, 1994.

D'Errico, Nicolas F. *American Corkscrew Patents 1921-1992.* Connecticut: D'Errico, 1993.

de Riaz, Yvan A. *The Book of Knives.* New York: Crown Publishers, 1981.

DeSanctis, Paolo, and Maurizio Fantoni. *I Cavatappi / Corkscrews.* Milan, Italy: Be-Ma Editrice, 1988.

DeSanctis, Paolo, and Maurizio Fantoni. *Le Collezioni Cavatappi.* Milan, Italy: Mailand, 1993.

DeSanctis, Paolo, and Maurizio Fantoni. *The Corkscrew, A Thing of Beauty.* Milan, Italy: Marzorati Editore, 1990.

Dippel, Horst. *Korkenzieher.* Hamburg, Germany: Ellert & Richter, 1988.

Doornkaat, Heinz ten. *Korkenzieher.* Germany: Doornkaat, 1991.

Giulian, Bertrand B. *Corkscrews of the Eighteenth Century.* Pennsylvania: White Space Publishing, 1995.

Goins, John. *Encyclopedia of Cutlery Markings.* Knoxville, Tennessee: Knife World Publications, 1986.

Heckmann, Manfred. *Korkenzieher.* Berlin, Germany: Fasanen Edition, 1979.

Kaye, Edward R., and Donald A. Bull. *The Handbook of Beer Advertising Openers and Corkscrews.* Sanibel Island: Kaye, 1984.

Levine, Bernard. *Levine's Guide to Knives and Their Values.* Iola, Wisconsin: Krause Publications, 1997.

MacLean, Ron. *A Guide to Canadian Corkscrew Patents.* Mississauga, Ontario, Canada: MacLean, 1985.

O'Leary, Fred. *Corkscrews: 1000 Patented Ways to Open a Bottle.* Atlgen, Pennsylvania, USA: Schiffer Publishing Ltd., 1996.

Olive, Guy. *Tire Bouchons Français Brevets 1828-1974.* France: Olive, 1995.

Paradi, Joseph C. *French Corkscrew Patents.* Ontario, Canada: Paradi, 1988.

Paradi, Monika. *Cookbook for Corkscrew Collectors.* Mississauga, Ontario, Canada: Canadian Corkscrew Collectors Club, 1991.

Perry, Evan. *Corkscrews and Bottle Openers.* Buckinghamshire, England: Shire Publications, Ltd., 1980.

Peters, Ferd. *German Corkscrew Patents and Registrations.* Holland: Peters, 1997.

Pickford, Ian. *Jackson's Hallmarks.* Suffolk, England: Antique Collectors' Club, 1997.

Pumpenmeier, Klaus. *Deutscher Gebrauchsmusterschutz für Korkenzieher 1891-1945.* Bad Salzuflen, Germany: Pumpenmeier, 1997.

Reichler, Mel, and Jim Egan. *Corkscrews.* New York: Reichler, 1996.

Rainwater, Dorothy T. *Encyclopedia of American Silver Manufacturers.* Atglen, Pennsylvania, USA: Schiffer Publishing Ltd., 1986.

Stanely, John., Edward R. Kaye, and Donald A. Bull. *The 1998 Handbook of United States Beer Advertising Openers and Corkscrews.* Chapel Hill, North Carolina: John Stanely, 1998.

Tweedale, Geoffrey. *The Sheffield Knife Book.* Sheffield, England: The Hallamshire Press, 1996.

Van Wieren, Dale P., Donald Bull, Manfred Friedrich, and Robert Gottschalk. *American Breweries II.* West Point, Pennsylvania, USA: Eastern Coast Breweriana Association, 1995.

Voyles, J. Bruce. *The American Blade Collectors Association Price Guide to Antique Knives.* Chattanooga, Tennessee: American Blade, Inc., Blade Books Division, 1990.

Wallace, Fletcher. *British Corkscrew Patents from 1795.* Brighton, East Sussex, England: Vernier Press, 1997.

Watney, Bernard M., and Homer D. Babbidge. *Corkscrews for Collectors.* London, England: Philip Wilson Publishers for Sotheby Parke Bernet Publications, 1981.

Articles

Danziger, Herb. *The Syracuse Ornamental Company.* Birmingham, Michigan: Danziger, 1983.

MacLean, Ron. *The Common Corkscrew / Diverse Executions.* Mississauga, Ontario, Canada: MacLean, 1988.

MacLean, Ron. *Common Corkscrews II.* Mississauga, Ontario, Canada: MacLean, 1989.

MacLean, Ron. *Common Corkscrews III.* Mississauga, Ontario, Canada: MacLean, 1990.

MacLean, Ron. *Common Corkscrews IV.* Mississauga, Ontario, Canada: MacLean, 1991.

Nugent, Robert P. *Knives with Corkscrews.* Hillsboro, New Hampshire: Nugent, 1987.

8/24